18/1/84
203

VOID

**Library of
Davidson College**

Library of
Davidson College

ADAM WODEHAM
AN INTRODUCTION TO HIS LIFE AND WRITINGS

STUDIES IN MEDIEVAL AND REFORMATION THOUGHT

EDITED BY

HEIKO A. OBERMAN, Tübingen

IN COOPERATION WITH

E. JANE DEMPSEY DOUGLASS, Claremont, California
LEIF GRANE, Copenhagen
GUILLAUME H. M. POSTHUMUS MEYJES, Leiden
ANTON G. WEILER, Nijmegen

VOLUME XXI

WILLIAM J. COURTENAY

ADAM WODEHAM

AN INTRODUCTION TO HIS LIFE AND WRITINGS

LEIDEN
E. J. BRILL
1978

ADAM WODEHAM

AN INTRODUCTION TO HIS LIFE AND WRITINGS

BY

WILLIAM J. COURTENAY

LEIDEN
E. J. BRILL
1978

ISBN 90 04 05267 4

Copyright 1978 by E. J. Brill, Leiden, The Netherlands

All rights reserved. No part of this book may be reproduced or translated in any form, by print, photoprint, microfilm, microfiche or any other means without written permission from the publisher

PRINTED IN ENGLAND

For Lynn

CONTENTS

Preface XI
List of Abbreviations XIV

Introduction 1

I. *Lecturae super Libros Sententiarum* 7
   A. Wodeham Studies, 1920–1970 7
   B. The Redactions of the Oxford Lectures on the *Sentences* . 12
      1. *Editiones media et longa* Reconsidered 15
      2. Vat. lat. 955: Main text and marginalia 20
      3. Vat. lat. 1110 23
      4. Caius College 281 25
      5. The *Ordinatio* 26
   C. The Norwich and London Lectures 30
      1. The Norwich Lectures 30
      2. The London Lectures 31
      3. Manuscript Possibilities 32
   D. Treatises on Quantity and the Continuum 34
   E. Summary 36

II. Oxford Thought in the Age of Wodeham: His Sources . . 39
   A. Biblical and Patristic Citations 40
   B. *Doctores antiqui* 42
   C. *Moderni* 45
      1. Franciscan Education in England 45
      2. Wodeham's "modern" sources 53
      Magister Abstractionum 54
      Peter of Baldeswell, OFM 56
      James of Ascoli, OFM 56
      Henry Harclay 56
      William of Alnwick, OFM 57
      Peter Aureol, OFM 58
      Walter Burley, Mertonian 59
      Richard Campsale, Mertonian 60
      Walter Beaufon, OFM 61
      John of Reading, OFM 62

	Richard Drayton, OFM	63
	William of Ockham, OFM	63
	Francis Mayronnis, OFM	65
	Henry of Costesey, OFM	65
	Ralph Pigaz, OFM	65
	Walter Chatton, OFM	66
	Gerard Odonis, OFM	74
	Richard Fitzralph	75
	Nigel of Wavere, Mertonian	81
	John of Rodington, OFM	82
	Nicholas of Hoyo, OFM	83
	Reppes	83
	Thomas Felthorp	85
	Richard Kilvington	86
3.	The *Socii*	89
	Monachus Niger: the Benedictine *socius*	90
	The Dominican *socius*: Robert Holcot, William Crathorn, and Roger Gosford	95
	Grafton: Edmund (OFM), Hugh (OSA), and William Chiterne, (OFM)	106
	William Skelton, Mertonian	109
	Richard of Radford	110
	The Carmelite Bachelor	111
D.	Summary	111

III. The *Lecturae* of Adam in Later Medieval Thought 113
    A. Early Reactions at Oxford, Paris, and Cologne 116
        1. England, 1334–1350 116
        2. Paris, 1342–1345 123
        3. Cologne, 1335–1348 133
    B. Wodeham in the Aftermath of the Condemnations of 1346 and 1347 135
    C. Parisian Theology, 1349–1364 137
    D. The Return of Marginalia, 1365–1400 140
    E. The Spanish Contribution 152
    F. Some Conclusions 156

IV. Wodeham's Academic Career 160
    A. The Early Years 160
        1. Studies under Ockham and Chatton 160

2. The Norwich Lectures		164
3. The London Lectures		166
B. The Oxford Lectures		171
1. *Collationes, Protestatio, Principia,* and *Quaestiones*		172
2. Wodeham's Style and Structure		177
C. *Baccalarius Biblicus et Formatus*		179
D. The Oxford Regency		180
E. Wodeham's Last Years		180
F. Epilogue		181
Appendix 1: *Reportatio et Ordinatio Oxonienses*		183
A. *Reportatio* (?) *Oxoniensis*		183
1. Description of Manuscript: Vat. lat. 1110		183
2. Incipits, Explicits, and List of Questions		183
B. *Ordinatio Oxoniensis*		186
1. Description of Manuscripts		186
a. Bruges, Bibl. de la Ville, 172		
b. Paris, Maz. 915		
c. Paris, Univ. 193		
d. Tarazona, Cat. 7		
e. Vat. lat. 955 (text)		
2. Incipits, Explicits, and List of Questions		187
C. Erfurt-Lüneburg Subredaction		198
1. Relation of Manuscripts		198
2. Description of Manuscripts and Order of Questions		199
a. Erfurt, CA 2° 133		
b. Lüneburg, Ratsbücherei, Theol. 4° 29		
Appendix 2: *Collectio brevis*, or the Second Redaction		202
A. Description of Manuscripts		202
1. Bruges, Bibl. de la Ville, 172		
2. Florence, Bibl. Naz., conv. soppr. A III 508		
3. Florence, Bibl. Naz., conv. soppr. B VII 1249		
4. Paris, Bibl. Nat. lat. 15 892		
5. Vat. lat. 955 (marginalia)		
B. Incipits, Explicits, and List of Questions		203
Appendix 3: *Lectura Secunda*		210
A. Description of Manuscript: Cambridge, Gonville & Caius, 281		210

B. Incipits, Explicits, and List of Questions 210

Appendix 4: *Fragmenta et Abbreviationes sive Extractiones* 215
　　A. Vat. lat. 869 215
　　B. The Cologne *Extractio* 215
　　　　1. Description of Text 215
　　　　2. Description of Manuscripts 216
　　　　　　a. Hannover, Stadtbibl., Ms. 1
　　　　　　b. Naples, Bibl. Naz. VII C 53
　　　　3. List of Questions 217
　　C. The Oyta *Abbreviatio* 223
　　　　1. List of Edition and Manuscripts 223
　　　　2. Incipits, Explicits, and List of Questions 223
　　D. Vat. lat. 946 228

Appendix 5: Table of Questions 229

Index of Manuscripts Cited 235
Index of Names 237

PREFACE

The following study has a somewhat unusual origin. It was begun in the spring of 1973 when, in order to use Adam Wodeham as a source in another work, I encountered the difficult and fundamental problem of determining which of the various redactions of his *Sentences* Commentary should be used as the principal text for his thought; or, to phrase the question more accurately, where in the life of Wodeham and the development of his thought should each redaction be placed and, consequently, what value or import should be assigned to each? This led me to investigate and eventually, I believe, solve many of the problems associated with the various redactions of Wodeham's Commentary on the *Sentences*. Initially (and naively) I hoped that what was to be only some background research for a small section in another work would take only a few weeks. Instead, it required a more thorough reading of Wodeham's Commentary, or commentaries, than first anticipated and, eventually, led to the examination of all the extant manuscripts of Wodeham that could be located and identified.

The material on Wodeham thus unearthed went well beyond my original needs. It not only made possible the chronological arrangement of the redactions of his *Sentences* Commentary, but shed considerable light on Wodeham's biography and, more importantly, on Oxford theology in the first third of the fourteenth century. This material should prove useful for anyone who might like to use Wodeham as a source, or for anyone who might give to Wodeham the more concentrated and extensive attention he deserves. I therefore expanded my "footnote" into the following study, in which form I hope it is able to provide a tentative map to guide the way into Wodeham research for other scholars.

A work that attempts to make order out of the literary remains of a famous but almost unstudied author is naturally indebted to a wide number of individuals and institutions. Such is the case with the present study. At the roots of the book stand the European libraries to which I would like to express my gratitude for allowing me access to the manuscripts of Wodeham or for providing microfilm copies of them. In particular, I would like to thank a number of librarians whose helpfulness to me exceeded the responsibilities of their offices: Professor Charles J. Ermatinger of the Vatican Film Library in St. Louis; Professor Astrik L. Gabriel of the Ambrosiana Microfilm Collection at Notre Dame; Dr.

Julian Plante of the Monastic Microfilm Library, Collegeville, Minn.; Sr. Dr. Don José Goñi Gaztambide, librarian of the Cathedral at Pamplona; M. I. Sr. D. Lc. Julian Ruiz Izquierdo, librarian of the Cathedral at Tarazona; and Fr. Dr. Winkler of the Ratsbücherei der Stadt Lüneburg.

I would also like to thank those who, through correspondence or by reading portions of the work, raised questions or made suggestions that altered some inaccurate assumptions or stimulated further thought and research. Most prominent within this group are Fr. Gedeon Gál of the Franciscan Institute at St. Bonaventure, N.Y.; Prof. Dr. Heinrich Schepers of the University of Münster; Dr. Damasus Trapp of the Institut für Spätmittelalter und Reformation at Tübingen; and Prof. James A. Weisheipl of The Pontifical Institute of Mediaeval Studies at Toronto. The evidence and interpretations presented in this work, however, are the responsibility of the author.

Ms. Elizabeth Zanichkowsky and Ms. Katherine Tachau-Auerbach helped improve the text by culling out inconsistencies and typographical errors and by calling my attention to some of the more glaring infelicities of style. In addition I am grateful to several graduate students at the University of Wisconsin who worked on the Wodeham texts with me or who fortuitously happened to be near the appropriate European library when I had a question that could not be answered through the microfilms: Ms. Carol Bargeron, Mr. Ronald Ferguson, Mr. Joseph Freedman, and Mr. Thomas Mitchell.

My greatest debt, however, is to those agencies whose belief in the present project was expressed through generous financial assistance. The American Council of Learned Societies and the Faculty Research Committee of the University of Wisconsin supported the archival research in Spain, France, and Germany and contributed the funds necessary to acquire the microfilms of the manuscripts. The Institute for Research in the Humanities at the University of Wisconsin, perhaps unknowingly, provided the time and setting in which this project was conceived and begun. Finally, the Faculty Research Committee at Wisconsin, the Alexander von Humboldt Stiftung, Prof. Dr. Heiko A. Oberman, and the Institut für Spätmittelalter und Reformation at Tübingen created the opportunity to complete the research and writing. I am particularly grateful to Prof. Oberman and the Humboldt Stiftung for permitting the final stages of this book to be drawn together in an environment that combined a congenial and quiet atmosphere with scholarly expertise and intellectual challenge. Together they enabled me to place my findings where they can be of service to others.

LIST OF ABBREVIATIONS

AFH	*Archivum Franciscanum Historicum*
AFP	*Archivum Fratrum Praedicatorum*
AHDL	*Archives d'histoire doctrinale et littéraire du moyen age*
BB	Baeumker, *Beiträge zur Geschichte der Philosophie und Theologie des Mittelalters*
BRC	Emden, *Biographical Register of the University of Cambridge*
BRO	Emden, *Biographical Register of the University of Oxford*
CIC	*Corpus Iuris Canonici*
CUP	*Chartularium Universitatis Parisiensis*
DTC	*Dictionnaire de théologie catholique*
EF	*Etudes Franciscaines*
FcS	*Franciscan Studies*
FzS	*Franziskanische Studien*
HLF	*Histoire littéraire de la France*
HTR	*Harvard Theological Review*
MedStud	*Mediaeval Studies*
PhilJahr	*Philosophisches Jahrbuch*
RepSent	Stegmüller, *Repertorium Commentariorum in Sententias Petri Lombardi*
RTAM	*Recherches de théologie ancienne et médiévale*
Statuta Oxon	Gibson, *Statuta Antiqua Universitatis Oxoniensis*
ZKT	*Zeitschrift für Katholische Theologie*

INTRODUCTION

Adam Wodeham, O.F.M. (d. 1358) has received only passing mention in the textbooks on the history of medieval philosophy. Although recognized as a major disciple of William of Ockham, he has suffered from the neglect given to medieval thought after Ockham, a neglect now beginning to disappear through the efforts of a number of scholars devoted to research in late medieval thought. We now possess preliminary assessments of the thought of numerous fourteenth-century authors of lesser reputation, but the comment of Etienne Gilson on Wodeham is as true today as when he wrote it: "his works are too little known to permit an estimate of the influence exercised by Ockham upon Adam's own thought."[1]

When one turns from the modern neglect or disinterest in Wodeham to the reputation he held among theologians and philosophers in the late Middle Ages, one is struck by the sharp contrast. Among late medieval authors, Wodeham was generally considered to be one of the two or three greatest minds in the fourteenth century (a period in which both Oxford and Paris produced gifted thinkers in abundance). One early sixteenth-century writer, humanist-trained but with a discernible bias in favor of Oxford theologians, ranked Wodeham among the two or three leading English men of letters since Bede.[2]

What explains such praise? Part of it was due to the fact that Wodeham was at the center of several theological, philosophical, and scientific controversies that reached the height of their English phase[3] during the years 1328 to 1335 and included, among others, such figures as Walter Chatton, Richard Fitzralph, Robert Holcot, Richard Kilvington, William Crathorn, William Skelton, Thomas Bradwardine, Thomas Buckingham, and Robert of Halifax. As the century progressed, the consensus emerged that Wodeham's analysis and solutions on various issues deserved more attention than those of most of his immediate contemporaries. His

---

[1] E. Gilson, *History of Christian Philosophy in the Middle Ages* (New York, 1955), p. 500.
[2] See John Major's introduction in Adam Wodeham, *Super quattuor libros Sententiarum*, abbreviated by Henry Totting of Oyta (Paris, 1512).
[3] Many of these questions were disputed with intensity at Paris during the decade 1340–50. As Michalski has already noted, the Parisian theology of this period was heavily indebted to the Oxford masters, particularly Fitzralph, Holcot, Wodeham, Buckingham, and Bradwardine.

reputation remained strong into the sixteenth century until, with the declining interest in linguistic logic and scholastic theology, Wodeham began to fade into oblivion. In the present century his name has reemerged through the growing interest in Ockham and late medieval thought, to which he contributed so richly. In spite of the lip service paid to his reputation and the acknowledgment that he ranks near the top of Ockham's followers, he has not received the level of attention paid to Fitzralph, Holcot, Bradwardine, or Rimini. If he was truly so important, why has he not been read more?

The major barrier to the study of Wodeham was and remains access to the proper sources. With many fourteenth-century authors, particularly the Franciscans, one is confronted not only with the survival of early *reportationes* and *lecturae annotatae* of one or more *Sentences* commentaries, but on occasion (and such is the case with Wodeham) the process of "re-editing" continued beyond the stage of the *lectura recollecta*, or *textus ordinarius*.[4] Moreover, the practice of reading the *Sentences* at a lesser school before (and sometimes after) reading at a major *studium generale* often produced a series of works that duplicate each other in part but which also must be viewed separately.

The various redactions of Wodeham's *Sentences* commentaries are a classic example of this problem, and the difficulties encountered are both fascinating and frustrating. Apart from the abbreviation of his *Sentences* Commentary made by Henry Totting of Oyta, and a brief treatise on indivisibles recently edited,[5] Wodeham's works are available only in manuscripts, which in turn reflect different redactions that have not yet been successfully identified or chronologically arranged within the known facts of Wodeham's life. To rely on the abbreviation is to rely on a work whose accuracy as a genuine reflection of Wodeham's thought is open to question. To go back to the manuscripts is to encounter the problem of the redactions: which ones best reflect Wodeham's thought and at what time in his life? Even where this effort has been made, following the lines laid down by Michalski,[6] Wodeham was found to be a very complex thinker whose intricate, somewhat involved structure made it difficult to sift out his major arguments and conclusions.

---

[4] For a discussion of the stages in editing *Sentences* commentaries, see D. Trapp, "Dreistufiger Editionsprozess und dreiartige Zitationsweise bei den Augustinertheologen des 14. Jahrhunderts?" *Augustiniana*, XXV (1975), 283–292.

[5] John E. Murdoch and Edward A. Synan, "Two Questions on the Continuum: Walter Chatton (?), O.F.M. and Adam Wodeham, O.F.M.," *FcS*, XXVI (1966), 212–288.

[6] See below, chapter one, pp. 7–10.

In a footnote in a recent article[7] I suggested that the dating and provenance of the various redactions of the *Sentences* commentaries of Wodeham could be established with a higher degree of probability than has heretofore been done. Although some aspects are still unclear, the following remarks are an attempt in that direction and supply a working hypothesis that can be tested and, if necessary, revised as new evidence is uncovered. The work intends only to be a prolegomenon: to identify and arrange Wodeham's writings in such a way that they can be more useful for our understanding of the content and development of his thought. It is primarily a codicological and biographical study. This approach may disappoint many readers who would like to be transported immediately to the major ideas of Wodeham and his contribution to medieval thought. However, before such interpretive studies can successfully be made, the texts must be established. In preparation for that task, this work should provide the necessary background and information for the selection of a text for the critical edition of Wodeham's Oxford Commentary on the *Sentences*. Even before that stage is reached, it is hoped that this arrangement of the sources and survey of their content will prove an adequate guide to Wodeham and thus remove one of the barriers that has hindered or delayed his being read and properly recognized.

In addition to simplifying the access to Wodeham's thought, the following work provides some new information on Wodeham's contemporaries. Wodeham was remarkable in his generation for his willingness to enter into controversy, to record contemporary opinions and attach names to them, and even to mention changes in opinion or development in thought in himself and others. We are becoming more aware in fourteenth-century studies of the importance of understanding and evaluating the thought of one thinker through the objections and counterarguments of his opponents. Scholastic opinions were not arrived at in a vacuum. Positions were refined, in some cases even altered, through an exchange of ideas among contemporaries. Thus it is important to know not only the final position adopted by a thinker but also his earlier positions and the development of his thought. It is only in this way that we can penetrate beyond *what* someone thought to the equally significant questions of *why* and *how*. It would not be wrong to say that for these questions Wodeham is the key to understanding English scholasticism in the crucial period from 1318 to 1338. He summarizes positions or cites

---

[7] "Some Notes on Robert of Halifax, O.F.M.," *FcS*, XXXIII (1973), 135–142.

passages from the works of more fourteenth-century authors than does anyone else in his period, and for some of these authors he is our sole source for their thought. In a similar way, how Wodeham is viewed and used by later thinkers offers some new perspectives on fourteenth-century thought after Wodeham.

The focus of the book, however, remains the life and writings of Wodeham, and our evidence is of three types. Of primary importance are the references in Wodeham's writings themselves. Although some of these may be comments of scribes, the majority appear to be by Wodeham himself and are of a personal and exact nature. The references made to Wodeham's work by other fourteenth-century authors constitute a second level of almost equal importance. Further removed but still of significance are the biographical notices of the sixteenth and later centuries, particularly the remarks of John Major in his preface to the 1512 Paris edition of the abbreviation of Wodeham's *Sentences* Commentary.

Of these three types of evidence, the witness of contemporary writers has been almost completely ignored, and the extant manuscripts as well as the question of the number of redactions of the *Sentences* Commentary of Wodeham have usually been approached through the *vita Adae* of John Major.[8] Fortunately, this procedure (somewhat questionable as a research method) has misled scholarship only in minor ways. Major's remarks were too brief to bear much interpretation, and scholars were unaware of the fourteenth-century traditions on Wodeham that provide the context for Major's remarks. Some interesting results, however, would have been obtained if all the remarks of Major had been examined closely in light of a knowledge of Wodeham's own remarks and in light of the fourteenth-century knowledge of Wodeham. Therefore, instead of understanding Wodeham by way of Major, it would be better to interpret Major by using the evidence from Wodeham and the fourteenth century. Such is the course we shall follow.

Before beginning that task, the unorthodox arrangement of the following work perhaps needs some explanation. In most studies of this type the facts of Wodeham's life, particularly his academic career, would be examined before his works. I have chosen to abandon that traditional order. The biography of Wodeham rests largely on internal evidence in the manuscripts, whose authenticity and chronological order must be established before we can evaluate and utilize the information extracted

---

[8] Adam Wodeham, *Super quattuor libros Sententiarum* (Paris, 1512), fol. ii^r.

from them. To avoid constructing a biography on the promise of evidence or using a tentative biography as a means of arranging the manuscripts, I have chosen to begin with the manuscripts themselves and allow the reader to follow what was my own path: through the manuscripts back to Wodeham.

The authenticity, dating, and arrangement of the manuscripts and redactions of Wodeham's Commentary on the *Sentences* will be approached in three ways: (1) internal evidence in the manuscripts themselves, reflecting the order of the redactions and the circumstances of their composition; (2) the chronological information contained in Wodeham's comments on contemporaries, especially Chatton, Fitzralph, and Holcot; and (3) references to and quotations from Wodeham's works by contemporary or subsequent authors. Only when these tasks have been done can one begin to reconstruct the academic career of Wodeham or use effectively the biographical details contained in the rich *scholion* of the opinions of those Wodeham heard in the schools at Oxford or whose works he read. Given the unusual amount of biographical material scattered throughout his works, it is amazing that the problem of the redactions of his *Sentences* Commentary has remained a mystery so long. However, the reconstruction of Wodeham's biography and the arrangement of his works are only necessary preliminaries that enable us to reach and begin to appreciate Wodeham himself. The rewards will be more than worth the effort. He gives us perhaps our most extensive view of contemporary English scholastic opinion, and he may well be the key to our understanding of one of the most crucial problems of that age: the dissemination of Ockham's thought in England and on the Continent in the fourteenth century.

CHAPTER ONE

LECTURAE SUPER LIBROS SENTENTIARUM

A. WODEHAM STUDIES, 1920–1970

The theory of the relationship of the redactions of the *Sentences* Commentary of Wodeham was primarily the work of Constantine Michalski, developed between 1920 and 1937.[1] It had long been known that Wodeham probably had been a student of Ockham, and that he had received his doctorate at Oxford.[2] John Major, whose biographical sketch of Wodeham was the source of these and other details about Wodeham, also asserted that Wodeham, while resident at London, Oxford, and Norwich, had given two series of lectures on the *Sentences*.[3] Ignoring the second half of this last statement, Michalski concluded that there were three separate commentaries, each more or less complete, and that they probably occurred in the order mentioned in Major. Thus began a search for manuscripts of these three *lecturae*.

On the basis of references at the beginning or end of several manuscripts, Michalski recognized that all of the manuscripts examined by him before 1927, including manuscripts of the abbreviation, represented or were based upon the Oxford lectures of Wodeham as *baccalarius sententiarius*. Eventually he broke these down into four redactions: a first

---

[1] Constantine Michalski, "Les courants philosophiques à Oxford et à Paris pendant le XIVe siècle," *Bulletin international de l'Académie Polonaise des Sciences et des Lettres*, classe d'histoire et de philosophie, 1919–1920 (Krakow, 1922), 71; "Les sources du criticisme et du scepticisme dans la philosophie du XIVe siècle," *International Congress of Historical Sciences* (La Pologne au Ve Congrès international des Sciences Historiques) (Brussels, 1923; Warsaw, 1924), 242; "Die vielfachen Redaktionen einiger Kommentare zu Petrus Lombardus," in *Miscellanea Fr. Ehrle*, Vol. I (Rome, 1924), 239–244; "Le criticisme et le scepticisme dans la philosophie du XIVe siècle," *Bulletin international de l'Académie Polonaise des Sciences et des Lettres*, classe d'histoire et de philosophie, 1925 (Krakow, 1927), 45–46; "Les courants critiques et sceptiques dans la philosophie du XIVe siècle," Ibid., 200–201; "Le problème de la volonté à Oxford et à Paris au XIVe siècle," *Studia Philosophica: Commentarii Societatis Philosophicae Polonorum*, Vol. II (Leopoli, 1937), 241–247.

[2] A. G. Little, *The Grey Friars in Oxford* (Oxford, 1892), pp. 172–173.

[3] Wodeham, *Super quattuor libros Sententiarum* (Paris, 1512), fol. ii^r: "... Oxoniensis academiae ... doctor, Londiniis anglorum regia, Oxoniae et Norwici plurimum moratus, quibus in locis duas Sententiarum lecturas peregit. Okam et Catonis contemporaneus, utrumque in scholis respondentem audivit."

redaction containing the original Oxford lectures, preserved only in Vatican lat. 955 (book I) and Vatican lat. 1110 (books II–IV); a later and longer redaction, preserved in Paris, B. N. lat. 15 892 (books I–IV) and including the additions that were written in the margin of Vat. lat. 955; a middle redaction, containing many but not all the marginal additions of Vat. lat. 955, preserved in Paris, Mazarine 915 (books I–IV); and the abbreviation of Wodeham's Commentary by Henry Totting of Oyta, compiled around 1375 and based on the middle edition.

The additions in the margins and on separate leaves in Vat. lat. 955 are one of the most intriguing but troublesome aspects of these manuscripts. For a time Michalski entertained the idea that Vat. lat. 955 might be a later, shorter text on whose margins the earlier, longer text had been written to improve its value and usefulness for its owner. Eventually, however, Michalski became convinced that the additions were authentic and that the main text of Vat. lat. 955 and its companion manuscript, Vat. lat. 1110 were the *redactio prima* out of which the other texts emerged.

Michalski's understandable fascination with the relation of text and marginalia in Vat. lat. 955 had the side effect of focusing attention on what he called the *editio prima* (Vat. lat. 955 and 1110) and the *editio longa* (B. N. lat. 15 892) to the neglect of the *editio media* (Mazarine 915). It was natural to suppose that what Wodeham originally said and what he finally said were more important than the middle stage. On the basis of Michalski's analysis one could only regret that Oyta chose to abbreviate the *editio media*, thus insuring that the text most accessible to modern scholars would be the least desirable basis for an assessment of Wodeham's thought.

Michalski made no attempt to date these various redactions apart from indicating that the *editio prima*, on the basis of the *explicit* in Vat. lat. 1110, had been completed in 1332.[4] The revisions must have taken place after that date, and there did not seem to be any way of knowing when. Michalski was more interested in discovering manuscript copies of the other two series of lectures given by Wodeham, namely the London and Norwich lectures. He knew from a statement at the beginning of book III in some manuscripts that Wodeham had lectured at London before Oxford and that in these earlier lectures he had commented on the first thirteen distinctions of book III.[5] In 1927 he announced the discovery of

---

[4] Vat. lat. 1110, fol. 135ᵛ: "Et sic finitur quartus liber fratris Adae Wodeham, doctoris in theologia, qui legit Oxoniae anno Domini MCCCXXXII."

[5] Many manuscripts, including Vat. lat. 1110 and Paris, B. N. lat. 15 892, lack this introductory explanation why Wodeham began his Oxford lectures on book three with

a new series of Wodeham lectures, contained in Cambridge, Gonville and Caius College, 281/674, fols. 105^r–250^v, covering books I and II. His initial reaction (1927) was that he had found the London lectures, in spite of the fact that book III, dist. 1–13, did not occur in the manuscript. By 1937 he had revised his judgment after discovering in the Paris lectures of Oyta a reference to the ninth question of the prologue of the London lectures.[6] Since the Caius manuscript contained only six questions in its prologue, he concluded it must be the Norwich lectures rather than the London lectures. Apart from the problem of which lectures they were, Michalski had every right to be proud that he had uncovered a new and exciting Wodeham source, one that concentrated as heavily on problems of the intellect and epistemology as the Oxford lectures had concentrated on problems of the will. In the meantime, Ehrle and Doucet had discovered two other commentaries that appeared to be by Wodeham, seemingly differing from each other as much as they differed from the Oxford lectures and the Caius manuscript.[7]

By 1937 Michalski had arrived at the following picture of Wodeham's academic career and the redactions of the *Sentences* Commentary. The London lectures, which preceded the Oxford lectures, were to be placed during the academic biennium 1328–1330.[8] In their proper form those lectures were lost, at least for the present. Assuming that an introductory note at the bottom of folio 1^v in Vat. lat. 955 referred to the text and not to the marginalia, Michalski concluded that parts of the London lectures

---

distinction 14. The introductory passage occurs in Paris, Maz. 915, fol. 167^r: "Circa istum librum tertium, qui alias Londoniae toto anno pertractavi quaestiones 13 primarum distinctionum, ideo nunc incipio a distinctione 14." The same words occur in Paris, Univ. 193, fol. 124vb and Tarazona, Cat. 7, fol. 131vb. No doubt because Oyta based his abbreviation on the redaction contained in Paris, Maz. 915, all copies of the Oyta abbreviation, e.g., Barcelona, Cat. 38, fol. 117^r, or Pamplona, Cat. 1, fol. 135^r, have this passage, and it was included in the printed edition of 1512, fol. 115^v. Michalski overlooked the fact that the Mazarine text referred to London after "alias", and unnecessarily based his information on F. Ehrle, *Der Sentenzenkommentar Peters von Candia des Pisaner Papstes Alexanders V* (Münster, 1925), p. 99, who in turn based his information on the printed edition of Oyta's abbreviation.

[6] Henry Totting of Oyta, *Quaestiones Sententiarum*, I, q. 1 (München, Staatsbibl., Clm 8867, fol. 20^r; Krakow, Bibl. Jag., 1362, fol. 20^r): "Adam, lectura Londoniensi, quaestione 9 prologi, articulo 3. . . ."

[7] Ehrle, *Der Sentenzenkommentar*, p. 97, called attention to Paris, Univ. 193 (44), and V. Doucet called attention to Vat. lat. 13002 in *AFH*, XXVIII (1935), 415, n. 1; XLVI (1953), 98, n. 3; *Commentaires sur les sentences. Supplément au Répertoire de M. Frédéric Stegmueller* (Florence-Quaracchi, 1954), 9.

[8] Michalski, "Le problème de la volonté," *Studia Phil.*, II, 247.

were incorporated into the Oxford lectures Wodeham gave as *sententiarius*.[9] Those Oxford lectures, in turn, were placed in the academic biennium 1330–1332, as established by the colophon in Vat. lat. 1110. Almost immediately the *editio prima* (Vat. lat. 955 and 1110) of those lectures was revised into the *editio longa* (Paris, B. N. lat. 15 892), since the Norwich lectures, read during the next academic biennium (1332–1334) and thought to be contained in Cambridge, Caius 281, included portions of the Oxford lectures according to the version of the *editio longa*.[10] That was sufficient proof for Michalski that Wodeham preferred the *editio longa*, which must therefore be the *ordinatio*.[11] Michalski was vague on whether the *editio media* (contained in Paris, Mazarine 915) stood chronologically between the *editio prima* and the *editio longa* (*ordinatio*) or whether it was an abbreviated version of the *editio longa*. In any event, its value was questionable, since the revised version Wodeham chose to incorporate into his Norwich lectures (and thus preferred) was the version of the *editio longa*. Inasmuch as the Norwich lectures reused material from the Oxford lectures, Wodeham may also have incorporated material from the London lectures, either directly or, more likely, as mediated through the Oxford lectures. In sum, the progression was: London (1328–30), then Oxford (1330–32), and finally Norwich (1332–34), and the *editio longa* was the *ordinatio* of the Oxford lectures.

Michalski's thesis about the redactions of Wodeham's Commentary

---

[9] Ibid., 245–246: "C'était là d'ailleurs sa méthode habituelle de travail comme en fait foi la note du Cod. Vat. lat. 955 qui sans aucun doute est de l'auteur lui-même, car elle se rattache organiquement à sa profession de foi, *protestatio*. Nous la rapportons ici textuellement pour l'interpréter à loisir: 'Incipit brevis collectio Wodeham super sententias apud Oxon, extracta ex leccionibus suis alibi et ex occurentibus aliis postea, dum se disponeret et eciam dum legebat.' fol. 1ᵛᵒ. A. Woodham veut signifier que sa *lectura* d'Oxford se compose 1) d'extraits choisis d'une *lectura* prononcée ailleurs—à Londres (extracta ex leccionibus suis alibi), 2) de parties nouvelles ajoutées soit au cours de la préparation de ses nouvelles leçons à Oxford, soit au cours même des leçons. Comme nous ne connaissons pas le *lectura* de Londres, il ne nous est pas possible d'indiquer exactement lesquelles de ses parties entrèrent dans le *lectura* ultérieure d'Oxford."

[10] Ibid., 246: "Je présume, en me basant sur la note rapportée plus haut du Cod. Vat. lat. 955, que le texte court date du temps de la préparation de la *lectura* d'Oxford (et ex occurentibus aliis postea, dum se disponeret), et qu'Adam Woodham y a adjoint les additions au moment même où il commentait Lombard (et eciam dum legebat), obtenant ainsi un nouveau texte, plus étendu dans l'ensemble. Le texte obtenu de cette façon passa en certaines de ses parties à la *lectura* ultérieure de Norwich."

[11] Ibid.: "Au cours de mes recherches sur la relation des deux dernières *lecturae* je suis parvenu à un important résultat, c'est à savoir qu'Adam Woodham a introduit dans la *lectura* de Norwich le texte long de la *lectura* d'Oxford, conservé dans les manuscrits du second groupe—et non le texte court du premier groupe. Nous avons là la preuve que l'auteur lui-même considérait le texte long comme l'*ordinatio* définitive."

on the *Sentences* and his evaluation of the manuscripts that contained them has gone almost unchallenged in subsequent scholarship. Ehrle, who discussed the pre-1925 version of Michalski's research into Wodeham, basically accepted his arguments, as did Lang.[12] Anneliese Maier made use of the Vatican manuscripts of Wodeham on some scientific questions, but her understanding of the redactions was based on Michalski.[13] As recently as 1966 John Murdoch, who has made one of the few recent additions to our knowledge of Wodeham, relied on Michalski's findings as they pertained to the *Sentences* Commentary.[14] The only doubts were raised by André Combes who, in 1961, pointed out that the *editio longa*, at least as found in Paris, B. N. lat. 15 892, was occasionally shorter, both in structure and content, than the Oyta abbreviation, which was based on the *editio media*.[15] In what sense, therefore, should it be called the *editio longa*? The problem was that Michalski had arrived at his view by tracing the marginalia of Vat. lat. 955 into the texts of Maz. 915 and B. N. lat. 15 892 and found that the latter included more of the marginalia than the former. He apparently did not compare the text of Vat. lat. 955 against the texts of Maz. 915 and B. N. lat. 15 892 on an individual question, in which case he would have found that the text of the first two manuscripts had been reduced in B. N. lat. 15 892. Combes did not carry his question that far. Instead, he confined himself to a comparison of B. N. lat. 15 892 and the Oyta text on only one question, and simply noted the possible inappropriateness of the title *editio longa*.

No one apart from Combes has sufficiently examined the manuscripts of Wodeham to raise questions about the Michalski thesis. Most scholars have relied on the Oyta abbreviation,[16] but some have not even penetrated beyond the information on Wodeham contained in Michalski's articles.[17]

---

[12] Ehrle, *Der Sentenzenkommentar*, p. 98; A. Lang, *Heinrich Totting von Oyta*, BB, xxxiii.4–5 (Münster i.W., 1937), pp. 54–61.

[13] A. Maier, *Die Vorläufer Galileis im 14. Jahrhundert*, Storia e Letteratura, xxii, 2nd ed. (Rome, 1966), pp. 174–176, 301; *Ausgehendes Mittelalter*, Vol. I (Rome, 1964), pp. 79, 252.

[14] J. E. Murdoch and E. A. Synan, "Two Questions on the Continuum: Walter Chatton (?), O.F.M. and Adam Wodeham, O.F.M.," *FcS*, XXVI (1966), 221.

[15] Jean de Ripa, *Lectura super primum sentientiarum. Prologi quaestiones I & II*, ed. André Combes (Paris, 1961), p. 399.

[16] For example, A. Lang, *Die Wege der Glaubensbegründung bei den Scholastikern des 14. Jahrhunderts*, BB, xxx.1–2 (Münster i.W., 1930), p. 151; A. Lang, *Heinrich Totting von Oyta*, pp. 54–61; P. De Vooght, *Les sources de la doctrine chrétienne* (Paris, 1954), p. 144; H. A. Oberman, *Archbishop Thomas Bradwardine. A Fourteenth Century Augustinian* (Utrecht, 1958), p. 47.

[17] For example, J. A. Robson, *Wyclif and the Oxford Schools* (Cambridge, 1961), pp. 78, 81–82.

A few have looked into the manuscripts but, it would appear, only to collate passages already found and interpreted through the printed edition.[18]

In order to test Michalski's thesis it is necessary to go back to the internal evidence contained in the Wodeham manuscripts. However, one must proceed here with great caution. Evidence sometimes has a way of confirming a preconceived hypothesis to the exclusion of other hypotheses that might also explain the evidence. The evidence Michalski looked at supported his thesis. It did not occur to him that it might also support a different thesis, nor did he construct tests that would disprove all other theses and thus unquestionably establish his own. Consequently, in order to avoid a circular argument that arranges the manuscripts chronologically according to our knowledge of Wodeham's career and then arranges that career according to information in the manuscripts, it is desirable to establish at the beginning the date, order, and relative merits of the various manuscripts and redactions of Wodeham on the basis of internal evidence alone.

B. THE REDACTIONS OF THE OXFORD LECTURES ON THE *Sentences*

Almost all the manuscripts of Wodeham's lectures on the *Sentences* belong to one of several redactions of the same work, as Michalski correctly ascertained. These manuscripts divide into five main groups, or redactions, to be discussed in more detail in the appendices.

The largest group comprises Erfurt, CA 2° 133; Lüneburg, Ratsbücherei, Theol. 4° 29; Paris, Mazarine 915; Paris, Université 193; Tarazona, Catedral 7; Vat. lat. 955; and portions of Bruges, Bibl. de la Ville 172. Within that group only Mazarine, Tarazona, and Université contain all four books. Moreover, they are almost identical in text and format. Although differing in format, the original (unaltered) text of Vat. lat. 955 is very close to the text of book I in these three manuscripts. Despite Michalski's assertion that Mazarine incorporated some of the marginal additions of Vat. lat. 955, I have been unable to find any significant differences between the original text of Vat. lat. 955 and the text of Mazarine, Université, and Tarazona. On occasion the last three manuscripts have material that is interlinear or marginal in Vat. lat. 955, but much of this shared material is, in Vat. lat. 955, in the hand of the original

---

[18] For example, G. Leff, *Bradwardine and the Pelagians* (Cambridge, 1957); G. Leff, *Gregory of Rimini* (Manchester, 1961); W. Dettloff, *Die Entwicklung der Akzeptations- und Verdienstlehre von Duns Scotus bis Luther*, BB, xl.2 (Münster i.W., 1963), pp. 329–332.

scribe and all of this shared material constitutes corrections of scribal errors, not additions to or revisions of the text. Other differences between Vat. lat. 955 and the other three manuscripts are not based upon the marginal revisions. Thus Vat. lat. 955 should not be considered a separate redaction from Mazarine 915. Michalski's theory may have been based less on the text of Vat. lat. 955 than on its relationship with Vat. lat. 1110, a problem that will be discussed below.

Within this same general group, Erfurt and Lüneburg, like Vat. lat. 955, contain only book I and possess rich marginal references. Although the marginal references of Lüneburg are usually a repetition of names that occur in the text, they do on occasion, as do those of Vat. lat. 955, identify anonymous arguments in the text. In the case of Walter Burley and John of Rodington, the Lüneburg manuscript identifies opinions that are ignored in the margins of Vat. lat. 955.[19] The relationship of the Lüneburg and Vatican manuscripts may be even closer. At one point they have the same geometric figure in the margin—the only two manuscripts to do so.[20]

However, the Lüneburg manuscript cannot be a direct copy of the Vatican manuscript, nor the Vatican of it. The order of questions differs radically in the Lüneburg manuscript, as does the order in the Erfurt manuscript. In the case of Lüneburg, some of this may be due to the shifting of text units before binding, but it is clear that in the Lüneburg arrangement, distinction 6 was to precede immediately distinction 33 (possibly thought of as distinction 7 for reasons that will become clear when we look at the second group). Similarly, distinction 3 was meant to follow immediately upon distinction 33 and to be followed, in turn, by distinction 8. The order of questions in the Erfurt manuscript (see appendix 1, section C) probably reflects what the Lüneburg manuscript was supposed to have looked like. Moreover, the Erfurt and Lüneburg manuscripts share readings not found in the other manuscripts, and thus form a subredaction within the first group. They probably stem from the same tradition as Vat. lat. 955, but with at least one intermediate text.

The Bruges manuscript contains a version of book IV that is all but identical with the text of Mazarine, Université, and Tarazona manuscripts. Both in readings and in the style of the hand it stands closest to Univ. 193.

A second major group consists of Paris, Bibl. Nat. lat. 15 892; Florence, Bibl. Naz., conv. soppr. B VII 1249; the marginal additions and insertions

---

[19] Lüneburg, Ratsbüch., theol. 4° 29, fols. 144va, 164ra, 181ra.
[20] Cf. Vat. lat. 955, fol. 19^r and Lüneburg 4° 29, fol. 14^v.

in Vat. lat. 955; and portions of Bruges, Bibl. de la Ville, 172, and Florence, Bibl. Naz., conv. soppr. A III 508.

Vat. lat. 1110 must be treated as a third and separate category. Its text differs in important respects from that of the previous two groups.

The final two redactions are extracts or abbreviations. One group is represented by Naples, Bibl. Naz. VII C 53, and Hannover, Stadtbibl. 1. The second group is the Oyta abbreviation, the manuscripts of which are listed in appendix 4.

There can be no doubt that this work, occurring in so many redactions, is the Oxford lectures of Adam Wodeham as *baccalarius sententiarius*. Most manuscripts identify Wodeham as the author, and passages quoted from Wodeham by other authors can be found in this work. Moreover, several manuscripts describe the work as the Oxford lectures, and at one point in the work Wodeham uses Oxford in an example that would be meaningful only if he were present there.[21] Wodeham also refers to the London and Norwich lectures, thus confirming that the work in question could not be either of those series of lectures.[22] Finally, Wodeham's numerous references to *socii baccalarii* in all four books establish that these lectures were delivered as a Franciscan bachelor at Oxford. The next step is to determine the dates of the various redactions.

The dating of Wodeham's Oxford lectures has depended almost exclusively on the colophon in Vat. lat. 1110, fol. 135^v: "Et sic finitur quartus liber fratris Adae Wodeham, doctoris in theologia, qui legit Oxoniae anno Domini MCCCXXXII." Michalski mistranscribed "qui legit" as "quem legit," and concluded that the fourth book was completed in 1332, and that Wodeham thus read in 1330–32 (if one believes it was a biennial reading) or 1331–32 (if one believes he read only for one academic year). But "qui", as the subject of "legit", refers to Wodeham,

---

[21] Wodeham, *Lectura Oxon*. I, dist. 2, q. 1, dub. 5 (Vat. lat. 955, fol. 105^r): "Verbi gratia, aliquando volo intrare villam [Oxford] tam ut intersim disputationi quam ut loquar scriptori, etc." And inserted on the margin: "Et potest esse quod indigerem ire ad loquendum cum scriptore, dato quod nulla tunc fieret disputatio. Et potest etiam tunc ita esse quod oporteret me tunc intrare villam pro disputatione audienda, dato quod nihil haberem facere cum scriptore." Paris, Maz. 915, fol. 65rb, and Paris, Univ. 193, fol. 78va lack the marginal addition. The Franciscan convent at Oxford, where Wodeham was lecturing, was located outside the walls of Oxford, commonly referred to as the *villa*. The point of the remark would have been lost on an audience unfamiliar with the geographical relation of the Grey Friars convent to the Oxford schools.

[22] There are numerous references to the London lectures in books III and IV of the Oxford lectures. See below, chapter four, note 30. Also in the Oxford lectures, books I, III & IV, there are references to the Norwich lectures. See below, chapter four, notes 19–23.

not the fourth book, and states that Wodeham read at Oxford but not necessarily that he read exactly the text that occurs on the previous 135 folios. Moreover, the date is not as helpful as it appears. Assuming that it is correct, it could be the year in which Wodeham began reading, the year in which he finished reading, one of the years in between, the date of the redaction contained in the manuscript, or possibly even the date of the manuscript.[23] This colophon can be helpful, but only when placed in the company of less ambiguous witnesses.

To arrive at a date for Wodeham's *Sentences* the usual procedure has been to assume that Vat. lat. 955 (book I) and Vat. lat. 1110 (books II–IV) are two consecutive volumes of the same redaction. After all, they both use a one-column structure, they both have rich marginalia, and they are found near each other on the shelves of the same library. Taking Michalski's suggestion that these two manuscripts contain the primitive text and relying on the colophon date of 1332 in Vat. lat. 1110, Wodeham scholarship has proceeded to view and interpret the other redactions in light of this foundation. However, in order to discover the order and date of the redactions rather than presuppose it, it is preferable to begin with the manuscripts in the first two groups and then interpret the Vatican manuscripts in light of their evidence.

1. *Editiones media et longa Reconsidered*

One of the most important dating devices in the Wodeham manuscripts was discovered by Albert Lang, but not fully explored.[24] It occurs in the fifth *dubium* of question 3, dist. 14, book III where Wodeham, in discussing the truth value and reference of temporal propositions against the position of Fitzralph, mentions the name of the then reigning pope. The passage does not occur in Vat. lat. 1110 or in Bruges 172, but it does appear in all other manuscripts of Wodeham's Oxford lectures that contain book III. The Tarazona manuscript gives the pope as John XXII, while, perpetuating what is undoubtedly a scribal error, Univ. 193 and

---

[23] Damasus Trapp, in working on the manuscripts of Gregory of Rimini, has argued that the date in the colophon: "... Gregorii, qui legit Parisius A.D. 1344" applies to the publication of the redaction, not to the year in which Gregory read the *Sentences*. See D. Trapp, "Gregory of Rimini Manuscripts, Editions and Additions," *Augustiniana*, VIII (1958), 425–443; "New Approaches to Gregory of Rimini," *Augustinianum*, II (1962), 115–130.

[24] A. Lang, *Heinrich Totting von Oyta*, p. 56.

Maz. 915 give John XXI.[25] B. N. lat. 15 892 and Florence, Bibl. Naz., conv. soppr. B VII 1249 (the only two complete manuscripts of the second group) name Benedict XII as the then reigning pope.[26] The Oyta abbreviation has Gregory XI.[27]

Thus the redaction contained in the Tarazona, Université, and Mazarine manuscripts, at least through book III, was completed before December 4, 1334 (the date of John's death). Moreover, it would appear that the redaction preserved in the two manuscripts of the second group

---

[25] In this section of Wodeham's Commentary, Paris, Maz. 915 is derived from Paris, Univ. 193 which, along with Tarazona 7, goes back to a lost exemplar. In the following passage the original text of the exemplar has been reconstructed as nearly as possible from the Université and Tarazona manuscripts, with the occasional help of later redactions that derive from the earlier exemplar. Since the passage is of crucial importance and the pattern of the individual *omissiones per homoeoteleuton* typical for this section of the *Lectura,* the texts of all three manuscripts have been given on page 29 to illustrate the relation of the manuscripts. Tarazona 7, fol. 142^{rD}, Université 193, fol. 184^{vD} (135vb), and Mazarine 915, fols. 179ra–179rb: "Praeterea, aliud falsum sumitur, videlicet quod tales in mente congregati termini 'rex Bohemiae primus futurus' vel 'summus sacerdos primus futurus', et sic de similibus, significent praecise illos qui primo succedent iam praesentibus, quia non plus quam iste terminus 'summus pontifex praesens' praecise significat Johannem 22, quia iste terminus congregatus non praecise significat nec praecise repraesentat menti Johannem 22, quamvis solum pro illo nunc vere supponat respectu verbi 'de praesenti', quia ita significat praeteritos et futuros, et menti repraesentat sicut illum. Alioquin haec esset falsa: 'Petrus fuit summus sacerdos praesens' vel '*a* erit summus sacerdos praesens' (sit *a* nomen alicuius futuri summi pontificis post Johannem), quae tamen verae sunt. Essent autem falsae nisi praedicatum 'praeteritos' et 'futuros' significaret vel ad minus repraesentaret, immo omnem sacerdotem et omnem summum repraesentat, quamvis vox haec expressa 'summus sacerdos praesens' aliquando distincte faciat recordari de Johanne apud unum et apud alium de alio praeterito vel futuro. Nec mirum cum solum ille de facto sit summus sacerdos."

[26] Paris, B. N. lat. 15 892, fol. 144rb; Florence, Bibl. Naz., conv. soppr., B VII 1249, fol. 110va: "Praeterea, aliud falsum sumitur, videlicet quod tales in mente congregati termini 'rex Angliae primus futurus' vel 'summus pontifex primus [futurus]', et sic de similibus, significent praecise istos qui primo succedant iam praesentibus, quia non plus hoc quam iste terminus 'summus pontifex praesens' significet Benedictum XII, quia iste terminus congregatus modo praecise significat nec praecise repraesentat menti Benedictum XII, quamvis pro illo nunc vere supponat respectu verbi 'de praesenti', quia significat praeteritos et futuros et menti repraesentat, sicut illum. Alioquin haec esset falsa: 'Petrus fuit summus sacerdos praesens' et similiter, '*a* erit summus sacerdos praesens' (sit *a* nomen alicuius futuri)."

[27] Oyta abbreviation (Paris, 1512), fol. 121vb: "Aliud falsum sumitur, videlicet quod tales conceptus in mente nostra congregati 'rex Bohemiae primus futurus' vel 'summus sacerdos primus futurus', et sic de similibus, significet illos qui primo succedent iam praesentibus, et non plus significant illos quam iste terminus 'summus pontifex praesens' significat praecise Gregorium XI, licet solum pro illo nunc vere supponat respectu verbi 'de praesenti', tamen ita significat praeteritos et futuros sicut istum. Alioquin haec esset falsa: 'Petrus fuit summus sacerdos praesens' vel '*a* erit summus sacerdos praesens', quod patet falsum."

should be dated after December 20, 1334 (the date of the election of Benedict XII) and before 1342 (the date of Benedict's death). Similarly, on the basis of this passage, Lang dated the Oyta abbreviation between 1370 and 1378.

While the *terminus ante quem* for the first group is certain, could not the mention of Benedict XII or Gregory XI have been inserted by a scribe, thus giving us an approximate date for the first manuscript in which these changes occurred but not for the redactions themselves? For several reasons it is unlikely that we have here a case of scribal updating. The period of the pontificate of Gregory XI as a date for the *Abbreviatio* accords perfectly with what we otherwise know of the life of Oyta, and no one has questioned Lang's dating. As for the two manuscripts of the second group, they derive independently from a lost exemplar. Thus their agreement in naming Benedict XII suggests that Benedict XII was also mentioned in at least one manuscript of this redaction earlier than the two we have. Furthermore, the introductory note in the margin of Vat. lat. 955 applies to the marginal revisions that contribute to the text of this second group and may indicate that some of their content was taken from lectures given after those of Oxford.[28] In all cases (and this is true for the first group of manuscripts as well as the Oyta abbreviation), the changes in the name of the reigning pope coincide with the changes in redaction, never with the date at which the manuscript was copied. That this passage provides a reliable dating device was already recognized by John Major, but he mistakenly understood it as a date for Wodeham, not Oyta: "Nota tempus quo Adam hunc librum composuit, quia de tempore Gregorii XI anno Domini MCCCLXX."[29]

Having placed these redactions in sequence, there are some characteristics worth noting. The redaction represented by the Mazarine, Tarazona,

---

[28] Vat. lat. 955, fol. 1ᵛ: "In nomine Domini incipit brevis collectio Wodeham super Sententias apud Oxoniam, extracta ex lectionibus suis alibi et ex occurrentibus aliis postea, dum se disponeret et etiam dum legebat." The meaning of *postea* in this context is unclear. It could mean lectures given after those delivered elsewhere (i.e., the Oxford lectures postdate the *lectiones alibi*), or it could refer to lectures given after the Oxford lectures. In the first interpretation the *aliis postea* is somewhat redundant and unnecessary; in the second interpretation, one could question why the author of this comment did not add "alibi" or "alias" after "postea" or "legebat". The fact that the second redaction can be dated after 1334 suggests that lectures after those of Oxford are intended. A slightly different form of this statement occurs in Bruges 172, fol. 27ᵛ: "In nomine Domini incipit brevis collectio Wodham super Sententias apud Oxoniam, extracta ex lectionibus suis et alibi occurrentibus, dum se disponeret et etiam dum legebat. . . ."

[29] Oyta abbreviation (Paris, 1512), fol. 121ᵛᵇ.

and Université manuscripts is the longest version, and it is a finished, polished production. Not only is the quality of the hand invariably precise, unhurried, and professional, but in the Université and Mazarine manuscripts there is also a marginal cyclic lettering system by question which served two purposes. First, it provided a second and shorter means by which Wodeham's text could be cited, namely by book, question, and letter rather than book, question, article, *dubium*, and response or, less useful, a folio reference. Secondly, at the bottom of almost every page, content summaries are provided for each letter, indicating the flow of the argument and permitting the reader to find a particular passage quickly. In Université 193 these summaries cease at book IV, q. 5, although the lettering system continues to the end.

Oyta's abbreviation was based on this redaction, but since it does not share many of the *omissiones per homoeoteleuton* found in Université and Mazarine, Oyta did not use these manuscripts. It is likely, however, that Oyta did use a copy that resembled the format of the Paris manuscripts. Some of the descriptive notes that occur at the bottom of the folios of the Mazarine and Université manuscripts were abbreviated and raised into the margin of the Oyta text at the appropriate point. In the printed edition, in turn, some of these marginal notes of the Oyta manuscripts were inserted into the body of Wodeham's argument.[30] Oyta's dependence on the form of Wodeham's Oxford lectures represented by these Parisian manuscripts is strong. As a comparison of the versions of the dating passage referred to above indicates, Oyta's reference to the King of Bohemia was based on this early redaction of Wodeham's text and was not his own inspiration. Thus the major evidence Lang used to support a Prague location for Oyta's abbreviation of Wodeham suggests instead a Paris location.[31] This may be why Oyta's reference to Wodeham occurs in his Paris lectures, not his Prague lectures.

The redaction represented by B. N. lat. 15 892 and Florence, Bibl. Naz., conv. soppr. B VII 1249 differs from the first redaction in a number of respects. First, the order of questions is different, as a glance at appendix 2 will show. This is not a result of the fact that the various text units could be bound together in different sequences, as we have seen with the Erfurt and Lüneburg manuscripts. The distinctions have been changed (e.g., dist. 33 has become dist. 7 and placed earlier), some questions have been

---

[30] Both Michalski and Combes have noted this difference between the Oyta manuscripts and the printed edition. See Jean de Ripa, *Lectura*, pp. 397–400.

[31] Cf. above, footnote 25, and Lang, p. 56.

removed, and other questions have been added. As in the case of the Erfurt manuscript (and possibly also in the Lüneburg manuscript before rearrangement and binding), the first book ends with dist. 17, the material on grace and merit, which is also the opening subject material of book II.

Second, as André Combes already noted, the text in many of the questions in this second redaction is shorter, both in structure (i.e., the number of arguments and counterarguments) and in content (i.e., individual arguments and responses have been reduced).[32]

Third, the quality of the manuscripts in the second redaction differs from those of the first redaction. They lack the finished, polished features, such as the cyclic lettering system and corresponding summaries, nor are they rubricated or ruled off as neatly. The hands are less careful and professional. There are also a greater number of scribal errors and bad readings.

Finally, it should be noted that the Florence and Paris manuscripts of this second redaction derive independently from an earlier manuscript of this tradition.[33] The lost manuscript that stands behind the Florence manuscript contained more folios than almost any extant manuscript of this work.[34]

---

[32] Ripa, *Lectura*, p. 399. Combes' edition of Oyta's abbreviation of Wodeham, *Lectura Oxon*. III, q. 1 provides a good opportunity to illustrate the reduction in structure (references in Combes are to the page and numbered line). The structure of the question from the beginning through article 2 is identical in Vat. lat. 1110, Paris, Maz. 915, and Paris, B. N. lat. 15 892. A few changes already appear in art. 2 in the Oyta abbreviation. The name of Grafton, whose opinions Wodeham discusses in art. 2, is garbled in the Oyta text to read "Grascon". With Wodeham's reply to Grafton, the structure begins to alter. The fourth through eighth replies to Wodeham were dropped by Oyta, as were the fifth principal argument and one that follows it. The most important changes, however, occur in art. 3. There Wodeham is attacking the opinions of Chatton (identified in the Oyta text as "Tricon"; Combes, 405.60, 406.95, 409.77) and the Benedictine bachelor, who argued 10 points in the previous year (Combes, 409.7–411.14). Not all these arguments are picked up for reply. Of the first 19 arguments, some of them belonging to Chatton, only fifteen are singled out for reply. However, all ten arguments of the Benedictine *socius* are answered, giving a total count of 25 in the Vatican and Mazarine manuscripts. In the Oyta abbreviation, those arguments and their corresponding replies are reduced to 22 (specifically 14, 15, and 19 having been removed). In the Paris, B. N. manuscript these are reduced to 13 arguments and replies. Moreover, a long section of conclusions and suppositions that appears in the Vatican, Mazarine, and B. N. manuscripts between the ninth and tenth replies, is missing in the Oyta abbreviation.

[33] See the discussion in appendix 2, pp. 202–203.

[34] Florence, Bibl. Naz., conv. soppr. B VII 1249, fol. 76va: "Dicendum est ergo, sicut supra praecedenti quaestione, fol. 100, quod tripliciter potest esse. . . ." Only in Univ. 193 would this reference back to dist. 17, q. 2 coincide with fol. 100, but the Florence and Université manuscripts belong to different redactions.

The original, pre-1334 redaction of Wodeham's *Sentences* Commentary as contained in the Paris and Tarazona manuscripts is the longer work, and its length suggests that these lectures were given across a two-year period, possibly interrupted by a year of lectures elsewhere.[35] This early form, following almost immediately upon the oral presentation, is one of the longest *Sentences* commentaries in the fourteenth century, running to almost a thousand columns of abbreviated text. There is also evidence to suggest that individual questions occupied more than one lecture period.[36] Even supposing Wodeham read on all legible days and during vacations as well, it would still be difficult to fit his Commentary into a year. A biennial reading is confirmed by Wodeham himself when in book III, referring to the opinions of a *socius* cited in book I, he states that those opinions (and thus his own lectures on book I) were given in *anno praeterito*.[37] Since the calendar year in fourteenth-century England extended into March, Wodeham would not have phrased himself thus if those opinions had been given in the fall semester of the academic year in which he lectured on book III.

There is every reason to believe that B. N. lat. 15 892 is an authentic redaction of Wodeham, but one done after 1334. Most of the changes that occurred between the first and second redactions cannot be viewed as corrections of scribal error, nor are they the type of changes that an abbreviator would make. Ultimately, the authenticity of B. N. lat. 15 892 depends on one's assessment of the additions in Vat. lat. 955.

2. *Vat. lat. 955: Main text and marginalia*

Michalski noted at the beginning of modern Wodeham research that all the material in the marginal additions of Vat. lat. 955 that he had checked appeared in the text of B. N. lat. 15 892. If that is so (and this has not yet been checked in every detail), then the marginalia of Vat. lat. 955 were added after 1334 whereas the main text, which coincides with Mazarine

---

[35] For a discussion of this point, see chapter 4, pp. 166–172.

[36] During his reading of question two of the prologue of his Oxford lectures Wodeham became aware of Fitzralph's change of opinion and was able to quote the revised version exactly. Therefore, there must have been at least one break in lecturing in the course of that question.

[37] Paris, Maz. 915, fol. 170va: "Item 16 potest sic argui, sicut fecit anno praeterito quidam bacallarius in hiis mediis fundans se quae hic sequitur. . . ." The reference is back to the opinions of the Benedictine bachelor cited in his prologue, quest. 2 (Vat. lat. 955, fol. 12^v–13^r; Paris, Univ. 193, fol. 10va–10vb) and in *Lectura Oxon.* II, q. 8 (Vat. lat. 1110, fol. 33^r–33^v; Paris, Univ. 193, fol. 166rb).

915, was written before that date. This solves one of the problems that bothered Michalski, namely whether Vat. lat. 955 was an early redaction on whose margins revisions were made that eventually became the redaction of B. N. lat. 15 892, or whether Vat. lat. 955 was a manuscript of a shorter and possibly later redaction on whose margins an owner had put the earlier, more authentic text. The text of Vat. lat. 955 precedes the marginalia.

We also know something about the circumstances that occasioned the marginalia. The famous introductory note of Vat. lat. 955 belongs with the marginalia and not with the original text: "In nomine Domini incipit brevis collectio Wodeham super Sententias apud Oxoniam, extracta ex lectionibus suis alibi et ex occurrentibus aliis postea, dum se disponeret et etiam dum legebat . . . ."[38] Although a fuller understanding of this statement must be postponed for the moment, we can note here that the revision that resulted in the redaction contained in B. N. lat. 15 892 took place while he was lecturing, probably after 1334.

There has been some question of the authenticity of the marginalia in Vat. lat. 955. That question, however, resulted from Michalski's initial indecisiveness as to whether the marginalia preceded or followed B. N. lat. 15 892. Eventually Michalski was persuaded, through a comparison of the questions in which Caius College 281 paralleled the Oxford lectures and invariably followed the version preserved in B. N. lat. 15 892, that the additions were authentic. To that argument can be added the fact that the additions in Vat. lat. 955 cannot have been copied from a completed revision, for they were themselves revised at several points. Consequently, we may view Vat. lat. 955 as a working copy of book I, probably *the* working copy that stands not between the *editio prima* and the *editiones media et longa* but between the redaction of the Mazarine text and the redaction of B. N. lat. 15 892. As such, the additions stem directly from Wodeham and may even be an autograph.[39]

The weight of evidence favors viewing the marginal notations and additions in Vat. lat. 955 as Wodeham's own handwriting, but the issue is by no means certain. Some of the remarks made in the additions are of a personal nature and are not only written in the first person but contain information that only Wodeham could have known. Moreover, most of the additions, whether they occur in the margins, between the lines, or on

---

[38] Vat. lat. 955, fol. 1ᵛ.
[39] A. Pelzer, *Codices Vaticani Latini*, Vol. II, pt. 1: *Codices 679–1134* (Vatican, 1931), p. 402, favored this interpretation.

separate *cedulae* inserted into the manuscript, are in the same hand, a cursive English book hand of the second quarter of the fourteenth century. This hand differs in style of characters, in speed, and in informality from the large, careful hand of the text scribe, also English. Some of the *cedulae* and marginalia are additions to additions and contain specific directions to the scribe on how to put the additions together and where they are to be inserted in the original text.[40] It is unlikely that a scribe would write such instructions to himself or to another scribe, and probably no scribe would have copied Wodeham's notes or taken dictation on such small scraps of parchment. Indeed, in some places it would appear that the length of the insertion was conditioned in part by the amount of blank parchment available. All this suggests that the man who was doing the writing was thinking and creating as he went along, not simply transcribing. It is interesting to note that while there are many copyist's errors in the main text of Vat. lat. 955, where the scribe either could not understand or could not read the copy from which he was working, I have found no such errors in the additions.

Only two things argue against viewing the additions as a Wodeham autograph. Why does the introductory note, in what would appear to be the same hand as the other marginalia, describe Wodeham in the third person, and why was a less polished text of the Oxford lectures used as the basis for revision when the edition contained in Mazarine 915 was already in existence? Is it possible that Wodeham, intending the introductory note to go into the revised redaction between the *collatio* and the prologue, felt the third person more appropriate? The preoccupation with historical sequence reflected in that note is in keeping with Wodeham's style. Moreover, the unpolished nature of Vat. lat. 955 may have been an advantage. The parchment was of an inferior quality and thus cheaper to use; the margins were originally large and empty; and the amount of text on each page to be reworked was almost half that of the more finished productions.

It is still possible that the additions could be in the hand of an appointed scribe, a Franciscan *socius* under the immediate supervision of Wodeham, but it is more likely that Wodeham wrote them himself. We know that he had a fairly competent hand and did copy manuscripts. He made a *reportatio* of Chatton's lectures while a student and continued to use it in

---

[40] E.g., Vat. lat. 955, fol. 21a^v: "Quaere in alia parte istius cedulae ibi ⊢⊣." Ibid., fol. 60^r: "Istud argumentum superius in margine scripsi, ignorans quod hic esset."

later years.[41] He may also have acted as Ockham's secretary.[42] Given his ability, it is difficult to imagine that Wodeham would not himself have written this complicated series of notes and changes that constitute the first draft of his revision.

3. *Vat lat. 1110*

Vat. lat. 955 and 1110 initially create a similar impression. They are both single-column texts of an unpolished type, the latter even more "primitive" in appearance than the former. They lack the lettered chapter divisions and the synopses found in the more polished manuscripts. The margins of both manuscripts teem with references to contemporary theologians and fellow *baccalarii*. The manuscripts appear in the same part of the Vatican collection and read consecutively.

On the other hand, there are differences that argue against taking them as two parts of the same redaction. The manuscripts are not by the same scribe. Indeed, the scribe responsible for Vat. lat. 1110 wrote neither the text nor the marginal additions in Vat. lat. 955. Moreover, Vat. lat. 1110 lacks the interlinear and marginal additions so important in Vat. lat. 955. The most significant difference appears when we compare these manuscripts with the redaction contained in the Tarazona or Université manuscripts. The original text of Vat. lat. 955 is almost identical with that of these other manuscripts of the pre-1334 redaction, but the text of Vat. lat. 1110 differs considerably. Moreover, Vat. lat. 1110 has the appearance of a *reportatio*, derived from lectures orally presented and based upon (or being) a copy of either those lectures or the lecturer's notes by an officially appointed scribe. In the questions I have examined, the structure of Vat. lat. 1110 is elaborate and detailed, a structure maintained or slightly reduced in the complete pre-1334 redaction and sharply reduced in the post-1334 redaction. Thus Vat. lat. 1110 cannot be an abbreviation of the redaction contained in B. N. lat. 15 892, because it follows the earlier, longer structure. Moreover, since the shift we saw between the pre- and post-1334 redactions was towards a simplification of the structure while maintaining and occasionally increasing the content, then Vat. lat. 1110

---

[41] See below, chapter four, pp. 162–164 and Vat. lat. 955, fol. 161^v; Paris, Maz. 915, fol. 214va.

[42] This possibility is discussed by Gedeon Gál in his introduction to William of Ockham, *Scriptum in Librum Primum Sententiarum Ordinatio*, ed. G. Gál and S. Brown, in William of Ockham, *Opera Philosophica et Theologica. Opera Theologica*, Vol. I (St. Bonaventure, N.Y., 1967), pp. 35*–37*.

stands closer to the pre-1334 redaction and may even reflect a version that predates its more polished form.

However, there is some evidence that argues against accepting Vat. lat. 1110 as the earliest redaction. Inasmuch as the colophons of books III (fol. 92^r) and IV (fol. 135^v) describe Wodeham as a doctor of theology, Vat. lat. 1110 must have been copied after Wodeham achieved that rank (sometime between 1335 and 1339). From that we know that the colophon date of 1332 cannot be the date of the manuscript. Moreover, William Skelton, the Mertonian *socius* of Wodeham, is referred to at one point in Vat. lat. 1110 (fol. 29^r) as "iste magister, scilicet Skelton," and we know from outside evidence that Skelton was still referred to as a bachelor of theology in 1335.[43] Since Wodeham usually refers to masters of theology as doctors, this probably means nothing more than that Skelton was a master of arts, which he certainly was when he read the *Sentences*. However, in the same passage, Fitzralph, who was a doctor of theology by the fall of 1330, is also referred to as "magister", thus paralleling the rank of Skelton. Since mendicants bypassed the arts degree, it may have been possible to refer to one's secular colleagues as *magistri*, whether they were masters of theology or not. But more than this is at stake in Vat. lat. 1110. On fol. 33^r Wodeham's Benedictine *socius* is referred to as "quidam magister nunc, tunc bachalarius," evidence which, if taken at face value, would mean that a *socius* of Wodeham was promoted to the doctorate while Wodeham plodded along with his lectures on the second book of the *Sentences*.

If one attempts to read these remarks as the *ipsissima verba* of Wodeham at the time he was lecturing on the *Sentences* as a bachelor at Oxford, our understanding of the degree program in theology at Oxford in the fourteenth century would have to be radically revised. Another theory, surely easier to accept, is that Vat. lat. 1110 was not only copied after 1335 but its content was "updated", either by Wodeham or by a scribe. In the two passages in question, neither of the *socii* is referred to as *magister* in the Tarazona, Université, or Mazarine manuscripts, whose content predates 1334.

That Wodeham himself updated the text preserved in Vat. lat. 1110 is suggested by the stylistic parallel between the reference to the Benedictine *socius* in Vat. lat. 1110: "quidam magister nunc, tunc bachalarius" and the reference to Fitzralph in Vat. lat. 955 (fol. 41^v) revised (in what is prob-

---

[43] A. B. Emden, *BRO*, III, 1707. See also *Calendar of Entries in the Papal Registers Relating to Great Britain and Ireland. Papal Letters*, Vol. II (London, 1895), 524.

ably Wodeham's own hand) to read: "unus nunc doctor, tunc bachalarius." The text in Vat. lat. 955 makes clear that while Fitzralph was a doctor at the time Wodeham was lecturing at Oxford, the opinion ascribed to Fitzralph predated his doctorate. The text in Vat. lat. 1110 suggests a viewpoint several years after Wodeham's Oxford lectures.

It would be a mistake to question categorically the importance and usefulness of all the references and cross references in Vat. lat. 1110. The problem of "the magisterial *socii*," however, should make us suspicious of accepting at face value evidence found only in Vat. lat. 1110, especially when that evidence conflicts with what we know from other sources. Moreover, it suggests that Tarazona 7 and Université 193 may reflect the original Oxford lectures better than Vat. lat. 1110.

Before leaving Vat. lat. 955 and 1110 one further aspect should be noted. In both manuscripts names of contemporaries and fellow bachelors occur in the text itself as well as in the margins, an unusual practice for the original redaction of a bachelor's commentary. But from all we know about Wodeham, this practice seems in character. While some of these references may be the result of later insertion, many of them are probably original to the Commentary.

4. *Caius College 281*

There can be no doubt that Cambridge, Gonville & Caius College 281 contains, on fols. 105^r–250^v, a commentary by Adam Wodeham on the first book of the *Sentences*. The style is Wodeham's, and the work begins with the distinctive identifying *collatio*: "Hic est liber generationis Adam." Moreover, although the work includes some material used in other works, such as the Oxford and London *Lecturae*, it appears to be a separate series of lectures, delivered as one unit, a fact attested to by numerous cross references. The manuscript has some of the characteristics of a *textus annotatus*, i.e., a manuscript prepared from a working copy, which was, in turn, to be revised into a *textus ordinarius*. Indications of the number of *quaterni* are included, and at one point Wodeham's directions to the scribe were placed in the text.[44] In the section where the Caius manuscript parallels the Oxford lectures, the version corresponds to Paris, B. N. lat.

---

[44] Cambridge, Caius 281, fol. 140va: ". . . Hoyn, doctor valens, supra aliqua unica operatione, etc. Quaere in nono [or 'novo'] quaterno! Istam habeo!" Fol. 105ra mentions that there are to be twelve *quaterni*, and fol. 142va refers to the fourth question of a *quaternus*. I would like to thank Fr. Trapp for calling these references to my attention.

15 892. Therefore, Caius 281 was compiled after 1334 and was probably delivered after that date. If one interprets the introductory note in Vat. lat. 955 ("ex occurrentibus aliis postea") to imply a series of lectures given after Oxford, this may refer to the lectures contained in Caius 281. If so, the revision of this portion of the Oxford lectures occurred first in these new lectures and subsequently became part of the post-1334 redaction, either directly or by way of the margins of Vat. lat. 955.

To what audience were these lectures given? They cannot be the pre-Oxford London lectures, as Michalski first supposed. The manuscript lacks the structure we know the London lectures to have had; it occasionally parallels the post-1334 redaction of the Oxford lectures while the pre-1334 redaction repeatedly cites the London lectures; and it also refers the reader back to the London lectures, which were delivered earlier.[45] Nor does the Cambridge manuscript contain the Norwich lectures, as Michalski eventually decided. References to the Norwich lectures in the pre-1334 redaction of the Oxford lectures confirm that the Norwich lectures preceded the Oxford lectures, while the lectures in the Caius manuscript came after 1334. A further discussion of the nature of Caius 281 and its relation to Wodeham's career must be postponed until after the evidence of contemporary witnesses has been examined.

5. *The Ordinatio*

After one has looked at the beautiful scholastic productions contained in Tarazona 7, Université 193, and Mazarine 915 and compared their text with that of Vat. lat. 1110 or B. N. lat. 15 892, there can be no doubt about which redaction best reflects Wodeham's bachelor lectures on the *Sentences* at Oxford. Vat. lat. 1110 appears to be a *reportatio*, and although extremely useful, it does not have the finishing touches of its author and shows subsequent updating. Vat. lat. 955, although it contains the same text of book I as the Tarazona, Université, and Mazarine manuscripts, lacks their polished, finished form. Unlike his master Ockham, Wodeham was able to complete an *ordinatio* version of his Oxford lectures. In that form the work exists in multiple manuscripts, but is best represented by the Université and Tarazona manuscripts, which for legibility, organization, and appearance (not to mention the accuracy of the text itself), stand near the top of scholastic book production.

---

[45] Ibid., fol. 143ra: "... ut alibi ostendi tertio Lond." "Tertio Lond." was Wodeham's standard way of citing his London lectures.

Until a complete text comparison is done, such as would be necessary in the preparation of the critical edition of Wodeham's *Lectura*, it is impossible to establish the *stemma* with complete accuracy. However, even at this early stage certain patterns can be detected that throw light on the value and interrelation of the manuscripts at various points and demonstrate the possibility and means of reconstructing the archetype from which the manuscripts of this redaction descend. Leaving aside differences between the manuscripts that are not clear cases of scribal error, such as changes in word order or the substitution of words of similar meaning, and concentrating on repeated cases of *omissiones per homoeoteleuton* or, more rarely, *homoeoarchon*, we gain some insight into the relation of our three copies of the complete pre-1334 redaction as well as the text of the archetype from which they ultimately derive.

The *stemma* for the manuscripts of Wodeham's *Lectura Oxoniensis* is complicated by the fact that the early copies seem to have been made from *peciae* or unbound text units that did not spring from an identical source. This is reflected by the fact that within each portion of the *Lectura* the relation of manuscripts remains the same, but the pattern differs between various portions. The editors of Ockham's *Summa Logicae* have pointed out that this is not an unusual occurrence with Franciscan texts in this period.[46] Where a work was circulated and copied from unbound text units and where there was such a high demand that a scribe could not wait for text units that belonged together as one codex, the *peciae* that stand behind a particular manuscript are not necessarily drawn from one "exemplar". This is not the same problem as contamination, where the scribe has two or more texts before his eyes. Instead, for purposes of the *stemma*, each manuscript must be treated as a series of separate manuscripts and the genealogical lines drawn for each portion.

For the text unit that contains the dating passage referred to earlier, one finds that Tarazona and Université stand closer to the original exemplar than does Mazarine. All three texts are very similar, and significant variants are infrequent. When the manuscripts differ in this text unit, however, we find that Université and Tarazona sometimes agree against Mazarine, and Université and Mazarine often agree against Tarazona, but that Tarazona and Mazarine never agree against Université. This finding, based on the comparison of numerous passages, places the Université

---

[46] William of Ockham, *Summa Logicae*, ed. Ph. Boehner, G. Gál, and S. Brown, in William of Ockham, *Opera Philosophica et Theologica. Opera Philosophica*, Vol. I (St. Bonaventure, N.Y., 1974), pp. 7*–8*.

manuscript in a middle position in relation to Mazarine and Tarazona, and also reveals that Université is closer to Mazarine than to Tarazona. Moreover, there are cases where Université has dropped a line or more of text that appears in Tarazona and where one can discount interpolation or contamination. Thus we know that Tarazona was not copied from the Université *pecia* but had access to a text unit genealogically earlier than Université. Similarly, there are cases where Tarazona has dropped a line that appears in Université and where one can again discount interpolation or contamination. Thus we know that Université was not copied from the Tarazona *pecia* but had access to a text unit genealogically earlier than Université. Mazarine, on the other hand, has in this text unit all the *omissiones per homoeoteleuton* found in Université in addition to a few of its own. One can conclude, therefore, that Université and Tarazona go back independently of one another to an earlier exemplar, while Mazarine has Université (or some manuscript like it) between itself and that exemplar.

In reconstructing the exemplar of this text unit, therefore, one cannot use agreement between Mazarine and Université (e.g., the mention of John XXI) to discredit the reading of Tarazona, while agreement between Tarazona and Université can be used to discount the reading of Mazarine. In fact, the individual readings of Mazarine can be ignored in this section except where the hand of Université or Tarazona proves difficult to read.

But if, as occasionally happens, Tarazona and Université disagree and where Mazarine, because it derives from the Université *pecia*, cannot be used to break the tie, how is one to establish the reading of the archetype, especially for books II and III, where we have no other copies of the *Ordinatio*? Fortunately, both the second redaction and the Oyta abbreviation, independently of one another, were based on a copy of the archetype that was at least as good as the Tarazona manuscript if not better. Thus, in those passages where revisions or abbreviations did not occur, these other two redactions can be of great use in establishing the text of the archetype.

To illustrate these points, the three versions of the dating passage are given below. The *omissiones per homoeoteleuton* are telling and reveal a pattern that can be seen in numerous other passages of this text unit. Here, for example, the Tarazona scribe skipped from one "praesens" to another, unaware that the following sentence made no sense without the missing phrase. On the other hand, the Université scribe skipped from one "John XXII" to another. Since the full text at that point as it occurs in Tarazona is garbled, one might argue that there is an unnecessary and meaningless addition in Tarazona rather than an omission in Université and Mazarine. But the text of B. N. lat. 15 892 (the later redaction but one based on an exemplar earlier than Université) has this passage and in a more readable form. One has the impression that in Wodeham's original hand or in a scribal copy the line was hard to read and was therefore rendered in several ways.

Tarazona, Cat. 7, fol. 142rb:

Praeterea, aliud falsum supponitur, videlicet quod tales in mente congregati termini, "rex Boemiae primus futurus" vel "summus sacerdos primus futurus" et sic de similibus, praecise significent illos qui primo succedent iam praesentibus; quia non plus quam iste terminus "summus pontifex praesens" praecise significat Johannem 22. Isti vero terminus congregatus iste non praecise significat nec praecise repraesentat menti Johannem 22, quamvis solum pro isto nunc vere supponat respectu verbi "de praesenti", quia ista significat praeteritos et futuros, et menti repraesentat sicut istum. Alioquin haec esset falsa: "Petrus fuit summus sacerdos praesens"
    (sit *a* nomen alicuius futuri summi pontificis post Johannem) quae tamen verae sunt. Essent autem falsae nisi praedicatum "praeteritos" et "futuros" significaret vel ad minus repraesentaret vere omnem sacerdotem et omnem summum repraesentat, quamvis vox haec expressa "summus sacerdos praesens" aliquando distincte faciat recordari de Johanne apud unum et apud alium de alio praeterito vel futuro. Nec mirum cum solum ipse de facto sit summus sacerdos.

Paris, Univ. 193, fol. 185[vb]:

Praeterea, aliud falsum sumitur, videlicet quod tales in mente termini congregati, "rex Bohemiae primus futurus" vel "summus sacerdos primus futurus" et sic de similibus, significent praecise illos qui primo succedent iam praesentibus; quia non plus quam iste terminus "summus pontifex praesens" praecise significet Johannem 21,

quamvis solum pro illo nunc vere supponat respectu verbi et "in praesenti," quia ita significat praeteritos et futuros, et menti repraesentat sicut illum. Alioquin haec esset falsa: "Petrus fuit summus sacerdos praesens" vel "*a* erit summus sacerdos praesens" (sit *a* nomen alicuius futuri summi pontificis post Johannem) quae tamen verae sunt. Essent autem falsae nisi praedicatum "praeteritos" et "futuros" significaret vel ad minus repraesentaret, immo omnem sacerdotem et omnem summum repraesentat, quamvis vox haec expressa "summus sacerdos praesens" aliquando distincte faciat recordari de Benedicto apud unum et apud alium de Johanne praeterito vel alio futuro. Nec mirum cum solum ille de facto sit summus sacerdos.

Paris, Maz. 915, fol. 179[ra]–179[rb]:

Praeterea, aliud falsum sumitur, videlicet quod conceptus tales in mente congregati "rex Boemiae primus futurus" vel "summus sacerdos primus futurus" et sic de similibus, significent praecise illos qui primo succedent iam praesentibus; et non plus quam iste terminus "summus pontifex praesens" praecise significet Johannem 21,

quamvis solum pro illo tunc vere supponat respectu verbi "est" et "in praesenti", quia ita significat praeteritos et futuros, et menti repraesentat sicut illum. Alioquin esset falsa: "Petrus fuit summus sacerdos praesens" vel "*a* erit summus sacerdos praesens" (sit *a* nomen alicuius futuri summi pontificis post Johannem) quae tamen verae sunt. Essent autem falsae nisi praedicatum "praeteritos" et "futuros" significaret vel ad minus repraesentaret, immo et omnem sacerdotem et omnem summum pontificem repraesentat, quamvis vox haec expressa "summus sacerdos praesens" aliquando distincte faciat recordari de Benedicto apud unum et apud alium de Johanne praeterito vel alio futuro. Nec mirum cum solum ille de facto sit summus sacerdos.

The establishment of the *Ordinatio* should not devalue the other manuscripts. Vat. lat. 1110 can and should remain important. Furthermore,

B. N. lat. 15 892 and Caius 281 are, in their way, also *ordinationes*, which means nothing more than an edition corrected by the author. The authenticity of the marginalia in Vat. lat. 955 confirms that B. N. lat. 15 892 is an approved redaction but one representing a later stage in Wodeham's thought. Moreover, the polished quality of Caius 281 suggests that it also is probably part of an *ordinatio*, not of the Oxford bachelor lectures but of some later series of lectures. Université and Tarazona should become the major text upon which Wodeham research depends, but the other redactions must be used as well.

Less important are the abbreviations of Wodeham's lectures, either the one contained in the Naples and Hannover manuscripts or the later one composed by Oyta. Since those versions were not authored by Wodeham himself, discussion of them has been left to the appendices. It should only be remarked here that when Oyta chose a text of Wodeham's Oxford lectures to abbreviate, he chose the text represented by the Paris and Tarazona manuscripts. That text can be considered the *ordinatio* of Wodeham's bachelor lectures at Oxford. On the basis of the foregoing analysis, although Wodeham scholarship has chosen to concentrate on the Vatican manuscripts or on B. N. lat. 15 892, the wisdom of Oyta's choice of a text to abbreviate is manifest.

C. THE NORWICH AND LONDON LECTURES

The search for the Norwich and London lectures has been one of the intriguing questions of Wodeham scholarship, but neither work has been discovered in its original form. Michalski thought he had found one or the other in the Caius manuscript, but as was demonstrated above, that manuscript is neither the Norwich nor the London lectures. Our knowledge of the content of these two series of lectures comes from two sources: Wodeham's cross references in the body of the Oxford lectures and references to or quotations from the London lectures in contemporary and subsequent authors. The testimony of outside witnesses will be discussed in chapter two, but it may be useful here to summarize the evidence Wodeham provides regarding the content of these lectures and to explore other possible leads in the manuscripts.

1. *The Norwich lectures*

Wodeham refers to his lectures given at Norwich in the first, third, and fourth books of his Oxford lectures. From Wodeham we know that these lectures covered the last three distinctions of book III (primarily devoted to an analysis of the Decalogue) and much of book IV.[47] These lectures not only preceded the Oxford lectures, but they can be dated in or close to 1329.[48]

Despite the fact that Wodeham directed his readers to these lectures, which must have been in circulation at one time, it is unlikely that they were widely read. Apart from the reference of John Major, who refers to Wodeham's presence in Norwich, not to his Norwich lectures, I have found no mention of these lectures outside the pages of Wodeham. One must assume, therefore, that they were not widely read. Moreover, the number of manuscript copies originally in circulation may have been quite small, restricted to two or three English Franciscan convents. Given our knowledge of some of the content of the work, it is possible that a copy may eventually be discovered, but the chances are not very good.

2. *The London Lectures*

With the London lectures the case is somewhat different. From Wodeham we know that they contained (and may have been limited to) the first thirteen distinctions of book III.[49] From outside witnesses we also know that they had a lengthy prologue (at least nine questions), some of which dealt with epistemology.[50] In the body of those lectures Wodeham

---

[47] *Lectura Oxon.* III, dist. 14, q. 12 (Tarazona 7, fol. 169ra; Paris, Univ. 193, fol. 207vb (158vb); Paris, Maz. 915, fol. 199ra): "Ad argumentum principale satis apte respondet Magister ibidem in littera, et in hoc tempore plus non dandae finiuntur conclusiones super tertium nisi quod alibi in lectura Norvicensi super tres ultimas distinctiones prosecutus sum quaestiones de praeceptis decalogi sigillatim." See also *Lectura Oxon.* I, dist. 33, q. 2 (Paris, Univ. 193, fol. 124ra); III, q. 11 (Paris, Univ. 193, fol. 203va (154va)); IV, q. 1 (Paris, Univ. 193, fol. 209va (160va)); IV, q. 3 (Paris, Univ. 193, fol. 214va (165va)); IV, q. 6 (Paris, Univ. 193, fol. 223va (174va)).

[48] This date is determined by the presence of Pigaz at Cambridge and the stages in the academic career of Wodeham. See below, chapter two, pp. 65–66 and chapter four, pp. 164–166.

[49] *Lectura Oxon.* III, dist. 14, q. 1 (Paris, Univ. 193, fol. 174vb (124vb); Tarazona 7, fol. 131vb; Paris, Maz. 915, fol. 167^r): "Circa istum librum tertium, quia alias Londoniae toto anno pertractavi quaestiones 13 primarum distinctionum, ideo nunc incipio a distinctione 14." With one possible exception, Wodeham always referred to his work as "in tertio Lond." Since there were at least nine questions in the prologue and some distinctions were given more than one question, the "13" seems to apply to "distinctionum" rather than to "quaestiones."

[50] See below, chapter three, pp. 123–130, 136–137, 146, and 155.

examined some of his favorite topics: fruition, quantity, and the continuum.

No manuscript corresponding to that material has yet been discovered, but the probabilities of finding one are much higher than in the case of the Norwich lectures. As will become evident in chapter three, a significant number of later writers had read the London lectures of Wodeham, thus attesting both to the popularity and availability of the work in England and on the Continent.

3. *Manuscript possibilities*

Vat. lat. 869, fols. 214vb–217vb, contains a *collatio* for book II, a question on future contingents, and a *replicatio* relating to the doctrine of the Trinity. The *collatio*, although it closely parallels the Oxford *collatio* II, differs at many points, and the question that follows it is not found in the Oxford lectures nor in the Caius manuscript. While it is probably authentic, it also probably belongs to some other series of lectures that included book II and a discussion of future contingents. Since the London lectures apparently did not include book II and since we already have the *collatio* II of the Caius manuscript, the most likely answer is that we have here some fragments of the Norwich lectures. It is possible, however, that some later "Wodehamist", possibly also called Adam (e.g., Adam Junior, or Adam of Ely), reworked a *collatio* of Wodeham and attached his own question to it.

Vat. lat. 13002 supposedly contains, on fols. 2^r–44^v, lectures by Adam Wodeham on the *Sentences* that differ both from the Oxford lectures and from the lectures contained in Caius 281. Since Doucet identified the commentary not only as belonging to Wodeham but as a commentary on the third book, it was my brief hope that Vat. lat. 13002 might contain the long-lost London lectures. I can say with some assurance now that Vat. lat. 13 002, fols. 2^r–44^v, does not contain the London lectures, and the commentary it does contain is probably not by Wodeham.

The work under discussion is a brief commentary (15 questions) on books III and IV of the *Sentences*. It begins (fol. 2^r): "Quia tactum est in lectione de caecitate generis humani quam incurrit homo propter peccatum.... Ideo sit prima quaestio de incarnatione: Utrum Christus idem praemium praecise nobis meruit per incarnationem suam, quod postea nobis meruit per suam passionem." Many of the questions concern sin, grace, and meritorious action. Book IV begins on fol. 23^r: "Utrum sacramenta veteris legis gratiam conferebant," and it ends with this question (fol. 43ʳ): "Utrum sufficientia [suffragia?] viatorum proficiant animabus defunctorum." The style is English, but beyond that there is little or nothing that could tie it to Wodeham. The end of the commentary (fol. 44ᵛ), often transcribed as: "Explicit Wo.", is: "Explicit Hic. Amen," or "Explicit Nic. Amen." The question on the sacraments of the Old Law seems out of step with Wodeham's sacramental theology, and Wodeham's penchant for citing and attacking his contemporaries is nowhere in evidence in this commentary. The only thing that in any way ties the work to Wodeham is the statement in the 1381 catalogue of the library of the Franciscan convent at Assisi, from which the manuscript came, describing this volume as: "Lecturae Adae Codam et plurium doctorum in Anglia."[51] There is reason to believe, however, that the manuscript in its present form does not contain all it once did.[52] Until some stronger evidence is uncovered, I see no reason to treat this as a work of Wodeham.

In the same manuscript (fols. 46ʳ–73ᵛ), however, there is another commentary (on book I) that seems closer to Wodeham's style. It treats the kinds of questions that interested Wodeham, and it takes a combative attitude toward the Carmelite bachelor, paralleling Wodeham's attitude toward his Carmelite *socius*. Nevertheless, it is unlikely that this work is Wodeham's, since we already possess his "bachelor" lectures.

Anneliese Maier suggested that an anonymous question in Vat. lat. 943, fols. 49ʳ–50ᵛ: "Utrum actus voluntatis fiat subito in instanti vel fiat in tempore" might be by Wodeham.[53] The author of this question refers to Fitzralph, who treated this subject under an almost identical title: "Utrum actus voluntatis fiat subito vel in tempore."[54] That fact places the question after 1327. It is similar to a question in Wodeham's Oxford Commentary: "Utrum voluntas possit simul et subito producere actum voluntarium et libere dilectionis,"[55] but this type of question was common in the fourteenth century, e.g. Robert of Halifax's: "Utrum aliquis actus voluntatis possit esse subito productus a voluntate."[56] Maier's

---

[51] L. Alessandri, *Inventario dell'antica Bibliothèca del convento di S. Francesco in Assisi* (Assisi, 1906), p. 109.

[52] See my "Alexander Langeley, O.F.M.," *Manuscripta*, XXXVIII (1974), 96–104.

[53] A. Maier, *Ausgehendes Mittelalter*, Vol. I (Rome, 1964), p. 252.

[54] Richard Fitzralph, *Lectura* I, q. 11, a. 2 (or q. 9, a. 2 in the numbering of Gordon Leff, *Richard Fitzralph* (Manchester, 1963), p. 195).

[55] Wodeham, *Lectura Oxon*. I, dist. 1, q. 8 (Paris, Maz. 915, fols. 31ᵛ–36ᵛ; Vat. lat. 955, fols. 51ʳ–60ʳ).

[56] Halifax, *Sent*. I, dist. 1, q. 2 (Paris, B. N. lat. 15 880, fols. 65ʳ–77ᵛ; Vat. lat. 1111, fols. 34ᵛ–43ʳ).

conjecture rests chiefly on the statement in the anonymous question: "Pro solutione istius argumenti . . . quaere in quaestionibus de divisione et compositione continui, quia ibi tractavi istam materiam."[57] However, several other authors wrote on the continuum after 1327, e.g., Walter Chatton (in a magisterial *determinatio*), Thomas Bradwardine, John the Canon, Nicolas Bonettus, and John Gedeonis.[58] If the question is by Wodeham, then it was written after his treatises on indivisibles, and it is surprising that the question does not occur in other manuscripts.

D. Treatises on Quantity and the Continuum

Although the lectures on the *Sentences* were and remain Wodeham's major contribution, he wrote several shorter works, some of which have survived. One of these is Wodeham's prologue to Ockham's *Summa Logicae*, a brief introductory note that has recently been re-edited as part of the critical edition of Ockham's *Logic*.[59] It is probable that Wodeham was the disciple who wrote chapter 51 of part I of that work.[60] He may also have been responsible for the final question in the fourth book of Ockham's *Reportatio*: "Utrum voluntas beata necessario fruatur Deo." In the margin of a manuscript of that work one reads: "Hic finitur reportatio super 4um Okam quae continetur in X praecedentibus quaestionibus, sequens vero superaddita fuit per reportatorem, scilicet Adam Guda, nunc magistrum tunc autem eius discipulum".[61]

More important and closely related to his *Sentences* Commentary are two treatises on the related problems of quantity and the continuum, written to attack the indivisibilists, or atomists, and more specifically directed against Walter Chatton. The shorter of the two treatises has been edited by Murdoch and Synan.[62] It is an early draft of, or is derived from, the first chapter of Wodeham's longer treatise on this subject, his *Tractatus de indivisibilibus*.[63]

---

[57] Vat. lat. 943, fol. 50vb.

[58] For a discussion of the authors who treated the continuum, see J. Murdoch and E. Synan, *FcS*, XXVI (1966), 212–225. Henry Harclay, Michael of Massa, and Gerard of Odo wrote before or at the same time as Fitzralph.

[59] William of Ockham, *Summa Logicae*, pp. 3–5.

[60] Ibid., pp. 162–166.

[61] Milan, Ambros. 281 inf., fol. 69rb. I am grateful to Fr. Gedeon Gál for calling my attention to this reference.

[62] J. Murdoch and E. Synan, *FcS*, XXVI (1966), 212–288.

[63] Florence, Bibl. Naz., conv. soppr. A III 508, fols. 135ra–147rb, and Florence, Bibl. Naz., conv. soppr. B VII 1249, fols. 133^r–143^r.

It is difficult to date these two treatises on quantity and the continuum. One possibility is suggested by the nature of the manuscripts in which the two copies of the longer treatise occur. Florence, Bibl. Naz., conv. soppr. A III 508 came from the Franciscan convent of Santa Croce and contains Fitzralph's Commentary on the *Sentences*, the Commentary of Monachus Niger, some questions of Adam Junior (of Ely?), and certain questions from Wodeham. All these works are of English origin and, in the form in which they occur there, cannot, with the possible exception of Wodeham, be dated before 1330.[64] Wodeham's *Tractatus de indivisibilibus*, fols. 135ra–147rb, is followed immediately by a question from Wodeham's *Lectura Oxon.*, I, dist. 1, q. 6: "Utrum voluntas necessario vel libere principiet actus suos." The text of that question is according to the post-1334 redaction. In Florence, Bibl. Naz., conv. soppr. B VII 1249, Wodeham's treatise occurs between books III and IV of his *Sentences* Commentary, again the post-1334 redaction. Although there is no reason to conclude that the treatise was written at Oxford while Wodeham lectured on books III and IV, one cannot discount the fact that the text tradition associates the treatise with the post-1334 lectures of Wodeham. The treatise and the questions it contains may well have been a quodlibetal disputation at Oxford while Wodeham was *magister regens* at the Franciscan convent. It has the structure of a *determinatio*, and we know that a manuscript of Wodeham's *Determinationes* once existed.[65]

Nevertheless, there is some evidence that the *Tractatus de indivisibilibus* was written earlier and may in fact be the earliest work of Wodeham. Wodeham formulated his views on quantity before 1324, probably while studying under Chatton.[66] His *Tractatus*, however, was probably written after 1325, since it cites Ockham's work on quantity, *De corpore Christi*, which (according to one assessment) was written in Avignon about that time,[67] but which in any event was written after Wodeham initially

---

[64] This manuscript contains the version of Fitzralph's *Lectura* revised ca. 1330; see below, chapter two, pp. 77–78.

[65] Little, *The Grey Friars in Oxford*, p. 173.

[66] When, in his *Tractatus*, Wodeham directed his reader to Ockham's discussion of quantity, he noted that he had himself developed these arguments before Ockham (Florence, Bibl. Naz., conv. soppr., A III 508, fol. 140ra): "Quaere prosecutionem in illo tractatu. Et haec argumenta fere omnia fuerant tua antequam Ockham aliquid scriberet de indivisibilibus." See G. Gál's introduction to William of Ockham, *Summa Logicae*, p. 54*.

[67] Ibid. On the provenance and date of Ockham's Eucharistic treatises on quantity, see C. K. Brampton, "Guillaume d'Ockham et la date probable de ses opuscules sur l'Eucharistie," *EF*, XIV (1964), 77–88.

expressed his views. In this work Wodeham reveals his close personal knowledge of the circumstances behind Chatton's two presentations of the problem of quantity in his *Reportatio* of 1321–23, but does not cite Chatton's *Determinatio*, given at Oxford between 1330 and 1332.[68] We know that Wodeham wrote on the continuum before he lectured on book II of the *Sentences* at Oxford.[69] This may have been as a separate treatise or as part of the Norwich or London lectures. If the *Tractatus* was originally part of the London lectures, which contained extensive criticisms of Chatton's views on quantity, that possibility could be explored by placing Wodeham's description of his discussion of the continuum in the London lectures alongside the text of the *Tractatus* and the shorter treatise edited by Murdoch and Synan. Until that is done, or some new evidence uncovered, a precise date cannot be given.

E. Summary

Much of the literary activity of Wodeham appears for the time being to have been lost. The Norwich lectures, the London lectures, the *Determinationes*, and the Commentary on the Song of Songs are those we know once existed, and there may well have been others. If we possessed all, we would have material from Wodeham's pen that would extend, almost without interruption, from his student days to the end of his teaching career. In the absence of a full record, we fortunately do have something from almost every period in Wodeham's life and have two separate *Sentences* commentaries that contain, between them, Wodeham's mature views on almost every major scholastic problem of his age.

The works that have survived cluster around three periods in his life. To the earliest period, when he was working with and/or studying under

---

[68] In book II of his *Reportatio* on the *Sentences*, written probably in the spring of 1322, Chatton posed this question (Paris, B. N. lat. 15 887, fol. 93^r; Florence, Bibl. Naz., conv. soppr. C V 357, fol. 187^r): "Utrum quantum componatur ex indivisibilibus, sive permanens sive successivum." In determining this question Chatton gave two separate solutions. Wodeham, who attended those lectures, wrote in his *Tractatus* (Florence, Bibl. Naz., conv. soppr. A III 508, fol. 136rb): "Aliter autem respondit frater Walter Chaton, et dupliciter: uno modo dum legit ante Pascha et alio modo post Pascha, habita deliberatione pleniori." Easter in 1322 fell on April 11. Chatton's *determinatio* can be dated after Wodeham began lecturing on the *Sentences* at Oxford and before Chatton left England.

[69] Wodeham, *Lectura Oxon.* II, q. 10 (Paris, Univ. 193, fol. 174rb (124rb)): "Explicit secundus liber, alias enim multas quaestiones secundi de motu, de tempore, de continuo et de individuatione et similibus alias seriosius pertractavi."

Ockham, belong the chapter that he contributed to Ockham's *Summa Logicae*, the preface he wrote for that work, probably the question that was added to Ockham's *Reportatio* (for which Wodeham may also have been the *reportator*), and possibly one or more of the treatises on quantity and the continuum.

The second period coincides with his bachelor lectures on the *Sentences* at Oxford. From this period only one redaction remains of which we can be certain. The completion of that redaction can be dated in or before 1334 and has survived in three complete copies: Tarazona 7; Paris, Univ. 193; and Paris, Maz. 915. Although there are some minor differences between Vat. lat. 955 and the text of book I in these three manuscripts, Vat. lat. 955 should not be considered a separate redaction. To put the matter in terms of Michalski's assessment, there is no *editio media* separate from the *editio prima*; Vat. lat. 955 and Maz. 915 belong to the same redaction, namely that which was completed before 1334. Vat. lat. 1110 is a separate redaction, but it is not clear whether it belongs to this period and, if so, whether it should be dated before or after the redaction represented by the other manuscripts.

The third period lies between 1334 and 1342. To this period belong the redaction of the Oxford lectures found in B. N. lat. 15 892 and Florence, Bibl. Naz., conv. soppr. B VII 1249. This redaction should not be called the *editio longa* but rather the "second redaction," which in actual fact is shorter than the pre-1334 redaction. Also belonging to this period is the *Sentences* Commentary contained in Caius 281, which may have been the lectures Wodeham was giving at the time he was preparing the second redaction of his Oxford bachelor lectures. An understanding of the context of those post-1334 lectures and a closer approximation of the date at which they were given must wait until we have examined the witness of contemporaries in chapter three.

The type of internal evidence examined so far allows us to see the order of the various redactions of Wodeham's *Sentences* commentaries and to assign approximate dates. In order to make the date of the Oxford bachelor lectures more precise, we must look at two other types of evidence, one internal and one external. The internal evidence consists of the names and writings of Wodeham's contemporaries, whom he is able to cite correctly and extensively in the body of his text (not simply marginalia, which could have been added later). Having now isolated the early redaction whose form was set by 1334 (our present *terminus ad quem*), a more precise *terminus a quo* can be established from Wodeham's familiarity with works by contemporary authors. The external evidence comes from those writers who are able, in turn, to cite Wodeham correctly and extensively. Where we have firm dates for the careers and writings of Wodeham's contemporaries, we can use these facts to date Wodeham's work. Thus, in the context of a broader examination of Wodeham's sources and the subsequent *Wirkungsgeschichte* of his thought, the next two chapters will also seek to define further the date and context of the *Sentences* commentaries of Adam Wodeham.

CHAPTER TWO

OXFORD THOUGHT IN THE AGE OF WODEHAM:
HIS SOURCES

It has always been important for intellectual historians to establish the sources of an author's thought. The character, uniqueness, and significance of an intellectual achievement are better understood by identifying and studying those who, in either a positive or negative way, influenced the ideas of a writer. In the case of Wodeham this is a particularly rich avenue for investigation because he so frequently mentioned contemporary and earlier thinkers whose writings, or at least ideas, he knew.

Beyond the obvious advantages of clarifying Wodeham's achievement by bringing into focus the intellectual milieu of his educational years and his teaching environment, his references to other authors and citations from their works provide useful information in dating the redactions of Wodeham's Commentary, since in some cases we have reasonably fixed dates for the careers and writings of his contemporaries. This is especially true when Wodeham's references to Fitzralph and Chatton are placed alongside our knowledge of the careers of those two authors. The authors and works Wodeham knew and in what redactions he knew them are thus important clues in dating the redactions of Wodeham's *Sentences*.

There is a further advantage to be gained from the study of Wodeham's sources. Wodeham was one of those few fourteenth-century authors whose excitement about contemporary theological and philosophical debate led him to mention, examine, and quote from the writings or lectures of a large number of contemporary and earlier authors, some of whom are barely known to us today, since their works are no longer extant. Wodeham, and others like him who filled their texts and margins with references to other authors, are among our most important sources for piecing together the history of fourteenth-century thought.

Before examining Wodeham's references to other authors, some methodological consideration needs to be given to the problem of assessing the importance of citations in an author's work. The most frequent method employed in determining the importance one author has for another has been to count marginal and/or text references. An exact numerical count of citations and the ranking of sources according to those figures look impressive to the intellectual historian, who may at times envy the apparent precision achieved by economic or social historians whose sources can more readily be approached through quantitative methods. Citation counting, however, can be misleading because it appears to tell us more than it actually does. For instance, we generally do not know whether the count was based on references in the body of the text, or on the margins, or both. Moreover, while the count may accurately reflect the number of citations, it may not reflect their importance. The name of one author on one issue might appear several times in the margin of a folio page, while a second author, whose ideas are more central to the discussion and whose work is extensively quoted, might be cited by name only once. Furthermore, name counting does not differentiate between an author renowned for and quoted repeatedly on one idea and an author quoted less frequently but on a variety of topics reflecting extensive knowledge of his work. Finally and most importantly, such lists do not differentiate between authors cited favorably and used as supporting authorities and those authors whose thought is generally being attacked.

Lists based upon citation counting can be of use to the historian of fourteenth-century thought as long as they are recognized for what they are, namely indications only of frequency of citation. The quantitative precision of these lists should not blind the reader to their severe limitations, and they should never be a substitute for the more difficult but more rewarding examination of texts to discover which sources are most important and how they are being used by an individual author.

In place of citation counting, the following chapter will attempt to deal individually with the fourteenth-century sources for Wodeham's thought, to see what works of other authors Wodeham knew and when he began to use them, to look at the topics in Wodeham in which their thought is introduced, and to consider Wodeham's general attitude toward these authors. Obviously, these brief examinations are no more than preliminary soundings, but by providing the references in Wodeham to other authors and indicating the topics under discussion, the groundwork is laid for future studies that can be of great importance for our understanding of fourteenth-century thought.

A. Biblical and Patristic Citations

Divisions are sometimes made between those fourteenth-century authors who consciously steeped themselves in and based much of their thought on the principal sources of the Christian faith, namely the Bible and the Fathers (particularly Augustine), and those authors whose interests in logic and in problems of contemporary philosophy caused them to neglect these historical sources. On which side of that division is Wodeham to be placed, or does a reading of Wodeham cause one to question the validity of that hypothetical division?

Biblical citations appear in Wodeham at those points where one would normally expect to find them. The four Oxford *collationes* and the two *collationes* in the Caius manuscript are almost exclusively Biblical in nature, as was customary. Moreover, Biblical citations are frequent in the opposing arguments that, in common scholastic style, form the introductory section of each of Wodeham's questions. In the remainder of the question Biblical references appear rarely, although they are certainly not absent. As one might expect, their presence is dictated to a large extent by the topic under discussion. In this regard Wodeham is typical of fourteenth-century scholastic style. Scriptural passages that seem to conflict with nature or theological doctrine provide a problem, a beginning point for discussion, and set boundaries within which a solution is to be found. They seldom constitute the solution itself. When a definitive or probable answer has been reached through argumentation, often elaborate and diffuse, it may be supported by references to passages in Scripture. Thus the Bible, in and of itself, does not provide answers to scholastic questions. Indeed, there is no reason to debate those questions it does answer decisively. The debatable question is by definition one that grows out of those issues on which Scripture seems to give no direct or unambiguous answer.

It can be said, therefore, that Wodeham shows himself to be thoroughly familiar with the Bible, which he was eventually to lecture on as *baccalarius biblicus* and as *magister regens*. In keeping with contemporary scholastic practice, however, he did not seed his work with extensive Biblical citations.

Wodeham's handling of patristic authorities is similar to his handling of the Bible. He makes use of a wide number of Fathers but they are generally restricted to the introductory and concluding portions of his questions. At one point or another most of the patristic authorities normally cited in the high and late Middle Ages appear in the pages of Wodeham. Of these, he shows particular fondness for Augustine, Anselm, and Gregory the Great, and to a lesser extent, Ambrose, Jerome, Boethius, Isidore, Hugh of St. Victor, and Bernard. It would appear that the majority of Wodeham's citations from patristic authorities are taken from Lombard's *Sentences*, canon law, or other scholastic authors.

Although Wodeham read some patristic writers firsthand, for example Augustine, that experience rarely contributed to a more sophisticated treatment of those authors or to the improvement of the structure of Wodeham's argumentations, as it would in the case of Gregory of Rimini.

In the continuum from those authors who consciously based their thought on a new and fresh reading of the early sources of the Christian faith to those who ignored Scripture and tradition through an exclusive concentration on problems of logic, Wodeham should be placed toward the middle, perhaps slightly in the direction of those with a primary commitment to logical argumentation and problems of contemporary philosophical interest.

B. Doctores Antiqui

When we come to Wodeham's use of scholastic authors before the fourteenth century we come upon a feature of his writing that does not seem typical of his age. Wodeham rarely cites authorities between Lombard and Scotus. He had great fondness for early twelfth-century authors, principally Anselm, whose interest in linguistic logic endeared him to many fourteenth-century authors. But, with the exception of William of Auxerre, one seldom finds mention of *doctores* active between 1160 and 1280. This tendency to ignore thirteenth-century authors was not a result of unfamiliarity. Wodeham knew Alexander of Hales' *Summa theologica*, Bonaventure's *Sentences* Commentary, and the major theological works of Thomas Aquinas, whom he generally cited as *Doctor communis*.[1] But Wodeham did not consider himself in dialogue with these thinkers. The *doctores* whose opinions interested Wodeham seem to begin with the generation of Richard Middleton, Henry of Ghent, and John Duns Scotus.

It is not clear what caused Wodeham's lesser interest in the thirteenth-century doctors whose careers preceded the Parisian condemnation of 1277. It was not based on the distinction between *antiqui* and *moderni*, which Wodeham used, and whose fourteenth-century meaning he may even have helped form.[2] For Wodeham, the *moderni* began with the

---

[1] For example, to take only one section of Wodeham's work, Bonaventure is cited in *Lectura Oxon.* I, dist. 33, qq. 1 & 4; the *Summa Halensis* in *Lectura Oxon.* I, dist. 33, q. 5; and Thomas Aquinas in *Lectura Oxon.* I, dist. 33, qq. 5 & 7, the last being a reference to Thomas' *Quodlibeta*.

[2] Wodeham appears to be using the term *modernus* as it was generally used in the fourteenth century, namely as a way of designating a contemporary. Despite the fact

generation of Ockham, or slightly earlier. Scotus, for whom Wodeham had great respect and whose opinions he sometimes favored, was an *antiquus*, while Campsale, who was a regent master in arts in 1308, was a *modernus*.[3] Nor was it strictly a predisposition on the part of Wodeham to favor Franciscans or those allied with the Franciscan school. Wodeham cites Thomas as often as Bonaventure. The answer seems to lie in another area, probably in a combination of age and geographical-academic attachment. Wodeham may have felt that theologians active in the second and third quarters of the thirteenth century were too recent to have the authoritative weight of Anselm, Hugh of St. Victor, or Lombard, and too distant to be a significant part of contemporary theological debate. Or Wodeham's disinterest may have resulted from an insularity that neglected earlier Parisian doctors. Although English theologians of the twelfth and thirteenth centuries made important contributions, they often made them on the Continent, at Paris. By contrast, English theologians dominate the half century from 1290 to 1340, a period in which Oxford

---

that the age difference between Campsale (a *modernus*) and Scotus (an *antiquus*) was not great, and despite the fact that Campsale seems to have died by the time Wodeham lectured at Oxford (see below, note 59), Campsale was a man of Wodeham's generation and Scotus was a man of the previous generation. The dividing line for Wodeham was approximately the year 1300, and that does not seem to vary according to method, school affiliation, or conclusions in epistemology, logic, or metaphysics. What has not been sufficiently noted, however, is that as one progresses in the fourteenth century from Wodeham (1330) to Gregory of Rimini (1342), to John Hiltalingen of Basel (1365), and even to Pierre d'Ailly (1375), Ockham's generation remains "modern" and the dividing line between *antiqui* and *moderni* seems still to be the opening years of the fourteenth century. One might say, therefore, that while the term *modernus* does not in the fourteenth century refer to a particular group, such as "nominalists" or "Ockhamists" nor is it used in a pejorative sense (save with Wyclif and a few others), it also does not continue to mean an exact contemporary. Between the equation *moderni*=contemporaries (1325) and *moderni*=*nominales* (1425) the term implied an historical periodization. As 1150 came to be the approximate boundary line between the "fathers" and the "ancient doctors", so 1300 came to be the approximate boundary line between the "ancient doctors" and the "modern doctors". It is not surprising, therefore, that when the conflict between *reales* and *nominales* developed in the course of the fifteenth century and the authority of Thomas and Albert was pitted against the authority of Ockham, that the distinction *antiqui-moderni* should begin to acquire the same meaning as *reales-nominales* in some universities. Such, however, was never its fourteenth-century meaning, as recent literature makes clear. See: *Antiqui und Moderni*, ed. A. Zimmermann, Miscellanea Mediaevalia, Vol. 9 (Berlin, 1974); E. Gössmann, *Antiqui und Moderni im Mittelalter* (München, 1974); A. Buck, *Die "Querelle des Anciens et des Modernes" im Italienischen Selbstverständnis der Renaissance und des Barocks* (Wiesbaden, 1973).

[3] Scotus' views are sometimes placed within a discussion of *opiniones antiquorum*. For

outshines Paris. Whatever the cause, Wodeham's interests gravitated to the ideas of those who made up his own and the immediately preceding generation. His interest in the full heritage of scholasticism, the accumulated opinions of the major representatives of earlier generations of doctors, took second place to his overriding interest in contemporary English thought, going back to Scotus and those authors in the last two decades of the thirteenth century who set the tone for early fourteenth-century thought.

Among the *antiqui*, Scotus was by far the most significant mind for Wodeham. He ranks alongside Ockham as the theologian most often cited in the *Lectura Oxoniensis* and the Caius manuscript. Wodeham was familiar with the entire corpus of Scotus. It was Wodeham's citation from the *Secundae Additiones secundi libri* that helped establish their authenticity.[4] Moreover, at the time Wodeham was lecturing at Oxford, the autograph of Scotus' *Ordinatio*, from which Assisi 137 was copied,[5] was still in the convent library. Twice in the Caius manuscript Wodeham referred to arguments written by Scotus in his own hand in the margin of his book.[6]

---

the reference to Campsale as a *modernus*, see *Lectura Oxon.* IV, q. 6, L (Paris, Univ. 193, fol. 222va (173va); Paris, Maz. 915, fol. 218va).

[4] C. Balić, *Les Commentaires de Jean Duns Scot sur les quatre livres des sentences*, Bibliothèque de la Revue d'Historie Ecclésiastique, Fasc. 1 (Louvain, 1927), pp. 116–127.

[5] Ibid., pp. 3–8.

[6] *Lectura secunda*, I, dist. 2, q. 1 (Cambridge, Caius 281, fol. 153ra): "Et hoc est quod iterum scribit, d. 37 primi, manu sua in margine: 'per speciem,' inquit, 'subiecti privari intellectionem passionis est passionem ut actu intellectam privari.'" = Scotus, *Ordinatio*, I, dist. 36 (Assisi 137, fol. 89va; *Opera Omnia*, Vol. VI, ed. C. Balić (Vatican, 1963), p. 286). Both the Assisi manuscript of Scotus and the Cambridge manuscript of Wodeham read 'privari intellectionem', not 'principari intellectam', as appears in the Balić edition. Moreover, the Balić edition does not indicate (as it usually does) that this passage is a marginal addition of Scotus. *Lectura secunda*, I, dist. 4 (Cambridge, Caius 281, fol. 181va): "Item, contra seipsum arguit Scotus in quadam additione in margine libri sui: 'Istud enim "de multiplici abstractione" quid valet? Haec humanitas non est humanitas et haec albedineitas non est albedineitas, et universaliter potest esse abstractio quantumcumque ultima; dum tamen conceptus abstractus sit communis,' 'quin abstractum dicatur de suo singulari per se.'" = Scotus, *Ordinatio*, I, dist. 5, q. 1 (Assisi 137, fols. 42va–42vb; *Opera Omnia*, Vol. IV, ed. C. Balić (Vatican, 1956), p. 21). The 'non's after the first 'humanitas' and the first 'albedineitas' are absent in the Assisi manuscript and in the Balić edition. For further remarks on the contents of the Franciscan library at Oxford, see my "Alexander Langeley, O.F.M.," *Manuscripta*, XVIII (1974), 100–104. The references to particular folios in Scotus found in Vat. lat. 13687 and Borgh. 346 may refer to volumes in the library of the Oxford convent. Cf. introduction to Duns Scotus, *Opera Omnia*, Vol. IV, ed. C. Balić (Vatican, 1956), pp. 7*–8*. On the reason for calling Caius 281 the *Lectura secunda*, see chapter three, pp. 123–130.

C. Moderni

Wodeham's commitment to contemporary thought is reflected in the fact that the majority of his citations from scholastic authorities are from the fourteenth century. For Wodeham, theology was an ongoing enterprise, and the opinions of recent doctors and masters were consequently of greater interest than those of the past. From the historian's standpoint this bias is fortunate, for through the abundant citations Wodeham drew from contemporaries we have a major avenue for reconstructing the thought of many authors whose works are otherwise lost to us. The interchange between Wodeham and his contemporaries also provides us with an additional check on the chronology of Wodeham's writings and career as well as the careers of several others.

1. *Franciscan Education in England*

Before embarking on an account of the thirty fourteenth-century authors cited by Wodeham, most of whom were Franciscan, it might be well to give some idea of what we know of the pattern of Franciscan education in fourteenth-century England. These details, in turn, will not need to be repeated as each new figure is introduced.

Originally one had to be eighteen to enter the Franciscan order, and that ideal may have lived on in the fourteenth century even while the need for competitive recruitment led the Franciscans to lower the age of entry to fourteen, to accept those deficient in grammar and logic, and even to accept oblates.[7] Recruitment of young children (given by parents) probably remained rare, but from 1316 on, the repeated prohibitions against accepting those below the age of fourteen suggests not only that fourteen had become the official age of entry but also that some were being received earlier. The inner life of the Franciscan convent must have

---

[7] For the thirteenth-century regulations prohibiting entry before the age of eighteen, see: *Decretales Gregorii IX*, L. III, tit. 31, c. 6 (*CIC*, II, 570): "Quia in insulis dura est congregatio monachorum, etiam pueros in eorum monasteriis ante XVIII annum suscipi prohibemus." M. Bihl, "Statuta Generalia Ordinis Edita in Capitulis Generalibus Celebratis Narbonae An. 1260, Assisii An. 1279 atque Parisiis An. 1292 (Editio critica et synoptica)," *AFH*, XXXIV (1941), 39, n. 2: "Ordinamus etiam, ut nullus recipiatur citra XVIII annum, nisi per robur corporis vel industriam sensus seu per excellentem aedificationem, a XV anno et supra, aetas secundum prudentium iudicium suppleatur." The Assisi Chapter of 1316 prohibited entry before the age of 14; for the fourteenth-century legislation on the required age and educational experience, see: M. Brlek, *De Evolutione Iuridica Studiorum in Ordine Minorum* (Dubrovnik, 1942), pp. 28–31; see also: *Decretales Gregorii IX*, L. III, tit. 31, c. 8 & 11 (*CIC*, II, 571–572).

been altered by this shift away from a strictly voluntary society and the corresponding increase in its involvement in elementary education. At the same time, however, younger recruitment brought to the Order some talented minds who may have progressed more rapidly in the concentrated educational environment of a major Franciscan convent. Peter John Olivi entered the Franciscan Order at age twelve.[8] Among others who entered while they were still *pueri*, i.e. thirteen or younger, William Woodford mentions William of Ware, Robert Cowton, Walter Chatton, and William of Ockham.[9]

Regardless of when one entered the Order, a one-year novitiate was required during which the study of philosophy and theology were forbidden.[10] Normally in the fourteenth century we may assume that this event immediately preceded or sometimes interrupted the eight-year study of philosophy, which was undertaken either in a local convent or, more commonly, in one of the custodial schools. In the early years of the fourteenth century Franciscans may have been completing their philosophical studies at Oxford or Cambridge, but it seems likely that by the second quarter of the fourteenth century, because of overcrowding at the university convents, friars were urged to complete their philosophical study at one of the recognized custodial schools. Such was the practice at Paris.[11]

By 1336 and probably for several years earlier the number of schools

---

[8] P. F. Callaey, "Olieu ou Olivi (Pierre de Jean)," *DTC*, XI (1931), 982.

[9] W. Woodford, *Defensorium*, cap. 62, quoted in A. G. Little, "The Franciscan School at Oxford in the Thirteenth Century," *AFH*, XIX (1926), 866.

[10] N. A. Fitzpatrick, "Walter Chatton on the Univocity of Being: A Reaction to Peter Aureoli and William Ockham," *FcS*, XXXI (1971), 140.

[11] The weight of the evidence suggests that the Oxford convent was principally if not exclusively a school of theology and canon law. This was true for the Dominicans; W. A. Hinnebusch, *The History of the Dominican Order*, Vol. II: *Intellectual and Cultural Life to 1500* (New York, 1973), p. 59: "Before coming to a university ... a Dominican would have studied and taught philosophy in the lesser schools of his province, and would have studied theology for two or three years in a provincial house of theology and one in a *studium generale*, either at Paris or elsewhere." That this was also the case for the Franciscans was the assumption of A. G. Little, *The Grey Friars in Oxford* (Oxford, 1892), p. 44: "A Friar usually completed his eight years' study of Arts, and often began his course of theology, at his native convent. On coming up to Oxford he at once entered on or continued his theological studies." See also Little, *AFH*, XIX, 825. The large number of friars at the Oxford convent (84 in 1317 according to Little) can be explained in part by the obligation of every convent, if at all possible, to send a friar to Oxford or Cambridge in addition to students from the Continent; see Little, *AFH*, XIX, 817–818. On the custom at Paris, see *AFH*, VII (1914), 497: "Nullus studens ... mittatur Parisiis pro studio, nisi prius in sua custodia probatus fuerit in lectione philosophiae vel logicalium, et etiam in moribus et conversatione."

at various levels of study had been determined. There were three major *studia generalia*: Paris, Oxford, and Cambridge. In addition, the Franciscan Order recognized several other *studia generalia*: Bologna, Toulouse, Cologne, and the *Curia romana*, or Avignon. Beneath that level were the *Studia secundae speciei*, or custodial schools, which in England were London (for the London custody), Norwich (for the Cambridge custody), Stamford (for the Oxford custody), Exeter (for the Bristol custody), Coventry (for the Worcester custody), York (for the York custody), and Newcastle (for the Newcastle custody). In addition there were lesser schools or "legibile" convents where teaching was done, such as Canterbury, Bristol, Hereford, and Leicester, but these did not qualify as places to read the *Sentences* before reading at Oxford or Cambridge.[12]

After having studied philosophy for eight years, and having reached the age of twenty-three, a Franciscan who was selected for the highest degree could be admitted to the convents of Oxford or Cambridge for the study of theology.[13] In many cases he would already have been ordained subdeacon by his diocesan. This was originally done at age twenty, but at the Council of Vienne (1312) the age limit was recognized as seventeen completed years, i.e., in the eighteenth year.[14] This change was promulgated in 1317.

---

[12] M. Bihl, "Ordinationes a Benedicto XII pro fratribus minoribus promulgatae per bullam 28 Novembris 1336," *AFH*, XXX (1937), 327–330, 349.

[13] To enter the theological program at Oxford it was necessary for the officials of the Order to swear under oath before the Chancellor that the candidate had studied philosophy for eight years; S. Gibson, *Statuta Oxon.*, p. 34: "Si autem non determinaverit audiat ad minus artes per octo annos ante suam inceptionem." Ibid., p. 49: "Et ideo supradicta universitas statuit et decrevit bachilarium facultatis theologie, quem liberalium artium honor magistralis minime decoravit, fore ad lecturam libri sententiarum nullatenus admittendum, nisi prius dictas liberales artes per octo annos integros in universitate vel alibi rite audierit, vel partim audierit partim legerit, per spacium temporis supradictum, solis philosophicis intendendo...." It was not required by statute that the Franciscan candidate be 23 years of age. This is an assumption based on the fact that those who took the arts degree normally completed their regency at age 23, and the preparation and experience of the religious candidate was supposed to be equivalent.

[14] The earlier practice can be found in the *Decretum*, I, dist. 77, c. 4 (*CIC*, I, 273): "Subdiaconus non minor viginti annorum ordinetur." The revised practice is in *Clem.*, L. I, tit. 6, c. 3 (*CIC*, II, 1140): "Generalem ecclesiae observantiam volentes antiquis iuribus in hoc parte praeferri... possit quis libere in decimo octavo ad subdiaconatus... promoveri." In light of the opening phrase, ordination to subdeacon at 17 may already have been in practice before the promulgation of this law in 1317. However, one cannot conclude that the earliest age permissible was the normal or only age for ordination. Many secular theologians were ordained subdeacons and deacons after they had read the *Sentences* at a major *studium generale*, e.g., Nigel of Wavere, Richard Radford, Richard Kilvington, William Skelton, and possibly Richard of Reppes.

At Oxford the Franciscan would be surrounded by a large number of fellow friars at various levels, many of whom would never attain the Oxford baccalaureate, let alone the *magisterium*. If A. G. Little is correct in his calculation of the ratio of king's pittance per friar,[15] the three glimpses we have into the Oxford Franciscan convent in the fourteenth century suggest that there must have been many students at the beginning stages of the study of theology or canon law, since the number of those at the level of bachelor or beyond was restricted.

Perhaps the mid-thirteenth century ideal of having a lecturer in every convent and every convent having one student at Oxford or Cambridge preparing for such a post partly explains this high number.[16] Not all convents, however, were either wealthy enough or possessed sufficient qualified candidates to fulfill this ideal. If we assume that of the fifty or sixty convents in England some thirty or forty students were supported at Oxford along with a number of foreign students from the Continent (where there was only one "official" major *studium generale* in theology in the first half of the fourteenth century), then one could conjecture forty to sixty theological students below the level of *sententiarius*. These certainly could not all read at Oxford, nor may that have been necessary in order to teach at a lesser school. One might leave Oxford in order to read at a custodial school and participate in debates there, acts that may have been considered sufficient to permit one to be appointed a lector at a local convent.

The tendency for younger friars from England and abroad to crowd into the university convents at Oxford and Cambridge presented a constant problem in the fourteenth century. One solution was to insist that students complete their philosophical training in a local convent or, more probably, in a *studium particulare*. This was the practice in France, and it seems unlikely that the English province would not have adopted this procedure.[17] A second means of curbing the growing numbers at the Oxford convent was to reduce the residency required for the theological degree. Franciscans, who like other mendicants did not take a university arts degree, were required to study theology for nine years before lecturing on the *Sentences* at Oxford. During the first six years of study

---

[15] Little, *AFH*, XIX, 819–820.

[16] Ibid., 814.

[17] *AFH*, VII (1914), 497: "Nullus studens... mittatur Parisiis pro studio, nisi prius in sua custodia probatus fuerit in lectione philosophiae vel logicalium, et etiam in moribus et conversatione."

they were required to attend lectures in the Bible and in the *Sentences*, but only one year before opponency need be spent in residence at Oxford or some major *studium generale*.[18] The others could be spent at a custodial school. A third procedure, adopted officially in 1336 but probably in use earlier, was to require candidates who aspired to lecture on the *Sentences* at Paris, Oxford, or Cambridge, to have lectured previously on the *Sentences* at some other *studium generale* or a custodial school.[19]

After the first six years of theological study, the friar was permitted to oppose in theological disputations (usually for two years), then to respond (usually one year).[20] It might be during the last year or two of the required nine years of theological study that a candidate might lecture for a year on the *Sentences* at some custodial school. In all probability he would not undertake this task before his seventh or eighth year of theological training, for he would not be sufficiently prepared.

The final three or four years of the theological program were spent lecturing and disputing at Oxford or Cambridge. The lectures on the *Sentences* as *baccalarius sententiarius* were usually completed in one academic year, but they might be stretched over a biennium.[21] After completing this task the friar remained at the university for two more years, lecturing

---

[18] Little, *AFH*, XIX, 825.

[19] *AFH*, XXX, 349: "Nullus quoque frater dicti Ordinis ad legendum in praememoratis studiis Sententias assumatur, nisi prius legerit IV Libros Sententiarum cum scriptis approbatorum doctorum in aliis studiis quae in eodem Ordine dicuntur generalia, vel in conventibus infrascriptis, videlicet . . . Londoniensi, Eboracensi, Northwicensi, Novi-castri, Stanfordiensi, Conventreiensi, Exoniensi. . . ."

[20] A. G. Little, *The Grey Friars at Oxford* (Oxford, 1892), pp. 44–45.

[21] In the thirteenth century a biennial reading had been the norm; P. Glorieux, "Sentences," *DTC*, XIV (1941), 1862: "Au XIIIe siècle, cette lecture est répartie sur deux années; encore faut-il qu'elles soient complètes." By the second quarter of the fourteenth century both these requirements were reduced. Some commentaries were produced only on one or two books, and most were read in the course of one academic year. The shift from a biennial to an annual reading is first reflected in the documents from the various mendicant general-chapter meetings, where a biennial appointment to read at Paris gives way to an annual appointment. The same is true for the Franciscans at Oxford by 1336 and probably even earlier; *AFH*, XXX, 346: "Qui autem ordinabuntur ad legendum Sententias Oxonii, duo assumantur duobus annis de provincia Angliae per ipsius provinciae capitulum eligendi; tertius autem pro anno tertio assumatur de aliis partibus Ordinis per generale capitulum vicissim tam de Cismontanis quam de Ultramontanis eligendus." A one-year reading was the rule at Balliol College by 1340; H. E. Salter, *The Oxford Deeds of Balliol College* (Oxford, 1913), p. 290 (dated 1340): "Et in nono vel decimo anno librum sententiarum legat et in duodecimo vel tertiodecimo anno in eadem facultate incipere teneatur, nisi ex causa legitima. . . ." The 1366 legislation at Paris (*CUP*, II, 700, §§ 32 & 38) sets the beginning weeks of October, January, March, and May for the *principia* on books I, II, III, and IV, respectively, which led Glorieux to

on the Bible as *cursor* and participating in disputations.²² At Oxford as well as Paris there could only be one *sententiarius* per order in any one academic year.²³ This meant that most of those who studied at Oxford or Cambridge could never complete their studies there.

Completion of the full twelve or thirteen years of theological study did not automatically bring promotion to the *magisterium*. That required appointment as lector to the Oxford or Cambridge convent, selected by the provincial chapter or the *curia* of the Minister General, usually at the request of those at the Oxford and Cambridge convents.²⁴ In the thirteenth century this term as *magister regens* lasted two years, but in the fourteenth century this was either reduced to one year or there was an overlap of an old and new lector.²⁵ This necessary period of regency, open only to a very few, was preceded by the ceremony of inception. It was

---

comment (*DTC*, XIV, 1862): "Ceci se rapportant à une époque où la lecture des Sentences ne durait plus qu'une année." The most explicit statement of this practice at Oxford comes at the end of the century; Gibson, *Statuta Oxon.*, p. 195 (dated 1407 or before): "Statutum est quod quilibet in futurum lecturus librum sententiarum, qui prius in artibus non rexerit Oxonie . . . per tres anni terminos suam lecturam continuet. . . ." It was also the assumption of Little, *The Grey Friars*, p. 46, that a one-year reading of the *Sentences* was the norm for fourteenth-century Franciscans.

²² S. Gibson, *Statuta Oxon.*, p. 50 (dated before 1350): "Post lecturam insuper libri sententiarum, ad minus per biennium vel fere studio incepturus insistat, antequam scandat cathedram magistralem." Cf. Little, *The Grey Friars*, pp. 46–47; *AFH*, XIX, 826–827.

²³ This practice is reflected in the lists of those appointed to read the *Sentences* at Paris for the various mendicant orders. It was specifically stated in the *Ordinationes Benedicti XII* of 1336, quoted in the previous note. The only university convent that permitted two *sententiarii* simultaneously was the Dominican house at Paris, which possessed two chairs of theology, one belonging to the Province of France and one filled from the other provinces. W. A. Hinnebusch, however, feels that only one Dominican bachelor at Paris "expounded the *Sentences* during any scholastic year"; see *History of the Dominican Order*, II, p. 60. For a contrary opinion see Guimaraes, "Hervé Noel. Etude biographique," *AFP*, VIII (1939), 30–32. Exceptions to the rule of one *sententiarius* per order per year were rare, but they did occur. The Dominicans Robert Holcot and William Crathorn read the *Sentences* at Oxford in the academic year 1330–31.

²⁴ Little, *AFH*, XIX, 822, 830–831.

²⁵ In the middle years of the thirteenth century the period of regency averaged three years. For the fourteenth century the number of names on Eccleston's list works out to approximately one lector per year. If the two-year rule was in force in the fourteenth century among the Franciscans, then one has to assume that a new master incepted when the senior regent master began his second year. Cf. Little, *AFH*, XIX, 830–831. It was S. Gibson's assumption that the regulation (dated before 1380) governing regency in the faculty of canon law revealed the period of regency in theology as well; *Statuta Oxon.*, pp. cxi, 178: "Item, statutum est quod incipiens in decretis de cetero non teneatur nisi ad lecturam annalem, excepto anno in quo incipit, sicut de artistis et theologis est statutum, antiquo statuto super lectura biennali decretistarum, excepto anno quo incipiunt, edito non obstante."

this act, if followed by a year or more as *magister regens*, that made one a master of theology at Oxford or Cambridge. One could teach at a convent or even at a custodial school without having attained that level. But one could not teach as master at Oxford, Cambridge, or Paris unless one had incepted and become regent.

As *magister regens*, the Franciscan lector, like the other *magistri regentes*, was expected to represent his convent or college in the solemn functions of the university, to oversee the progress of the *baccalarii*, to lecture on the Bible, and to participate in certain debates.[26] In addition to these duties, he could also give theological lectures on selected topics, *Quaestiones disputatae*, or *Quaestiones ordinariae*. He might during this time revise his earlier bachelor lectures on the *Sentences* into an *ordinatio*. However, with the exception of the Biblical lectures, which were taken very seriously among the mendicants, there was an increasing tendency by the end of the thirteenth century for the masters to concern themselves solely with directing the students or participating in the public functions of the university.[27]

Some *Quaestiones ordinariae* from the thirteenth, fourteenth, and fifteenth centuries were organized according to the plan of the *Sentences* and consequently have the appearance of magisterial lectures on the *Sentences*.[28] Because "reading the *Sentences*" was normally the exclusive right of a newly-formed bachelor, scholars have chosen to view these works as *Quaestiones disputatae* that only have the appearance of *Sentences* commentaries. However, as Glorieux has remarked, this genre has received little attention, and its study may hold some surprises for us.[29] We know that if a bachelor was not available to "read the *Sentences*," it would be incumbent upon the master to provide the instruction that was

---

[26] Little, *The Grey Friars*, p. 52; *AFH*, XIX, 831; cf. Beryl Smalley, *English Friars and Antiquity* (Oxford, 1960), pp. 139–140.

[27] P. Glorieux, *Répertoire des Maîtres en Théologie de Paris au XIIIe siècle*, Vol. I (Paris, 1933), p. 23.

[28] P. Glorieux, "Sentences," *DTC*, XIV, 1877: "On le comprend d'autant mieux que, parallèlement à la lecture des *Sentences*, oeuvre du bachelier, ont dû se développer des *Quaestiones super Sententias*, oeuvre du maître. Leur présence est parfois difficile à déceler, surtout en tant que distinctes du commentaire proprement dit. Elle est pourtant incontestable et remonte même assez haut. Un des premiers exemples qu'on en peut citer est contemporain de saint Thomas: ce sont les *Questiones* proposées par Gérard d'Abbeville, suivant le plan des *Sentences*, mais pourtant sans aucun doute oeuvre de maître."

[29] Ibid.: "L'étude de ce genre littéraire n'a pu encore être entreprise méthodiquement. Elle réserve sans doute plus d'une surprise."

necessary for students in theology.[30] In such exceptional cases the master would in effect lecture on the *Sentences*. It may also have been possible on other occasions for a master to give to his *Quaestiones*, if he so chose, the structure of a *Sentences* commentary. In such circumstances it may only be a matter of definition whether we choose to call these works *Quaestiones disputatae* or *Quaestiones magistrales super Sententias*. Examples are rare. Weisheipl has recently called attention to the examples of Alexander of Hales, Roland of Cremona, Hugh of St. Cher, and Richard Fishacre, and Glorieux has examined the cases of Gerard d'Abbeville, Peter John Olivi, and John Baconthorp.[31] Nicholas of Dinkelsbühl read the *Sentences* for a second time (1409–1413) at Vienna as *magister regens*, and these lectures on all four books were known as his *Quaestiones magistrales*.[32] When Gabriel Biel read the *Sentences* at Tübingen in 1484, he did so as professor of theology.[33] It may be in this light that we should view some of Wodeham's remarks. Wodeham cites the "ordinary" lectures of John of Reading on the *Sentences*, seemingly differentiating these from his bachelor lectures.[34] He also refers to the revised *Sentences* Commentary of Richard Fitzralph as a *lectura*, although it was done while Fitzralph was *magister regens*.[35] Finally, it would appear that Adam Wodeham lectured on the *Sentences* after he gave his bachelor lectures at Oxford, and even through this work, known as a *lectura*, need not have been given at

---

[30] This was certainly true at the provincial schools of theology; W. A. Hinnebusch, *History of the Dominican Order*, II, p. 29: "When a lector had no bachelor under his direction, he himself was obliged to give two theological lectures daily, the first expounding the Scriptures, the second the *Sentences*." This may also have been the reason Gabriel Biel read at the newly founded University of Tübingen.

[31] J. A. Weisheipl, "The Johannine Commentary of Friar Thomas," *Church History*, XLV (1976), 185–188, is of the opinion that magisterial lectures on the *Sentences* were given at Paris only in the period from 1222–1235, after which time Parisian masters lectured exclusively on the Bible and were not allowed to lecture on the *Sentences*. The only Oxford example he lists comes from the same period (1245). For Glorieux's discussion see: *DTC*, XIV, 1877; "Pour une édition de Gérard d'Abbeville," *RTAM*, IX (1937), 74–78.

[32] The example of Dinkelsbühl probably led A. Madre, *Nikolaus von Dinkelsbühl*, BB, XL.4 (Münster i.W., 1965), p. 21, to the following assumption: "Als Erstes war dem neu promovierten theologischen Magister die Aufgabe gestellt, zum zweiten Mal die Sentenzen des Petrus Lombardus zu kommentieren."

[33] Cf. H. A. Oberman, *The Harvest of Medieval Theology* (Cambridge, Mass., 1963), pp. 16–20; *Collectorium circa quattuor libros Sententiarum*, Vol. I, ed. W. Werbeck and U. Hofmann (Tübingen, 1973), pp. xiv–xv; Vol. IV.1 (Tübingen, 1975), pp. ix, 3.

[34] Wodeham, *Lectura secunda*, dist. 4, q. un. (Cambridge, Caius 281, fol. 181va). But Wodeham also cites Ockham "in suis responsionibus ordinariis" (Vat. lat. 955, fol. 185^r), and Ockham was never *magister regens*.

[35] See below, pp. 77–78.

Oxford, one cannot without examination exclude the possibility that it may belong to this genre of *Quaestiones disputatae super Sententias*.³⁶

When a new master incepted, the one who had held that position became *magister non regens*. In that capacity he might remain at the university convent for a year or two longer before undertaking tasks elsewhere.³⁷

2. *Wodeham's "modern" sources*

In the following discussions of those figures cited in the pages of Wodeham's commentaries on the *Sentences*, the number and location of citations must be considered illustrative rather than exhaustive. For some authors, such as Ockham, Wodeham's citations are so numerous and extensive that their cataloging and description would amount to an annotated summary of the entire contents of Wodeham's commentaries. For less frequently cited authors, however, I have tried to isolate as many references as possible, but additional ones will no doubt turn up as further work is done in the Wodeham manuscripts. What follows is thus no more than a beginning.

The space devoted to each author does not reflect his importance to Wodeham. I have taken the liberty of treating at length those authors for whom the Wodeham manuscripts offer additional biographical information. Moreover, I have restricted the footnote references to one or two manuscripts, but these citations can be found in other manuscripts of the same redaction.

It has not been possible to identify with certainty all the *moderni* cited by Wodeham. In some cases Wodeham cites a name that could apply to more than one of his contemporaries. In other cases the spelling that occurs in the Wodeham manuscripts approximates but is not identical to the standard form by which an author is known. Therefore these identifications are probable, but not certain. This applies to Peter of Baldeswell, Walter Beaufon, Nigel of Wavere, Nicholas Hoyo, Richard of Repps, and Hugh Grafton. Only one author has remained unidentifiable, a

---

³⁶ See chapter one, pp. 25–26, chapter three, pp. 123–130, and chapter four, p. 180.
³⁷ E. Ypma, *La formation des professeurs chez les ermites de Saint-Augustin de 1256 à 1354* (Paris, 1956), pp. 120–122; "Le 'Mare Magnum'. Un code médiévale du couvent augustinien de Paris," *Augustiniana*, VI (1956), 275–321; "La résompte incomplète des 'Quaestiones Vesperiae' d'Alphonse Vargas O.E.S.A. est-elle retrouvée?" in *Scientia Augustiniana. Festschrift ... Adolar Zumkeller OSA zum 60. Geburtstag*, ed. C. P. Mayer and W. Eckermann (Würzburg, 1975), 257–266.

certain "E" cited at several points in the Cambridge manuscript,[38] which for reasons that will become apparent in chapter three will be cited in the notes as *Lectura secunda*. Those authors who have some identity outside the pages of Wodeham are arranged below in approximate chronological order.

MAGISTER ABSTRACTIONUM

Although the identity of this author has not yet been definitely determined, he has, like the Monachus Niger, achieved a certain notoriety in the current literature, and we know considerably more now than we did a decade ago. He is certainly not Francis Mayronnis, to whom that honorific title was eventually applied. Working from the side of fourteenth-century evidence, Fr. Gedeon Gál has pointed out that the opinions of the *Magister Abstractionum* are mentioned before 1324, when Mayronnis became a master of theology, and cannot be found among the known works of Mayronnis.[39] L. M. de Rijk, on the other hand, established that a logical work known as *Abstractiones* was written by a certain Richard Sophista, whom de Rijk believed to be Richard Fishacre.[40] Recently J. Pinborg made the fortunate discovery that the *Abstractiones* of Richard Sophista contains the opinions of the *Magister Abstractionum*, thus tying together work and author.[41]

The *Abstractiones* of Richard Sophista exists in four manuscripts, some of which appear to be written in a thirteenth-century hand.[42] It seems unlikely, however, that Richard Fishacre was its author. If the Richard in question was Fishacre, it is surprising that he would be known as a theologian under the name "Fishacre" and known as a logician under the title *Magister Abstractionum*. Moreover, since Fishacre was active in the middle of the thirteenth century, it is strange there are no references to the *Abstractiones* or to the *Magister Abstractionum* before the second decade of the fourteenth century.

In a private communication Fr. Gál has noted that the language used by the *Magister Abstractionum* suggests he might be a disciple of Henry of

---

[38] For example, *Lectura secunda*, I, dist. 1, q. 1 (Cambridge, Caius 281, fol. 130vb).

[39] See the introduction in William of Ockham, *Summa Logicae*, ed. Ph. Boehner, G. Gál, and S. Brown (St. Bonaventure, N.Y., 1974), pp. 50*–53*.

[40] L. M. De Rijk, *Logica Modernorum*, Vol. II, Pt. 1 (Assen, 1967), pp. 62–72.

[41] Prof. Pinborg made his discovery known to several scholars by letter, and it has proven correct.

[42] Oxford, Bodleian Library, Digby 24, fols. 61ra–90rb; Oxford, Bodleian Library, Digby 2, fols. 122^{r}–140^{v}; Bruges, Bibl. de la Ville, Ms. 497, fols. 74–95; and Paris, Bibl. Nat. lat. 14 069, fols. 26ra–33ra.

Ghent and, considering those who knew his work best, was probably a Franciscan. Fr. Gál has suggested two candidates: Richard of Conington (who could have written a *Sophismata* as early as 1290 or as late as 1320) or Richard Rufus of Cornwall, a younger contemporary of Richard Fishacre.

References to the *Magister Abstractionum* begin around 1320. He is cited by Ockham in his *Summa Logicae*,[43] by the Pseudo-Campsale in his *Logica contra Ockham*,[44] by John of Reading in his *Sentences* Commentary,[45] and by Adam Wodeham. Wodeham's earliest reference to this author seems to be in the context of the discussion of the habit of grace in the first book of his Oxford lectures, when considering the fallacy of the consequent.[46] Later, in treating the problems raised by the conflict between Aristotle's logic and the doctrine of the Trinity, the views of the *Magister Abstractionum* are frequently repeated.[47] The *Magister*

---

[43] *Summa Logicae*, III–1, c. 4, lin. 35–40.

[44] *Logica contra Ockham*, caps. 51 and 54; cf. introduction in William of Ockham, *Summa Logicae*, p. 51*.

[45] *Sent.* I, prol., q. 8; cf. Ockham, *Summa Logicae*, pp. 51*–52*.

[46] Wodeham, *Lectura Oxon.* I, dist. 17, q. 1, CC (Paris, Univ. 193, fol. 98ra; Vat. lat. 955, fol. 133^v): "Exemplum: neuter oculus requiritur ad hoc quod videas haec est vera sicut inductive patet. Et tamen non sequitur: igitur neutrum oculum habendo potes videre quod patet per eius exponentes communiter datas et etiam in abstractionibus quae falsae sunt, quia exponitur sic, id est, dum neutrum habens potes videre, vel quia neutrum habens, vel si neutrum haberes posses videre, quae falsae sunt per naturam saltem. Et tamen singularia antecedentis inferunt modo quo prius singularia consequentis. Nam sequitur: iste oculus demonstrato dextro non requiritur ad hoc quod videas, igitur istum oculum non habendo potes videre. Et iste oculus non requiritur ut videas demonstrato sinistro, igitur istum oculum non habendo potes videre. Et tamen non sequitur ultra: igitur neutrum oculum habendo potes videre, quia notatur quod nec hunc nec istum habendo potes videre, id est si nec hunc nec istum haberes posses videre, quod non est verum. Et haec responsio quoad falsitatem consequentis est ratio Magistri Abstractionum ad Sophisma praetactum. Et per consequens similem daret ad propositionem." The reference is to *abstractio* 62 (De Rijk, *Logica Modernorum*, p. 64).

[47] Wodeham, *Lectura Oxon.* I, dist. 33, q. 1, F (Paris, Univ. 193, fol. 117rb; Vat. lat. 955, fol. 173^v): "Contra has opiniones et similes ponitur conclusio praemissa iam negativa, licet enim apud Magistrum Abstractionum sicut apud eos haec consequentia sit bona: Sortes est, et non est omnis homo, igitur differt seu distinguitur ab omni homine. Et tunc similiter: tu es, et non es idem cuilibet, igitur differs a quolibet, sicut tenet et exprimit Magister iste Abstractionum." The reference is to *abstractio* 19 (De Rijk, *Logica Modernorum*, p. 63). Wodeham's references to the Magister Abstractionum in *Lectura Oxon.* I, dist. 33, q. 2, S (Paris, Univ. 193, fol. 124ra; Vat. lat. 955, fol. 185^r)= *abstractio* 10 (De Rijk, *Logica Modernorum*, p. 62) and in *Lectura Oxon.* I, dist. 33, q. 3, N (Paris, Univ. 193, fol. 128vb; Vat. lat. 955, fol. 192^v) have been transcribed in the introduction to William of Ockham, *Summa Logicae*, pp. 52*–53*.

Abstractionum also appears in the pages of Wodeham's commentary found in the Cambridge manuscript.[48]

Peter of Baldeswell, OFM

In the Caius manuscript Wodeham refers to the thought of another logician, a certain Baldeswell (Baldiswil) in his discussion of the fallacy of accident.[49] Wodeham does not seem to refer to this author elsewhere. In all probability he meant Peter of Baldeswell, OFM, who was the Oxford lector around 1302–1303 and subsequently Parisian lector, although it is possible Wodeham might have been referring to a later Franciscan, Roger Baldiswell, who was associated with the Cambridge convent and who died in 1366.[50] Baldeswell appears in this question in Wodeham alongside references to Ockham, Chatton, and Aureol.

James of Ascoli (Esculo), OFM

Ascoli, master at Paris in 1309–10, was among the earliest defenders of the teaching of Scotus. He is cited by Wodeham in his Oxford lectures in his discussion of the Trinity.[51] There, on the question of whether the divine persons are equal according to power, the fifth question of the Quodlibet of Jacobus de Esculo is mentioned alongside references to Scotus and Ockham.[52]

Henry Harclay (Harkeley)

In contrast to Baldeswell and Ascoli, who played a small role among the authors cited by Wodeham, Harclay[53] was a significant theologian,

---

[48] *Lectura secunda*, dist. 3, q. 4 (Cambridge, Caius 281, fol. 172vb)=*abstractio* 11 (De Rijk, *Logica Modernorum*, p. 62). This passage has also been transcribed in William of Ockham, *Summa Logicae*, p. 52*.

[49] *Lectura secunda*, dist. 26, q. 2 (Cambridge, Caius 281, fol. 250va).

[50] On Peter Baldeswell see A. B. Emden, *BRO*, I, 96; on Roger Baldiswell see Emden, *BRC*, p. 33.

[51] *Lectura Oxon.* I, dist. 33, q. 5 (Paris, Univ. 193, fol. 134ra).

[52] On James of Ascoli see: P. Glorieux, *Répertoire des maîtres en théologie de Paris au XIIIe siècle*, Vol. II (Paris, 1933), pp. 236–237.

[53] On Henry of Harclay: F. Pelster, "Heinrich von Harclay, Kanzler von Oxford, und seine Quästionen," *Studi e Testi*, XXXVII (1924), 307–356; J. Kraus, "Die Universalienlehre des Oxforder Kanzlers Heinrich von Harclay in ihrer Mittelstellung zwischen skotistischen Realismus und Ockhamistischen Nominalismus," *Divus Thomas* (Fribourg), X (1932), 36–58, 475–508; XI (1933), 76–96, 288–314; A. Maurer, "Henry of

whose atomistic position on the problem of the continuum drew criticism from Wodeham in various works. Harclay, as with so many of Wodeham's opponents, was a northerner, coming from the area around Carlisle, as did Chatton. He was already a master of theology when he was elected Chancellor of Oxford in 1312. He died in Avignon in 1317, and probably was not personally known to Wodeham.

It would appear that Wodeham was not concerned with the opinions of Harclay at the time of his Oxford lectures. I have not come across a single reference to Harclay in that work. However, Harclay is cited repeatedly in the Cambridge manuscript and in both of his treatises on the continuum. In the Commentary in the Caius manuscript, Wodeham has a generally favorable view of Harclay, using him as a supporting authority on problems of logic, epistemology, and the doctrine of the Trinity.[54] For Wodeham, Harclay is closely associated with Scotus and Peter Aureol. By contrast, Wodeham is critical of Harclay in the two treatises on the continuum, where he attacks his indivisibilist position.[55] If, as has been argued, Harclay stands in a tradition of developing nominalism from Scotus to Ockham, Wodeham would seem to place Harclay nearer to Scotus, both chronologically and ideologically.

WILLIAM OF ALNWICK, OFM

Alnwick was a Franciscan contemporary of Harclay and also came from the north of England.[56] He began the study of theology in the custodial school at Newcastle on Tyne and subsequently studied at

---

Harclay's Question on the Univocity of Being," *MedStud*, XVI (1954), 1–18; A. Maurer, "Henry of Harclay's Question on Immortality," *MedStud*, XIX (1957), 79–107; C. Balić, "Henricus de Harcley et Ioannes Duns Scotus," *Mélanges offerts à Etienne Gilson* (Toronto, 1959), 93–121, 701–702; A. Maurer, "Henry of Harclay's Questions on the Divine Ideas," *MedStud*, XXIII (1961), 163–193; G. Gál, "Henricus de Harclay: Quaestio de Significato Conceptus Universalis (Fons Doctrinae Guillelmi de Ockham)," *FcS*, XXXI (1971), 178–234.

[54] Cambridge, Caius 281, fol. 136ra: "Ad quem dicit unus doctor et credo quod verum dicit, scilicet Hark., prima quaestione primi Sententiarum, quod quaedam propositiones . . .;" Ibid., fol. 149ra: "Item respondet Hark., prima quaestione prologi super primum Sententiarum, et bene mihi videtur, licet hoc tenere non auderem absque teste auctoritate . . .;" Ibid., fols. 238va, 239va, and 241rb.

[55] For Wodeham's references to Harclay on the continuum, see: J. E. Murdoch and E. A. Synan, "Two Questions on the Continuum: Walter Chatton (?), O.F.M. and Adam·Wodeham, O.F.M.," *FcS*, XXVI (1966), 271–272.

[56] For biographical data and bibliography on Alnwick, see Emden, *BRO*, I, 27.

Oxford and Paris. Between 1303 and 1308 he was closely associated with Scotus, attending his lectures at Paris and Oxford and acting as his secretary at Paris. After Scotus' death in 1308, he oversaw the definitive edition of the *Opus Oxoniense* and the *Reportatio Parisiensis*. By 1314 he had given his own lectures on the *Sentences*, possibly at Paris, and around 1316 he became the Franciscan *magister regens* at Oxford. After 1317 he seems to have returned to the Continent, where he lectured at Paris (as regent master), Montpellier, Bologna, and Naples. He died at Avignon in 1333.

During Wodeham's academic career Alnwick was no longer in England and probably exercised little direct influence on Oxford theology after 1322, since he remained in Italy and southern France. As with Ockham a few years later, his theological reputation in England was based on his earlier writings, particularly his *Sentences* Commentary, his *Quaestiones disputatae*, and his *Quodlibets*.

As might well be expected, Wodeham grouped Alnwick with Scotus. He is not referred to separately in Wodeham's *Lectura Oxoniensis* and, to my knowledge, is not referred to at all in the other works.[57]

Peter Aureol, OFM

Among Franciscans and even outside that circle Peter Aureol was the most influential theologian in the period between Scotus and Ockham.[58] Except for his years as *sententiarius* and *magister* at Paris (1316–1320), his career was centered in Provence and northern Italy. He died in Provence in 1322, when Wodeham was in the first years of his theological training.

In view of Aureol's reputation by 1330 and the impact his *Sentences* Commentary made almost upon publication, it is not surprising that Aureol appears frequently in the text and margins of Wodeham. He is one of a handful of authors (Scotus, Aureol, Ockham, Chatton, and Fitzralph) whom Wodeham cited repeatedly. By contrast, Wodeham

---

[57] Wodeham, *Lectura Oxon.* I, dist. 33, q. 1 (Vat. lat. 955, fol. 173^r; Paris, Univ. 193, fol. 117ra; Paris, Maz. 915, fol. 102ra): "Istum sensum ponit Scotus in quaestione sua de hac materia, quae vocatur 'Logica Scoti', et Alnwick [texts read: Abilnoik and Alerwik] in additionibus Scoti super primum Sententiarum, dist. 33, q. 1." I am grateful to Fr. G. Gál for bringing this reference to my attention. Wodeham's hand must have been difficult to read at this point, for the Vatican manuscript has Abilnoik and Univ. and Maz. have Alerwik.

[58] The best biographical sketch of Peter Aureol can be found in Peter Aureoli, *Scriptum super primum sententiarum*, Vol. I, ed. E. M. Buytaert (St. Bonaventure, N.Y., 1953), pp. vii–xvi. The literature on Aureol is well known and, in any event, too vast to permit citation here.

seems never to have cited Aureol's major contemporary, Durand of St. Pourçain.

Wodeham refers to Aureol in nine questions of the Oxford lectures and seventeen questions in the Caius manuscript.[59] The topics for which he is important are wide-ranging: epistemology, knowledge of God, love of God, the Trinity, grace, the power of creation, and the problem of quantity. Of these, the central issue, one that occupies much of the Caius manuscript, concerns the problems of logic and language that follow from the doctrine of the Trinity.

WALTER BURLEY, MERTONIAN[60]

Walter Burley is generally viewed as a major opponent of Ockham in the area of logic. Burley's negative reaction, when it came, was so strong that its presence or absence in particular works has been used to date them. One might expect, therefore, that Burley would be recognized by Wodeham to be a major opponent against whom Wodeham would defend the teaching of Ockham. Such, however, is not the case. Burley is rarely cited by Wodeham. When he is, it is as an authority on logic, a reputation based on his supposedly pre-1320 works. In this manner Wodeham cites Burley's opinions in relation to the doctrine of the Trinity, and one of his two citations is from Burley's *De Fallaciis*.[61]

---

[59] Wodeham, *Lectura Oxon.* I, dist. 1, q. 2 (Vat. lat. 955, fol. 21^v; Paris, Univ. 193, fols. 16va, 17va); I, dist. 1, q. 5 (Vat. lat. 955, fol. 31^r; Paris, Univ. 193, fols. 23va, 23vb, 24rb); I, dist. 17, q. 2 (Vat. lat. 955, fol. 136^v; Paris, Univ. 193, fol. 99vb); I, dist. 33, q. 2 (Vat. lat. 955, fol. 181^v); I, dist. 33, q. 5 (Paris, Univ. 193, fols. 132rb, 132va (twice), 132vb); II, q. 1 (Paris, Maz. 915, fol. 130vb); II, q. 2 (Vat. lat. 1110, fols. 6^r, 6^v); IV, q. 1 (Paris, Univ. 193, fol. 212rb); IV, q. 5 (Paris, Univ. 193, fol. 221rb); *Lectura secunda*, prol., q. 3 (Cambridge, Caius 281, fols. 113rb, 113va); Prol., q. 4 (Caius 281, fols. 115vb, 116rb, 116va, 116vb); prol., q. 5 (Caius 281, fol. 119vb); dist. 1, q. 1 (Caius 281, fol. 131va); dist. 1, q. 4 (Caius 281, fols. 142va, 144ra, 144va, 144vb (twice), 145va); dist. 2, q. 1 (Caius 281, fols. 153rb, 153va); dist. 4 (Caius 281, fols. 178ra, 178rb, 180ra); dist. 6, q. 1 (Caius 281, fol. 187ra); dist. 7, q. 1 (Caius 281, fols. 190va, 193rb, 194va (twice), 198va); dist. 7, q. 2 (Caius 281, fol. 199vb); dist. 10 (Caius 281, fols. 213rb, 215ra); dist. 17, q. 1 (Caius 281, fols. 220rb (twice), 221rb, 225vb); dist. 23 (Caius 281, fol. 233va); dist. 24, q. 1 (Caius 281, fols. 235va, 235vb, 236va); dist. 24, q. 2 (Caius 281, fols. 238va, 239va, 239vb, 241rb (twice), 241va, 242vb, 243va); dist. 26, q. 1 (Caius 281, fol. 248ra); dist. 26, q. 2 (Caius 281, fol. 250ra).

[60] On Walter Burley, see: J. A. Weisheipl, "Ockham and some Mertonians," *MedStud*, XXX (1968), 174–188; "Repertorium Mertonense," *MedStud*, XXXI (1969), 185–208.

[61] Wodeham, *Lectura Oxon.* I, dist. 17, q. 3 (Lüneburg 4° 29, fol. 144va); I, dist. 33, q. 2, a. 2 (Vat. lat. 955, fol. 183^v; Paris, Univ. 193, fol. 123rb); I, dist. 33, q. 3 (Paris, Univ. 193, fol. 127va). By the title *De Fallaciis* Wodeham was probably referring to Burley's *Tractatus de modo arguendi*. See Hester Gelber, *Logic and the Trinity: A Clash of Values in*

It is difficult to know how to interpret Wodeham's complete silence on Burley's anti-Ockhamism, which appeared a decade before Wodeham lectured at Oxford. Burley was almost a full generation older than Wodeham, having been born probably in 1275, and was already a Parisian doctor of theology by 1324. During Wodeham's student years (which coincide with Burley's attack on Ockham), Burley was active on the Continent, first at Paris and then in the south of France. By 1333 he had returned to England and had joined the circle of scholars who surrounded Richard de Bury, Bishop of Durham.

It is possible that Burley's post-1320 writings, having been composed on the Continent, did not circulate widely in English Franciscan circles and that Wodeham was simply unaware of Burley's critique of Ockham at the time of his Oxford lectures. It is also possible, however, that scholarship may have over-stressed Burley's critique of Ockham. Perhaps in the period following 1320 Burley continued to be read as a logician of standing whose critique of Ockham, if known in England, did not rank high alongside those of John of Reading or Walter Chatton.

RICHARD CAMPSALE, MERTONIAN

Campsale may well have completed his teaching career by the time Wodeham arrived at Oxford to finish his theological study.[62] As will be argued in chapter four, Wodeham was at the Franciscan convent in London when Campsale was "sacrae theologiae professor."[63] By the time Wodeham lectured on the *Sentences* at Oxford, Campsale was dead.[64]

Wodeham, however, was familiar with the life and writings of Campsale. He knew the stages in the controversy between Campsale and Chatton over the logic of the Trinity.[65] He was familiar with Campsale's logical treatises as well as his theological writings. In fact, Wodeham's

---

Scholastic Thought, 1300–1335, unpublished doctoral dissertation, University of Wisconsin (Madison, 1974), p. 228.

[62] For the life and writings of Richard Campsale, see: E. A. Synan, "Richard of Campsall, an English Theologian of the 14th Century," *MedStud*, XIV (1952), 1–8; *The Works of Richard of Campsale*, 2 vols. (Toronto, 1968 ff.); J. A. Weisheipl, "Repertorium Mertonense," *MedStud*, XXXI, 208–209; C. H. Lohr, "Medieval Latin Aristotle Commentaries," *Traditio*, XXVIII (1972), 391.

[63] Weisheipl, *MedStud*, XXXI, 208.

[64] Wodeham, *Lectura Oxon.* I, dist. 33, q. 2 (Vat. lat. 955, fol. 184^v; Paris, Univ. 193, fol. 124ra) calls Chatton a "doctor iam existens" to distinguish him from Campsale, who must therefore have died in or before the academic year in which Wodeham was writing, i.e., 1330–31.

[65] See Gelber, *Logic and the Trinity*, pp. 203–204, 208–211, 229–230.

citations of Campsale's theological opinions are of special value, since so little remains of that side of Campsale's career.

Wodeham respected Campsale as a logician and theologian, although he was occasionally critical of specific views. We encounter Campsale both in the Oxford lectures and in the Caius manuscript. Wodeham cites him on the nature of volition, on the doctrine of grace, on the logic of the Trinity, and on cognition.[66]

WALTER BEAUFON, OFM

Beaufon (*alias* Bonfon, Benfon, Beafou, Benson, Biensu) was the thirty-seventh lector at the Franciscan convent at Cambridge, an office which he held ca. 1317–1319.[67] His works have not been recovered, which in part explains why he is so unfamiliar to modern historians of fourteenth-century thought. He appears to have been cited and opposed by Ockham on the problem of the Trinity, inasmuch as Padua Univ. 927 identifies an "alia opinio" in the text of Ockham as "Gualteri Beaufon."[68] Wodeham cites Beaufon three times, if we are justified in assuming that several variants in spelling refer to one person. In *Lectura Oxon.* I, dist. 1, q. 12, Wodeham refers to the opinion of a certain Biensu on the doctrine of the Trinity.[69] There he is associated with Ralph Pigaz (Pigam) and the Cambridge convent. Later, in *Lectura Oxon.* I dist. 33, q. 1, toward the beginning of an extensive treatment of the doctrine of the Trinity, he again cites "Benfon" or "Benson".[70] Finally, in his shorter treatise on

---

[66] Wodeham, *Lectura Oxon.* I, dist. 1, q. 6 (Vat. lat. 955, fol. 33^r; Paris, Univ. 193, fol. 24va; Vat. lat. 955, fol. 39^r; Vat. lat. 955, fol. 39^v; Paris, Univ. 193, fol. 29vb): "Haec erat responsio in puncto Magistri Richardi Camsale." Ibid. (Vat. lat. 955, fol. 42^v; Paris, Univ. 193, fols. 31va–31vb): "... respondet Camsale et bene...." *Lectura Oxon.* I, dist. 1, q. 9 (Vat. lat. 955, fol. 61^r; Paris, Univ. 193, fol. 44vb); I, dist. 17, q. 5 (Paris, Univ. 193, fol. 110vb); I, dist. 33, q. 2 (Vat. lat. 955, fols. 183^r, 184^r; Paris, Univ. 193, fols. 123ra, 123vb): "Ars Camsale"; II, q. 2 (Paris, Maz. 915, fol. 133rb); III, q. 3 (Naples, Bibl. Naz. VII C 53, fol. 81rb; ref. by abbreviator, not by Wodeham); IV, q. 6 (Paris, Univ. 193, fol. 222va; Paris, Maz. 915, fol. 218va); *Lectura secunda*, dist. 3, q. 4 (Cambridge, Caius 281, fols. 174vb, 176va).

[67] Emden, *BRC*, p. 46. Emden prefers the spelling "Beafou".

[68] William of Ockham, *Ordinatio* I, dist. 2, q. 11, in William of Ockham, *Opera Philosophica et Theologica*, Vol. II (St. Bonaventure, N.Y., 1970), pp. 361–363.

[69] Paris, Univ. 193, fol. 65ra, and Tarazona, Cat. 7, fol. 46ra, have "Biensu". Paris, Maz. 915, fol. 54rb, reads "Biensa", and Vat. lat. 955, fol. 71^r, reads "Bensu".

[70] Vat. lat. 955, fol. 172^r, reads "Benfon". Paris, Univ. 193, fol. 116va, and Tarazona, Cat. 7, fol. 84ra, read "Benson". Paris, Maz. 915, fol. 101va, reads "Lenson".

the continuum, Wodeham refers to the argument of "Benfon".[71] Given the similarity in late gothic bookhands between "s" and "f", and between "n" and "u", it is easy to see how "Beaufon," or "Beufon," can become "Benson" or for that matter, how "Benson" can become "Beufon".

John of Reading, OFM

John of Reading was among the most noted defenders of Scotism at Oxford at the time of Ockham and Wodeham.[72] Wodeham called him Scotus' "discipulus et sequax valentissimus frater Johannes de Radingia, magister."[73] He was probably a few years Ockham's senior, and around 1320 he became the forty-fifth lector at the Oxford convent.[74] Reading was also among the earliest opponents of Ockham, and the redactions of the *Sentences* commentaries of Ockham and Reading trace the stages of a heated debate over the differences between the teachings of Scotus and Ockham.[75] Wodeham may never have known him personally, since by 1322 Reading had moved to Avignon, where he acted as a theological adviser to John XXII and may have been lector of the Franciscan convent there. He died in Avignon, and there is no evidence to suggest that he returned to England after 1322.

Wodeham not only continued to defend Ockham against Reading, but he also pursued Reading on points other than those treated by Ockham. His interest in Reading even seems to have grown across his teaching career, since we find Reading appearing more frequently in the margins of the Caius manuscript than in the *Lectura Oxoniensis*.[76] Wode-

---

[71] London, Brit. Mus., Harley 3243, fol. 55vb, reads "Bēfon", which might be read as "Benfon" or "Beaufon". For the text, see: J. Murdoch and E. Synan, *FcS*, XXVI (1966), 276.

[72] Emden, *BRO*, III, 1554; F. Longpré, "Jean de Reading et le Bx. Jean Duns Scot," *La France franciscaine*, VII (1924), 99–109.

[73] *Lectura Oxon*. I, dist. 1, q. 12, H (Vat. lat. 955, fol. 70^{v}; Paris, Univ. 193, fol. 65ra; Paris, Maz. 915, fol. 54ra; Tarazona, Cat. 7, fol. 45vb). Wodeham was probably referring to Reading when, in *Lectura secunda*, dist. 7, q. 3 (Cambridge, Caius 281, fol. 205ra), he listed several "rationes Rad."

[74] Little, *The Grey Friars*, p. 168.

[75] S. Brown, "Sources for Ockham's Prologue to the *Sentences*," *FcS*, XXVI (1966), pp. 36–51; S. Brown and G. Gál, introduction to William of Ockham, *Scriptum in librum primum sententiarum ordinatio*, in William of Ockham, *Opera*, II, pp. 18*–34*.

[76] *Lectura Oxon*. I, dist. 1, q. 6 (Vat. lat. 955, fol. 43^{r}); I, dist. 1, q. 12 (Vat. lat. 955, fol. 70^{v}; Paris, Univ. 193, fol. 65ra); *Lectura secunda*, Prol., q. 2 (Cambridge, Caius 281, fols. 111vb, 112rb); dist. 1, q. 1 (Caius 281, fol. 130vb, 131vb); dist. 1, q. 4, a. 3 (Caius 281, fol. 144ra); dist. 1, q. 5 (Caius 281, fol. 147ra); dist. 3, q. 3 (Caius 281, fol. 172va); dist. 4, q. un. (Caius 281, fols. 181rb, 181va).

ham shows himself familiar with both the *Ordinatio* and the *Quodlibeta* of Reading.⁷⁷ At one point Wodeham seems pleased to note that this most distinguished disciple of Scotus "sibi planissime contradixit."⁷⁸

RICHARD DRAYTON, OFM

Richard Drayton was the forty-seventh lector at the Franciscan convent in Oxford around 1324.⁷⁹ His works are not extant, and our only means of reconstructing portions of his thought is through citations in the works of others. His close contemporary, John of Reading, quoted sections from his writings.⁸⁰ He appears once in the Cambridge manuscript in a discussion of beatific fruition in relation to the soul and the intellect.⁸¹

WILLIAM OF OCKHAM, OFM

Ockham was the most creative and influential mind in the fourteenth century, a fact attested to not only by the citations and controversies of the fourteenth and fifteenth centuries but by the attention he has received from modern historians.⁸² To Wodeham he was both teacher and friend. Therefore, it should come as no surprise to anyone that Ockham was, for Wodeham, the most authoritative voice among contemporary theologians. References to him abound throughout the redactions of Wodeham's *Sentences* Commentary.⁸³ It should be noted, however, that

---

⁷⁷ *Lectura secunda*, dist. 1, q. 1 (Caius 281, fol. 130ᵛᵇ): "Et ideo concedunt isti quod Deus est significabilis i[n] con[ceptu] proprio mentali, licet non vocali, scilicet E. et Red., Quodlibet suo, q. 5, tractando et probando conclusionem suam secundam." Ibid., dist. 4, q. un. (Caius 281, fol. 181ᵛᵃ): "Huic tamen respondit Redingg in lectionibus ordinariis quod omnis talis. . . ."

⁷⁸ *Lectura Oxon*. I, dist. 1, q. 12 (Vat. lat. 955, fol. 70ᵛ; Paris, Univ. 193, fol. 65ʳᵃ).

⁷⁹ Emden, *BRO*, I, 593.

⁸⁰ Longpré, *La France franciscaine*, VII (1942), 107; G. Gál, "Quaestio Ioannis de Reading de necessitate specierum intelligibilium, defensio doctrinae Scoti," *FcS*, XXIX (1969), 66–156.

⁸¹ Cambridge, Caius 281, fol. 138ʳᵇ: "Hanc viam tenuit Drayton in determinando quod nisi a Deo non recipit actu inherentia."

⁸² For guides to the literature on Ockham, see: V. Heynck, "Ockham-Literatur 1919–49," *FzS*, XXII (1950), 164–183; J. P. Reilly, "Ockham Bibliography, 1950–67," *FcS*, XXVIII (1968), 197–214; H. Junghans, *Ockham im Lichte der neueren Forschung* (Berlin and Hamburg, 1968). An excellent recent study is G. Leff, *William of Ockham* (Manchester, Engl., 1975).

⁸³ Wodeham, *Lectura Oxon*. I, dist. 1, q. 4 (Paris, Univ. 193, fol. 22ʳᵇ, 22ᵛᵃ; Vat. lat. 955, fol. 27ʳ); I, dist. 1, q. 6 (Vat. lat. 955, fol. 45ʳ; Paris, Univ. 193, fols. 33ᵛᵇ, 34ᵛᵇ, 35ʳᵃ);

Wodeham did not consider his own thought derivative of Ockham's, nor is there any indication that he felt himself to belong to a school of *Ockhamistae*. On occasion he was critical of Ockham's solutions, and at one point he notes that many of Ockham's arguments on the problem of quantity were formulated by Wodeham himself at an earlier date.[84] In addition to the known works of Ockham, with which Wodeham had intimate knowledge and some editorial relation, Wodeham cites some of the unpublished opinions of Ockham.[85]

I, dist. 1, q. 7 (Paris, Univ. 193, fol. 36ra); I, dist. 1, q. 10 (Paris, Univ. 193, fols. 49va, 52vb; Vat. lat. 955, fols. 67^r, 73^v); I, dist. 1, q. 12 (Vat. lat. 955, fol. 89^v: "Ockham respondet aliter sed obscure"; Paris, Univ. 193, fols. 65rb, 65vb, 66rb, 66va, 67ra, 67rb, 67va, 69ra); I, dist. 2, q. 1 (Vat. lat. 955, fols. 101^v, 103^r, 105^r, 106^r); I, dist. 3, q. un. (Vat. lat. 955, fol. 107^r); I, dist. 17, q. 2 (Vat. lat. 955, fols. 136^v, 138^v; Paris, Univ. 193, fols. 99vb, 100va, 101rb); I, dist. 17, q. 4 (Vat. lat. 955, fol. 152^v); I, dist. 17, q. 5 (Vat. lat. 955, fols. 159^r, 161^v, 163^r; Paris, Univ. 193, fols. 110rb, 110va, 111ra, 111rb, 111va, 111vb, 112ra, 112rb, 112va); I, dist. 33, q. 1 (Vat. lat. 955, fol. 177^r; Paris, Univ. 193, fols. 116va, 116vb, 117ra, 117rb, 119ra, 119rb, 119va, 121rb, 121va); I, dist. 33, q. 2 (Vat. lat. 955, fols. 181^v, 183^r: "Ockham in suis responsionibus ordinariis"; Paris, Univ. 193, fols. 123rb, 123va); I, dist. 33, q. 4 (Vat. lat. 955, fols. 97^v–98^r); I, dist. 33, q. 6 (Paris, Univ. 193, fols. 134vb, 135rb); I, dist. 33, q. 7 (Paris, Univ. 193, fol. 136vb); II, q. 1 (Vat. lat. 1110, fol. 1^v; Paris, Maz. 915, fols. 127rb, 127va, 127vb, 129ra, 129rb, 131ra); II, q. 2 (Vat. lat. 1110, fols. 6^r, 8^v, 9^r; Paris, Maz. 915, fols. 131vb, 132vb, 133ra, 133va, 136rb); II, q. 3 (Paris, Maz. 915, fols. 136va, 140ra, 141ra); II, q. 7 (Vat. lat. 1110, fols. 31^r, 32^v; Paris, Maz. 915, fol. 157vb); III, q. 2 (Vat. lat. 1110, fols. 48^v, 50^r; Paris, Univ. 193, fols. 179va, 179vb, 180va, 181ra); III, q. 3 (Vat. lat. 1110, fols. 53^v, 54^r; Paris, Univ. 193, fol. 183ra); III, q. 8 (Vat. lat. 1110, fols. 70^v–71^r; Paris, Univ. 193, fol. 196vb); IV, q. 1 (Vat. lat. 1110, fol. 96^v); IV, q. 4 (Vat. lat. 1110, fol. 107^v); IV, q. 6 (Paris, Univ. 193, fols. 223rb, 223va); *Lectura secunda*, prol., q. 1 (Cambridge, Caius 281, fols. 106rb, 107vb, 108rb, 108va); prol., q. 2 (fols. 109ra, 109rb, 111ra, 111rb, 111vb, 112ra, 112va, 112vb); prol., q. 4 (fols. 115va, 118rb); prol., q. 5 (fols. 119ra, 119rb); prol., q. 6 (fols. 123rb, 123va, 124va, 125ra); dist. 1, q. 2 (fols. 132va, 132vb, 133va, 136rb); dist. 1, q. 4 (fols. 140ra, 141vb, 142rb, 142va, 143rb, 143va, 144ra, 144vb); dist. 1, q. 5 (fol. 146ra); dist. 2, q. 1 (fols. 150va, 151va, 158rb, 159va); dist. 3, q. 1 (fols. 164rb, 166vb); dist. 3, q. 3 (fols. 170ra, 170rb, 170va, 171ra, 171rb); dist. 3, q. 4 (fol. 173vb); dist. 4, q. un. (fols. 178ra, 181vb, 182va, 182vb); dist. 6, q. 1 (fols. 184ra, 187ra, 187rb); dist. 7, q. 1 (fols. 192ra, 194rb, 195ra, 195rb, 195vb, 196ra, 198va); dist. 7, q. 2 (fols. 199va, 199vb); dist. 7, q. 3 (fols. 204va, 205ra); dist. 8, q. un. (fols. 206vb, 207rb); dist. 9, q. un. (fol. 210va); dist. 10, q. un. (fol. 213vb); dist. 11, q. un. (fol. 216ra); dist. 12, q. un. (fols. 217rb, 217vb); dist. 13, q. un. (fol. 219rb); dist. 14, q. un. (fol. 219vb); dist. 17, q. 1 (fols. 220va, 221vb, 222ra, 224va); dist. 17, q. 3 (fol. 226rb); dist. 20, q. un. (fol. 228va); dist. 22, q. un. (fols. 230va, 231vb); dist. 23, q. un. (fol. 235ra); dist. 24, q. 1 (fols. 237ra, 238ra); dist. 24, q. 2 (fols. 238rb, 238va, 238vb, 239rb, 239va, 240vb); dist. 26, q. 1 (fol. 247rb); dist. 26, q. 2 (fols. 250ra, 250rb, 250va, 250vb).

[84] Florence, Bibl. Naz., conv. soppr. A III 508, fol. 140ra: "Quaere prosecutionem in illo tractatu. Et haec argumenta fere omnia fuerant tua antequam Ockham aliquid scriberet de indivisibilibus."

[85] *Lectura Oxon.* I, dist. 17, q. 5 (Vat. lat. 955, fol. 161^v): "Ad 14m respondet Ockham (manu sua in margine reportationis meae [Chattonis]) quod ille [Chatton] male intellexit articulum. . . ." *Lectura Oxon.* I, dist. 33, q. 1 (Paris, Univ. 193, fol. 121rb; Paris, Maz.

Francis Mayronnes, OFM

Francis Mayronnes was a noted Parisian Scotist who became master in 1324 and died sometime after 1328.[86] He did not play as important a role in Wodeham's thought as was once believed. Gál and De Rijk have demonstrated that Mayronnes was not the *Magister Abstractionum* cited frequently by Ockham, Wodeham, and others.[87] That title was applied to him much later. However, Mayronnes does appear once in the first book of Wodeham's Oxford lectures, on the issue of the identity of the soul and its powers.[88]

Henry of Costesey, OFM

Although Henry Costesey may have had some connection with Oxford, his principal association was with the Cambridge convent, where he was the 46th lector ca. 1325–26.[89] In March of 1330 he was summoned to Avignon for his opposition to *Ad conditorem canonum*. There is no indication in Wodeham that Costesey's opinions were suspect. Wodeham cited him in *Lectura Oxon.* III, q. 3[90] (probably delivered in the fall semester of 1331) and in the Caius manuscript, dist. 7, q. 2.[91]

Ralph Pigaz (or Pigam), OFM

Pigaz is another fourteenth-century author from whom we have no surviving works and whose thought we can only partially reconstruct from discussions in Wodeham and others. Wodeham and Pigaz knew each other at Norwich, where Pigaz was resident, probably shortly before he became the forty-ninth lector of the Franciscan convent at Cambridge,

---

915, fol. 105va): "Hanc rationem approbat Ockham reputans eam efficacem, et ideo cum Scoto concordat in conclusione, dist. 2 primi, quaest. ultima, licet aliter tenuerit respondendo in scolis."

[86] On Mayronnes (or Meyronnes) see: Ch.-V. Langlois, "François de Mayronnes, Frère Mineur," *HLF*, XXXVI (1924–27), 305–342, 652; B. Roth, "Franz von Mayronis und der Augustinismus seiner Zeit," *FzS*, XXII (1935), 44–75; *Franz von Mayronis OFM, sein Leben, seine Lehre vom Formalunterschied in Gott* (Werl i.W., 1936).

[87] L. M. De Rijk, *Logica Modernorum*, Vol. II, Pt. 1 (Assen, 1967), pp. 62–72; William of Ockham, *Summa Logicae*, pp. 50*–53*.

[88] Wodeham, *Lectura Oxon.* I, dist. 17, q. 5 (Paris, Univ. 193, fol. 112ra): ". . . tenetur Parisie a multis reputatis . . . et hoc plane tenet Magister Francis Maronis, lib. 3, q. 45."

[89] Emden, *BRO*, I, 495; *BRC*, p. 161.

[90] Vat. lat. 1110, fol. 56^r.

[91] Cambridge, Caius 281, fol. 200vb.

around 1329.⁹² Wodeham noted certain Platonic elements in Pigaz' thought, especially as concerned the problem of applying Aristotelian logic to the doctrine of the Trinity. Although occasionally critical of Pigaz, Wodeham informed his readers that Pigaz, his senior, sometimes supported his views.⁹³ Wodeham's references to Pigaz seem to be confined to the first book of the Oxford lectures.⁹⁴ There Pigaz often appears in the company of Fitzralph or Burley.

WALTER CHATTON, OFM

Chatton was one of the two most important theologians in Wodeham's immediate environment, and the one with whom he had the longest contact.⁹⁵ They had met by 1321, when Wodeham attended the lectures of Chatton on the *Sentences* and criticized his handling of certain philosophical problems.⁹⁶ One of the major points of conflict was the under-

---

⁹² On Pigaz see: Emden, *BRC*, p. 454. The spelling of Ralph's last name differs in the manuscripts. In Eccleston's list it appears as "Pigaz", but in Paris, Univ. 193, it often appears as "Pigam", "Pigā" (which would usually be read as "Pigam"), and "Piga3" (which could be read as "Pigam" or "Pigaz"). On occasion one also finds "Pigas" or "Picas". The name is probably Pigaz, as Eccleston has it, but one has to recognize the possibility that the original spelling might have been "Pigam" (or "Pigham"), which in the form "Piga 3" was transcribed as "Pigaz" or "Picas".

⁹³ *Lectura Oxon.* I, dist. 33, q. 2 (Vat. lat. 955, fol. 185ʳ; Paris, Univ. 193, fol. 124ʳᵃ): "Aliud dubium: an sufficiat illa distinctio de deitate singulorum et singulis deitatis quam tenet Pigaz, et mihi multum placuit, tum quia bene accessit ad veritatem, tum forsitan quia multum concordabat sententiae quam prius tenueram in lectione Nor."

⁹⁴ *Lectura Oxon.* I, dist. 1, q. 12 (Vat. lat. 955, fol. 71ʳ; Paris, Maz. 915, fol. 54ʳᵇ; Paris, Univ. 193, fol. 65ʳᵃ); I, dist. 33, q. 1 (Vat. lat. 955, fol. 177ᵛ; Paris, Univ. 193, fols. 119ʳᵇ, 120ᵛᵇ, 121ᵛᵇ); I, dist. 33, q. 2 (Vat. lat. 955, fols. 185ʳ, 185ᵛ; Paris, Univ. 193, fols. 124ʳᵃ, 124ʳᵇ, 124ᵛᵃ, 124ᵛᵇ); I, dist. 33, q. 3 (Paris, Univ. 193, fols. 125ʳᵃ, 127ᵛᵃ): ". . . sed vult ipse [Plato] quod eius sequaces cuiusmodi sunt hodie adhuc Burley, Pigam, et alii, et Parisienses non pauci quorum opinio Philosophi et veritas reprobat . . . ;" I, dist. 33, q. 4 (Paris, Univ. 193, fols. 129ᵛᵇ, 130ᵛᵃ).

⁹⁵ Chatton has been the focus of considerable scholarly attention of late. Of particular importance are: L. Baudry, "Gauthier de Chatton et son commentaire des sentences," *AHDL*, XIV (1943–45), 337–369; C. K. Brampton, "Gauthier de Chatton et la provenance des mss. lat. Paris Bibl. Nat. 15886 et 15887," *EF*, XIV (1964), 200–205; G. Gál, "Gaulteri de Chatton et Guillelmi de Ockham Controversia de Natura Conceptus Universalis," *FcS*, XXVII (1967), 191–212; N. Fitzpatrick, "Walter Chatton on the Univocity of Being: A Reaction to Peter Aureoli and William Ockham," *FcS*, XXXI (1971), 88–177; G. Gál, in the introduction to William of Ockham, *Summa Logicae*, pp. 47*–56*.

⁹⁶ The *Reportator* of Chatton noted the criticisms of Wodeham. Paris, Bibl. Nat. lat. 15 887, fol. 65ʳᵃ: "Item, dicit unus, scilicet Wod., quod omnes minores quas accipio in argumento,—quod solum argumentum dixi esse ponderis—sunt falsae apud Aristotelem; igitur ipse non habuit unde moveri ad conclusionem." Ibid.: "Sed dicit aliquis,

standing of the *praedicamentum* "quantity", especially as it related to the divisibility of the continuum. The debate over that issue and others continued in subsequent years, providing content for some of Chatton's magisterial disputations and filling the margins of Wodeham's *Sentences* commentaries at Oxford and elsewhere. Toward the end of Wodeham's academic career, in the Commentary contained in the Caius College manuscript, the views of Chatton were attacked more than those of any other contemporary writer.

Reconstructing the biography of Chatton has proved to be a difficult task, despite the fact that we have several fixed dates and events in his career. We know that he joined the Franciscans before the age of 14.[97] We also know he was, on May 20, 1307, ordained subdeacon at Dalston, just south of Carlisle, by John of Halton, Bishop of Carlisle.[98] In the period from 1321 to 1323 he was lecturing on the *Sentences* at a Franciscan convent other than Oxford, probably London.[99] In 1329 he was at the Franciscan convent in Oxford holding a position of authority, presumably as regent master.[100]

On the assumption that young mendicants were ordained at the earliest possible age, Brampton and Fitzpatrick have placed Chatton's birth around 1285, his ordination to the subdeaconate in 1307 at age 22, his bachelor lectures on the *Sentences* at Oxford in 1318–1319, and viewed the *Reportatio* of 1321–23 as post-Oxford lectures.[101] Several factors, however, bring this account into question. In the opening years of the fourteenth century the earliest age for ordination to the subdeaconate was

---

scilicet Wod., quod Aristoteles diffusius tradit artem et doctrinam suam de relativis modo unius quam de aliis, et de illis currunt quasi omnia dicta et exempla sua tam in Praedicamentis quam in V Metaphysicae." Wodeham states he developed his arguments on quantity against Chatton before Ockham wrote his work on quantity, that is, before 1326; Florence, Bibl. Naz., conv. soppr. A III 508, fol. 140ra. Wodeham also showed his personal copy of Chatton's *Reportatio* to Ockham; Vat. lat. 955, fol. 161^v.

[97] William Woodford (*Defensorium*, c. 62) states that Chatton was one of those who joined the Order as a *puer*. This must mean before the age of 14. In the early fourteenth century it was possible to join the Franciscans at age 14 and, in the case of the *oblati*, even earlier. See Little, *AFH*, XIX, 866.

[98] *The Register of John of Halton, Bishop of Carlisle*, Canterbury and York Society Publications, Vol. XII (London, 1913), p. 279; Emden, *BRO*, I, 395.

[99] Cf. Baudry, *AHDL*, XIV (1943–45), 341; Brampton, *EF*, XIV (1964), 200–205; G. Gál, in the introduction to William of Ockham, *Summa Logicae*, pp. 53*–56*.

[100] *Munimenta Civitatis Oxonie*, Oxford Historical Society, Vol. LXXI (Devizes, 1920), pp. 80–81.

[101] C. K. Brampton, "The Probable Date of Ockham's *Lectura Sententiarum*," *AFH*, LV (1962), 367–374; C. K. Brampton, "Gauthier de Chatton et la provenance des mss. lat. Paris Bibl. Nat. 15886 et 15887," *EF*, XIV (1964), 200–205; N. Fitzpatrick, "Walter Chatton on the Univocity of Being," *FcS*, XXXI (1971), 140–141.

20, not 22. Even allowing for that difference, this chronology would make Chatton 42 when he was regent master at Oxford, seven years beyond the minimal age for attaining the *magisterium*. Why would a gifted man, who was already a friar by age 13, have to wait ten years between his baccalaureate and his regency? This picture is further complicated by the fact that some scholars view Chatton's *Reportatio* as pre-Oxford lectures, that is, lectures given elsewhere, probably at London, in preparation for his bachelor lectures on the *Sentences* at Oxford.[102] However, if he was 20 in 1307, then he was 36 in 1323 and should have completed his studies at Oxford several years earlier.

One solution to this problem is to suppose that the drop in the age of ordination to the subdeaconate from 20 to 17 may already have been permitted in 1307 and that the Council of Vienne did not change the law but simply recognized present custom.[103] This assumption would solve most of the problems. If Chatton was 17 in 1307 and began his theological training at the not-unreasonable age of 24, then the *Reportatio* of 1321–23 would coincide exactly with the biennium during which he could appropriately be lecturing on the *Sentences* at one of the custodial schools, namely his eighth and ninth years of theological study.[104]

On the basis of our present knowledge, it is difficult to decide between the opposing *curricula vitae* constructed by Brampton and Gál. Because the *Reportatio* cannot have been given at Oxford, we must place Chatton's bachelor lectures either four years earlier than 1321 or one year later than 1323, thus producing a six-year variation. The dating of Chatton's bachelor lectures has important ramifications. When did Chatton's opinions begin to circulate, and when did he become critical of Campsale and Ockham? Was Chatton an academic contemporary of Ockham and thus thirteen or fourteen years more advanced than Wodeham, or did Chatton stand academically between Ockham and Wodeham, being only seven or eight years older than the latter?

If these questions cannot presently be answered, there are some other aspects of Chatton's career that are certain. First, Chatton was a northerner, having been born at the village of Catton, in the hill country west of Durham.[105] Although his village was located in a jurisdictional island

---

[102] See G. Gál's introduction to William of Ockham, *Summa Logicae*, p. 55*.

[103] This suggestion was made in a private communication from Fr. G. Gál. Cf. above, note 14.

[104] See above, p. 49

[105] Emden, *BRO*, I, 395–396. In view of the animosities between northerners and southerners at Oxford, it may be of significance that both Ockham and Wodeham were from the south.

belonging to the diocese of York, Chatton's early contact with the Franciscans was not at York nor at Newcastle (in the diocese of Durham), but at Carlisle, where he probably professed. There, close to the Scottish border, he may have been especially influenced by the thought and reputation of the then leading theologian of the Franciscan Order, John Duns Scotus, who was born in the neighboring region to the north.

Much, perhaps all, of Chatton's philosophical training was received in the north, either at the convent of Carlisle or at one of the two northern custodial schools, Newcastle or York. By the time of his ordination as subdeacon he had not yet come south to London or Oxford.[106]

In the period between 1315 and 1321, during which time Ockham lectured on the *Sentences* at Oxford, Chatton was probably present at the Franciscan convent in that town, either attending lectures as a beginning student of theology or completing his program there.[107] Whatever his rank may have been, he made his views known. Either through questions in the classroom or through his bachelor lectures, Chatton criticized Campsale's treatment of the problem of non-identity in statements about the persons of the Trinity. Both Chatton and Wodeham report that Campsale was sufficiently moved by Chatton's comments to adapt an Anselmian rule to solve the problem.[108] By the time we reach Chatton's *Reportatio* in 1321, several stages in this controversy had already taken place. We may assume, therefore, that Chatton had already made something of a reputation for himself, and this reputation may have been based in part on a critique of Ockham.

The *Reportatio* of Chatton, probably delivered at London, can be dated

---

[106] Chatton must have completed at least half of his philosophical studies before his ordination, at which time he was still at Carlisle. At one point in his *Reportatio*, however, Chatton mentions Oxford in such a way that some scholars have inferred he studied philosophy there. Paris, Bibl. Nat. lat. 15 887, fol. 73ra, and Florence, Bibl. Naz., conv. soppr. C V 357, fol. 171vb: "Tertio opinio, quae currebat in villa tempore ille quo audivimus in villa philosophica [Paris reads: prophetica] Romanorum iam dictis quod quando accipis 'antichristus erit', 'Sortes sedebit in *a*', ista potest vel asserere se esse veram vel sententia de inesse fore veram." On the basis of this passage we may conclude that Chatton studied at Oxford before 1321. Furthermore, he is claiming to have heard philosophy at Oxford, but not necessarily while enrolled in the arts program. Although some aspects of the text are unclear, it would not appear that he is claiming to hold an arts degree from Oxford. One must keep in mind that Chatton entered the Order as a *puer*, and Franciscans were not allowed to take the arts degree.

[107] This can be conjectured from the "audivimus in villa" in the previous note as well as Chatton's debate with Richard Campsale before 1321.

[108] On the stages in the controversy between Chatton and Campsale before 1321, see H. Gelber, *Logic and the Trinity*, pp. 201–204.

to the biennium 1321–23.[109] The date of completion depends not only on Chatton's failure to mention the "Cum inter nonnullas" of 1323, but on the fact that Wodeham, who audited those lectures, made a copy, which he showed to Ockham before Ockham left England for Avignon in the summer of 1324.[110]

We have no record of Chatton between 1323 and 1329, during which time he either completed his theological training or simply waited for an opportunity to become regent master at Oxford or Cambridge. He achieved this final stage in the academic year 1329–30 and probably remained at the Oxford convent for the next two years, first as regent master and then as *magister non regens*. According to Wodeham, Chatton had already attracted followers by 1330.[111] Wodeham attended a *determinatio* of Chatton at Oxford during this period.[112] Subsequently, Chatton left England for Avignon, possibly never to return. He was certainly in Avignon in January, 1333.[113]

This brings us to the date and circumstances of Chatton's second (?) lectures on the *Sentences*, known as his *Lectura*.[114] Since this work quotes from Ockham's *Summa Logicae*, it can be dated after 1323,[115] and since

---

[109] Baudry established the dates for this work, and his conclusions have not been overturned. In the third book of the *Reportatio* Chatton mentions that the papal constitution, "Ad conditionem canonum" of John XXII, dated December, 1322, was recent. Because Chatton failed to mention the "Cum inter nonnullas" of November, 1323, Baudry concluded that books III and IV of the *Reportatio* were written in 1322–23, and books I and II were written in 1321–22. It should be noted, however, that failure to cite an important papal pronouncement, even where the author in subsequent works cited it frequently, is not solid evidence for a *terminus ante quem*. For example, Ockham did not read the papal decree on apostolic poverty until the end of his stay in Avignon, although it was available to him and he had a strong interest in the topic. Baudry's assumption that these lectures were given at Oxford was subsequently disproved by Brampton, and recently, in his introduction to Ockham's *Summa Logicae*, Fr. Gál has made a persuasive case that these lectures were given in London.

[110] Vat. lat. 955, fol. 161^v.

[111] *Lectura Oxon.* I, dist. 1, q. 2 (Vat. lat. 955, fol. 23^r, in margin; Paris, B. N. lat. 15 892, fol. 17va): ". . . et adhuc est aliquorum modernorum, Chat. scilicet et eius sequacium, et Aegidii." *Lectura Oxon.* IV, q. 5 (only in Vat. lat. 1110, fol. 114^v): "Si autem tu, Chatton, cum sequacibus tuis ponderem . . ., nam tu ponis. . . ."

[112] *Lectura Oxon.* III, q. 11 (Vat. lat. 1110, fol. 84^r; Paris, Maz. 915, fol. 193va); *Lectura Oxon.* IV, q. 5 (Vat. lat. 1110, fol. 112^v; Paris, Maz. 915, fol. 211vb; Paris, B. N. lat. 15 892, fols. 157rb–157va).

[113] Emden, *BRO*, I, 395–396.

[114] Paris, B. N. lat. 15 886, fols. 2ra–191vb; Florence, Bibl. Naz., conv. soppr. C V 357, fols. 1^r–151^v.

[115] Chatton, *Lectura* (Paris, B. N. lat. 15 886, fols. 175ra, 175rb; Florence, Bibl. Naz., conv. soppr. C V 357, fols. 107ra–107rb, 119vb, 121vb); see introduction to William of Ockham, *Summa Logicae*, p. 37*.

Wodeham was familiar with the work, its *terminus ante quem* must be 1330.¹¹⁶ Brampton, working on the assumption that Chatton had read the *Sentences* at Oxford in 1318–19, believed that Chatton's *Lectura* was a reworking, an *ordinatio* version of his earlier Oxford lectures.¹¹⁷ Fr. Gál, on the other hand, along with others, prefers to see the *Lectura* as the Oxford lectures themselves and to date Chatton's baccalaureate in 1323–24 or slightly later.¹¹⁸ Whatever the ultimate solution to this problem, it is certain that the *Lectura* was written a few years before or possibly even during the regency of Chatton.

By the time Wodeham lectured on the *Sentences* at Oxford, he had known Chatton for a decade and had argued at length against several of his opinions. He had raised questions in Chatton's classroom and had discussed Chatton's views in both the Norwich and London lectures. The controversy was continued at Oxford, during which time Wodeham attended one or more of Chatton's magisterial disputations.

Chatton's name appears in seventeen questions in the first book of Wodeham's Oxford lectures. Occasionally Chatton's name is cited in the text, but he is usually referred to as "iste doctor" or "C." and identified in the margin as "Catho.", "Caton", or "Chat.". Although Wodeham frequently disagreed with Chatton, he sometimes favored his opinions when he found them "reasonable" and "beautifully stated". For Wodeham, Chatton was an authority whom he contrasted variously with Aureol, Campsale, Ockham, and Fitzralph. The topics on which Wodeham felt Chatton's views were important varied widely. One encounters Chatton on the questions of fruition,¹¹⁹ the necessity of grace,¹²⁰ the

---

¹¹⁶ See Gelber, p. 203: "... Adam Wodeham, writing in 1330–31, cites material found in the *Lectura*, but not in the *Reportatio*." Cf. Wodeham, *Lectura Oxon.* I, dist. 33, q. 2, a. 2 (Vat. lat. 955, fol. 183ʳ) and Chatton, *Lectura*, I, dist. 2, q. 6, a. 4 (Florence, Bibl. Naz., conv. soppr. C V 357, fol. 79ᵛᵇ); *Reportatio*, I, dist. 2, q. 5 (Paris, B. N. lat. 15 887, fols. 16ʳᵃ–16ʳᵇ).

¹¹⁷ C. K. Brampton, *EF*, XIV, 200–205.

¹¹⁸ See G. Gál's introduction to William of Ockham, *Summa Logicae*, p. 55*.

¹¹⁹ *Lectura Oxon.* I, dist. 1, q. 2 (Vat. lat. 955, fols. 22aᵛ, 23ʳ); I, dist. 1, q. 3 (Vat. lat. 955, fol. 24ʳ); I, dist. 1, q. 4 (Vat. lat. 955, fols. 27ᵛ, 28ᵛ); I, dist. 1, q. 12 (Paris, Maz. 915, fol. 55ʳᵃ; Paris, Univ. 193, fols. 66ʳᵇ, 69ʳᵃ).

¹²⁰ *Lectura Oxon.* I, dist. 1, q. 10, a. 1 (Vat. lat. 955, fols. 67ʳ, 71ᵛ, 73ᵛ; Paris, Maz. 915, fol. 41ʳᵇ); I, dist. 17, q. 3, a. 1 (Vat. lat. 955, fol. 144ʳ); I, dist. 17, q. 4 (Vat. lat. 955, fol. 152ᵛ; Paris, Maz. 915, fol. 94ᵛᵃ; Paris, Univ. 193, fols. 92ᵛᵃ–93ʳᵇ); I, dist. 17, q. 5 (Vat. lat. 955, fols. 160ᵛ, 161ᵛ). This last reference is the place where Wodeham brings forward against Chatton the rebuttal that Ockham had written in the margin of Wodeham's *reportatio* of Chatton's lectures.

problem of causality,[121] the freedom of the will in relation to its acts,[122] divine attributes,[123] the divine essence, the generation of the Son, and the procession of the Holy Spirit.[124]

Chatton does not appear to be cited in book II, but Wodeham returned to him in books III and IV of the Oxford lectures. In book III he appears in questions 1, 3, 5, 6, and 11, on topics ranging from the two natures of Christ in relation to the possibility of sin and the extent of Christ's knowledge of future contingents, to the central problem of the continuum and quantity.[125] In book IV Chatton appears in questions 5, 10, and 11, particularly associated with the problem of quantity.[126]

At some time between the end of the London lectures and Wodeham's lecture on question 11 of book III at Oxford, Wodeham attended a disputation at Oxford in which Chatton defended the thesis that the continuum was made up of atoms (indivisibles).[127] Chatton's *determinatio* was directed against Ockham's position on quantity, but Wodeham took it as a personal challenge. Not without humor he noted that Chatton had not improved his arguments since he treated the issue of quantity a decade earlier in his *Reportatio*. Wodeham attacked Chatton's position in the third book of his Oxford lectures, giving particular attention to the

---

[121] *Lectura Oxon.* I, dist. 2, q. 1 (Vat. lat. 955, fols. 100^v, 102^r, 104^r; Paris, Maz. 915, fol. 62rb; Paris, Univ. 193, fols. 74vb, 75vb, 76ra–76vb, 77rb).

[122] *Lectura Oxon.* I, dist. 1, q. 7 (Vat. lat. 955, fol. 48^r); I, dist. 3, q. un. (Vat. lat. 955, fol. 112^r).

[123] *Lectura Oxon.* I, dist. 6, q. 1, a. 2 (Vat. lat. 955, fols. 118^v, 119^v).

[124] *Lectura Oxon.* I, dist. 33, q. 1 (Paris, Univ. 193, fol. 117rb); I, dist. 33, q. 2 (Vat. lat. 955, fols. 183^r, 184^v; Paris, Maz. 915, fols. 107rb, 107va, 108rb); I, dist. 33, q. 4 (Vat. lat. 955, fol. 198^r); I, dist. 33, q. 5 (Vat. lat. 955, fol. 199^v); I, dist. 33, q. 6 (Vat. lat. 955, fols. 202^v, 203^r).

[125] *Lectura Oxon.* III, dist. 14, q. 1 (Vat. lat. 1110, fols. 44^v, 45^r; Paris, Maz. 915, fols. 170^r, 170^v); III, dist. 14, q. 3 (Vat. lat. 1110, fol. 54^v; Paris, Univ. 193, fols. 184vb, 185ra); III, dist. 14, q. 5 (Vat. lat. 1110, fols. 61^v, 62^r); III, dist. 14, q. 6 (Paris, Univ. 193, fols. 140va, 141rb); III, dist. 14, q. 11 (Vat. lat. 1110, fol. 84^r; Paris, Maz. 915, fol. 193va). In André Combes' edition of Oyta's abbreviation of Wodeham's *Lectura Oxon.* III, dist. 14, q. 1 (see above chapter one, note 32) the reference to Tricon (p. 405) should read Chaton; see Vat. lat. 1110, fols. 44^v–45^v; Maz. 915, fols. 170^r–170^v.

[126] *Lectura Oxon.* IV, q. 5 (Vat. lat. 1110, fols. 112^v, 113^v; Paris, Maz. 915, fol. 211vb); IV, q. 10 (Vat. lat. 1110, fol. 128^v); IV, q. 11 (Vat. lat. 1110, fol. 132^r).

[127] *Lectura Oxon.* III, dist. 14, q. 11 (Paris, Maz. 915, fol. 193va), referring to what he eventually describes as "Chatton in quadam determinatione Oxon. quod continuum non componitur ex partibus divisibilibus," says that ". . . quae audivi postquam illam materiam Londoniae pertractavi." This disputation or another is referred to again by Wodeham, *Lectura Oxon.* IV, q. 5 (Paris, Univ. 193, fols. 220va–220vb), and IV, q. 10 (Vat. lat. 1110, fol. 128^v).

arguments recently put forward in the *determinatio*.¹²⁸ Later, in the fifth question of the fourth book, Wodeham again attacked Chatton's view of quantity, mentioning the *determinatio*, and apparently responding to new arguments Chatton posed against Wodeham.¹²⁹

At the time of his *determinatio* Chatton may not have been aware of the objections to his position Wodeham had raised in the London lectures. In Wodeham's reply to Chatton's *determinatio*, he gave no indication that Chatton's arguments were "contra me." In the fifth question of the fourth book, however, Wodeham quoted the objections Chatton raised against the response Wodeham had made in the eleventh question of book III.¹³⁰ The arguments Wodeham attempted to refute had been specifically directed against him by Chatton. Wodeham's reply was couched in very personal terms, as the frequent insertion of "tu Chatton", "tu arguis", or "per te" reflects.

One may infer from this that Chatton was present in Oxford while Wodeham was lecturing on book III of the *Sentences*. This gives us a *terminus ante quem* for most of Wodeham's Oxford lectures. Chatton was in Avignon by January of 1333 and remained there for some time. In order to allow time for Chatton to have heard or read Wodeham's attack and to have responded to it, we must place book III, q. 11 no later than the fall of 1332.

It is certain that Wodeham challenged Chatton directly. There is some evidence to suggest that Chatton couched his reply in less personal terms, answering the individual points raised by Wodeham but aiming his comments at the "divisibilists" in general or at Ockham in particular. In this regard there is an important difference between Vat. lat. 1110 and the *ordinatio* version of the *Lectura Oxon.* IV, q. 5. In Vat. lat. 1110

---

¹²⁸ *Lectura Oxon.* III, dist. 14, q. 11 (Paris, Maz. 915, fol. 193ᵛᵃ): "Ponam igitur quattuor argumenta Cattonis . . . ; secundo, argumenta quattuor in contrarium, et reducam illa contra responsiones Chattonis; tertio, solvam argumenta Chattonis."

¹²⁹ *Lectura Oxon.* IV, q. 5 (Paris, Maz. 915, fol. 211ᵛ): "Quod sic videtur per argumenta cuiusdam doctoris [Chatton] alias facta contra me. . . . Secundo, ponam magistri praenotati contra meas responsiones sua argumenta reducentes et positionem meam impugnantes. . . . Quinto, ponam rationes . . . quibus arguit contra me."

¹³⁰ Compare, for instance, the second article of *Lectura Oxon.* III, q. 11 (Paris, Univ. 193, fol. 203ʳᵃ): "Secundo, argumenta quattuor in contrarium, et reducam ista contra responsionem Chaton"; and (fol. 203ᵛᵇ): "Ad tertium dicendum quod illud est multo fortius contra eum [Chatton], sicut in responsione ad praecedens deduxi et reductionibus rationis tertiae contra eum"; to the second article of *Lectura Oxon.* IV, q. 5 (Paris, Maz. 915, fol. 211ᵛ): "Ponam magistri praenotati [Chatton] contra meas responsiones sua argumenta reducentes et positionem meam impugnantes."

Chatton is not as clearly identified nor are his arguments as personally directed against Wodeham as in the *ordinatio* version. Instead, Chatton's comments appear to have been directed more at Ockham than at Wodeham. In the *ordinatio* version Chatton's arguments are reported as having been directed specifically against Wodeham. It is difficult to know which version accurately reflects Chatton's reply to Wodeham. The differences between the two versions may have resulted from nothing more than the failure of the *reportator* to record the personal remarks Wodeham included in his lecture.[131]

In the Caius manuscript Chatton continued to play an important part. In the number of citations he is barely surpassed by Ockham and Scotus. Although Wodeham remained critical of Chatton's views, he also at times found Chatton's arguments convincing.[132]

GERARD ODONIS, OFM

Gerard Odonis, or Guiral Ot, was a contemporary of Chatton and a fellow indivisibilist, or atomist.[133] He read the *Sentences* at Paris in 1326[134] and subsequently lectured on the Bible at the Franciscan convent in Toulouse. On June 10, 1329, in the midst of the crisis in the Order over apostolic poverty and John XXII's teaching on the beatific vision, the

---

[131] As a brief sample of the differences between the *Reportatio* (?) and the *Ordinatio*, the following will suffice. The "videtur quod sic, quia sic se habet" of Vat. lat. 1110, fol. 108^r, becomes "quod sic videtur per argumenta cuiusdam doctoris alias facta contra me, quia sic se habet" in the other manuscripts. The "secundo ponam aliqua argumenta contra meam responsionem sive responsiones" of Vat. lat. 1110, fol. 108^r, becomes "secundo ponam magistri praenotati contra meas responsiones sua argumenta reducentes et positionem meam impugnantes" in the other manuscripts. The "quinto ponam rationes 8 quibus argui potest quantitatem esse rem distinctam a substantia et qualitate" of Vat. lat. 1110, fol. 108^r, becomes "quinto ponam rationes 6 [or 7, in some manuscripts] quibus arguit contra me quantitatem . . ." in the other manuscripts.

[132] *Lectura secunda*, prol., q. 1 (Cambridge, Caius 281, fol. 107vb); prol., q. 2 (fols. 109vb, 111rb, 111vb, 112ra, 113ra); prol., q. 3 (fols. 113vb, 114rb); prol., q. 5 (fols. 119va, 122va); prol., q. 6 (fols. 124rb, 124va, 124vb, 128va); I, dist. 1, q. 1 (fols. 128va, 129va: "ipse super primum Perihermenias, quaestione 2", 130va); dist. 1, q. 2 (fols. 133ra, 135rb, 136rb, 137rb); dist. 1, q. 4 (fols. 140ra, 141ra, 142va, 145va: "respondet Chatton et bene"); dist. 1, q. 5 (fols. 146ra, 146va, 147vb); dist. 2, q. 1 (fols. 151ra, 158va, 160ra, 160rb); dist. 3, q. 1 (fols. 163ra, 164rb, 168ra, 170va); dist. 4, q. 1 (fols. 181ra, 181vb); dist. 6, q. 1 (fol. 184va); dist. 7, q. 1 (fols. 196va, 198va); dist. 7, q. 3 (fols. 202vb, 203rb); dist. 10 (fol. 214va); dist. 11 (fol. 216rb); dist. 17, q. 1 (fols. 222rb, 223va); dist. 22 (fol. 231ra); dist. 23 (fol. 233va); dist. 24, q. 2 (fol. 240vb); dist. 26, q. 2 (fol. 250vb).

[133] On Odonis, see *DTC*, XI (1932), cols. 1658–1663; *HLF*, XXXVI (1927), 203–225; J. A. Murdoch and E. A. Synan, *FcS*, XXVI (1966), 213–214.

[134] Madrid, Bibl. Nac., Ms. lat. 65, fol. 203^v.

Chapter at Paris, under the influence of Bertrand de la Tour, made him Minister General of the Order to replace Michael of Cesena.

Gerard remained the Franciscan Minister General during the period of Wodeham's Oxford *Lectura* and the completion of his Oxford residency. Wodeham was familiar with Gerard's Parisian lectures on the *Sentences* and possibly some of his logical treatises. Wodeham cited Odonis three times in the course of his lectures on the first two books of the *Sentences* at Oxford. Odonis appeared in the context of the problem of quantity and on the Trinity.[135]

RICHARD FITZRALPH

Chatton was not the only Oxford *magister regens* that Wodeham, as a bachelor, challenged. Fitzralph was Wodeham's major opponent and, on occasion, ally. Except for Ockham, Fitzralph was the most frequently cited *modernus* in Wodeham's Oxford lectures, appearing in the margins or text of over forty of Wodeham's seventy questions.

Fitzralph was probably about four years older than Wodeham, if we may judge by the time between their readings of the *Sentences* at Oxford. When Fitzralph visited Balliol College on July 25, 1325, he was already a master of arts, had previously vacated a fellowship in that college, and must have been studying theology for a number of years.[136] By 1329, when he went to Paris for a year, he was *baccalarius theologiae* and thus had already read the *Sentences*,[137] and before May 24, 1331, he was *magister theologiae*.[138] In May of the following year his election to the chancellorship of Oxford was confirmed by the Bishop of Lincoln.[139]

---

[135] *Lectura Oxon.* I, dist. 33, q. 5 (Paris, Univ. 193, fol. 132va): "Geraldus"; I, dist. 33, q. 8 (Paris, Univ. 193, fol. 138va): "... sicut etiam tenet Geraldus Odonis ..."; II, q. 7 (Vat. lat. 1110, fol. 31^v; Paris, Maz. 915, fol. 157vb): "... probabiliter arguit frater Geraldus Odonis, libro III, dist. 14, q. 1."

[136] Emden, *BRO*, II, 692–693. Fitzralph could not have begun the study of theology in 1325, as Gordon Leff has suggested (*Richard Fitzralph: Commentator of the "Sentences". A Study in Theological Orthodoxy* (Manchester, 1963), p. 1), inasmuch as seven years of theological study and disputations were required of a master of arts before he could advance to reading the *Sentences*, a task Fitzralph had completed by 1329.

[137] He is so described in a letter from Bishop Grandisson of Exeter to an unnamed professor at the University of Paris, introducing Fitzralph, who spent the academic year 1329–30 in Paris as tutor to John of Northwode, a young nephew of Bishop Grandisson. *The Register of John de Grandisson, Bishop of Exeter, 1327–1369* (3 vols.; London and Exeter, 1894–99), I, 233. Emden, *BRO*, II, 693.

[138] *The Register of John de Grandisson*, II, 616. See also *Calendar of Entries in the Papal Registers Relating to Great Britain and Ireland. Papal Letters*, Vol. II (London, 1895), 355; A. Gwynn, "Richard Fitzralph, Archbishop of Armagh," *Studies*, 22 (1933), 389–405.

[139] Emden, *BRO*, II, 693.

Normally, a minimum of three years of Oxford residency was required between the beginning of the reading of the *Sentences* and the granting of the doctorate: one year lecturing on the *Sentences*, and two further years lecturing on the Bible and participating in advanced disputations.[140] Since Fitzralph was not yet a bachelor of theology in July of 1325 and had finished reading the *Sentences* by 1329, his reading must have taken place during one of the four academic years between 1325 and 1329. In view of his absence in Paris during the academic year 1329–30 and the date of his regency, to be established in a moment, Fitzralph's bachelor lectures on the *Sentences* can reasonably be placed in 1326–27.

Fitzralph's tenure as regent master in theology can be dated precisely. He could not have incepted before the summer of 1330, because, when he left England in the autumn of 1329 for a year in Paris, he was still a bachelor of theology. Moreover, William Crathorn, in his opening lecture on the *Sentences* in the fall of 1330, cites him as "Magister Richardus filius Radulphi" and "iste doctor."[141] Since there is no evidence Crathorn's Commentary was updated or revised at a later time, we may take its references to contemporary figures and events, such as the eclipse of the sun on July 16, 1330, as valid at the time of his writing. Thus Fitzralph's regency began in or about the summer of 1330 and lasted at least a year and possibly into the spring of 1332. The benefice granted him on May 24, 1331, was not directly connected with his inception, which must have occurred by October, 1330. When he was elected Chancellor of the University in May, 1332, he had completed his required regency.

As Chatton's response to question 11, book III of Wodeham's Oxford lectures provides us with a *terminus ante quem* for Wodeham's *lectura*, so Wodeham's references to Fitzralph provide us with a *terminus post quem*. When Wodeham referred to Fitzralph in the opening questions of the Oxford lectures, Fitzralph was already a doctor of theology, i.e., had incepted and had entered upon his activities as regent.[142] Consequently, the beginning of Wodeham's Oxford lectures cannot be dated before the fall of 1330. In light of the fact that these lectures occupied two years, we can date Wodeham's Oxford lectures to the biennium 1330–32, or to the years 1330–31 and 1332–33, if interrupted by the London lectures.

There are some indications that this first dating is preferable. At no

---

[140] Little, *AFH*, XIX, 826–827.
[141] Crathorn, *Sent*. I, Prol., q. 1 (Basel, Univ. Bibl. B V 30, p. 29); *Sent*. I, dist. 3, q. 2 (Basel, Univ. Bibl. B V 30, p. 107(105)).
[142] Vat. lat. 955, fols. 4^r, 8^r, 10^r, 24^r–24^v, 27^r, 29^r, 41^r–41^v, et passim.

point in the four books of the Oxford lectures does Wodeham cite Fitzralph as the Chancellor of the University. Although arguments from silence seldom have much force, there is more reason to accept one here, since Wodeham did show great care in acknowledging titles. During Wodeham's second year on the *Sentences*, he mentioned Fitzralph's high reputation in the University but did not indicate that he was Chancellor, a fact that would have strengthened his argument. Finally, the colophon in Vat. lat. 1110 indicates that Wodeham read (completed?) the *Sentences* at Oxford in 1332.[143]

If our knowledge of Fitzralph helps us to date Wodeham's Oxford lectures, a reading of Wodeham throws considerable light on Fitzralph's regency and the manuscripts of his *Sentences* Commentary. As we have seen in the case of Chatton, Wodeham did not shrink from attacking the opinions of those who were senior in rank and age. Although probably not unique in this regard, he was perhaps unusual. In his Oxford lectures Wodeham challenged the opinions of Fitzralph more than those of any other living author. When Wodeham began his Oxford lectures he was familiar with the text of Fitzralph's bachelor lectures, which he may well have attended as a theological student.[144] However, while lecturing on the second question of his prologue, he became aware that Fitzralph had changed his position on the capacity of the soul for beatitude. The position Wodeham had criticized toward the beginning of his question was abandoned by Fitzralph in favor of a "corrected" opinion.[145]

---

[143] Vat. lat. 1110, fol. 135^v.

[144] Vat. lat. 955, fols. 4^r–4^v; Paris, Univ. 193, fols. 5ra–5rb; Paris, Maz. 915, fols. 3ra–3rb; Tarazona, Cat. 7, fols. 2vb–3ra. This passage occurred in the original redaction of Fitzralph and was retained in the corrected version. Compare Wodeham's quotation with Fitzralph, *Lectura*, q. 11, a. 3 (Paris, B. N. lat. 15 853, fol. 81vb; Florence, Bibl. Naz, conv. soppr. A III 508, fol. 47vb; Oxford, Oriel 15, fol. 53vb). Wodeham also records an opinion that occurred in the original version and was removed in the corrected version; see *Lectura Oxon.*, prol., q. 2 (Vat. lat. 955, fol. 8^r; Paris, Univ. 193, fol. 7vb). Wodeham heard Fitzralph respond and dispute at Oxford between 1326 and 1329. *Lectura Oxon.* I, dist. 1, q. 6 (Vat. lat. 955, fols. 41^r–41^v): "Ad primum respondet et bene in disputatione unus nunc doctor, tunc bachalaurius [in margin: Responsio Hyb.]...." Cf. Paris, Maz. 915, fol. 26rb; cf. Florence, Bibl. Naz., conv. soppr. B VII 1249, fol. 27ra. *Lectura Oxon.* III, q. 6 (Paris, Univ. 193, fol. 193ra): "Praeterea sic arguit Fir., licet respondendo in scolis tenuit illam responsionem...." Many of the details on Wodeham's citations from Fitzralph were worked out with the help of Ms. Katherine Tachau-Auerbach, who has also verified the manuscripts of the *Opus correctum*.

[145] Vat. lat. 955, fol. 10^r: "Ideo aliter videtur posse dici, sicut nunc scribit unus doctor modernus [in margin: Hibernicus], corrigens responsionem suam aliam contra quam supra ponitur [8^r] illa conclusio necessaria. 'Dico,' inquit, 'sine praeiudicio meliorum sententiae quod....'"

It is not clear whether Fitzralph changed his position because of the critique of Wodeham, the Franciscan *baccalarius sententiarius*. It is certain, however, that Fitzralph was just then in the process of making a new and to his mind improved edition of his *Sentences* Commentary. It is also clear that Wodeham had immediate access to the text of that revision. He was able to quote lengthy passages from Fitzralph verbatim. Fitzralph must have been well along in his revision. The corrected section that Wodeham saw early in the fall of 1330 occurs toward the middle of Fitzralph's Commentary.

We know, therefore, that one of the activities that engaged Fitzralph's attention during the academic year 1330–31 was the completion of the revision of his bachelor lectures on the *Sentences*. Much of the earlier lectures was retained, although the arguments may have been rearranged. Other passages were deleted and new arguments substituted. In all probability the work of revision was never completed into a finished *ordinatio*. The occasional confusions and double argumentations in Fitzralph's Commentary may be due to Fitzralph's (or his scribe's) retention in the revised work of passages that were part of his earlier lectures.

Wodeham continues to refer to Fitzralph's *Opus correctum* as distinct from his bachelor lectures until almost the end of Wodeham's lectures on book I of the *Sentences*. From that point on, the text of Fitzralph's *Sentences* Commentary is referred to as the *Lectura*. If we attribute Wodeham's Commentary on book I to the academic year 1330–31, then it would appear that Fitzralph completed his *Opus correctum* by the spring of 1331, after which time Wodeham referred to it as the *Lectura*.[146]

Despite the differences among the manuscripts of Fitzralph's Commentary, all are versions of the *Opus correctum*, or *Lectura*, and none contains the version Fitzralph gave as a bachelor of theology. This is clear from the fact that all manuscripts of Fitzralph's *Sentences* Commentary contain the passages that Wodeham says are unique to the *Opus correctum*.

Fitzralph's change of opinion did not cease with the completion of his revised *Lectura*. Between the summer of 1331 and the fall of 1332 he wrote another work, which Wodeham knew as his *Quaestio Biblica*. In that work Fitzralph radically revised his views on the problem of future contingents.[147] Whether or not Fitzralph's thinking was being aided by

---

[146] In normal usage "Lectura" should refer to lectures as they were originally presented in the classroom and never to a revised version. However, by Fitzralph's "Lectura" Wodeham meant the *Opus correctum*.

[147] The *Quaestio Biblica* cannot be the Bible lectures that Fitzralph undoubtedly gave as a bachelor at Oxford upon completion of his lectures on the *Sentences*. In his *Quaestio*

the criticisms of Wodeham, it is true that Wodeham disagreed with Fitzralph's treatment in his *Lectura* and generally agreed with his revised position in the *Quaestio Biblica*. No manuscripts of this work of Fitzralph appear to be extant, and Fitzralph scholars seem thus far to have been unaware of its existence. It is possible, however, to reconstruct some of its content from the extensive quotations provided in Wodeham.[148]

According to Wodeham, Fitzralph also wrote a commentary or gloss on the *De Trinitate*, presumably that of Augustine but possibly that of Boethius or of Richard of St. Victor. Wodeham's citation to this work is brief and may not be sufficient to identify this work among the anonymous manuscripts.[149]

Finally, Fitzralph held magisterial *determinationes* during his regency. Some of these have survived, and one of them is cited by Wodeham.[150]

Biblica Fitzralph rejected opinions that appear in the corrected version of the *Lectura*. Therefore, the *Quaestio Biblica* can be dated to 1331–32, after the *Opus correctum* was completed and before Wodeham reached the fifth question of book III of his Oxford lectures (in the fall of 1332, at the latest). The following passages, all dealing with the problem of future contingents, show that the *Quaestio Biblica* was written after Fitzralph's *Lectura*. Wodeham, *Lectura Oxon*. III, q. 6 (Paris, Univ. 193, fol. 193va): "... in quaestione sua biblica, in arguens multipliciter ac tenens quod..., quam in lectura tenuit, repudiat." *Lectura Oxon*. III, q. 7 (Paris, Univ. 193, fol. 194va): "... confirmatur in sua lectura, licet contradixit in quaestione biblica." *Lectura Oxon*. III, q. 8 (Paris, Univ. 193, fol. 195va): "... repudiavit hanc responsionem [given in the *Lectura*] sicut irrationalem in sua quaestione biblica." *Lectura Oxon*. III, q. 8 (Paris, Univ. 193, fol. 196ra): "Sed haec posset dici, sicut respondet Fir.... in lectura.... Similiter ipsemet [Fitzralph] repudiavit hanc responsionem sicut irrationalem in sua quaestione biblica." *Lectura Oxon*. III, q. 9 (Paris, Univ. 193, fol. 198rb): "... et sicut credit etiam in lectura, licet... ipsemet improbat in quaestione sua biblica illud quod tenuerat in lectura."

[148] Wodeham, *Lectura Oxon*. III, q. 5 (Paris, Univ. 193, fols. 187vb, 188va); III, q. 6 (Paris, Univ. 193, fols. 192vb, 193va); III, q. 7 (Paris, Univ. 193, fol. 194va); III, q. 8 (Paris, Univ. 193, fols. 195va, 196ra, 196rb, 197ra); III, q. 9 (Paris, Univ. 193, fol. 198rb).

[149] Wodeham, *Lectura Oxon*. I, dist. 33, q. 1 (Vat. lat. 955, fols. 179^v–180^r; Paris, Univ. 193, fol. 119vb): "... et haec est etiam via Firauf in Lectura et similiter in Glosulis super 5 Trinitate, c. 19...." Fourteenth-century commentaries on Augustine's works were not unusual. John of Rideval, the 54th lector at the Franciscan convent in Oxford (ca. 1330–31), wrote commentaries on Augustine's *De Civitate Dei* and *Confessions*. See Little, *The Grey Friars*, p. 171; B. Smalley, *English Friars and Antiquity* (Oxford, 1960), pp. 109–110, 121–132. Earlier, Thomas Waleys wrote a commentary on *De Civitate Dei* (Smalley, *English Friars*, pp. 88–100). One recalls also Francis Mayronnes' *florilegium* from Augustine.

[150] Wodeham, *Lectura Oxon*. II, q. 6, a. 1 (Paris, Univ. 193, fol. 163ra; Paris, Maz. 915, fol. 156rb): "Et propter hoc respondet doctor iste in determinatione quod...." Some of Fitzralph's *Determinationes* can be found in Florence, Bibl. Naz., conv. soppr. A III 508, fols. 109vb–129vb; see description in G. Leff, *Richard Fitzralph*, p. 192. It is possible that the seventh *determinatio*, fols. 129ra–129vb: "Utrum sit possibile antichristum fore bonum pro omni tempore quo conversabitur in terra" belonged to the *Quaestio Biblica*.

Fitzralph was a frequent target for Wodeham in the Oxford lectures.[151] It should be noted, however, that at the points where Wodeham was critical of Fitzralph's opinions (and this is generally the rule), Wodeham was respectful of Fitzralph and often acknowledged the quality of Fitzralph's arguments, even if he did not agree with them. Occasionally Wodeham had considerable praise for Fitzralph's opinions. This is particularly true with regard to the disputation attended by Wodeham when Fitzralph was a bachelor.[152] Once Wodeham even traded on the high regard in which Fitzralph was held by the University, an attitude he insisted he shared, in order to undermine the opinion of a *socius* whom Fitzralph had also attacked.[153] It would, therefore, be incorrect to give

---

[151] Wodeham, *Lectura Oxon.*, prol., q. 1 (Vat. lat. 955, fol. 4^r; Paris, Univ. 193, fol. 5ra; Paris, Maz. 915, fol. 3ra); prol., q. 2 (Vat. lat. 955, fols. 8^r, 10^r; Paris, Maz. 915, fol. 6va; Paris, Univ. 193, fols. 7vb, 8vb); I, dist. 1, q. 3 (Vat. lat. 955, fols. 24^r–24^v, 25^v, 26^r, 26^v, 27^r, 29^r; Paris, Maz. 915, fols. 15rb–17rb); I, dist. 1, q. 6 (Vat. lat. 955, fols. 41^r–41^v; Paris, Maz. 915, fol. 26rb); I, dist. 1, q. 8 (Vat. lat. 955, fols. 53^v, 54^v, 55^v, 60^r; Paris, Maz. 915, fols. 33ra, 33va, 34rb, 36vb); I, dist. 1, q. 9 (Vat. lat. 955, fol. 65^r; Paris, Maz. 915, fol. 40ra); I, dist. 1, q. 10 (Vat. lat. 955, fols. 69^r, 79^r; Paris, Univ. 193, fols. 50va, 51ra, 51rb); I, dist. 1, q. 11 (Vat. lat. 955, fols. 82^r, 82^v, 83^r, 86^v; Paris, Maz. 915, fol. 49va); I, dist. 1, q. 12 (Vat. lat. 955, fol. 92^v); I, dist. 1, q. 13 (Vat. lat. 955, fols. 94^v, 95^r, 95^v); I, dist. 1, q. 14 (Vat. lat. 955, fols. 98^v, 100^r; Paris, Univ. 193, fol. 74ra); I, dist. 3, q. un. (Vat. lat. 955, fols. 108^v, 111^r, 113^r, 113^v, 114^v); I, dist. 17, q. 2 (Paris, Univ. 193, fol. 101ra); I, dist. 17, q. 3 (Vat. lat. 955, fol. 148^v); I, dist. 17, q. 5 (Vat. lat. 955, fol. 159^v); I, dist. 33, q. 1 (Vat. lat. 955, fol. 177^r; Paris, Univ. 193, fol. 120vb); I, dist. 33, q. 2 (Vat. lat. 955, fols. 185^r, 185^v; Paris, Maz. 915, fols. 108va, 109ra; Paris, Univ. 193, fol. 124ra); I, dist. 33, q. 3 (Paris, Univ. 193, fol. 125ra); I, dist. 33, q. 4 (Paris, Univ. 193, fol. 130va); I, dist. 33, q. 6 (Vat. lat. 955, fol. 202^v); I, dist. 33, q. 8 (Vat. lat. 955, fol. 207^v; Paris, Univ. 193, fol. 138rb); II, q. 1 (Paris, Maz. 915, fol. 128va); II, q. 2 (Paris, Maz. 915, fol. 135va); II, q. 3 (Paris, Maz. 915, fol. 137rb; Vat. lat. 1110, fols. 12^r–12^v, 14^r–14^v); II, q. 5 (Paris, Maz. 915, fol. 146va; Vat. lat. 1110, fol. 21^v); II, q. 6 (Paris, Maz. 915, fol. 156ra–156rb); II; q. 7 (Vat. lat. 1110, fol. 31^v); II, q. 9 (Vat. lat. 1110, fol. 38^v); III, q. 2 (Vat. lat. 1110, fol. 50^r); III, q. 3 (Paris, Univ. 193, fol. 184va); III, q. 5 (Paris, Univ. 193, fols. 187vb, 188va; Paris, Maz. 915, fols. 181^v, 182^r, 184^r; Vat. lat. 1110, fols. 59^r, 60^r); III, q. 6 (Paris, Univ. 193, fols. 189ra, 190ra, 191vb, 192rb, 192vb, 193ra, 193rb, 193va; Vat. lat. 1110, fols. 65^r–65^v); III, q. 7 (Paris, Univ. 193, fols. 194ra, 194rb, 194va); III, q. 8 (Paris, Univ. 193, fols. 195rb, 195va, 196ra, 196rb, 196vb, 197ra; Paris, Maz. 915, fols. 187^r, 187^v; Vat. lat. 1110, fols. 70^r, 71^r); III, q. 9 (Paris, Univ. 193, fols. 197rb, 197vb, 198rb; Paris, Maz. 915, fol. 188^r; Vat. lat. 1110, fol. 72^v); III, q. 10 (Vat. lat. 1110, fol. 79^r); IV, q. 2 (Paris, Univ. 193, fols. 212va, 212vb); IV, q. 4 (Paris, Maz. 915, fol. 210^v; Vat. lat. 1110, fols. 106^r–106^v); IV, q. 7 (Paris, Univ. 193, fols. 223va, 224va); IV, q. 8 (Paris, Univ. 193, fol. 224va); IV, q. 9 (Paris, Univ. 193, fols. 227vb–228rb, 228va, 228vb).

[152] Vat. lat. 955, fols. 41^r–41^v.

[153] *Lectura Oxon.* II, q. 5 (Vat. lat. 1110, fol. 21^v): "Sed alius doctor certe non minus imputatus in hac universitate scribit et dicit quod haec opinio non est bene sana." (Paris, Maz. 915, fol. 146^v): "Sed alius doctor [margin: Sir'] cui non minus [than in William of Auxerre] credo nec minus creditur in hac universitate scribit quod non videtur opinio haec esse sana."

the impression that Wodeham was a committed adversary of Fitzralph.

In view of the central place Fitzralph held in the Oxford lectures, it is surprising that Fitzralph does not seem to appear in the Caius manuscript. If it were not for the fact that where this Commentary parallels the Oxford lectures it is according to the post-1334 redaction, one might use the absence of Fitzralph citations as evidence that the *Sentences* Commentary in the Caius manuscript preceded the Oxford lectures. However, since it is subsequent to the Oxford lectures, we must assume that Wodeham considered Fitzralph's thought less significant at that time, or did not challenge him for reasons of ecclesiastical or academic polity.

Nigel of Wavere, Mertonian

In book three of his Oxford *Lectura* Wodeham referred to a "Magister Nigellus" who had criticized Fitzralph's position on future contingents, apparently as stated in the *Quaestio Biblica*.[154] No further information is provided in any of the manuscripts, but the identity of this figure can be ascertained with some degree of certainty.

Wodeham usually cited authors by surname or place of origin, but the comparative rarity of the name Nigel permitted him to use a first name without being misunderstood. Wodeham himself is among a small circle of authors to be cited subsequently by Christian name. Nigel is a Celtic name and usually English in this period. The link with Fitzralph suggests an Oxford setting for his academic career. Moreover, he was at least master of arts by the time Wodeham was lecturing on book III and had probably already lectured on the *Sentences* (the first serious opportunity for one theologian to criticize the ideas of another).

From what we now know, there was only one "Master Nigel" who would have been immediately recognized by an Oxford audience at the time Wodeham was lecturing. While there were several masters by that name at Cambridge, they all, with the exception of Nigel of Thornton,[155] lived well before or after Wodeham and Fitzralph. At Oxford, by contrast, there was only one Nigel whose name has survived, namely Nigel of Wavere, whose career coincides well with the person to whom Wodeham

---

[154] *Lectura Oxon.* III, q. 8 (Paris, Univ. 193, fol. 195va; Tarazona, Cat. 7, fol. 154ra; Vat. lat. 1110, fol. 70^v).

[155] Emden, *BRC*, p. 584. Thornedon was a fellow of University Hall (Clare Hall) in '1326 and gave a copy of Giles of Rome's *Super libros de generatione* to the College. There is no evidence that he became a theologian nor that he was known at Oxford.

referred.[156] Wavere was from the diocese of Lichfield and Coventry. He was attached to Merton College as early as 1312. By 1327 he was a bachelor of theology, and by 1330, when he was elected Chancellor of the University, he was a licentiate in theology. His term as Chancellor immediately preceded Fitzralph's, although his reading of the *Sentences* may have coincided with or followed Fitzralph's by a year or two. Wavere would have been well-known to any Oxford audience around 1332, and as a theologian and secular master of arts, it would not have been unusual for him to have been known as "Master Nigel." Unfortunately, Wavere's work has not survived.

JOHN OF RODINGTON, OFM

In the judgment of contemporary and subsequent theologians, John of Rodington was among the major thinkers of the fourteenth century.[157] To date, however, his thought has been little studied.[158] He was the 56th lector at the Oxford convent and was a close contemporary of Fitzralph and Wodeham. He became regent master of the Franciscans before Wodeham completed his Oxford lectures on the *Sentences*.[159]

Since we are reasonably certain of the dates for Wodeham's Oxford lectures, it may be possible to provide more precise dates for the regencies of several Franciscan lectors. First, we know that Rodington incepted before Wodeham completed his lectures on book IV. Thus, the latest date at which he could have been regent master would have been 1332–1333. Second, Walter Chatton was probably regent master when, in the spring of 1330, he answered a summons to the Mayor's Court. Thus, the earliest year in which Chatton could have been lector would have been 1329–30. Since there were two lectors between Chatton and Rodington,

---

[156] Emden, *BRO*, III, 2000.

[157] After Wodeham, Rodington was cited by Robert Halifax, Alphonsus Vargas of Toledo, John of Mirecourt, John Hiltalingen of Basel, and others.

[158] On Rodington's life and writings, see Little, *The Grey Friars*, pp. 171–172; Emden, *BRO*, II, 1583; Michalski, "Le criticisme et le scepticisme dans le philosophie du XIVe siècle," in *Bulletin International de l'Académie Polonaise des sciences et des lettres* (Krakow, 1927), 77–79; "Le problème de la volonté à Oxford et à Paris au XIVe siècle," *Studia Philosophica* (Leopoli, 1937), 247, 267–268; J. Lechner, *Johann von Rodington, OFM und sein Quodlibet de conscientia*, BB, Suppl. III.2 (Münster i.W., 1935), pp. 1125–1168; "Die Quästionen des Sentenzkommentars des Joh. v. Rodington O.F.M.," *FzS*, XXII (1935), 232–248; M. M. Tweedale, *John of Rodynton on Knowledge, Science and Theology*, unpublished doctoral dissertation, University of California (Los Angeles, 1965).

[159] Wodeham, *Lectura Oxon.* IV, q. 6 (Paris, Univ. 193, fol. 222vb): "Ad istam potest argui argumento Rodintonis in sua inceptione. . . ."

the sequence would have run: Walter Chatton (1329–30), John of Rideval (1330–31), Lawrence Briton (1331–32), and John of Rodington (1332–33). Illness, however, might have shortened the term of one or more of these men, so that the sequence might not have been one year apiece. A few years after his regency, Rodington was made Provincial Minister of the Order in England (ca. 1336), an office that he held until ca. 1340. His later activities seem to have paralleled Wodeham's, for we find Rodington in Basel in July of 1340.[160]

Wodeham cited Rodington in the first and fourth books of his Oxford lectures as well as in the Caius manuscript.[161] Rodington seems to have been of primary interest to Wodeham for his opinions on the sacrament of penance and on the power of the soul in relation to its acts. Since Wodeham was critical of Rodington and the latter has sometimes been seen along with Wodeham as a disciple of Ockham, a comparison of their ideas would make an interesting study.

NICHOLAS OF HOYO, OFM

In the Caius manuscript Wodeham refers to a certain Hoyn as *doctor valens*.[162] The person so designated must have been a master of theology at the time Wodeham was writing. By the name Hoyn, Wodeham was probably referring to the Franciscan master, Nicholas de Hoyo (Huy in Belgium), who was one of the *viri solemnes*, along with Walter Chatton, who helped draw up the legislation of 1336 for the Franciscans.[163] Only two questions on the Immaculate Conception have survived from his writings.[164]

REPPES

The name "Reppes" or "Resipis" occurs several times in the Oxford *Lectura* of Wodeham.[165] The person so designated is the same in each case,

---

[160] *Analecta Franciscana*, III (1897), 638.
[161] *Lectura Oxon*. I, dist. 1, q. 8 (Vat. lat. 955, fols. 57^v, 59^r; Paris, Univ. 193, fol. 42va); I, dist. 1, q. 9 (Vat. lat. 955, fols. 60^r–60^v, 64^r; Paris, Univ. 193, fol. 47ra); I, dist. 17, q. 6 (Lüneburg 4° 29, fol. 164ra); I, dist. 33, q. 3 (Lüneburg 4° 29, fol. 181ra); IV, q. 6 (Paris, Univ. 193, fol. 222vb); *Lectura secunda*, I, dist. 1, q. 5 (Cambridge, Caius 281, fol. 147ra).
[162] *Lectura secunda*, I, dist. 1, q. 4, a. 2 (Cambridge, Caius 281, fol. 140va).
[163] M. Bihl, "Ordinationes a Benedicto XII pro fratribus minoribus promulgatae per bullam 28 Novembris 1336," *AFH*, XXX (1937), 324, 334; XLVI (1953), 87. I owe this suggestion to Fr. Gedeon Gál, OFM.
[164] *AFH*, XLVII (1954), 420.
[165] Wodeham, *Lectura Oxon*. I, dist. 1, q. 13 (Vat. lat. 955, fol. 98^r; Paris, Univ. 193, fol. 72rb; Paris, Maz. 915, fol. 60rb; Tarazona, Cat. 7, fol. 51rb): "Rep̄p". *Lectura Oxon*.

but who this might be outside the pages of Wodeham is not yet certain. Repps is a village in Norfolk and also the name of several Cambridge theologians. Wodeham might have been referring either to John Reppes[166] or that Reppes who died around 1334 and was associated with the Norwich convent.[167] The two most likely candidates, however, are both Franciscans, Bartholomew of Rippes and Richard of Reppis.

Bartholomew of Rippes, or Repps, was the 52nd Franciscan master at Cambridge (numbered 51st in the Eccleston list).[168] Moorman places the date of his regency ca. 1332–33.[169] Subsequently he went as master to Norwich, where around 1337 he gave a *determinatio*, which has survived along with another question.[170]

Richard of Reppis was connected with the Cambridge convent when, in December, 1331, he was ordained deacon in the diocese of Rochester.[171] Nine years later, in January of 1341, we still find him in the Cambridge area, being licensed to hear confessions in the diocese of Ely.[172]

Both Bartholomew and Richard could have been at Cambridge or Norwich at the time Wodeham was resident at the Norwich convent around 1328 and came in contact with the opinions of several Cambridge

---

III, q. 9 (Tarazona, Cat. 7, fol. 156rb; Paris, Univ. 193, fol. 197rb; Paris, Maz. 915, fol. 188rb; Vat. lat. 1110, fol. 73^{r}): "Et ita videtur Reppis [Univ.: 'Rep'; Vat.: 'Respis']. . . . Sed in contrarium arguit Sirad [Fitzralph]. . . . Sed huic leviter respondet Reppis [Univ.: 'Rep'; Maz.: 'Vesperis'] quod concederet conclusionem si illud argumentum Sirad non esset in rerum natura, et haec arguit sic. . . ." Ibid. (Tarazona, Cat. 7, fol. 156va; Paris, Univ. 193, fol. 197va; Paris, Maz. 915, fol. 188va; Vat. lat. 1110, fol. 73^{v}): "Sed haec responsio videtur ponere opposita, sicut arguitur Reppis [Univ.: 'Rep.'; Vat.: 'Respis'] dicendo. . . ." *Lectura Oxon.* III, q. 12 (on motion *in vacuo*) (Paris, Maz. 915, fol. 197vb; Tarazona, Cat. 7, fol. 167vb; Paris, Univ. 193, fol. 206vb; Vat. lat. 1110, fol. 90^{v}): "Hic quidam bachalarius, scilicet Reppes [Univ.: 'Repces', or 'Reptes'; Vat.: 'Resipis' and 'Resipreis' in margin]." Ibid. (Tarazona, Cat. 7, fol. 168ra; Paris, Maz. 915, fol. 198ra; Paris, Univ. 193, fol. 208ra): ". . . quid dicunt aliqui, ut Reppes [Univ.: 'puta Repp.']. . . ." *Lectura Oxon.* IV, q. 9 (Paris, Maz. 915, fol. 224ra; Tarazona, Cat. 7, fol. 196va; Paris, Univ. 193, fol. 227vb): "Ad primum respondet Reppis [Tar.: 'Rippis'; Univ.: 'Risperis']. . . ."

[166] There is no evidence that John of Reppes was a theologian. For the few biographical details that have survived see Emden, *BRC*, p. 477. The Carmelite John Reppys lived a generation later and cannot be the one referred to by Wodeham; see Emden, *BRC*, p. 477.

[167] *Collectanea Franciscana,* I (1914), p. 151.

[168] See Emden, *BRC*, p. 482; J. R. H. Moorman, *The Grey Friars in Cambridge* (Cambridge, 1952), pp. 145, 204; V. Doucet, "Le studium franciscain de Norwich," *AFH*, XLVI (1953), 95.

[169] Moorman, p. 145.

[170] V. Doucet, *AFH*, XLVI, 95.

[171] Emden, *BRC*, p. 477.

[172] Ibid.

theologians, such as Henry Costesey and Ralph Pigaz. Moreover, the date of Richard's ordination to the diaconate does not necessarily mean he was only 25 at the time and thus too young to have read the *Sentences*. When, on June 6, 1327, Nigel of Wavere was ordained subdeacon, he was already a bachelor of theology. Richard of Radford was ordained subdeacon ten years after he read the *Sentences*. Similarly, Richard Kilvington was ordained subdeacon and priest at approximately the time he read the *Sentences*, and William Skelton was ordained priest two or three years after he had read the *Sentences*. If the Franciscans tended to have their members ordained as early as possible, one cannot assume that this was true in all cases.

The major problem, however, in identifying Wodeham's Reppes with either Bartholomew of Rippes or Richard of Reppis is that Wodeham's theologian must have been a bachelor sometime between 1326 and 1332, and must either have been at Oxford or in close communication with it. This is required by the stages in the debate between Fitzralph and Wodeham's Reppes. The latter had criticized certain opinions of Fitzralph (possibly in Fitzralph's bachelor lectures, ca. 1326–27). Fitzralph in turn, possibly in a magisterial debate, had replied with a countercritique to which Reppes subsequently responded. While it is true that Ockham, while at Oxford, criticized Beaufon, whose opinions were put forth at Cambridge only a short while before, it is difficult to imagine this debate between Fitzralph and Reppes taking place without both participants being in the same place. We can also assume that Wodeham's Oxford audience was familiar with the bachelor Reppes, for otherwise many of Wodeham's remarks would lose their edge.

Nothing associates either Bartholomew or Richard with Oxford, but since Wodeham refers in 1332 to the "bachelor Reppes" and Bartholomew became regent master at Cambridge later in the same year, perhaps Richard is our better candidate. Whatever the solution to this problem, the Reppes cited by Wodeham would appear to be of more than passing interest. He was engaged in a lively debate with Fitzralph, and he was important for Wodeham on the subjects of the Trinity, future contingents, motion in a vacuum, and the sacrament of penance.

THOMAS FELTHORP

Felthorp was a southerner from the diocese of Norwich.[173] He was already a fellow of Balliol College in 1321, when he was regent in arts.

---

[173] On Felthorp, see Emden, *BRO*, II, 676.

Shortly thereafter he began the study of theology and probably lectured on the *Sentences* between 1331 and 1333, thus a close contemporary of Wodeham but academically a year or two his junior. Between 1337 and 1343 he became a master of theology, after which we lose sight of his career. His works are not extant.

Wodeham does not cite Felthorp in his *Sentences* Commentary and in 1330–32 may have been as yet unaware of his ideas. However, in the short treatise on the continuum, Wodeham does refer to Felthorp's opinions.[174] Since Felthorp probably had not become a bachelor of theology when Wodeham began his lectures on the *Sentences*, Wodeham may have become aware of Felthorp after 1332. If true, this suggests that Wodeham's short treatise on the continuum should also be placed after 1332.

RICHARD KILVINGTON

Wodeham was the first author to cite Kilvington, and the meaning of this fact for the biography of Kilvington has been variously interpreted.[175] Michalski took Wodeham's references to Kilvington as evidence that Kilvington had read the *Sentences* before Wodeham.[176] Since, on the basis of the colophon in Vat. lat. 1110, he assigned the date of 1332 to Wodeham's *Lectura*, he placed Kilvington's period as *sententiarius* before 1331. On the other hand, A. B. Emden pointed out that as late as 1331 Kilvington was still described simply as a master of arts, and the first reference to him as a bachelor of theology was not until 1335.[177] Moreover, his ordination to the subdiaconate was only in 1333, and the first reference to him as a doctor of theology occurs in 1350. This would seem to suggest a slightly later academic career and would place the *Sentences* Commentary of Kilvington after that of Wodeham.

There were two Richard Kilvingtons at Oxford in this period. Although all the biographical data may not have been sorted out correctly between these two figures, the main facts for the career of the Kilvington Wodeham cited are clear. He was a northerner, from the diocese of York, and was the son of a priest, a fact that initially hampered his financial and ecclesiastical preferment and may also have slowed the progress of his

---

[174] Murdoch and Synan, *FcS*, XXVI (1966), 282–283.
[175] Emden, *BRO*, II, 1050–51.
[176] Michalski, "Le problème de la volonté," *Studia Philosophica* II, 250; cf. A. Maier, *Die Vorläufer Galileis im 14. Jahrhundert*, 2nd ed. (Rome, 1966), pp. 174, 301–303.
[177] Emden, *BRO*, II, 1050.

academic career. By 1333, the year in which he was ordained subdeacon and priest, he was already a fellow of Oriel College.

During the first year in which Wodeham lectured on the *Sentences* at Oxford, 1330–31, he cited the opinions of Kilvington seven times in four different questions,[178] but these citations all appear to be from Kilvington's *Sophismata*,[179] a work that must therefore be dated before 1330 and was probably written while Kilvington was still in the arts faculty. On the other hand, in book II, quest. 3, Wodeham cites what appears to be a passage from Kilvington's *Sentences* Commentary. Since Wodeham was lecturing on this question in the spring or fall of 1331, that would place Kilvington's *Sentences* Commentary in 1331–32.

An examination of all the manuscript evidence bearing on this particular passage in Wodeham reveals that Wodeham is not necessarily referring to Kilvington's *Sentences* Commentary and may, in fact, not have been referring to Kilvington at all. In this section of Wodeham's question, he was attacking Fitzralph's understanding of the augmentation of charity. In order to refute Fitzralph, Wodeham cited an opinion on proportional units of time to the effect that continual meriting does not necessarily augment grace. In some manuscripts the opinion that Wodeham uses against Fitzralph is attributed to Kilvington.[180]

It must be noted that this reference to Kilvington may be a scribal error for Skelton. In the *ordinatio* version of this question, which includes a passage written by Wodeham after the lectures on book II were completed, Wodeham remarks that he is responding to Fitzralph with the words of Skelton. He now holds with Skelton the affirmative side of the question, although on other aspects of the same issue he disagrees with

---

[178] Wodeham, *Lectura Oxon.* I, dist. 1, q. 6 (Vat. lat. 955, fols. 34^r, 35^r, 35^v, 36^r); I, dist. 8 (Vat. lat. 955, fol. 124^r: "... valet Sophismata Kil. 32^m"); I, dist. 17, q. 4 (Vat. lat. 955, fol. 153^v); I, dist. 33, q. 2 (Vat. lat. 955, fol. 182^r). Wodeham also refers to Kilvington in *Lect. Oxon.* II, q. 3 (Vat. lat. 1110, fol. 14^v) and II, q. 4 (Paris, Maz. 915, fol. 143vb).

[179] There is as yet no critical edition of the *Sophismata*, but the contents of the work have been summarized in C. Wilson, *William Heytesbury. Medieval Logic and the Rise of Mathematical Physics* (Madison, 1956), pp. 163–168.

[180] Vat. lat. 1110, fol. 14^v: "Hic respondetur per Kilvinton, et ego cum eo, quod non in omni parte proportionali temporis tantum facit ad augmentum gratiae actus continuo [should read: continuatio], sicut ipsius instantanea causatio. Immo additur quod sequitur continuatio meriti non augmentat gratiam." Bruges 172, fol. 89va: "Ad illud respondet Kil. quod non in omni. . . ." Florence, Bibl. Naz., conv. soppr. B VII 1249, fols. 87vb–88ra, does not have Kilvington in the text, but in the margin one reads: "Re[sponsio] Kylvi[n]t." Interestingly enough, only the *reportatio* and the second redaction have Kilvington.

Skelton, referring his reader ahead to question 6.[181] Of the three manuscript copies of the *Ordinatio*, two have Skelton and one has Chatton.[182] When one looks ahead to question 6, one finds neither Chatton nor Kilvington, but there are extensive discussions of Skelton with cross references back to this section of question 3.[183]

This confusion in attributing arguments to the proper author may be explained in one of two ways. It would appear that Wodeham intended to credit Skelton with the opinion, and it is possible that a poorly written sKeLTON might be misread by a scribe as KiLvinTON, while another might read it as CH'TON (especially considering the number of times Chatton appears). Another possibility is that the opinion originated with Kilvington, and that in some versions Wodeham acknowledged the original source "per Kilvinton" while in other versions he admitted that he was relying on Skelton, who may in turn have been quoting Kilvington.

Kilvington does deal with this topic, namely the division of time into proportional units, in the second question of his *Sentences* Commentary.[184] However, that may not be the source upon which Wodeham drew. Since Kilvington is still referred to as a master of arts in 1331 and not called a bachelor of theology until 1335, it is likely that he read the *Sentences* after Wodeham, not before. Furthermore, I have not been able to find in Kilvington's *Sentences* Commentary the exact passage Wodeham cited. If ultimately found there, it would have to be proved that it was *only* there, and not also in Kilvington's earlier work, the *Sophismata*, with which Wodeham was familiar.

Wodeham had a strong interest in the ideas and arguments of Kilvington, especially (or exclusively?) as reflected in his *Sophismata*. Moreover,

---

[181] Paris, Univ. 193, fol. 149vb, and Maz. 915, fol. 140ra: "Hic respondetur, ut recitat doctor iste [Fitzralph], et verum est quod ita respondit Skelton, et ego iam in parte sustinui illud idem, licet in multis de merito continuationis vel frequentationis actuum discordem ab ipso et improbem eum, sicut patebit in sexta quaestione huius distinctionis. Dico ergo ad propositum illud: quod non in omni proportionali parte temporis tantum facit ad augmentum gratiae actus continuatio, sicut ipsius instantanea libera causatio; immo additur quod sola continuatio meriti non augmentat gratiam."

[182] Paris, Univ. 193 and Maz. 915 read "Skelton", while Tarazona, Cat. 7, fol. 109ra reads: "Hic respondetur per Chatton, et ego iam in parte sustinui. . . ."

[183] Wodeham, *Lectura Oxon.* II, q. 6 (Paris, Univ. 193, fol. 161vb; Maz. 915, fol. 155ra): "Hic essent duo videnda. Primum est: An possibile sit viatori mereri subito. Secundo . . . . De primo teneo primam conclusionem, alias distinctione prima primi seriosius persecutam, quod homo existens in gratia potest mereri per subitas causationes bonarum volitionum, sicut satis probant media praetacta et rationes multas in contrarium ibi solvi et septimo dubio, tertio quaestione distinctionis praesentis, et in hac conclusione concordat mecum Magister W. Skelton, sed in aliis quibusdam contradicat."

[184] Cf. Paris, B. N. lat. 14 576, fols. 140va, 149vb.

Wodeham usually cited Kilvington favorably. At the present time we can only say that Wodeham knew Kilvington as a logician, not as a theologian. Until further evidence is uncovered, it would seem best to place Kilvington's period as *sententiarius* between 1332 and 1335.

3. *The Socii*

Unlike the term *baccalarius*, which could describe any contemporary who was lecturing or had lectured on the *Sentences* but who had not yet incepted, the term *socius* was generally a technical term describing a fellow *baccalarius sententiarius*, i.e., one who was reading the *Sentences* in the same year or years as the person using the term and with whom he was expected to engage in debate. Except in unusual circumstances, each convent or theological college could present only one candidate each year to read the *Sentences*, and these *sententiarii* would challenge the opinions of each other in their principal debates and at various points in their lectures. This technical meaning of the term has led some scholars to take any reference to a *socius* as hard evidence that the author and the person so cited were reading the *Sentences* together in exactly the same year.

The evidence behind this view is strong, but there are some indications in Wodeham that the term may have been used somewhat more flexibly. It seems it was possible for those who *began* reading together to read for different lengths of time, so that their activities no longer paralleled. While Wodeham was lecturing on book II of the *Sentences*, one of his *socii* had completed the *Sentences* and was lecturing on the Bible. The same thing happened to Holcot. It is possible that all these *socii* began reading in the same year and progressed at different rates. It is also possible that the term *socius* applies more broadly to those bachelors who were not yet *baccalarii formati* and who could attack the opinions of other bachelors, whether they were reading the *Sentences* or reading on the Bible.

Challenging the opinions of others, a requirement for the *baccalarii sententiarii*, was not, however, limited to them. There is ample evidence in Wodeham to suggest that the *baccalarii* could and did challenge the opinions of the *magistri regentes*, who in turn responded to the arguments of the bachelors. We have already seen that Wodeham challenged both Chatton and Fitzralph, when the former had probably just completed his regency and the latter had just begun his. We know that Chatton responded to Wodeham, but we do not know whether Fitzralph responded or changed the arguments in his *Opus correctum* as a result of Wodeham's arguments. Wodeham does tell us, however, that the bachelor Reppes attacked Fitzralph, who responded to him. Reppes may have been *respondens* under Fitzralph. Similarly Skelton, as bachelor, attacked Fitzralph, as master. Moreover, in the passage in which Wodeham speaks about Fitzralph's reputation in the University, it is in support of Fitzralph for having called the opinion of one of Wodeham's *socii*, Grafton, unhealthy. It would seem, therefore, that the *magistri regentes*, or at least Fitzralph, took an active part in the debates among and with the bachelors.

We know only a few of Wodeham's *socii*. It is possible that Reppes may have been among them, although Wodeham consistently calls him a bachelor, never a *socius*. Among those he named as *socii*, three are identified by order: a Benedictine (*monachus niger*), a Carmelite (*Carmelita*), and a Dominican (*Praedicator*). Three others are William Skelton, a Mertonian, Richard of Radford, and a certain Grafton, whose identity is not as obvious as was once thought.

Monachus Niger: The Benedictine *Socius*

The first *socius* to appear in the pages of Wodeham is the Benedictine bachelor, who is identified on the margin of Vat. lat. 955 in the second question of the prologue.[185] The topic under discussion—a central one to all of Wodeham's *socii*—was the knowledge of God in relation to fruition and the beatific vision. The *monachus niger* had either given his principial lecture before Wodeham, or Wodeham had seen a prepared text, such as were frequently circulated in advance of the formal *principium*. In his *principium* the Benedictine had argued a point against Fitzralph that Wodeham felt was justified.[186] While some of the supporting arguments of the Benedictine bachelor were approved by Wodeham, others were rejected.

The Benedictine *socius* next appears in *Lectura Oxon*. II, q. 8, where many of the same issues are introduced.[187] Wodeham's *socius* is not identified, but Wodeham's reference back to the arguments in the second question of the prologue leaves no room for doubt. Here Wodeham is answering the Benedictine's reply to the criticisms Wodeham raised in

---

[185] Vat. lat. 955, fol. 12^v; see also Paris, Univ. 193, fol. 10va.

[186] Vat. lat. 955, fol. 13^r: ". . . sicut probavit socius iste [monachus niger] contra Magistrum Hybernicum [Fitzralph] et bene arguit hic et secum idem teneo."

[187] Vat. lat. 1110, fol. 33^r–33^v; Paris, Univ. 193, fol. 166rb; Paris, Maz. 915, fol. 159va.

his prologue. Later, in the opening question of book III,[188] Wodeham again refers to the opinions of this bachelor, who by then had responded to Wodeham's counterattack in book II, q. 8. In book III, the original arguments of this *socius* are listed as having been given in "anno praeterito", evidence that Wodeham's lectures on book III were given in the year following his lectures on book I.

The arguments of Wodeham's Benedictine *socius* caught the attention of at least one later writer. We find them repeated in John Capreolus,[189] who was aware that the *socius* referred to in *Lectura Oxon*. III, q. 1, was the same person referred to in prol., q. 2. Capreolus, however, did not know that the writer in question was a Benedictine. Capreolus used Wodeham's arguments against this "quidam" and added a few of his own.

We do not know the name of Wodeham's Benedictine *socius*, for he is not further identified in the text or margins of the Wodeham manuscripts. We know far too little about the Benedictine theologians at Oxford in this period, about life in the Benedictine schools, Gloucester and Durham Colleges, and about their relation with the major monasteries, such as Canterbury, St. Albans, Bury St. Edmunds, Malmesbury, Glastonbury, Gloucester, and Worcester. These last two in particular supplied a large number of scholars at Gloucester College which, being the larger of the two Benedictine colleges in the first half of the fourteenth century, may well have housed Wodeham's *socius*.

It is intriguing to speculate on whether the Benedictine *socius* of Wodeham is the same as the famous (or infamous) Monachus Niger, whose opinions were criticized by Gregory of Rimini in 1342.[190] Some years ago Damasus Trapp discovered Gregory's quotations from "Monachus" in a Fribourg manuscript of an anonymous *Sentences* Commentary, thereby tying together work and author.[191] Through the research of Trapp and others, we now know of several manuscript copies of this work.[192] But

---

[188] *Lectura Oxon*. III, dist. 14, q. 1 (Paris, Univ. 193, fol. 176ra; Paris, Maz. 915, fol. 170^v): "Item 16 potest sic argui, sicut fecit anno praeterito quidam bacalarius in hiis mediis fundans se quae hic sequuntur. . . ." Cf. Vat. lat. 1110, fol. 45^r.

[189] John Capreolus, *Defensiones theologiae divi Thomae Aquinatis*, Vol. V (Turin, 1904), pp. 179–183, 198–205 = Capreolus, *Sent*. III, dist. 14, q. 1.

[190] Gregory of Rimini, *Super primum et secundum sententiarum* (Venice, 1522; Reprint: St. Bonaventure, N.Y., 1955), I, 149 P; I, 171 D; II, 43 F.

[191] D. Trapp, "Augustinian Theology of the Fourteenth Century," *Augustiniana*, VI (1956), 201–213, 235–239.

[192] Bruges, Bibl. de la Ville, Ms. 503, fols. 106^r–115^v; Erfurt, Stadtbücherei, CA 2° 132, fols. 39va–73ra; Florence, Bibl. Naz., conv. soppr. A III 508, fols. 189ra–239ra; Fribourg, Cordeliers 26, fols. 82^r–142^v; Paris, B. N. lat. 15 561, fols. 251ra–266ra.

before considering whether Wodeham's "monachus niger" might be Rimini's "Monachus," it might be well to review the evidence on the latter and to reject some unwarranted conjectures that have been circulated.

First, we know that by 1342 Gregory had read a theologian whom he identifies only as *Monachus*. Gregory's citations came from a *Sentences* Commentary that has survived in several manuscript copies. Therefore the "monk" in question must have read the *Sentences* in or before 1342 (if at Paris) or before 1342 (if not at Paris).

Second, the *Sentences* Commentary of this monk is similar in structure and style to English commentaries of the 1330–1350 period, and this work appears only in manuscripts that contain primarily or exclusively English authors. Moreover, when the author uses an example of a city, he invariably uses London, or London and Rome.[193] The Latin of the work shows a marked degree of Anglicizing, as Trapp noted.[194] The author uses examples that would be most meaningful to an English audience, such as his references to London and the fogs in England. Consequently, it would seem almost certain that the author was English and lectured on the *Sentences* between ca. 1330 and 1342. Since the form of a *Sentences* commentary reflects the educational environment more than the country of birth, we may also assume an English university setting. He may or may not be identical with the Oxford theologian whom John Major knew as "Monachus Anglicanus".[195]

Third, the probabilities are very high that this *monachus* was a Benedictine. John Hiltalingen of Basel refers to a passage in the *Sentences* Commentary of Monachus and attributes the opinion to "Monachus Niger".[196] However, one must admit the possibility that Hiltalingen

---

[193] E.g., Monachus Niger, *Sent.*, q. 1, a. 1 (Erfurt, CA 2° 132, fol. 40ra); q. 4, a. 1 (Erfurt, CA 2° 132, fol. 54ra).

[194] *Augustiniana*, VI, 235.

[195] John Major, *Historia Maioris Britanniae* (Paris, 1521), fol. 8r.

[196] Hiltalingen, *Sent.* I, q. 15 (Munich, Staatsbibl., Clm 26 711, fol. 95rb): "Ex hoc apparet quod Monachus niger non bene dicit, ut videtur dicendo quod existens in peccato tenetur credere se esse extra caritatem, et tenetur credere se esse in caritate." Monachus Niger, *Sent.*, q. 1, a. 1 (Erfurt, CA 2° 132, fol. 40ra): "Prima conclusio: quod aliquis homo simul tenetur credere se esse in caritate et se esse extra caritatem. Haec patet, quod aliquis homo existens in peccato mortali tenetur credere se esse extra caritatem, quia tenetur credere esse se in peccato mortali; igitur tenetur credere se esse extra caritatem. Et quod tunc teneatur se esse in caritate patet, quia tunc tenetur esse in caritate; igitur non tenetur de aliquo mortali peccato; igitur non tenetur credere se esse in mortali, et per consequens tenetur se credere esse in caritate." Cf. also Hiltalingen, *Sent.* II, q. 18 (Clm 26 711, fol. 196rb) and Monachus Niger, *Sent.*, q. 3, a. 2 (Erfurt, CA 2° 132, fol. 56vb; Fribourg, Cord. 26, fol. 102v).

might have been misled. Through the *Sentences* Commentary of his fellow Augustinian John Klenkok, Hiltalingen was familiar with the Benedictine *socius* of Klenkok, Ulcredus of Durham, otherwise known as Uthred of Boldon.[197] If he assumed that the *monachus niger*, Uthred, was the same as the Monachus whose commentary he was using, he may have added the *niger* himself. It seems more likely, however, that Hiltalingen knew the truth of the matter. He had read the *Sentences* Commentary of Monachus, for the passage he cites is not cited by any earlier author. Furthermore, he knew Gregory's references to Monachus and would have known that the Oxford *socius* of Klenkok some ten years earlier could not be the Monachus cited by Gregory over twenty years earlier. One could also argue that since Gregory did not further identify his author, e.g. as *monachus albus* (i.e., Cistercian), he also implied a Benedictine. If the supposition of an English origin of the Commentary is correct, then the author was likely an Oxford Benedictine, for English Cistercians in this period often did their theological study at Paris, whereas English Benedictines studied at one of their two schools at Oxford.

This profile of Monachus Niger narrows the possibilities and excludes a number of conjectures that have been made in the past. Part of the problem has been that any reference to a *monachus niger* has been viewed as a reference to *the* Monachus Niger, overlooking the fact that many Benedictines read the *Sentences* at Oxford and Paris in this period. It was customary in the *Sentences* commentaries of both universities to identify one's *socii* by their order rather than by name. Thus one finds references to "Praedicator", "Cordatus", "Carmelita", etc. Not all references to *monachus albus* designate John of Mirecourt, and not all references to *monachus niger* refer to the author of the *Sentences* Commentary found in the Fribourg manuscript.

Therefore, on chronological grounds alone, Rimini's Monachus cannot be John Normannus, the Benedictine *socius* of John of Mirecourt, who read the *Sentences* at Paris in 1344-45; nor can he be Uthred of Boldon,[198] the Benedictine *socius* of John Klenkok, who read the *Sentences* at

---

[197] Hiltalingen, *Sent.* IV, q. 9 (Clm 26 711, fol. 339vb): "Secundum corollarium contra Ulcredum nigrum [or: magistrum] monachum: Nullus homo ex puris naturalibus cum adiutorio Dei quale semper est sibi, potest viam ad aeternam vitam invenire vel mereri."

[198] On Uthred see: D. Knowles, "The Censured Opinions of Uthred of Boldon," *Proceedings of the British Academy*, XXXVII (1952), 305-352; Emden, *BRO*, I, 212-213. It distorts the biography of Uthred to credit him with the authorship of the *Quaestiones Monachi*. This work is an English *Sentences* commentary, written before 1342 and probably before 1340 (to allow time for copies of it to cross the Channel). There is no reason to

Oxford in 1354–55. It is not surprising that none of the quotations from these authors can be found in the *Sentences* Commentary of Rimini's Monachus.[199]

If we are looking for an English Benedictine who could have read the *Sentences* between 1330 and 1342, we might better look to the Benedictine *socius* of Wodeham, or the *socius* of Richard Kilvington, or possibly Roger Swineshead of Glastonbury,[200] or the Benedictine "Wicierus" referred to in one of the *Reprobationes errorum* on Nicholas of Autrecourt.[201]

The first possibility is unlikely. I have not been able to locate any parallels between the opinions of Wodeham's Benedictine *socius* and the *Sentences* Commentary of Monachus Niger. The correlation between Kilvington's Benedictine *socius* and the *Quaestiones* of Monachus Niger is much stronger, for similar ideas are being discussed and similar terminology used.[202] While no parallel passages have been discovered as yet, the similarities are close enough to warrant further and more intensive investigation.

suppose it was written merely to "look like" a *Sentences* commentary or that it was extracted from or based upon Nicholas of Autrecourt's Commentary. Its *Sitz im Leben* is English, and it has no more in common with Autrecourt's ideas than half a dozen other commentaries in the period immediately preceding Autrecourt. Thus it is not necessary to suppose that in 1339–40 Uthred was in Paris studying under Autrecourt. But it is also unlikely that Uthred could have written this work in England. As his academic and ecclesiastical career reveal, Uthred was only about 18 when, in 1338, he left northern England to go to London and Oxford. He did not become a monk until August, 1341, and he probably did not begin the study of theology until he entered Durham College in 1347. He took the full nine years of theological study required of those who had not done a formal Arts degree, and he was admitted to read the *Sentences* in 1355. While it is true that Uthred could have lectured on the *Sentences* at some cathedral chapter before reading at Oxford, this would have been in the two or three years prior to his Oxford *Lectura*, not fifteen years earlier, when he had not even begun the study of theology. In addition to believing Uthred to be exceptionally precocious, we would have to believe Gregory omniscient to be aware at Paris in 1342 that the *Quaestiones* he held in his hands had been authored by a young Englishman who had become a monk at the Durham Cathedral Priory only in the previous year.

[199] Trapp recognized that there were only occasional similarities and no direct parallels between the citations from Uthred and the *Quaestiones Monachi*. The similarities may be due to nothing more than a Benedictine's familiarity with the works of his earlier coreligious. This type of dependence and interrelation was common among the Augustinians and other orders.

[200] On this Swineshead, not to be confused with Richard Swineshead, the Mertonian Calculator, see: J. A. Weisheipl, "Ockham and Some Mertonians," *MedStud*, XXX (1968), 207–213; J. Coleman, "Jean de Ripa O.F.M. and the Oxford Calculators," *MedStud*, XXXVII (1975), 150–152.

[201] J. Lappe, *Nicolaus von Autrecourt*, BB, VI.2 (Münster i.W., 1908), p. 41*.

[202] Compare Kilvington, *Sent.*, q. 3 (Bruges 188, fol. 35vb; Paris, B. N. lat. 14 576, fol. 157va; Paris, B. N. lat. 15 561, fol. 218va) with Monachus Niger, *Sent.*, qq. 1–2.

In the case of Roger Swineshead, we have no citations from his *Sentences* Commentary to check against the text of Monachus Niger. However, as his Commentary reveals, Monachus Niger was first and foremost a logician who was heavily influenced by the tradition of *sophismata*, and that interest corresponds with the known works of Roger Swineshead. Moreover, if Swineshead was a regent in arts around 1330, he could certainly have become a Benedictine and lectured on the *Sentences* before 1340. Perhaps the cross references in the *Quaestiones Monachi* to opinions in logic and physics discussed earlier in other works can provide a means of testing the possible identification of Monachus Niger with the author of *De insolubilibus* and *De motibus*.[203] There is also the distant possibility that Roger Swineshead could have been the Benedictine *socius* of Kilvington, but this would require moving Swineshead's regency in arts back to 1328 and moving Kilvington's baccalaureate in theology forward to 1335—both possible but unlikely.

Finally, we have no citations from a *Sentences* Commentary of "Wicierus", and thus no means of checking his possible authorship of the *Quaestiones*. In fact we know nothing about him, save his respect for Nicholas of Autrecourt. The chances are good that he was at Paris, not at Oxford, and only by being imaginative with the spelling of his name, his location, and the time he is mentioned can one identify him with Ulcredus, or Uthred of Boldon.

One must keep in mind that there may have been as many as twenty Benedictine *sententiarii* produced at Oxford in the period under consideration, although we only know two or three. Nevertheless, it is still to be hoped that a more definite date and specific author can be found for the *Quaestiones* of Monachus Niger.

The Dominican *Socius*: Robert Holcot, William Crathorn, and Roger Gosford

Wodeham's Dominican *socius* appears twice in the Oxford lectures: once in the prologue[204] and once toward the middle of book II.[205] When he first makes his appearance, it is to attack the opinions of the Benedictine *socius*. Whether the Dominican bachelor had heard the Benedictine's

---

[203] For example, in discussing the augmentation of forms, Monachus Niger states (Erfurt, CA 2° 132, fol. 54va): ". . . quia alias tetigi . . . , quia sicut alias ostendi, non oportet quod. . . ."

[204] *Lectura Oxon.* prol., q. 2 (Vat. lat. 955, fol. 14^v; Paris, Univ. 193, fol. 12ra).

[205] *Lectura Oxon.* II, q. 6, a. 2 (Paris, Maz. 915, fol. 156va; Paris, Univ. 193, fol. 163rb).

principium or had read it in a form circulated in advance, it would appear that Wodeham had heard or read the Dominican's attack on the Benedictine and that Wodeham thus followed the Dominican in the order of those reading.

In this early section Wodeham quotes extensively from the Dominican. While Wodeham was partially critical of the Benedictine, accepting some of the latter's arguments against Fitzralph and rejecting others, he rejects all the opinions of the Dominican bachelor, or at least he lists only those he intends to reject. When the Dominican *socius* reappears in the sixth question of book II, we find that he has recently replied to Wodeham's arguments against him. Wodeham makes his counterreply and again attempts to refute the arguments of the Dominican bachelor. It should be noted that although Wodeham sometimes supports the opinions of his other *socii*, e.g. the Benedictine bachelor or William Skelton, his Dominican *socius* stands forth as a major opponent whom he never cites favorably.

Who was Wodeham's Dominican *socius*? Unlike the case of the Benedictine *socius*, where we have no names for Benedictines reading at Oxford in the years 1330–33, we know of several Dominicans who were reading at this time. Robert Holcot[206] and William Crathorn[207] were both lecturing on the *Sentences* in 1330–31(–32?), and Robert Gosford (or Gofford)[208] followed Holcot as *sententiarius* in 1331 or 1332. The precise dating of these *baccalarii* is important for Wodeham's biography and requires further examination.

Holcot had given his bachelor lectures on the *Sentences* at Oxford during one, or more likely, two academic years. In his *Sermo finalis*, which he gave on the completion of his reading of the *Sentences*, he indicated he had

---

[206] Holcot has been the subject of considerable attention in recent years. In particular, see: Beryl Smalley, "Robert Holcot, OP," *AFP*, XXVI (1956), 5–97; Smalley, *English Friars and Antiquity in the Early Fourteenth Century* (Oxford, 1960), pp. 133–202; H. A. Oberman, "Facientibus quod in se est Deus non denegat gratiam. Robert Holcot, O.P., and the Beginnings of Luther's Theology," *HTR*, LV (1962), 317–342; Fritz Hoffmann, "Robert Holcot: Die Logik in der Theologie," in *Die Metaphysik im Mittelalter*, 2nd International Congress of Medieval Philosophy, Köln, 1962 (Berlin, 1963), pp. 624–639; Hoffmann, *Die theologische Methode des Oxforder Dominikanerlehrers Robert Holcot*, BB, Neue Folge, Vol. V (Münster i.W., 1972); Heinrich Schepers, "Holkot contra dicta Crathorn," *PhilJahr*, LXXVII (1970), 320–354; LXXIX (1972), 106–136.

[207] Much of the research on Crathorn overlaps with the studies on Holcot. In addition to Schepers' extensive article listed in the previous note, see: J. Kraus, "Die Stellung des Oxforder Dominikanerlehrers Crathorn zu Thomas von Aquin," *ZKT*, LVII (1933), 66–88; and F. Hoffmann, "Der Satz als Zeichen der theologischen Aussage bei Holcot, Crathorn und Gregor von Rimini," *Der Begriff der Repraesentatio im Mittelalter*, Miscellanea Mediaevalia, 8 (Berlin, 1971), 296–313.

[208] Emden, *BRO*, II, 794.

entered upon his baccalaureate in "anno praeterito".²⁰⁹ This might mean he had become the designated *sententiarius* at the end of the previous school year and had taken one year to fulfill that obligation; or it could mean he had begun reading in the previous school year and had, therefore, taken two years to complete the *Sentences*. Holcot's Commentary is long, but not as long as Wodeham's; therefore one cannot decide this issue on length alone.

If we accept a biennial reading, Holcot's second year as *sententiarius* (and possibly his first as well) coincided with the reading of the *Sentences* by Crathorn, whom we know began his lectures on the *Sentences* in the autumn term of 1330.²¹⁰ After completing his lectures on the *Sentences*, Crathorn gave his lectures on the Bible in which he attacked positions Holcot had maintained in his *Sentences* Commentary. Holcot responded to Crathorn in the first three of his *Sex Articuli*, a work which was written almost two years after Crathorn began his *Sentences* Commentary.²¹¹

On the basis of the above facts, Heinrich Schepers has constructed what is certainly the most likely chronology.²¹² On the assumption that the two years separating Crathorn's first lecture on the *Sentences* and Holcot's *Sex Articuli* are the same two years separating Holcot's first lecture on the *Sentences* and his *Sermo finalis*, Schepers maintains that Holcot and Crathorn read the *Sentences* simultaneously across the biennium 1330–32. Crathorn finished reading before Holcot in the spring of 1332. In the following summer semester Crathorn gave his Biblical lectures, to which Holcot responded in his *Sex Articuli*, also written in the summer of 1332. In the following February, 1333, Holcot gave his lectures on Matthew. By 1334 Holcot had qualified to become appointed *magister regens*, an event that must be placed in or after 1334.

While that chronology best explains the known facts, there are some aspects for which it does not adequately account. It was against common

---

²⁰⁹ *Sermo finalis*, ed. J. C. Wey, "The *Sermo Finalis* of Robert Holcot," *MedStud*, XI (1949), 220: ". . . anno praeterito fidem dedi de faciendo cursus in dicto certamine cum eadem. . . ."

²¹⁰ The opening lectures of William Crathorn on the *Sentences* can be dated precisely by his reference to an eclipse in the previous summer. This important discovery was made by Heinrich Schepers. See Erfurt, Wiss. Stadtbibl., CA 4° 395, fol. 5ʳᵃ; and Schepers, *PhilJahr*, LXXVII, 325. In his *Sermo finalis* Holcot stated that he and another Dominican (Crathorn) had been reading concurrently in that year; *MedStud*, XI, 221: "Et licet de domo Praedicatorum isto anno in lectura sententiarum cucurrerunt duo simul, ille tamen alius discipulus, qui Granton nominatur. . . ."

²¹¹ *Sex Articuli*, art. 1, M: "Unde principalis conclusio quam iste iam per biennium nisus est probare. . . ."

²¹² Schepers, *PhilJahr*, LXXVII, 340–354.

practice for two bachelors from the same order to begin reading the *Sentences* in the same year. Moreover, Crathorn seems to have read only the first book of the *Sentences*.[213] His Commentary in the form that has survived is less than a quarter the size of Wodeham's lectures on book I. If Crathorn lectured on the *Sentences* across almost two years, it is strange that the resulting Commentary is so brief. It is also strange that Holcot could charge Crathorn with not having "run the full course,"[214] since a biennial reading seems to have become the exception rather than the rule by 1330.[215]

Because of the size of Crathorn's Commentary and Holcot's suggestion that Crathorn received a university dispensation to shorten his reading, it is possible that 1330–31 was not only the first year for Crathorn but was also his only year as *sententiarius*. Holcot's remark that he began his own task in "anno praeterito" suggests a biennial reading, but it is not necessary to assume that Crathorn read simultaneously with him in both those years. When Holcot speaks of two Dominicans reading concurrently, it is in "isto anno", the year that is concluded with the *Sermo finalis*.[216]

This leads one to conjecture a different sequence of events. Holcot may have read the *Sentences* in 1329–31, the second year of which coincided with Crathorn's reading. Crathorn finished in less than a year, moving Holcot to his invidious and somewhat gratuitous observation. Holcot's reference in his *Sermo finalis* to the unrest at Oxford between northern and southern students cannot be taken as solid evidence that the *Sermo finalis* should be placed in 1332, nearer the secession of northern students to Stamford in the autumn of 1333. The conflict between the Boreales and the Australes was long-standing, and although there was unrest in the

---

[213] Holcot, *Quodlibeta* (Cambridge, Pembroke 236, fol. 182va): "Igitur si socius iste numquam in aliquo doctore legit de gratia animam informante, sequitur quod numquam legit secundum librum sententiarum, quod absit, quia tunc est periurus."

[214] *Sermo finalis, MedStud,* XI, 221: ". . . ille tamen alius discipulus, qui Granton nominatur, usus favore, quia gratiam universitatis de cito terminandis lectionibus habuit, citius praecucurrit . . . ad quiescendi tempus et locum. Ego autem . . . statum tempus implevi, et multiplicem cursum feci. . . ."

[215] By the end of the fourteenth century the one-year rule was in force; Gibson, *Statuta Oxon.,* p. 195: "Statutum est quod quilibet in futurum lecturus librum sententiarum, qui prius in artibus non rexerit Oxonie, ad hoc, quod huiusmodi lectura sibi cedat pro forma, per tres anni terminos suam lecturam continuet. . . ." It is the feeling of most scholars that this was already the practice by the second decade of the fourteenth century; see above, note 21.

[216] *Sermo finalis, MedStud,* XI, 221; see above, note 210.

spring of 1332, a year and a half before the secession, it was already present in the spring of 1331.[217]

According to this chronology, Crathorn's Biblical lectures in which he attacked Holcot could be placed in the summer semester or the autumn term of 1331. Holcot's response in his *Sex Articuli* need not have followed immediately. Between the end of his lectures on the *Sentences* and the beginning of his lectures on Matthew, Holcot suffered a period of illness and had to attend to non-academic affairs.[218] He began his Biblical lectures on February 10, in 1332 or 1333.[219] The earlier date seems more likely, both because they would have begun on a Monday and because some of Holcot's quodlibetic debates, which cannot have occurred before he was *baccalarius formatus* and had completed his Biblical lectures, can be dated to the academic year 1332–33.[220] If the *Sex Articuli* were delivered in the

---

[217] H. E. Salter arrived at this conclusion working from other evidence. See "The Stamford Schism," *English Historical Review*, XXXVII (1922), 249–253; A. B. Emden, "Northerners and Southerners in the Organization of the University to 1509," in *Oxford Studies Presented to Daniel Callus* (Oxford, 1964), 1–30.

[218] Holcot, Opening lecture on the Gospel of Matthew (London, Brit. Mus., Royal 10 C VI, fol. 136va): "Ego autem, occupatione temporali distractus de dispositione corporali confractus, exilem illam oblationem, quam volui facere, non valui usque modo."

[219] Ibid.: "Iam autem, postquam illa Virgo, cuius semper spero praesidium, cuius semper imploro subsidium, cuius habitum semper geram, cuius regnum quaeram, puerum Iesum praesentavit in templo, quem attulit et intulit et optulit (attulit in Ierusalem, intulit in templum, et optulit Deo Patri), iam, inquam, ultra procrastinare non audeo, sed statim 'Ierusalem evangelistam dabo,' actumque istum scholasticum die Scholastice virginis, quae tunc valde convenienter evenit, inchoabo." This lecture could not have been given in 1331, since February 10 (feast of St. Scholastica) in that year fell on a Sunday. By February 10, 1333 (which fell on a Wednesday), Holcot was probably *baccalarius formatus* and was already engaging in quodlibetal disputes. In 1332 February 10 fell on a Monday and the Purification of Mary was the last major feast.

[220] On the basis of a reference to the age of the world, Michalski was able to date one of Holcot's quodlibets (and thus a group of them) to the year 1332. The date in the early printed version "fere Mdxxxii" differs from what is found in the manuscript "6531" and is obviously corrupt. Conjecturing that "fere" was a misreading of the Roman numeral for 5000, Schepers has argued that the correct reading is 6532, and that the Quodlibet should be dated to 1333. One could argue, however, that the Roman numeral for 5000 was simply dropped, and that the "fere" should be taken seriously, referring to the academic year 1332–33.

It may seem unusual that Holcot could engage in a quodlibetal dispute, indeed a *determinatio*, in a year in which he could not yet be *magister regens*. In the thirteenth century the determination in a quodlibetal dispute was only given by a master. Quodlibets were by nature magisterial debates. By the late fourteenth century it seems that quodlibetal debates occurred among the bachelors in the year or two before their inception. We do not know when in the fourteenth century this change took place, but it was well before mid-century. William of Ockham engaged in quodlibetal disputes,

spring of 1332, his audience would still be familiar enough with Crathorn's remarks for Holcot's "sicut audistis" to be relevant.[221] It would also be true for Holcot to say about one of Crathorn's conclusions: "iste iam per biennium nisus est probare."[222]

The only difficulties with this chronology are that it requires placing the *Sex Articuli* after Holcot's Commentary on Matthew and requires a space of about six months between Crathorn's "prima lectio super Bibliam" and Holcot's *Sex Articuli*. However, it solves other problems. Only one Dominican bachelor would begin reading the *Sentences* in any one year: Holcot in 1329 and Crathorn in 1330. Furthermore, it would explain why Crathorn's Commentary is so brief and why Holcot could say Crathorn finished before the required time and had never reached the second book of the *Sentences*. It would also permit us a better date for the opening of his lectures on Matthew and make the *Quodlibeta* correspond better with Holcot's period as a formed bachelor.

For purposes of Wodeham's chronology, it is important to know whether Holcot was still *sententiarius* in 1331–32 or whether Robert Gosford had already succeeded him in that office by the autumn of 1331. We know almost nothing of Robert Gosford save that he followed Holcot as Dominican *sententiarius* and that he was a northerner, from Coupland in Northumberland. His Commentary on the *Sentences* has not survived, and, with the possible exception of Wodeham, there are no references to his opinions. If Wodeham began his lectures on the *Sentences* as late as 1331–32, then his Dominican *socius* might have been Gosford. If, however, as seems far more likely, Wodeham began in the autumn term of 1330, then his Dominican *socius* must have been either Holcot or Crathorn.

Throughout the literature on fourteenth-century thought the names of Holcot and Wodeham have been linked as the two major representatives of Ockhamism in England after the Venerable Inceptor left his homeland in 1324. William Crathorn, on the other hand, has been identified as one

---

although he was never a master regent. His quodlibets seem to have been given at London after he had completed his residency at Oxford and while he was still *baccalarius formatus*. In the introduction to his first group of Quodlibets, Holcot refers to his *socii*, which suggests that these debates occurred among the *baccalarii formati*. See London, Brit. Mus., Royal 10 C VI, fol. 152rb.

[221] Schepers, *PhilJahr*, LXXVII, 344 has pointed to this audience-reference in the *Sex Articuli*: "In der Mehrzahl der Manuskripte liest man: 'Contra tres primos articulos arguit quidam socius reverendus in sua prima lectione super Bibliam sicut audistis' und wenig später: 'Et ad argumenta mea in oppositum respondit sicut audistis.'"

[222] *Sex Articuli*, art. 1, M.

of Holcot's two major opponents, and his thought has recently been characterized as radical nominalism, in contrast to Holcot.[223] Thus one has clearly differentiated "schools." On the one side stand Wodeham and Holcot, representing the Ockhamist tradition. On the other side stand Chatton, a major opponent of Ockham, Holcot, and Wodeham and purportedly a representative of Scotism; and Crathorn, a major opponent of Holcot and a representative of what appears on the surface to be realism but which can also be viewed as more "nominalist" than Ockham, Holcot, or Wodeham.

One would expect, therefore, that the Dominican *socius* whom Wodeham attacked was William Crathorn. That would in fact solidify our picture of Oxford thought in this period and make it more understandable and exciting: Ockham's two disciples, Holcot and Wodeham, fighting back to back against common enemies: Chatton, Crathorn, and probably Fitzralph, and they, in turn, fighting the spread of Ockhamism at Oxford. This assumption finds support in the margin of one manuscript, Mazarine 915, where the opinions of Wodeham's Dominican *socius* are identified as belonging to the "Praedicator Cathorn."[224]

Under test, however, this theory encounters severe problems. The arguments of the Dominican bachelor quoted by Wodeham do not appear in Crathorn's Commentary in its present form, which seems to be its original form. Moreover, the opinions of the Franciscan bachelor quoted by Crathorn do not appear to be in Wodeham's *Lectura Oxoniensis* in any of its present forms. It is possible, of course, that this material occurred in principial debates that are no longer part of the manuscripts, but this seems unlikely.

When one turns to Holcot, the results are different. Some of the opinions Wodeham attributes to his Dominican *socius* are found in Holcot, both in his *Sentences* Commentary and in his *Quodlibeta*, although the supporting arguments of Wodeham's Dominican *socius* are not found there verbatim.[225] From the other side, Holcot quotes directly from

---

[223] H. Schepers, *PhilJahr*, LXXVII, 320–321; LXXIX, 106–136.
[224] Paris, Maz. 915, fol. 156va.
[225] Holcot, *In Quatuor Libros Sententiarum Quaestiones* (Lyon, 1518), I, q. 3, arg. prin. 13, HH: "Et consequens similiter ad istum intellectum, potest libere antequam peccet facere peccatum et non facere peccatum; non ita quod possit libere vitare peccatum postquam peccavit, sicut probat venerabilis Anselmus *de libertate arbitrii*, cap. ii." "Ad tertiam formam, quando arguitur: si homo potest vitare peccatum, aut peccatum praesens aut futurum, dico quod nec sic, nec sic. Sed dicitur quod homo potest vitare peccatum, loquendo secundum in sensu diviso, sicut dictum est ad istum intellectum quod potest vitare ne peccet in futurum."

Wodeham's *Lectura Oxoniensis*, but only in his *Quodlibeta*, where Wodeham's arguments are attributed to a *quidam modernus*. In fact, two of the quodlibets of Holcot seem to have been directed against Wodeham, and

---

Wodeham, *Lectura Oxon.*, prol., q. 2 (Vat. lat. 955, fol. 15^r; Paris, Univ. 193, fol. 12ra; Paris, Maz. 915, fol. 9va): "'Praeterea, dixi quod homo potest ultra omnem gratiam habitam proficere ultra ad maiorem vel meliorem; ergo cum aliqua gratia viae, ut videtur possit tanta esse quod illa habita potest homo ex tunc vivere sine hoc, quod peccet mortaliter vel venialiter. Igitur aliquis viator ex gratia viatoribus communiter possibili et puris naturalibus cavere posset omne peccatum tam mortale quam veniale.' Sed consequens est falsum apud me, ut probabo; et minor vera, ut probavit secundus socius [Praedicator]; igitur mea maior falsa. Quod minor sit vera arguebatur sic: Primo Augustinus in libello *de bono virginali* non multum ante finem libri dicit sic: 'Non contendo cum illis qui asserunt hominem posse in hac vita sine ullo peccato vivere: nec commendo nec contradico.'"

Holcot, *Determinatio* IV (Lyon ed., A; Cambridge, Pembroke 236, fols. 173va–174rb; Oxford, Balliol 246, fols. 234rb–235ra): "Circa primum dicit quidam modernus positionem hanc: Non est in potestate naturali hominis etiam existentis in gratia transire vitam istam sine peccato veniali, nisi fiat aliquod speciale miraculum circa eum, quale factum fuit circa virginem gloriosam. Non tamen negat quin homo potest esse sine omni peccato per aliquod tempus. Ad istam conclusionem arguit multipliciter. Primo per Augustinum in libello *de bono virginali* non multum ante finem ibi: 'Non concedo,' dicit, 'qui asserunt hominem posse in hac vita sine ullo peccato vivere; non concedo, et non contradico.' Et parum ante dicit sic: 'Vigilantibus nobis peccata subrepunt,' etc. Unde licet Augustinus dicit se ibi velle contendere contra dicentes contrarium, sententia sua est quod homo non potest vitare omne peccatum. Secundo sic ibidem probat Augustinus per illud I Ioh. 1: 'Si dixerimus quod peccatum non habemus, ipsi nos seducimus,' etc. Non dicit illis vel illis, sed christianis omnibus. Tertio ad idem per Augustinum, *de libero arbitrio*, cap. xxix: 'Sunt,' inquit, 'quaedam necessitate facta improbanda, ubi vult homo recte facere, et non potest. Nam vera sunt illius voces: Non quod volo bonum hoc facio, sed quod nolo malum hoc ago. Et dicit plane quod de talibus non intelligit, quando dicit quod nullus peccat in eo quod vitare non potest." "Quarto per illud *de fide ad Petrum*: 'Firmissime tene et nullatenus dubites, etiam iustos atque sanctos homines exceptis parvulis iam baptizatis sine peccato hic neminem vivere.'" ". . . et haec via communis antiquorum doctorum. Alius modus dicendi posset esse, tenendo oppositum, videlicet quod homo existens in gratia potest vitare quodlibet peccatum tam veniale quam mortale. Sed quia mihi illa via pro nunc melius placet, adducam circa hoc quasdam rationes. Secundo ponam circa eam quasdam conclusiones; et tertio respondebo ad rationes iam factas in contrarium." "Secundo circa illum modum dicendi quem nunc teneo, pono in oppositum conclusiones. Prima est: quod sine miraculo de lege communi homo potest vitare quodcumque veniale per liberum arbitrium adiutum per gratiam. Secunda est: quod dubium est an hoc aliquis fecerit de facto. Tertia est: hoc facere est multum difficile." "Ad primum: si Augustinus in illo dicit quod homo non potest vitare quodlibet peccatum, accipit 'non posse' non pro omnino non posse, sed pro difficulter posse. Ad secundum quando dicit Augustinus et probat hoc per dictum illud apostoli: 'Si dixerimus' etc., planum est auctoritas est glossanda. . . ."

Wodeham, *Lect. Oxon.* II, q. 6, a. 2 (Paris, Univ. 193, fol. 163rb; Paris, Maz. 915, fol. 156va): "Secundus articulus principalis habet duo dubia. Primum est: An viator existens in gratia potest producere vitam suam totalem sine privilegio speciali sine hoc

one manuscript names Wodeham in the margin, although the verbatim quotation from Wodeham in the text sufficiently identifies it.[226]

---

quod peccet venialiter. Et videtur quod sic per argumenta quibus probat hoc et tenet socius quidam cuius conclusionem improbavi in lectione mea prima. Tenuit enim nuper replicans contra me quod homo existens in gratia potest vitare omne peccatum imputabile ad culpam. Et hoc probatur primo sic, quia homo existens in gratia potest omni temptationi resistere; igitur potest omne peccatum vitare." Then follows a series of arguments taken from the Dominican's reply to Wodeham. "Et tamen dixi ego [Wodeham] quod Augustinus dicens in *de bono virginitatis*: 'cum illis qui asserunt hominem vivere sine peccato; non contendo nec contradico;' licet sic dicat Augustinus quod non vult contendere, etc., cum mens sua est ad contrarium. . . . Contra cautus doctor non debuit dissimilare ex quo tunc fuisset terminus loquendi et ubi de materia illa specialiter mentio habeatur. . . . Et cum arguitur per auctoritatem Iohanni: 'Si dixerimus' etc., glossat quod nullus est sine peccato, id est sine causa peccati nec etiam sine debito, quia quibus manet obligatus pro peccato aliquo, et si non actuali saltem originali. Secundo principaliter allegavi contra eum illud Augustini, *de libero arbitrio*: 'sunt etiam aliqua necessario facta improbanda', 'dico,' inquit, 'quod hac dicit quia vix, et tamen difficultate evadere talis necessitas. Tertio argui potest per illud Augustini, *de fide ad Petrum*: 'Firmissime tene et nullatenus dubita exceptis parvulis neminem hic posse vivere sine peccato.' 'Verum est,' inquit iste, 'Id est sine dispositione propinqua ad peccatum, non tamen originali quod quibus actualiter habeat peccatum. Consimiliter glossat alias pulchre. . . ."

The work of Augustine that Wodeham knew as *de bono virginali* appears in Migne as *de sancta virginitate* (PL 40, 426). This work is not excerpted in Gratian's *Decretum* nor in Lombard's *Sentences*. The accuracy with which Wodeham locates this passage in the work indicates that he had first-hand knowledge of this Augustinian text.

[226] Holcot's citation from Wodeham in *Determinatio* IV is given in the previous note. In addition, compare Wodeham, *Lectura Oxon.*, prol., q. 1 (Vat. lat. 955, fol. 4ᵛ; Paris, Univ. 193, fol. 5ʳᵇ): "Aliter igitur mihi videtur dicendum quod et capacitas animae est finita, quia ista non est nisi ipsa substantia animae, et quod ipsa de quavis forma in ea receptibili de cuius specie non est dare maximam possibilem repleri potest proportionaliter in spiritualibus secundum intensionem, sicut vas corporeale repleri potest secundum extensionem aqua vel alio liquore, ita quod non potest simul sine speciali miraculo plus illius speciei recepi hic et ibi."

"Unus modus possibilis hoc salvandi bene gressus esset iste, quod sicut non obstante quod cyphus posset repleri aqua ita quod plus de aqua non sit in eo sine miraculo receptibile, tamen per illud miraculum quo Deus posset ponere plura corpora in eodem loco, posset Deus in eodem cypho aqua priori remanente aliam aequalem priori vel minorem simul ponere, et pari ratione si sibi placeret tertiam et quartam, et sic sine statu; ita in proposito non obstante quod aliqua anima, puta 'a', possit repleri gratia ita quod plus de tali gratia secundum speciem non possit simul sine speciali miraculo naturaliter recipi in ea, tamen per miraculum similem proportionaliter priori poterit Deus ponere in ea, si ipsa homo meruerit, aequalem priori simul cum priori et tertiam et quartam et sic sine fine, et proportionaliter in alia vita de praemio. Et sic evadere utrumque inconveniens ante tactum.

"Alius modus possibilis sine tali miraculo et subtilior priori esset quod sicut vas corporale, puta cyphus, non possit plus naturaliter recipere una vice de aqua quam certam quantitatem, puta ciphatum, tamen ipse posset de meliori liquore, puta de vino, tamdem recipere aqua abiecta, et illo abiecto adhuc tamdem de meliori. Et sic non esset finis quin Deus ultra omnem liquorem possibilem posset facere liquorem in duplo meliorem vel

Since Wodeham's debate with Chatton in books III and IV of the Oxford lectures makes it unlikely that Wodeham could have begun his Oxford lectures any later than the fall of 1330, it is all but certain that Holcot is the Dominican *socius* of Wodeham. One might ask, however, why Wodeham's direct quotations from his Dominican *socius* do not appear verbatim in Holcot's *Sentences* Commentary if that is indeed their source. Holcot's work shows signs of later re-editing, and it is possible that the supporting arguments of the *socius* cited by Wodeham could have

---

melioris speciei, tunc totus liquor una vice in eo naturaliter receptibilis numquam posset esse ita bonus quin adhuc meliori posset repleri."

Cf. Holcot, *Determinatio* II, a. 1 (Cambridge, Pembroke 236, fols. 162ra–162rb; Oxford, Balliol 246, fols. 221rb–221va): "Est tamen de isto articulo alius modus dicendi apud modernos, dicunt enim quidam quod non est dare gradum summum meriti quem Sortes potest acquirere, et tamen anima humana non est infinitae capacitatis, ad quod declarandum ponunt exempla: vas enim potest impleri aqua ita quod sine miraculo plus continere non potest. Manente tamen eadem liquore in alio vase, potest Deus alium liquorem ibidem ponere et 3, et 4, et sic infinitum, et tamen capacitas illius vasis est praeter infinitis, cum non sit aliud quam ipsum idem vas. Sic dicunt quod capacitas animae non est nisi ipsa anima. Unde est finita capacitas, et ideo potest impleri gratia sic quod non potest naturaliter de tali gratia secundum speciem plus recipere. Supernaturaliter tamen et per miraculum bene potest duplam et triplam et sic in infinitum.

"Aliud exemplum ponunt subtilius: Videmus quod vas licet non potest de quolibet liquore plus recipere nisi unum ciphatum, una vice potest tamen ciphatum aquae recipere, et abiecta aqua recipere de meliori liquore (ut puta de vino) alium ciphatum, et abiecto illo ad hunc alium ciphatum de meliori liquore in infinitum cum ultra quodlibet liquorem potest Deus causare meliorem. Sic anima potest recipere diversas passiones secundum speciem respectu diversi et diversi amoris fruenti secundum speciem respectu Dei, ita quod quacumque fruitione data vel posita in anima respectu Dei, potest Deus in eadem anima causare perfectiorem alterius speciei in anima viatoris. Ex quibus patet quod non est dare perfectissimam caritatem receptabilem nec perfectissimam beatitudinem in anima alicuius.

"Alii dicunt aliter, scilicet quod est dare maximum gradum meriti et praemii et si Deus conservaret hominem ultra quemcumque terminum cito deveniret ad summum gradum meriti. Et si ultra continuaret bona opera nullum novum praemium novis actibus corresponderet, sed idem praemium quod prius mereretur multiplicius ut de Christo, Magister, libro tertio, dist. 18.

"Sed contra tunc secundum istum modum dicendi. Repugnat enim bono iudicio rationis quod propter novum meritum non debetur novum praemium, quia nec pari ratione nec propter novam malitiam debetur nova poena, et sic bonus posset tantum mereri quod Deus non posset sibi retribuere et malus tantum demereri quod Deus non posset eum iuste punire, quia non posset vel non foret capax maioris poenae. Secundo sic, quanto opus bonum procedit ex maiori caritatis ceteris paribus, tanto est de acceptis, igitur cum deventis fuerit ad summam caritatem frustra, igitur ulterius bene operatur nisi aliquod novum praemium corresponderet. Tertio, per unam decretalem quae ponitur in capitulo De Hereticis, Ad Nostram, ubi damnatur sententia Begardorum, dicentium quod homo in hac vita tantum mereri posset quod amplius in gratia proficere non valeret."

been part of an early redaction but were dropped before the work achieved its present form. Similarly, the arguments the Dominican *socius* "gave recently" and which Wodeham attacked in book II, q. 6 may have been revised before they appeared in a *determinatio* form. The fact remains that the *opinions* Wodeham attacks are found in Holcot.

What, then, is one to do with the reference in the margin of Mazarine 915, identifying Wodeham's Dominican *socius* as Crathorn? I can only conjecture that the scribe, knowing that Crathorn read about the same time as Wodeham, assumed that he was the person intended.

Wodeham's attack on his Dominican *socius* and the fact that the ideas of the latter can be found in Holcot leaves us with the remarkable and somewhat inconvenient conclusion (over against our present understanding of fourteenth-century Oxford thought), that Wodeham and Holcot might not be two interchangeable representatives of an Ockhamist or nominalist school in England but, instead, were opposed to one another on several important issues. Therefore, it might be well to overstep the self-imposed biographical and codicological limits of this chapter and examine in more detail the differences of opinion between Holcot and Wodeham. Among a variety of issues, there are two that stand out by reason of the space both writers devote to them. The issues concern sin and grace.

The first of these is whether a *viator*, in a state of grace, is able to avoid all sins, both venial and mortal. Holcot argued that one can. Since God commands man not to sin, man must be able to fulfill that command.[227] If man can fulfill God's command through one unit of time, he can fulfill it through more, indeed through all time.[228] Wodeham, in a surprisingly Augustinian frame of mind, rejected that position and argued that without the special help of God, i.e. additional grace such as God gave Mary, the *viator* is unable to remain sinless throughout life.[229] Wodeham's position is described by Holcot as the "via communis antiquorum doctorum."

---

[227] Holcot, *Determinatio* IV (Lyon, 1518, A): "Arguit primo sic: Deus praecipit homini; ergo consulit quod vitet omne peccatum; ergo homo potest hoc facere cum adiutorio gratiae. Consequentia videtur esse nota, quia irrationabile esset quod Deus praeciperet aliquid homini quin illud sibi consuleret."

[228] Ibid.: "Secundo sic: Creet Deus hominem perfectum in naturalibus. Iste statim potest incipere mereri si habeat gratiam. Et pono quod Deus conservet vitam illius per unum diem tantum. Tunc arguo sic: Per primam huius diei horam potest vitare omne peccatum. Manifestum est etiam secundum eos, dicunt enim quod homo per aliquid tempus potest esse sine quocumque peccato. Sed eadem ratione potest vitare peccatum secunda; sub eadem ratione et tertia; et sic per totum diem. Ergo per totam vitam suam."

[229] See above, note 225.

The second issue is whether the soul can merit unlimited additional grace, indefinitely and infinitely. Richard Fitzralph had maintained that one could, and on this issue Wodeham attacked him frequently, possibly forcing Fitzralph to revise his wording although not his opinion.[230] Wodeham's position is that the capacity of the soul for grace and beatitude is nothing other than the soul itself and thus has a finite capacity.[231] If it is able to accommodate additional infusions of grace beyond its natural capacity, that can only be done supernaturally and miraculously by God. In the early printed version of Holcot's treatment of this question, he describes both Fitzralph's and Wodeham's positions and appears to remain noncommittal.[232] However, in the only two manuscript copies of this question, Holcot seems inclined towards Fitzralph's opinion.[233]

These differences can be reduced to one major issue. Wodeham views as Pelagian the position to which Holcot adheres, a rather remarkable fact considering that Wodeham is singled out by Gregory of Rimini and by recent historians as the archetypal semi-Pelagian of the fourteenth century. It is too early to say in how many areas of philosophy and theology Holcot and Wodeham were opposed or where we find agreement. Much groundwork has still to be done. But this contrast in their understandings of sin and grace should make us cautious about placing them together as two faithful and almost identical disciples of Ockham.

GRAFTON: EDMUND (OFM), HUGH (OSA), AND WILLIAM CHITERNE (OFM)

Wodeham's *socius* Grafton appears for the first time in the fifth question of book II,[234] in the company of the Mertonian, William Skelton, and the Carmelite bachelor, who is otherwise not identified. Grafton was among those who attacked Wodeham for the position he took in the prologue to his Commentary, specifically on the capacity of the soul for beatitude. When we meet Grafton in book II, however, we find he has already

---

[230] Richard Fitzralph, *Lectura*, q. 11, a. 3 (Paris, B. N. lat. 15 853, fol. 81vb; Florence, Bibl. Naz., conv. soppr. A III 508, fol. 47vb; Oxford, Oriel 15, fol. 53vb). Adam Wodeham, *Lectura Oxon.*, prol., q. 1 (Vat. lat. 955, fols. 4^{r}–4^{v}; Paris, Univ. 193, fols. 5ra–5rb); *Lectura Oxon.*, prol., q. 2 (Vat. lat. 955, fols. 8^{r}, 10^{r}).

[231] See above, note 226.

[232] Robert Holcot, *Determinatio* II, a. 1 (Lyon, 1518, K–L).

[233] Ibid., Cambridge, Pembroke 236, fols. 162ra–162rb; Oxford, Balliol 246, fols. 221rb–221va.

[234] *Lectura Oxon.* II, q. 5 (Vat. lat. 1110, fols. 20^{r}, 21^{r}, 27^{v}, 28^{r}; Paris, Maz. 915, fols. 145ra, 146vb, 154vb).

completed his lectures on the *Sentences* and has attacked Wodeham in the opening question of his Biblical lectures.[235] Later, Grafton appears again in the first question of book III of Wodeham's Oxford lectures.[236] He is almost certainly the *socius* cited in book III, q. 10.[237] Finally, there is the possibility that he is referred to in the sixth question of book II.[238]

There are two problems in relation to Grafton: his identity and his similarity with Crathorn. Most scholars have assumed that Wodeham referred to Edmund Grafton, the fifty-ninth lector at the Franciscan convent at Oxford.[239] As unusual as the practice would be for two bachelors from the same convent to read in the same year, we know this was the case with Holcot and Crathorn and it might be true in the case of Wodeham and Grafton. The fact that Crathorn's citations from his Franciscan *socius* cannot be found in Wodeham's *Lectura Oxoniensis* and differ from the opinions we know Wodeham held, suggests that there may have been two Franciscan *socii*, parallel with the two Dominicans.

While it is not impossible that Edmund Grafton read in the same year as Adam Wodeham, this conjecture is not without problems. Heinrich Schepers has accumulated evidence that suggests that the Franciscan *socius* of Holcot reading in 1330–31 was William Chiterne (or Chitterne), who subsequently received license to hear confessions in the diocese of Sarum (Salisbury).[240] If Wodeham and Grafton also read in 1330–31, that would mean there were three Franciscan *sententiarii* in the same year, which is highly improbable, not to mention improper. This difficulty could be mitigated somewhat by suggesting that Grafton, like Wodeham, read across a biennium, and that the second year of one *sententiarius* coincided with the first year of another from the same convent. That

---

[235] Ibid. (Paris, Maz. 915, fols. 145vb–146ra; Paris, Univ. 193, fol. 154va; Tar. 7, fol. 113ra): "Item alius socius in principio lectionis suae biblicae arguit contra me. Primo contra illud quod dixeram, quod anima repleta cognitione una alicuius speciei respectu alicuius obiecti potest illa stante recipere cognitionem alterius speciei, ut pote si cognosceret rem aliquam improprio genere posset cum cognitione tali ipsam replente aliam rem cognoscere in verbo, sicut lac quemcumque esset album non obstante quin posset esse dulce album. . . ."

[236] *Lectura Oxon.* III, q. 1 (Paris, Univ. 193, fol. 175ra; Paris, Maz. 915, fol. 169va; Vat. lat. 1110, fol. 44^{r}): "Dices forte uno modo concedo, sicut dicit Grafton, quod anima illa est infinite beata sicut et Deus, et ulterius etiam dicit Grafton quod uniri hypostatice verbo est videre et frui visione et fruitione increata."

[237] *Lectura Oxon.* III, q. 10 (Paris, Univ. 193, fols. 198vb–199ra; Paris, Maz. 915, fols. 189va–189vb; Tar. 7, fol. 158rb; Paris, 1512 ed., fol. 133ra).

[238] *Lectura Oxon.* II, q. 6 (Vat. lat. 1110, fol. 30^{v}).

[239] Emden, *BRO*, II, 799.

[240] Emden, *BRO*, III, 2161; H. Schepers, *PhilJahr*, LXXVII, 351–354.

might explain why, in Wodeham's second year, his *socius* Grafton had completed the *Sentences* and had begun his commentary on a book of the Bible.

There is, however, another possibility. There was, contemporary with Wodeham at Oxford, an Austin Friar, Hugh Grafton.[241] We know little about him save that he was at the Augustinian convent at Oxford in 1328. The supposition that he was the *socius* of Wodeham would reduce the concentration of Franciscans reading at Oxford in 1330–32.[242]

The second problem in identifying Grafton lies in the similar biographies of Wodeham's *socius* Grafton and Holcot's *socius* Crathorn. Both Grafton and Crathorn completed the reading of the *Sentences* before their respective *socii*, Wodeham and Holcot. Moreover, in their introductory lectures on the Bible, Grafton criticized Wodeham and Crathorn criticized Holcot, and the attacks were on similar subjects.[243] Finally, the spelling of Crathorn's name in some manuscripts comes very close to Grafton.[244] Is it possible that under the name "Grafton" Wodeham was really referring to Crathorn or, vice versa, that Holcot's *socius* was either Hugh Grafton or Edmund Grafton, not William Crathorn?

The parallels between Holcot's quotations from his *socius* and the *Sentences* Commentary of Crathorn make it certain that Holcot was

---

[241] Emden, *BRO*, II, 799.

[242] If the order in which the bachelors read at Oxford in 1330 were known, it might be possible to test further the plausibility of this conjecture. In book II, q. 5, Wodeham cites and keeps in order three *socii*: the Carmelite bachelor, Skelton (the Mertonian), and Grafton. At Paris it was customary for the bachelors each year to begin reading the *Sentences* and debating one another in a strict sequence, based on the date at which their convents or colleges were "established" at the University. Cf. *CUP*, II, 700, n. 38; P. Glorieux, "Sentences," *DTC*, XIV (1941), 1862: "L'ordre de préséance auquel on s'astreint est soigneusement établi: ce sont les carmes qui commencent: les dominicains qui terminent." If we assume that in Wodeham's year such a system was observed at Oxford and that the sequence began with the older foundations (and not, as at Paris, with the most recent), then we would expect the Carmelite to precede the Mertonian, and the Mertonian to be followed immediately by the Augustinian. Such may, however, not have been the case.

[243] Cf. Wodeham, *Lectura Oxon.* II, q. 5 (Paris, Maz. 915, fol. 145vb; Paris, Univ. 193, fol. 154va; Tar. 7, fol. 113ra): "Item alius socius [Grafton] in principio lectionis suae biblicae arguit contra me." Holcot, *Sex Articuli*, art 1 (Lyon, 1518, A; Oxford, Oriel 15, fol. 207rb; Cambridge, Pembroke 236, fol. 105(107)^{rb}; Florence, Bibl. Naz., conv. soppr. J VI 20, fol. 62ra; Prague, Univ. Bibl. III B 10, fol. 306(290)^{ra}): "Et contra tres primos articulos arguit quidam socius reverendus in sua prima lectione super Bibliam."

[244] In the manuscripts of Holcot's *Sermo finalis*, the name of his Dominican opponent and fellow bachelor is written as "Grā" or "G^a". The *socius* mentioned in the first of the *Sex Articuli* is written as "Grathon" in Vat. Ottob. 591, fol. 69rb, but as "Crathon" on fol. 70rb of the same manuscript.

generally referring to Crathorn. However, it is still possible that when Holcot cited "quidam socius introitu Bibliae sic posuit", he was referring to Grafton and not Crathorn. It is similarly possible that Wodeham's Grafton might be none other than Crathorn, although again it has proven impossible to find the opinions of Wodeham's Grafton in the *Sentences* Commentary of Crathorn.

WILLIAM SKELTON, MERTONIAN

The most important of Wodeham's *socii*, if we are to judge by the number of times his name appears in the *Lectura Oxoniensis*, was William Skelton.[245] He was a northerner by background and had been resident in Oxford for many years. This may be the reason why, on the margin of one manuscript, he is called "William of Oxford."[246] He was a fellow of Merton College at least since 1319. Wodeham usually referred to him as "Master Skelton" and once as "Master William Skelton",[247] thus recognizing his degree in arts and perhaps his reputation in philosophy. Later, in December of 1339, he was appointed Chancellor of the University, a position which he held until June, 1341. He died at Avignon in 1342.

Despite the regional differences between Wodeham and Skelton, Wodeham frequently cited Skelton favorably.[248] Skelton, like Wodeham, had attacked the opinions of Fitzralph, and Wodeham felt that many of Skelton's arguments against Fitzralph were well conceived. In most of the citations to Skelton's opinions, as was customary among the *socii*, one finds Skelton and Wodeham taking opposite sides of an issue.

Although the heaviest discussion of Skelton is centered in the *Lectura Oxoniensis*, book II, q. 5 and subsequent passages that refer back to this question, the opinions of Skelton are found scattered throughout that

---

[245] Emden, *BRO*, III, 1707.
[246] Paris, Maz. 915, fol. 146va.
[247] Paris, Univ. 193, fol. 161vb.
[248] The total references to Skelton in the *Lectura Oxoniensis* where he is identified by name in the text or margin are as follows: *Lectura Oxon.* I, dist. 17, q. 3, dub. 5 (Vat. lat. 955, fol. 149^v; Paris, Maz. 915, fol. 90vb); II, q. 3, dub. 8 (Vat. lat. 1110, fols. 15^v, 16^r (twice); Paris, Maz. 915, fols. 140ra, 140vb, 141ra, 141rb, 141va); II, q. 5 (Vat. lat. 1110, fols. 20^v, 25^r, 27^v; Paris, Maz. 915, fols. 145ra, 145rb, 145va, 145vb, 146va, 147va); II, q. 6 (Vat. lat. 1110, fols. 28^v–29^r; Paris, Maz. 915, fols. 155ra, 155rb, 156ra, 156va); II, q. 7 (Paris, Maz. 915, fol. 158rb); III, q. 4 (Florence, Bibl. Naz., conv. soppr. B VII 1249, fol. 113va); IV, q. 4 (Paris, Maz. 915, fol. 210ra; Paris, Univ. 193, fol. 216ra); IV, q. 8 (Paris, Univ. 193, fols. 224vb, 225ra); and probably IV, q. 12 (Paris, Univ. 193, fol. 232rb; Vat. lat. 1110, fol. 134^v), although this last reference may be to Richard Radford.

work and even appear in the Caius manuscript.[249] In fact, Skelton is the only *socius* of Wodeham who appears in this later Commentary.

Skelton's works have not survived under his name nor have they been identified among the anonymous works of that period. Wodeham gives the impression that he considered Skelton one of his most gifted contemporaries, ranking alongside Kilvington and perhaps superior to him. At one time there probably existed works in logic and a *Sentences* Commentary. The extensive quotations from his writings found in the pages of Wodeham may provide enough authentic texts through which to identify at least Skelton's *Sentences* Commentary, if it has survived in any manuscript.

RICHARD OF RADFORD

In the second book of his Oxford lectures, Wodeham cited a series of arguments on the augmentation of merit that in the margin of Vat. lat. 1110 are attributed to a certain Radford.[250] It has generally been assumed that Wodeham was referring to one of two Franciscans, either Thomas of Ratford,[251] who was the 63rd lector at the Oxford Franciscan convent around 1340, or more likely to John of Radford,[252] the 51st lector of the Franciscans at Oxford around 1328. Wodeham undoubtedly knew John of Radford personally and probably heard him lecture and debate. Moreover, it has been assumed that the Radford cited in Wodeham might well be the Radford who authored the three theological questions in Ms. Digby 216.[253] A closer look at the Wodeham manuscripts, however, clarifies certain aspects of this problem and invalidates a number of previous conjectures.

First of all, the Radford intended by Wodeham was Richard Radford, master of arts and fellow bachelor of theology at the time Wodeham was reading.[254] This Radford was a northerner from the diocese of York. He

---

[249] Cambridge, Caius 281, fol. 142ra.

[250] *Lectura Oxon.* II, q. 5 (Vat. lat. 1110, fol. 24^r).

[251] Emden, *BRO*, III, 1548.

[252] Ibid., III, 1548. Emden was not certain whether the three questions found in Oxford, Bodl., Digby 216, fols. 40^r–41^r or the citation in Wodeham's Oxford lectures referred to John de Ratforde (Radford) or to Thomas Ratforde.

[253] Oxford, Bodl., Digby 216, fols. 40^r–41^r. The vocabulary and style of argumentation seem to reflect the theological climate of 1335–40 rather than 1320–25. I would therefore be inclined to attribute these questions to Thomas Radford rather than John Radford.

[254] Paris, Univ. 193, fol. 158ra–158rb: "... ego probavi et alius etiam socius, Magister R. Retforde, hoc arguit mecum primo sic...." On Richard Radford see Emden, *BRO*, III, 1541.

studied arts at Oxford, and by 1321, at which time he was a fellow of Balliol, he was regent in arts. By 1325 he had left Balliol and was engaged in the study of theology, possibly as a fellow of University College. To the biographical material assembled by Emden, we can now be certain on the basis of Wodeham's citation that he read the *Sentences* around 1331. In August of 1335 he was still addressed as a bachelor of theology and thus had not yet incepted.

Secondly, it is unlikely that the Radford cited by Wodeham, i.e. Richard Radford, is identical with the author of the three theological questions found in Digby 216. Although the ideas cited by Wodeham are surprisingly similar in one or two instances to opinions found in the Digby questions,[255] there are no exact parallels. Moreover, the Digby questions are attributed by the scribe who copied them to "Ratford Frater", a title that could refer to Thomas or John, but certainly not to Richard of Radford. Until further evidence is uncovered, it is advisable to sever the connection between Wodeham's Radford and the author of the Digby questions.

It is surprising in a sense that Richard of Radford figures so marginally. Most of Wodeham's *socii* appear in his *Lectura* more than once. However, the opinions of Richard of Radford as quoted in Wodeham are worthy of study and are the only insights we presently have into the thought of this secular theologian.

The Carmelite Bachelor

The last of Wodeham's *socii* was the Carmelite, who has not otherwise been identified. He is mentioned only in book II, q. 5 of the *Lectura Oxoniensis*, where Wodeham answers the Carmelite's arguments brought against him on the basis of his discussion of beatitude in his prologue to the Oxford lectures.[256]

D. Summary

Wodeham centered his attention on the generation of theologians between Scotus and himself, and within that group he cited the writings of thirty or more authors. That makes Wodeham the richest single source

---

[255] For example, compare Vat. lat. 1110, fol. 24^r or Paris, Univ. 193, fol. 158^r with Oxford, Bodl., Digby 216, fol. 40^v.

[256] Vat. lat. 1110, fols. 20^r, 25^r.

for Oxford thought of the early fourteenth century. For the authors whose works have survived, Wodeham provides one context or perspective through which to view their opinions and achievements. For those whose works have not survived, Wodeham is one of the few means available for reconstructing their thought or, as is to be hoped, the means for identifying their works among the large numbers of anonymous texts.

The sources used by Wodeham narrow the chronological boundaries of his Oxford lectures. Through his references to Fitzralph as "Magister" and his references to Fitzralph's *Opus correctum* and *Quaestio Biblica*, Wodeham's *Lectura Oxoniensis* must have a *terminus post quem* of 1330. On the other end, the direct quotations from Wodeham found in the *Quodlibets* of Holcot place a *terminus ante quem* of 1332 on at least book I of the *Lectura Oxoniensis*. Moreover, the debate with Chatton in books III and IV suggests that those books cannot be placed beyond 1332–33. Further precision in this matter, however, must await evidence and discussion that will be presented in chapters three and four, particularly the witness of Gregory of Rimini and the relation of the London lectures to those of Oxford.

CHAPTER THREE

THE *LECTURAE* OF ADAM IN LATER MEDIEVAL THOUGHT

The problem of sorting out and properly identifying the various redactions of Wodeham's lectures on the *Sentences* does not depend entirely on the internal evidence of the manuscripts. Fortunately, there is also the evidence of contemporary and subsequent authors who were familiar with Wodeham's thought and who were aware that there were several different *lecturae*. References to and quotations from Wodeham are abundant in the later scholastic literature, and where the redaction is in some way identified, these references provide an additional, important check in determining what lectures are reflected in a particular group of manuscripts.

The utilization of contemporary and subsequent references to an author or a work has proved useful in solving problems of authenticity and chronology in fourteenth-century manuscript studies. The advantages of this method can be seen in the work of Boehner, Brampton, Brown, and Gál, particularly as applied to the works of Ockham.[1] Used carelessly, however, this method can jumble the facts for many fourteenth-century biographies.[2] Despite its visible rewards, the procedure of approaching authors through the writings of their contemporaries as well as through their own work has generally been limited to a comparison of those writing at the same time. The references to one author have not been traced into later writers, since those later citations are of little help in solving questions of priority and date. How an author is used by later thinkers, though, can be as important a question as his own sources. Thus, in addition to a list of doctors and authorities one writer cites, i.e., his sources, we need a list of places, frequencies, and

---

[1] The benefits of a rigorous and critical application of this approach are best reflected in the introduction to the critical edition of Ockham's *Ordinatio* and in recent articles by the two editors of that edition, Stephen Brown and Gedeon Gál.

[2] For example, the problems caused through the erroneous assumption that all references to Bradwardine's thought must postdate the publication of the final redaction of his *Summa de causa Dei* (1344), or the similarly erroneous assumption that references to the thought of Kilvington are to his Commentary on the *Sentences* (ca. 1335) and not to his earlier but equally important *Sophismata* (pre-1330).

contexts in which that same writer is cited in subsequent discussions, i.e., the authors for whom he became a source. This approach would not only demonstrate how and why some thinkers continued to be quoted and thus increased in reputation, but it might also be useful in sorting out the manuscripts that are usually products of subsequent generations.[3]

The case of Wodeham provides a good illustration of this method. Through these outside witnesses the major significance of the Oxford lectures (as opposed to the Norwich and London lectures) is further established, an importance to which the extant manuscripts of Wodeham also testify. More importantly, it is through other authors that we learn which redactions of the Oxford lectures were in circulation and how they were designated. Only through a comparison of quotations from the "Lectura secunda" or the "Lectura Londoniensis" with the manuscripts of Wodeham can it be determined what, if anything, is extant from the London lectures or to what works the names "Lectura prima" and "Lectura secunda" refer. Furthermore, references to the London lectures are the only way, apart from Wodeham's own cross references, of establishing the general structure and particular content of that work.

Beyond providing a key to the various redactions of Wodeham's lectures on the *Sentences,* outside references also help determine what about Wodeham's thought was of interest to contemporaries and later generations. Was Wodeham known for his position on only a few limited issues and, if so, what were these? Was Wodeham's name linked with a standard set of topics, or did the conception of what was valuable in Wodeham change as the century progressed? Did subsequent authors consider Wodeham a major figure and, if so, why? Was he considered primarily a reflection of or an extension of Ockham, or was he viewed as a separate thinker whose solutions to certain questions merited attention in their own right? Was he considered radical or unorthodox, or was he quoted favorably by a wide group of later scholastics, even those generally considered conservative?

In addition to the works, redactions, and ideas of Wodeham that appealed to later authors, this type of material shows *how* Wodeham's

---

[3] It is surprising how long this question or approach has been ignored. We have several studies now on the attitude toward and evaluation of Ockham in modern research. We have no comparable work on the use of Ockham by subsequent medieval authors, in spite of the crucial importance such a study would have for understanding the association of Ockham and nominalism that developed in the fifteenth century or the pejorative attitude toward Ockham found in certain sixteenth-century writers.

thought was passed down through succeeding generations. For example, it reveals those who continued to read Wodeham and quote directly from him, but it also reveals those who borrowed their references and quotations indirectly through other authors. More significantly, it points to the important role played by the University of Paris and, in particular, the Augustinian Hermits in preserving and transmitting the thought and writings of Wodeham.

As a byproduct of this approach one is able to confirm impressions about other authors already gleaned from the manuscripts. What later scholastics found in Wodeham is often a guide to their own interests and approach, especially since the sections and issues quoted from Wodeham differ among later authors. Moreover, the distinction between authors who refer frequently and exactly to contemporary opinion and authors who ignore or only make oblique reference to such opinion is further documented, as is the distinction between authors who quote directly and reflect a fresh and thorough reading as opposed to authors whose references and quotations are not exact or who borrow their material from some indirect source. It should be remembered, however, that while listing the number of times Wodeham was cited by another author may indicate the importance Wodeham held in his eyes, it does not indicate whether the other author generally agreed or disagreed with Wodeham, which is a crucial consideration.

It should also be kept in mind that failure to cite an important author can also be meaningful. However, one must be careful not to exaggerate the difference between those who do and those who do not quote Wodeham. Some writers, for example Thomas Buckingham or Nicholas Aston, rarely mention anyone, and thus there is nothing particularly significant in their failure to cite Wodeham. Moreover, the absence of a direct reference from Wodeham by a later author does not mean that Wodeham exercised no influence on his thought, for there may indeed be an unacknowledged influence. This is especially true for authors who seldom acknowledge their sources.

In searching for references to Wodeham among authors in the fourteenth and fifteenth centuries, I have been greatly aided by the pioneering work done on fourteenth-century scholastic manuscripts and, in particular, the lists of "authors cited" compiled by Xiberta, Zumkeller, Trapp, and others. The following treatment does not contain all authors who mention Wodeham, nor does it claim to have isolated every reference to Wodeham in a particular author. The field of fourteenth-century studies is too new and the number of little-known authors available in manuscripts too great to permit that degree of thoroughness. For our purposes, however, the material collected includes the major authors and is sufficient to show the knowledge and transmission of Wodeham's thought and writings up to the Reformation.

A. Early Reactions at Oxford, Paris, and Cologne

Out of the three or four lecture series that Wodeham gave on the *Sentences* and the multiple redactions that some lectures underwent, how much has come down to us and in what form? As was stated earlier, the majority of manuscripts reflect the Oxford lectures in the form of the first complete redaction, the post-1334 redaction, or one of the *extractiones* or *abbreviationes,* principally that of Oyta. No manuscripts have been successfully identified as either the London or the Norwich lectures. When Wodeham was quoted by his own and future generations, however, no references were made to anything called the "Oxford lectures". In cases where the lecture series was indicated, the earliest references differentiate between what are called the *Lectura Londoniensis* and the *Lectura secunda*. Later authors, moreover, differentiated between what they called the *Lectura prima* and the *Lectura secunda*. This latter designation was adopted by John Major who referred in his *Vita Adae* to two courses of lectures on the *Sentences* given by Wodeham while he was in residence at London, Oxford, and Norwich. Since the London lectures circulated separately, the implication would be that lectures similar in structure and content were given at Norwich and Oxford. Should one assume from this account that there were only two series of lectures, not three, and that the *Lectura secunda* refers to the Oxford lectures while the *Lectura prima* is a later name for the London lectures? This can only be determined by a detailed examination of these references to Wodeham's writings.

1. *England, 1334–1350*

The dramatic exchanges of opinion reflected in the pages of Wodeham and the frequency and openness with which contemporary names are mentioned do not set the style for later English writers. Indeed, with the English tendency to reduce the commentary on the *Sentences* to a few select questions treated at great length, there was also a tendency to exclude the names of any source or authority after Scotus. University statutes encouraged this reticence, especially for bachelors while they read. Wodeham is an exception to that rule. However, there was a reluctance among English scholastics after Wodeham to break that silence in the margins of manuscripts or when bachelor lectures were revised in later life, as generally they were. Controversy continued and in some cases was quite heated, but names of opponents were shrouded under such broad and anachronistic labels as *Pelagiani* or *Ciceroniani*. It is therefore of interest that one of those names that appear so rarely is Wodeham.

While Wodeham was reading at Oxford or shortly thereafter, THOMAS BRADWARDINE, a fellow of Merton College, lectured on the *Sentences*.[4] Within a decade, largely because of the controversial nature of his thought, Bradwardine became widely read and quoted, taking his place alongside Ockham, Fitzralph, and Wodeham as one of the most frequently cited English authors of the century. He was the only one to appear in the pages of Chaucer. In his widely read *Summa de causa Dei,* written during the period 1332-1340, based on his lectures as a *sententiarius,* and published in its final form in 1344, Bradwardine attacked those he considered to be Pelagian on the issues of free will, grace, and divine foreknowledge.[5] Although Bradwardine does not mention those he is

---

[4] In light of the date at which Bradwardine matriculated at Merton College (1323), the date at which he is first mentioned as a bachelor of theology (1333), and the date at which he left Oxford (1335), his reading of the *Sentences* can be placed between 1330 and 1333, but probably a year or two after Wodeham began reading.

[5] Most scholars have assumed that Bradwardine's *Summa* was completed in 1344 at London and therefore accessible to others only after that date. But the weight of evidence is against that view. Robert of Halifax referred to Bradwardine's *Summa* in a passage that is an integral part of his Commentary on the *Sentences* and thus could not have been inserted by a later scribe. Moreover, Gregory of Rimini cited both Halifax and Bradwardine in sufficient detail to show he had access to Bradwardine's *Summa* and Halifax's *Sentences Commentary.* These references in Rimini occur in the version of his Commentary that was read in 1342 and "published" in 1344 as established by Trapp. To allow time for Halifax to gain access to Bradwardine's work, and for the works of both Halifax and Bradwardine to cross the Channel and be read by a bachelor lecturing on the *Sentences* in 1342, Bradwardine's work must have been accessible in England in some form similar to its present structure before 1340, possibly as early as 1336.

If this is true, how is one to interpret the frequent colophon in the manuscripts of Bradwardine's *De causa Dei*: "Perscriptum London. 1344"? It is true that this date does not refer to the transcription of a particular codex but is rather the date of publication, as Weisheipl has correctly argued. However, the date of publication is not the date of writing and indeed applies only to the release of a particular and, in this case, polished redaction. References to the work before 1344 suggest that portions of Bradwardine's *Summa* were released into circulation earlier, although the completed *ordinatio* edition may not have been circulated until 1344.

This evidence means that we need not place after 1344 all sources that refer to the

attacking, most scholars feel that two of his major opponents were William of Ockham and Adam Wodeham. Indeed, the elaborate discussions of fruition apart from grace, of human free will, and of future contingents in relation to divine foreknowledge by such Ockhamists as Holcot and Wodeham at Oxford and London in the years between 1330 and 1334 may well have stimulated Bradwardine's expansion of his bachelor lectures into his monumental *Summa*.

Toward the middle and latter part of that same decade, well before the publication of the final form of Bradwardine's work in 1344, several critics of Bradwardine's position emerged who attempted to steer a middle course between what appeared to be the theological determinism or divine omnivolence of Bradwardine and the semi-Pelagianism of the disciples of Ockham, particularly Adam Wodeham. One of these was the Franciscan, ROBERT OF HALIFAX, who was among the earliest authors to quote Wodeham by name.[6] For Halifax, Wodeham was already a person

---

Summa of Bradwardine. Although no one has argued that Rimini's Commentary was written after 1344, there is no further need to explain away his references to Bradwardine. Moreover, the date for Alexander Langeley's Commentary on the *Sentences*, which cites Bradwardine frequently, can now be placed before 1340, thus corresponding to the other known facts of his life. Similarly, there is no longer any need to bend the biographical data on Thomas Buckingham by placing his *Sentences* after 1344. Buckingham became chancellor of Exeter Cathedral in 1346, a fact that, in combination with his citation of Bradwardine in his *Sentences* Commentary, has led some scholars to squeeze Buckingham's *Sentences* Commentary into the year 1345, thus crediting Buckingham with perhaps the fastest promotion on record from *sententiarius* to *magister*, and on to a position as *chancellarius*, in violation of university statutes. At the earlier end of his academic career, that theory would mean Buckingham had remained a theological student from 1324 to 1344 without having progressed to the point of reading the *Sentences*. Even more remarkable would be the omniscience of Rimini, who was familiar with Buckingham's Commentary in 1342 although the work was supposedly not written until 1345. Surely something is wrong here!

In a recent article on John of Mirecourt (*RTAM*, XXXIX (1972), 224–256; XL (1973), 147–174) I suggested a different biographical sketch which includes a period of teaching at Paris sometime between 1340 and 1346, attested to by Thomas of Cracow. Here I only wish to suggest that Buckingham read before 1340, possibly as early as 1336. Since there are no references in Buckingham to Aston or Osbert, nor do Aston or Osbert refer to Buckingham as a *socius*, there is no reason to assume that they read in the same year. The dating of the *Sentences* commentaries of Aston and Pickingham will be discussed below in note 14.

[6] Paris, B. N. lat. 15 880, fol. 58^r (the earlier text), corrected according to Vat. lat. 1111, fol. 32^r, Milan, Ambrosiana E 55 inf., fol. 47^v, and Paris, B. N. lat. 14 514, fol. 295^v (the later text): "Hic tamen est opinio cuiusdam valentis [*opinio Adae* initially in margin and eventually in text] qui dicit quod, stante cognitione Dei enigmatica in universali et in particulari, voluntas viatoris potest in se causare active dilectionem Dei, et super omnia et propter se, et fruitionem Dei sine gratia et sine aliquo dono super-

whose opinions carried weight.[7] Although Halifax was critical of both Bradwardine and Wodeham, it is his treatment of the latter that is of interest to us. Halifax's quotation from Wodeham was taken from the Oxford lectures, I, dist. 1, q. 10, a. 1, concl. 1.[8] He attacked Wodeham on the point that was to become central in the debate over Wodeham's semi-Pelagianism, namely the thesis that man *ex puris naturalibus* is able to do good works apart from the infused habit of grace. The passage in Wodeham to which Halifax refers does not seem to occur in the Caius College manuscript and consequently should probably be placed before 1334. However, from the quotation it is impossible to tell

---

naturaliter dato, ita quod voluntas viatoris sine caritate vel quocumque dono supernaturali infuso potest habere et elicere actum talem secundum speciem qualem nobis praecipitur et qualem voluntas potest elicere mediante caritate infusa, quia sic est de habitibus acquisitis, quia idem actus secundum speciem potest elici a potentia sine habitu qualis cum habitu elicitur." Wodeham was cited earlier by Halifax, as is indicated by the marginal note in Vat. lat. 1111, fol. 7va; cf. Paris, B. N. lat. 14 514, fols. 253^r–253^v; Paris, B. N. lat. 15 880, fols. 10^r–10^v. For a further discussion of Halifax see my "Some Notes on Robert of Halifax, O.F.M.," *FcS*, XXXIII (1973), 135–142.

[7] The term *valens* was used to describe a contemporary whose opinion carried weight. It seems to have been used only when the proper name was not included in the text. The audience or reader would probably know who was intended by the content of the citation. In his *Quodlibeta* (Cambridge, Pembroke 236, fol. 185rb; Oxford, Balliol 246, fol. 246rb–246va) Holcot refers to the "opinio cuiusdam valentis" that an article concerning the future, once revealed, was no longer contingent but would happen of necessity. Wodeham applied the title "valens" to a bachelor with whom he agreed (Vat. lat. 955, fol. 22a^v). He also applied it to Fitzralph and others (Vat. lat. 955, fol. 8^r). The scholastic use of this term in the first half of the fourteenth century may cast some light on the meaning of the phrase "pars valentior" in the political thought of Marsilius of Padua.

[8] Vat. lat. 955, fol. 66^v; Paris, Univ. 193, fol. 49rb; Paris, Maz. 915, fol. 41ra: "Prima conclusio primi articuli est haec: Quod in via, stante cognitione viatoris enigmatica in universali vel in particulari, voluntas potest causare in se active dilectionem Dei super omnia et propter se sive fruitionem Dei, quia voluntas potest se conformare recto dictamini intellectus. . . ." And later in the same article, Vat. lat. 955, fol. 67^v; Paris, Univ. 193, fol. 49vb: "Ad primum istorum concedendum mihi videtur quod etiam sine infusione doni supernaturalis posset voluntas viatoris mediante dictamine possibili haberi de Deo in via libere in se causare dilectionem Dei super omnia. . . . Utrum autem talem qualis nobis praecipitur et qualis potest elici mediante caritate infusa dubitatio bona ulterior esset, et dico pro modo quod sic talem in specie, quia sic (V: sicut) est de habitibus adquisitis, quia (V: quod) idem actus secundum speciem elici potest a potestate sine habitu qualis cum habitu licet non ita perfectus ceteris paribus, ita est de habitibus infusis a multo fortiori, quia licet sint ponendi, tamen cadunt partim sub experientia nostra. . . . " Wodeham felt his position differed from that of Pelagius because he (Wodeham) was talking about some acts, not all acts, and because he was talking about good acts in conformity to God's law, not meritorious acts which depend upon divine acceptation. See note 24. Cf. Michalski, "Le problème de la volonté," *Studia Philosophica*, p. 293.

which redaction Halifax was using. In the passage in question there are only minor differences among the various redactions, and Halifax appears to be paraphrasing rather than quoting verbatim. It is entirely possible that Halifax had attended the lectures of Wodeham and may have been quoting from his own notes or from memory. In any event, Halifax throws no light on the London lectures or the redactions of the Oxford lectures.

Wodeham's name again appears in the *Sentences* Commentary of another Franciscan in England, ROGER ROSETUS (or Roseth), writing around 1335.[9] Rosetus, who also cited Bradwardine,[10] joined Wodeham's

---

[9] One copy of Rosetus' *Sentences* Commentary was made at Norwich in 1337 (Vatican, Chigi B. V. 66, fol. 14ᵛ), and thus these lectures must have been given before that date. Inasmuch as Rosetus cites Wodeham and calls him *unus valens,* he must have lectured after 1332, probably after 1334. The style and content of Rosetus' *Sentences* Commentary is English, and it was probably written at Oxford or Cambridge.

Unlike most English theologians of this period, Rosetus does not begin appearing in the margins of other *Sentences* commentaries for almost thirty years. When he does, there is ample evidence that he was being read extensively. We find him quoted frequently by John Hiltalingen of Basel and in the anonymous *Sentences* Commentary contained in Vat. lat. 986. Indeed, Hiltalingen borrowed at least one of his quotations from Wodeham through the pages of Rosetus. There is reason to believe, however, that Rosetus was considered an important theologian even earlier. Doucet conjectured that Adam of Ely may have read Roger's Commentary at Norwich in 1337–38. If so, this would be one of the earliest examples of reading the *Sentences secundum alium*. This may also explain why the Commentary of Rosetus was sometimes attributed to Swineshead, presumably Richard Swineshead, the Merton *Calculator*. Most recent scholars have assumed that this mistake occurred on the Continent and resulted from a confusion between the supposed similarity of the names Roseth and Suisset. While this seems plausible, especially since one manuscript (Oxford, Bodl., Canon. Misc. 177, written in 1395 at Padua) of the opening section of Rosetus' *Sentences* Commentary is ascribed to "Rugerio Suiscepto sive Roseto in studio Anglicano," it should be noted that the only extensive manuscript of Rosetus' *Sentences* Commentary attributed to Swineshead is Oxford, Oriel 15, written in 1389 in England. There can be no doubt that the scribe believed the commentary belonged to an author named Swineshead, for on every folio in that portion of the manuscript he copied that name in the margin, Swynissete or, more frequently, Swynished. This fact, noted by many scholars, has not yet been adequately explained.

A solution to this problem may lie in the fact that Oriel 15 is closely related to and in part derives from the same source as London, Brit. Mus., Royal 10 C VI, which belonged to Gloucester Abbey and is therefore of Benedictine provenance. Oriel 15 was also a Benedictine manuscript, copied for a monk of Glastonbury Abbey in 1389 (fol. 210ʳᵇ). With the exception of a theological treatise of Nicholas of Oresme, Oriel 15 contains only Oxford theologians: Fitzralph, Holcot, Aston, and Swineshead (Rosetus). In light of the Benedictine provenance of Oriel 15, perhaps the Swineshead intended by the scribe was not Richard Swineshead, the Mertonian, but Roger Swineshead, the monk of Glastonbury, who distinguished himself as a logician (before 1335) and eventually as a theologian. Given the strong interest in logic, mathematics, and physics reflected in the pages of Rosetus' Commentary, it is not unlikely that a theological bachelor,

socii in attacking Adam's use of the *vas miraculose* example in the prologue of his Oxford lectures.[11] Interestingly, Rosetus also referred to Wodeham as *unus valens*, indicating the growth of Wodeham's reputation among the Franciscans before 1337. While Rosetus was critical of Wodeham and Bradwardine, he did not center his objections on the issues of grace and salvation.

A more vociferous English critic of Bradwardine was the fellow Mertonian, THOMAS BUCKINGHAM, who lectured on the *Sentences* toward the end of the 1330's. Although Buckingham frequently cites authorities and knows Fitzralph and Bradwardine, I have found no mention by name of an author later than Scotus.[12] However, if Wodeham

---

possibly already a Benedictine at that time, unquestionably interested in those same topics, and perhaps sharing the same point of view, would choose to read, *secundum alium*, the Commentary of a respected Franciscan master, Roger Roseth, and that a Benedictine scribe would naturally attribute the work to Roger Swineshead, O.S.B., instead of Roger Roseth, O.F.M. Close ties between the Benedictines and the Franciscans were not unusual. Christ Church, Canterbury, relied for a long time on the services of a Franciscan lector, and the author of the poem, *De laude Universitatis Oxoniae* (probably written around 1367–70) which includes a eulogy to Roger Swineshead of Glastonbury, was none other than Richard Trevytlam, O.F.M. In the conflict between the monks and friars, Roger Swineshead may have appeared as an exemplary figure to Trevytlam perhaps because of Swineshead's appreciation for and dependence on Franciscan theology. On Rosetus and the Chigi B. V. 66 manuscript, see V. Doucet, "Le Studium Franciscain de Norwich en 1337 d'après le MS Chigi B. V. 66 de la Bibliothèque Vaticane," *AFH*, XLVI (1953), 89–93; on Roger Swineshead see: J. A. Weisheipl, "Roger Swyneshed, O.S.B., Logician, Natural Philosopher and Theologian," in *Oxford Studies Presented to Daniel Callus*, O.H.S., n.s. XVI, (Oxford 1964) 231–252, and "Ockham and Some Mertonians," *MedStud*, XXX (1968), 207–213.

[10] Rosetus, *Sent.*, q. 1, a. 2 (Oxford, Oriel 15, fjl. 254ra): "Ad illud respondet Bradwardyn quod tam 'a' quam 'b' est falsum..."; Rosetus, *Sent.*, q. 2, a. 3 (Oxford, Oriel 15, fol. 277vb).

[11] Rosetus, *Sent.* I, q. 2, a. 1 (Oxford, Oriel 15, fol. 268rb): "Addit unus valens Adam Wodam quod capacitas animae finita est, et ideo repleri potest per aliquam formam receptabilem in ea, ita quod sit dare maximam formam talis speciei, quia maiorem non [potest] recipere quoad extensionem...." Ibid., fol. 268va.

[12] Anneliese Maier called attention to one citation of Bradwardine in Buckingham's *Sentences* Commentary, Vat. lat. 4353, fol. 50^v: "Ad idem arguo et faciam formam quam fecit doctor noster Bardvardinus [sic!] anno proximo ad istam eandem conclusionem." While it is certain the passage refers to Bradwardine, the fact that the citation is missing in the other manuscripts and in the printed edition suggests, along with the use of the phrase "doctor noster," that it was a later insertion, an example of "marginalia shift" to which Trapp has alerted us. See A. Maier, *Die Vorläufer Galileis im 14. Jahrhundert*, 2nd. ed., Storia et Letteratura, xxii (Rome, 1966), p. 96, n. 27. A reference to Fitzralph is probably intended in the statement in Buckingham's *Sentences,* question 6: "et fuit haec opinio reverendi doctoris, et non diu est cancelarii." J. A. Robson, *Wyclif and the Oxford Schools* (Cambridge, 1961), p. 41, states that Buckingham cites Chatton and Holcot, but without giving references to the Buckingham manuscripts. So far, I have not found Chatton and Holcot cited by name.

was one of the "Pelagians" attacked by Bradwardine, then Buckingham was certainly aware of that fact. In criticizing Bradwardine's thought he describes positions maintained by Wodeham, although he never cites him by name and does not subscribe to his position.

In the years after 1335 there were other critics of Bradwardine in England, but like Buckingham they rarely, if ever, cited Wodeham. One of these was the Franciscan, ALEXANDER LANGELEY. He cited few contemporaries, so it is perhaps not surprising that he failed to cite Wodeham. He did, however, openly criticize Bradwardine by name.[13] Nor does Wodeham appear in the *Sentences* commentaries of NICHOLAS ASTON or OSBERT PICKINGHAM, both of whom lectured at Oxford between 1345 and 1350, probably closer to the later date.[14] In general, Aston adopted Buckingham's practice of not citing by name any source later than Scotus, the only exception being his frequent citations of Bradwardine, under the honorific title "Doctor profundus".[15] Osbert, a Carmelite contemporary of Aston, was somewhat less reticent. He

---

[13] For these citations as well as a biographical sketch of Langeley, see my "Alexander Langeley, O.F.M.," *Manuscripta,* XVIII (1974), 96–104.

[14] It has been suggested that Aston and Pickingham were *socii* and read in 1345. This date was based on the assumption that Buckingham was a *socius* of Osbert (and thus Aston) since they debated each other, and if Buckingham's lectures on the *Sentences* had to be placed between the publication of *De causa Dei* (1344) and his becoming chancellor of Exeter Cathedral (1346), then the date for all three would have to be 1345. But, as was argued in note 11 above, Buckingham had to have read before 1340. We also know that Aston, a fellow of Queen's College, was still a bachelor of theology in 1350 (Cf. Robson, *Wyclif and the Oxford Schools,* p. 106), and thus he must have read the *Sentences* in or shortly before that year. Moreover, Aston refers to Bradwardine as "doctor profundus," an honorific title that does not seem to have come into use until after 1344. Osbert was a close contemporary but may not have read in the same year as Aston. Osbert refers to Buckingham as a master and doctor, and the impression is that he debated Buckingham while the latter was in Oxford, i.e., before 1346 (when Buckingham became chancellor of Exeter Cathedral) or more likely after 1349 (when Buckingham left that post and eventually reappeared in the documents of Merton College). Cf. Robson, *Wyclif and the Oxford Schools,* pp. 11, 46. Gregory of Rimini, John of Mirecourt, Hugolino of Orvieto, and Peter Ceffons, all of whom knew Buckingham and most of the English doctors, never refer to Osbert or Aston. Osbert is first mentioned in 1354 in the *Sentences* Commentary of John Klenkok. Aston is first mentioned in the *Sentences* commentaries of John Hiltalingen of Basel and the anonymous author whose work is found in Vat. lat. 986. Both of those works date around 1365. Osbert also seems to have had a student whose opinions were examined by a papal commission in 1371, an event that again suggests Osbert taught later than 1345.

[15] Oxford, Oriel 15, fols. 214^r, 217^r, 219^v, 220^r, 221^r. These references were first pointed out by Trapp, "Augustinian Theology of the 14th Century," *Augustiniana,* VI (1956), 229.

mentioned Baconthorp, Buckingham, and Aston by name and referred obliquely to Bradwardine. However, he did not cite either Ockham or Wodeham.[16]

Excluding references to *socii*, Wodeham and Bradwardine—the two poles in an important theological controversy—are almost the only two *moderni* cited by English authors in the period from 1334 to 1350. By 1350 Oxford was no longer the great intellectual center it had been in the first half of the fourteenth century, surpassing even Paris. With few exceptions it could claim no men whose reputations traveled outside England, and the intellectual history of the second half of the fourteenth century is strikingly non-English. Intellectual prominence was recaptured by Paris in the years 1340–45, a position which it held until the Great Schism drove German scholars homeward to strengthen newer educational foundations there. But the Parisian dominance from 1340 to 1380 was erected on the foundations of English theology and science, and Adam Wodeham played as important a part in the development of Parisian thought in the third quarter of the fourteenth century as he did in the development of Oxford thought in the second quarter. It was at Paris that Wodeham came to be more fully appreciated, and through Paris he was transmitted to the later Middle Ages. His strong reputation on the Continent is reflected in the distribution of Wodeham manuscripts, only one of which is now found in England.

2. *Paris, 1342–1345*

In contrast to Oxford theologians, there was a willingness on the part of Parisian scholars, at least in the final editions of their lectures on the *Sentences,* to indicate contemporary sources. In that atmosphere citations from Wodeham appear frequently. In fact, almost all Parisian authors between 1342 and 1345 cite Wodeham.

The first of these authors is GREGORY OF RIMINI, who commented on the *Sentences* in 1342–43. The information that can be gleaned from Gregory is far more useful for our purposes than the single citation from Halifax, for Gregory shows extensive and exact knowledge of Wodeham's various lecture series. Among his numerous references to Wodeham, some quotations are designated as coming from the *Lectura Londoniensis,* some from the *Lectura secunda,* and several others without

---

[16] On the life and writings of Osbert see B. M. Xiberta, *De scriptoribus scholasticis saeculi xiv ex ordine Carmelitarum* (Louvain, 1931), pp. 241–284.

any specific identification. The meaning of the *Lectura Londoniensis* is clear, and Gregory is the first author, outside Wodeham himself, to refer to that series of lectures. With the *Lectura secunda* and the undesignated references we encounter a problem. Is *Lectura secunda* another name for the London lectures, a title for the Oxford lectures, or a reference to a third set of lectures? Do the undesignated references come from the same series of lectures or could they be taken from one of several series? Since all of Gregory's references to Wodeham which list no series title conform to what we have in the Oxford lectures, and since most of the references from the *Lectura secunda* and the *Lectura Londoniensis* do not, it is tempting to conjecture that there were in Gregory's time at least three series of Wodeham lectures in circulation on the Continent: the London lectures, the Oxford lectures, and a series called the *Lectura secunda*. This last title might refer to the Norwich lectures (if they were delivered between the London and Oxford lectures) or to a second series of lectures delivered at Oxford or London.

All the references in which Gregory indicates no lecture series conform, either exactly or in paraphrase, with the text of the revised version of the Oxford lectures. In some of these Gregory includes phrases found in the margins of Vat. lat. 955 but which appear in other manuscripts of the pre-1334 redaction. His quotations differ enough in word order to suggest that he may have been citing a slightly different text from the one preserved in either the pre-1334 or the post-1334 redactions. Because of that, it is impossible to judge which of the revised texts he was using. Gregory's familiarity with the Oxford lectures indicates a wide knowledge and a close reading. Gregory paraphrases or quotes directly from Wodeham's prologue, question 2;[17] book I, dist. 1, qq. 10 (twice) and 11 (twice);[18] book II, q. 9;[19] book III, dist. 14, q. 5;[20]

---

[17] Gregory of Rimini, *Super primum et secundum sententiarum* (Venice, 1522; Reprint: St. Bonaventure, 1955), II, 56 J corresponds to Wodeham, *Lectura Oxon.*, prologue, quaest. 2, art. 2, ad dub. 6 (Vat. lat. 955, fol. 11^v f.).

[18] Rimini, II, 97 E–F: "Error Pelagii fuit, quia posuit quod ex puris naturalibus possumus mereri. Hoc autem non dicit opinio tenens partem illam affirmativam. Nam quamvis concedat nos ex puris naturalibus posse elicere bonos actus moraliter, non tamen in potestate nostra est quod Deus illos acceptet ad vitam aeternam, quia hoc semper est de mera gratia sua. . . . Pelagius voluit nos ex puris naturalibus posse implere praecepta divina. Hoc autem est error, quia non est in potestate nostra facere aliquid ex huius praeceptis, cum in potestate nostra non sit quod illa sint praecepta." Wodeham, *Lectura Oxon.* I, dist. 1, q. 10, a. 1 (Vat. lat. 955, fol. 67^v; Paris, Univ. 193, fol. 50ra; Maz. 915, fols. 41va–41vb): "Et cum dicit [Chatton] quod tunc [i.e., if Wodeham's position were accepted] possem ex puris naturalibus implere praeceptum Dei et vitare omnia peccata omissionis et commissionis, dico quod non sequitur, tum quia non est in

and book III, dist. 14, q. 11, dub. 2.[21] The section to which Halifax referred appears in Gregory, but in much greater detail.

As we would expect, neither of Gregory's references to the London lectures corresponds to anything in the Oxford lectures. Both are references to questions from the prologue of that series of lectures and thus provide, alongside Oyta's reference to the same portion of that work, further knowledge of Wodeham's thought and additional clues that may prove helpful in eventually identifying a manuscript of that work.

While the material that Gregory attributes to the London lectures does not occur in the Oxford lectures, it does appear in the Caius College manuscript referred to earlier. Moreover, Gregory's citations from what he knows as the *Lectura secunda* correspond even more closely with the

---

potestate nostra aliquid facere ex huius praecepto, quia non est in potestate nostra quod praeceptum sit; tum quia nec cum caritate nec sine caritate possumus vitare ex communi statu omnia peccata. . . . Concedo tamen quod multa peccata mortalia et etiam venialia vitare posset homo sine caritate infusa, nec propter hoc erravit Pelagius, sed quia dixit quod 'omnia' et quod 'mereri etiam possumus ex puris naturalibus,' ut aestimo et hoc falsum est, quia licet sit in potestate nostra elicere multos actus bonos ex genere, tamen non est in potestate nostra quod Deus illos acceptet ad vitam aeternam, quia hoc semper est de mera gratia sua. . . ." Rimini considered this opinion worse than that of Pelagius. While this passage does not show which redaction Gregory was using, it is certain he was not using the Mazarine manuscript, which dropped a line Gregory has.

Rimini, II, 97 O–P corresponds to *Lectura Oxon.* I, dist. 1, q. 10, a. 1 (Vat. lat. 955, fol. 67^v; Paris, Univ. 193, fol. 49vb). Cf. above, note 8.

Rimini, I, 29 0–30 A corresponds to *Lectura Oxon.* I, dist. 1, q. 11, a. 1 (Vat. lat. 955, fols. 80^v–81^r). The quotations from patristic authority in this section occur in Wodeham, although Rimini has in some cases supplied an exact reference. Some of the material Rimini uses in his response to Wodeham (Rimini, I, 30 G–K) is borrowed from Wodeham; see Vat. lat. 955, fol. 80^v. Rimini, I, 31 B–C corresponds to *Lectura Oxon.* I, dist. 1, q. 11, a. 1 (Vat. lat. 955, fols. 81^r–81^v). Unfortunately for our purposes, Rimini does not quote from those sections that were altered in the post-1334 redaction.

[19] Rimini, I, 113 D, 115 D–117 A depends, in part, on Wodeham, *Lectura Oxon.* II, q. 9 (Vat. lat. 1110, fols. 36^r–40^v; Paris, Maz. 915, fols. 163ra–166rb; Paris, Univ. 193, fols. 169rb–172rb).

[20] Rimini, I, 166 D corresponds to *Lectura Oxon.* III, dist. 14, q. 5, dub. 2 (Paris, Maz. 915, fol. 182^r f.).

[21] Rimini, II, 36 P–Q: "Quidam vero doctor alius solvit praedictam rationem dicendo quod non est simul dandum quod in continuo sint huiusmodi partes proportionales infinitae et quod omnes possint illo modo in certo tempore transiri cum talibus quietibus interceptis." Wodeham, *Lectura Oxon.* III, dist. 14, q. 10, dub. 2 (Paris, Univ. 193, fol. 200ra; Paris, Maz. 915, fol. 191va): "Istud argumentum bene probat quod non est simul dandum esse in continuo dando partes huiusmodi proportionales infinitas et quod omnes possint isto modo in certo tempore transiri cum talibus quietibus interceptis, sicut imaginatur argumentum."

Caius manuscript. Since Gregory's citations seem to hold the key to identifying the Caius manuscript and placing it within what we know of Wodeham's life, this problem must be examined in detail, evaluating all possible theories carefully.

First, could Gregory be using two titles for the same work? Could the Caius manuscript contain the first book of the London lectures which, if they were delivered between the Norwich lectures (his first?) and the Oxford lectures (his third and final reading?) might also have circulated under the name *Lectura secunda*? Would this not explain why material cited from the London lectures by Gregory can be found in Caius 281, why that manuscript contains references that point ahead to future discussions,[22] and why Fitzralph, whom Wodeham may not yet have read when he lectured in London, is not cited in the Caius manuscript?

Attractive as this theory might be, the weight of the evidence is against it. The London lectures, either as cited in Wodeham's Oxford lectures or as known and read in the fourteenth century do not correspond to the Cambridge manuscript. At the opening of the third book of the Oxford lectures, Wodeham states that he lectured for a year on the first thirteen distinctions of book III at London.[23] All of Wodeham's fifty some odd references to his London lectures, with one possible exception, are to the third book.[24] Gregory refers to questions 2 and 7 of the prologue, and Oyta refers to the prologue, quest. 9, and to the third book. There are no references within or outside Wodeham to books I, II, or IV of the London lectures. All that we know, and it is considerable, suggests that they consisted solely of a lengthy prologue (at least nine questions) and a commentary on the first thirteen distinctions of book III. Neither of those features are found in the Caius manuscript, whose prologue has only six questions and whose commentary is devoted exclusively to book I. The division in the Caius manuscript between the prologue and dist. 1 is the intended structure and not a scribal error.[25] But the form in which the London lectures circulated and were read by later authors

---

[22] For example, Cambridge, Caius 281, fol. 246va: "Et ego nondum tractavi materiam de univocatione entis, ideo differo hanc difficultatem donec istam materiam pertractem...."

[23] See above, chapter one, note 48.

[24] The one possible exception is a reference Wodeham makes to opinions he held in London (Paris, Univ. 193, fol. 133ra). There is no indication of a particular book.

[25] Cambridge, Caius 281, fol. 128rb: "Habito ex quinta quaestione quod..., nunc sexta quaero et ultimo quoad prologum...."

had a prologue of at least nine questions. Consequently, Rimini and Oyta could never have cited the London lectures as they did if they were using a manuscript that resembled the Caius manuscript.

It must also be noted that Gregory of Rimini was careful about his sources. He did not quote the same work under two separate names, and he seldom made errors when he gave an exact reference. However, of the two citations Gregory provides from the London lectures, neither is found in the Caius manuscript at the location given by Gregory. For example, the material Gregory locates as coming from quest. 2 of the prologue does not occur at that point, although the substance of the passage can be found in quest. 1.[26] But Gregory's citation has all the appearance of a direct quotation, which cannot be found at all in the Caius manuscript. Similarly, Gregory's reference to the seventh question of the prologue can be found in the Caius manuscript, verbatim, at quest. 7, art. 2, but only if one disregards the shift from the prologue to dist. 1 and simply counts the number of questions from the beginning of the manuscript.[27]

To those points must be added several other facts. The Caius manuscript cites William Skelton, who read concurrently with Wodeham at Oxford.[28] Moreover, that manuscript contains material from the Oxford lectures in a form that postdates 1334,[29] and the London lectures are repeatedly cited in books III and IV of the Oxford lectures, which were given before 1334. Finally, the Caius manuscript, as was noted in chapter one, cites the London lectures.

Although the Caius manuscript cannot, therefore, be identical with the London lectures, it does contain material directly borrowed from the London lectures, at least in its prologue and the early questions of dist. 1. Thus, although we may not yet have the London lectures in their proper form, we do have portions of those lectures on topics of considerable importance to Wodeham studies.

---

[26] Compare Rimini, II, 88 B with Cambridge, Caius 281, fol. 105vb; cf. 108vb.

[27] Rimini, I, 13 K: "Tertio: sic esse sicut significatur per conclusionem dependet a sic esse sicut significatur per praemissas in essendo; igitur et in cognoscibile essendo. Nam unumquodque sicut se habet ad entitatem, ita se habet ad veritatem et scibilitatem, secundo *Metaphysicae*." Cambridge, Caius 281, fol. 131va: "Item: sic esse sicut significatur per conclusionem dependet a sic esse sicut significatur per praemissas in essendo; igitur et in cognoscibile essendo. Nam unumquodque sicut se habet ad entitatem, sic se habet et ad veritatem et scibilitatem, ex secundo *Metaphysicae*." The quotation from Peter Aureol (Rimini, I, 13 L) was borrowed from Wodeham, fol. 131va.

[28] Cambridge, Caius 281, fol. 142ra.

[29] *Lectura secunda*, dist. 1, q. 4 (fols. 137va–145vb).

A second possibility is that the Caius manuscript contains the Norwich lectures of Wodeham, as Michalski eventually concluded. Michalski's theory, however, was based on the false assumption that the Norwich lectures followed rather than preceded the Oxford lectures. All the information we have on the Norwich lectures indicates that they included or were entirely composed of questions on the last three distinctions of book III and much of book IV. Again, no such material is found in the Caius manuscript. Moreover, since some of the text of the Caius manuscript conforms to the post-1334 version of the Oxford lectures, that manuscript cannot contain the Norwich lectures, which precede book I of the Oxford lectures. However, in view of the extensive discussion of the Trinity in the Caius manuscript, it is possible that, as with the London lectures, this manuscript contains questions from the Norwich lectures, which dealt largely with that theme.

When we compare Gregory's references to the *Lectura secunda* with the Caius manuscript a surprising fact emerges. Not only can Gregory's quotations from Wodeham's *Lectura secunda* be found there verbatim, but the location of the quotations corresponds exactly with the structure of the Caius manuscript.[30] Therefore, while Gregory's citations from both the *Lectura Londoniensis* and the *Lectura secunda* can be found in the Caius manuscript, only the *Lectura secunda* citations can be found at the *place* cited. It is true that one of Gregory's citations from the *Lectura secunda* also appears in the Oxford lectures, but this occurs at a point where the Oxford lectures and the Caius manuscript are parallel both in content and structure.[31]

What are we to conclude from this? The logical deduction is that the lectures contained in the Caius manuscript are identical with the work Gregory knew as the *Lectura secunda*. But before accepting this explanation, one final possibility must be examined. Could not the Caius manuscript be a *textus conflatus,* a collection of questions from other works? Could it not be that the Caius' *Lectura*, composed after 1334, drew upon

---

[30] For example, Rimini (I, 3 M) has a marginal note: "Adam in secunda lectura, quaest. 6 prologi in fine." The entire passage (3 M—N) is found at that point in the Caius manuscript, fols. 128ra–128rb. Similarly, Rimini's reference (I, 36 G–H) to the *Lectura secunda,* prologue, quaest. 4, corresponds to the Caius manuscript, fol. 117va. This last reference was located by Fr. Gedeon Gál.

[31] Rimini, I, 25 H–L, refers to the *Lectura secunda,* I, dist. 1, q. 3 and the quotation can be found in Caius 281, fol. 140va (listed as question 4 in the manuscript but question 3 in order; see appendix three) and also in the *Lectura Oxon.* I, dist. 1, q. 3, a. 2, concl. 2 (Vat. lat. 955, fols. 24^v–25^r).

earlier works, upon the London lectures, the Norwich lectures (=*Lectura secunda*?), and the Oxford lectures, as revised after 1334? Perhaps it is sheer coincidence that the questions from the *Lectura secunda* are found in the same place in the Caius manuscript, while those from the London lectures are not.

This fourth theory explains the mixture of materials from various periods in Wodeham's career, but it does not explain the structure and style of the Caius manuscript, nor does it explain what the title *Lectura secunda* could mean if it does not refer to the Caius manuscript. First, as was argued in chapter one, the Caius manuscript is a separate commentary on book I of the *Sentences*. Both in its style and in the frequent internal cross references it reveals itself to be a distinct work of Wodeham, not a compilation assembled by some scribe or later disciple. It has features that can only have resulted from oral presentation, although Wodeham incorporated material from earlier lectures. Second, one of Gregory's citations from the *Lectura secunda* is exactly one of those sections of the Oxford lectures that appears in the Caius manuscript.[32] The particular passage that Gregory cites was left unchanged in the second redaction, but it is a passage that must have originated with the Oxford lectures, since it depends not only on Wodeham's debate with Fitzralph but upon Fitzralph's *Opus correctum*. If Gregory could quote under the title *Lectura secunda* a passage that could not have existed before the Oxford lectures, then the *Lectura secunda* cannot be the Norwich lectures but must also date after the Oxford lectures.

If we are to avoid positing pluralities without necessity, we may safely assume that the *Lectura* of the Caius manuscript and the *Lectura secunda* referred to by Gregory are identical. But when were they delivered and to what audience? Because the Caius' text contains the revisions that were made subsequent to the Oxford lectures, the completion of Wodeham's theological studies at Oxford becomes the *terminus post quem* for the *Lectura secunda,* namely 1334. Gregory's citations from this work place the *terminus ante quem* at 1342 or slightly earlier, allowing time for knowledge of the work (and at least one copy) to reach Paris.

The location of the lectures is limited by the title Gregory knew: *Lectura secunda*. These cannot be the second lectures Wodeham ever gave, since they were delivered after the Oxford lectures and were, therefore, at least the fourth series of lectures on the *Sentences*. So, in what

---

[32] Compare Rimini, I, 25 H–L; Vat. lat. 955, fols. 24^v–25^r; Paris, Univ. 193, fol. 19ra; Cambridge, Caius 281, fol. 140va.

sense were they Adam's "second" lectures? The most likely solution is that they were the second lectures on the *Sentences* that Wodeham gave in a particular place. Since Gregory was distinguishing them from a lecture series he already knew, they are probably either the second London lectures or the second Oxford lectures.

At this point it is well to return to the introduction that prefaced the post-1334 redaction of the Oxford lectures.[33] According to that statement, the second redaction of the Oxford lectures, known as the *collectio brevis*, was based on his original Oxford lectures but included material from lectures given elsewhere and from lectures given subsequently. The "lectures given elsewhere" could be either the Norwich or the London lectures, or possibly an earlier series unknown to us, although that seems unlikely. If the "lectures given subsequently" means subsequent to the Oxford lectures and not subsequently to the "lectures given elsewhere", then these "later" lectures are in all probability the *Lectura secunda*. In the Bruges manuscript version of this *introductio*, the "lectures given elsewhere" and the "lectures given subsequently" are the same, which might well suggest a site other than Oxford: probably London.

The evidence is on the side of locating the *Lectura secunda* in London or some other custodial school between 1334 and 1340. While *Quaestiones ordinariae super Sententias* may, on rare occasions, have occurred in the fourteenth century, and while it is true that Wodeham, in his first *collatio* in the Caius manuscript speaks of the four books of the *Sentences* "de quorum praerogativa inter doctores",[34] the way Wodeham follows through book I, distinction by distinction, suggests that he was still a bachelor of theology at the time this work was written. Moreover, the Caius manuscript contains a reference to Oxford that would be more appropriate for a non-Oxford audience.[35]

Whatever the audience of the *Lectura secunda,* some of the questions, perhaps many of them, were written earlier. We have already noted the material borrowed from the London and Oxford lectures, and the possibility that it may contain material from the Norwich lectures as well. Perhaps a comparison of the text of the later portions of the *Lectura secunda* with Wodeham's description of the positions he maintained in the Norwich lectures will uncover a valuable correspondence.

Two years after Gregory read the *Sentences* at Paris, three others

---

[33] See Appendix two, page 203.
[34] Cambridge, Caius 281, fol. 105rb.
[35] Ibid., fol. 124rb.

read whose works are available to us: the Italian Carmelite, Paul of Perugia (Perusino); the Spanish Augustinian, Alphonsus Vargas of Toledo; and the French Cistercian, John of Mirecourt.

The first of these, PAUL OF PERUGIA, does not mention Wodeham, although he does cite Ockham.[36] Why this happens is difficult to say, for Paul was not reticent about naming bachelors or doctors close to his own age. Moreover, he seems to have been especially fond of the Franciscan tradition, citing, in addition to Ockham, Aureol, Landulph, Mayronnis, Francis of Marchia, and Peter John Olivi. Moreover, both of the English writers cited, namely Ockham and Burley, are cited favorably. Recent doctors, however, do not figure largely in his Commentary, and his reliance on the English tradition is minor.

When we turn to ALPHONSUS VARGAS we encounter a person familiar with Wodeham, but one who makes less extensive use of him than did Gregory.[37] The quotations from Wodeham that appear in Vargas indicate a first-hand knowledge and a fresh reading of his work. The Augustinian Vargas did not borrow Rimini's footnotes. In the only quotation from Wodeham they share, a reference to book I, dist. 1, q. 3 of the Oxford lectures, Alphonsus knows that it is article 2 (information not given in Gregory) and his quotation follows the text of the Wodeham manuscripts available to us at points where Gregory's quotation departs from it.[38] It would appear that Vargas may have brought Gregory's occasional paraphrase or re-wording back into line with the text of Wodeham. The remainder of Vargas' quotations do not parallel those selected by Gregory.[39] Moreover, there is no evidence that Vargas was familiar with the London lectures.

A third bachelor commenting at Paris in 1344–45 was JOHN OF MIRECOURT, the contents of whose *Sentences* Commentary provided the propositions that were condemned by the theological faculty of Paris in 1347 and thus formed the basis for the second, or new list of Parisian

---

[36] See B. M. Xiberta, *De scriptoribus,* pp. 285–316.

[37] J. Kürzinger, *Alfonsus Vargas Toletanus und seine theologische Einleitungslehre,* BB, xxii. 5–6 (Münster i.W., 1930). D. Trapp, "Augustinian Theology," *Augustiniana,* VI (1956), 213–222.

[38] Alphonsus Vargas of Toledo, *In primum sententiarum* (Venice, 1490; Reprint: New York, 1952), col. 183 corresponds to *Lectura Oxon.* I, dist. 1, q. 3, a. 2, concl. 2 (Vat. lat. 955, fols. 24^v–25^r). As was stated above, this passage also occurs in the Caius manuscript.

[39] Vargas, col. 236 corresponds to *Lectura Oxon.* I, dist. 1, q. 9, a. 1, concl. 8 (designated incorrectly in the Vargas text as q. 7) (Vat. lat. 955, fol. 60^r–60^v); Vargas, col. 301 corresponds to *Lectura Oxon.* I, dist. 1, q. 14, a. 2 (1512 edition, fol. 46^v).

condemned articles.⁴⁰ Mirecourt shows a greater familiarity with English theologians than did Vargas and a stronger interest in those of recent vintage. In the margins and occasionally in the text of his *Sentences* Commentary appear the names of Rodington, Fitzralph, Holcot, Wodeham, Bradwardine, Halifax, and Buckingham. However, his familiarity with and use of English sources is far greater than these references reflect. In his question on the fruition of God Mirecourt uses and criticizes the arguments of Wodeham, which were rapidly becoming a familiar part of such discussions.⁴¹ In the ninth question of his second book Mirecourt paraphrases a section of Wodeham, book II, question four of the Oxford lectures.⁴² His use of Wodeham at that point is favorable. The uniqueness of this second quotation tells us that Mirecourt, like Halifax, Rimini, and Vargas, had direct access to the Wodeham texts.

On the basis of the foregoing discussion one can say that the texts of most of Wodeham's works must have been available in Paris by 1340, certainly before 1342. Some of these works were probably in the library of the Austin Friars. If the close relationship noted by Trapp between the Augustinians and Cistercians at Paris dates back to this period, Mirecourt may have had access to the same library Rimini used. This may also explain why English authors are so seldom cited by the Carmelite bachelor of 1344. Rimini, Vargas, and Mirecourt had read at least portions of Wodeham's Oxford lectures in the form of the *Ordinatio* or the post-1334 redaction. It is possible that one of the texts they used is among the three manuscripts of these redactions still extant at Paris. One of those is in a gothic cursive that shows English influence and the other two are in *littera Parisiensis,* all dating from the middle of the fourteenth century or slightly earlier. Moreover, Rimini was familiar with the text of the London lectures and of the *Lectura secunda,* which must also have been available in Paris or, at least, on the Continent, since

---

[40] On Mirecourt see G. Tessier, "Jean de Mirecourt," in *HLF*, XL, offprint issued separately (Paris, 1966); W. J. Courtenay, "John of Mirecourt and Gregory of Rimini on Whether God can Undo the Past," *RTAM*, XXXIX (1972), 224–256; XL (1973), 147–174.

[41] Mirecourt, *Sent.* I, q. 14 (Krakow 1184, fol. 35^r): "Argumentum Adae de Wodeham." Cited in A. Birkenmajer, "Ein Rechtfertigungsschreiben Johanns von Mirecourt," in *Vermischte Untersuchungen, mittelalt. Philos.,* No. 4, BB, xx.5 (Münster i.W., 1922), p. 96.

[42] Mirecourt, *Sent.* II, q. 9 (Paris, B. N. lat. 15 883, fol. 45va; Bologna, Archiginnasio A 921, fol. 81vb; Lilienfeld 148, fol. 200ra).

as far as we know Rimini never traveled to England. If Wodeham had made some impression on English theology in the 1330's, his impact on Parisian theology was even stronger. His reputation continued to grow in the next academic generation at Paris.

3. *Cologne, 1335-1348*

Before continuing with the development at Paris in the next generation, we must consider the presence of Wodeham's thought at one other Continental center of learning: Cologne. It has generally been assumed that the spread of Ockham's philosophical and theological thought into Germany came by way of Paris in the 1380's. "O felix schisma," as Henry of Langenstein phrased it,[43] brought back to German universities some of the best minds of that age, all trained in Parisian thought. And most of them had a thorough knowledge of—and sympathy for—the philosophical and theological ideas of Ockham and his followers, particularly Adam Wodeham.

But the presence of Ockhamist thought in Germany is much earlier and may have its own history there, apart from Parisian influence. Ockham's presence in Munich during the last twenty years of his life may have had some effect, although his concerns during that period were almost exclusively political and ecclesiological. There is evidence that Wodeham was in Basel in 1339,[44] and the Lüneburg sub-redaction of Wodeham's *Ordinatio*, the only copies of which are found in Germany, was done before 1350.[45]

The most interesting evidence, however, comes from Cologne, where a disciple of Wodeham, probably a Franciscan and possibly English (considering his love of Wodeham and knowledge of Campsale) read the *Sentences* before 1348 *secundum Adam*. The redaction of Wodeham's Oxford Commentary contained in the manuscripts from Hannover and Naples is an *Extractio* within which one finds, interspersed in the reduced Wodeham text, the comments of the person "rereading." In the dating passage discussed in chapter one, the compiler of the *Extractio* replaced

---

[43] Henry of Langenstein, Letter to Friedrich von Brixen, ed. Gustav Sommerfeldt, "Zwei Schismatraktate Heinrich von Langenstein," *Mitteilungen des Institut für österr. Geschichtsforschung*, Erg.–Bd. VII (1904), 469; Letter to Count Ruprecht, ed. Gustav Sommerfeldt, "Ruprecht III. von der Pfalz und die deutsche Publizistik," *Zeitschrift für Geschichte des Oberrheins*, XXII (1907), 311.

[44] *Analecta Franciscana*, II (1887), 177; III (1897), 630, 631, 637.

[45] See chapter one, p. 13 and appendix one, pp. 198–201.

the example of the then reigning pope with a certain "Comes Adolphus de Monte."[46] Berg (Mons), on whose western edge Cologne was situated, ceased to be a county in 1380, after which time it was not held separately, and in any case its possessor would be referred to as "dux" (Herzog), not "comes" (Graf).[47] Between the time Wodeham read the *Sentences* at Oxford and the end of the County of Berg, there was only one Count Adolf, namely Adolf IX, who reigned from 1308 to 1348. That places the *Extractio* between 1334 and 1348. Moreover, the example would only be meaningful for an academic audience located in or near the County of Berg. Cologne is the only place that fits this description.

From this discovery several important things follow. Wodeham was known in at least one German *studium* before his death. Therefore Wodeham was not only being read at Paris by 1342, but was known in some parts of Germany in the same period, long before he was cited by John of Basel and long before Henry Totting of Oyta made an *Abbreviatio* of his work. Moreover, he was not simply being read, but one theologian was reading lectures *secundum Adam,* a fact that speaks for the high reputation of Wodeham on the one hand and, on the other, establishes that the practice of *lecturae secundum alium* goes back before the middle of the fourteenth century.

Perhaps most important, however, is the fact that these lectures were being read at Cologne, a center that comes to be associated with the *via antiqua,* with Albertism and Thomism, in the fifteenth century. The date and location of this *Extractio* may be connected with Ockham's presence at Munich or Wodeham's brief presence at Basel in this period. But it may also indicate that the channel of academic contact between Oxford and Cologne, already there in John Duns Scotus, remained open and alive in the fourteenth century, bringing newer ideas and works directly from England to Germany. In combination with the fact that Gabriel Biel in the mid-fifteenth century acquired the works of Ockham (and perhaps much of his Ockhamism) at Cologne and not at Heidelberg or Erfurt as once imagined, we should perhaps not see Cologne as a center exclusively devoted to the *via antiqua* (except for the period 1415–1425) but as a center that remained, despite official pronouncements to the

---

[46] Naples, Bibl. Naz., Cod. VII C 53, fols. 80^(va)–80^(vb); Hannover, Stadtbibliothek, Cod. 1, fol. 24^(va).

[47] Wilhelm Karl Prinz von Isenburg, *Stamm-Tafeln zur Geschichte der europäischen Staaten,* I (Berlin, 1936), tables 186–188; Hellmuth Rössler and Günther Franz, *Sachwörterbuch zur deutschen Geschichte* (München, 1958).

contrary, interested in Ockham and his followers and was perhaps even an important source for the dissemination of Ockhamism within German universities and lesser *studia*.

B. WODEHAM IN THE AFTERMATH OF THE CONDEMNATIONS OF 1346 AND 1347

Inasmuch as Wodeham was one of the sources for the thought of Mirecourt and part of the highly speculative discussion of philosophical and theological topics at Paris in the years before 1347, one might expect that Wodeham's reputation would have suffered through the condemnations that occurred in 1346, 1347 and, probably, across the next two or three years. If a quieter, less critical atmosphere were desired, would not Wodeham be among the first authors to be expunged?

Interestingly enough, Wodeham's name was one of those that remained in discussion when other names began to drop out. Moreover, Wodeham was not attacked as a radical or unorthodox mind. Instead, he was quoted favorably as an authority of great value, even by those who have been placed within the more conservative, Augustinian tradition in the fourteenth century.

PETER CEFFONS was a Cistercian whose respect for Mirecourt and dislike for the instigators of his condemnation, although veiled in cautious and sometimes cryptic language, show through his Commentary on the *Sentences* (1348–49).[48] Ceffons' references to Wodeham are favorable, although he does not link his name with Mirecourt in any way. For Ceffons, Wodeham is one of the chief authorities of the previous academic generation, alongside Landulph, Buckingham, and Rimini. Ceffons shares the interest in and respect for English theologians already found in Rimini, Vargas, and Mirecourt. In fact, Ceffons shows a greater familiarity with English theologians after Ockham than any of his Parisian predecessors. He shows a firsthand knowledge of Ockham, Chatton, Rodington, Fitzralph, Holcot, Wodeham, Kilvington, Bradwardine, Halifax, Buckingham, and Langeley, thus missing only Crathorn (who seems to have been unread at Paris) and Pickingham and Aston, who were just then reading the *Sentences* at Oxford.

Ceffons' references to Wodeham reveal that certain changes had taken place in the form of Wodeham citations since the time of Rimini.

---

[48] D. Trapp, "Peter Ceffons of Clairvaux," *RTAM*, XXIV (1957), 101–154.

Ceffons' quotations from Wodeham, often of considerable length, are exclusively devoted to problems of epistemology.[49] Several of these quotations are identified as coming from the *Lectura prima,* a designation for a lecture series of Wodeham that appears for the first time in Ceffons' Commentary. Beyond an occasional "in prima lectura," the locations of his Wodeham citations are not further identified. From their content it is clear they do not come from the Oxford lectures. Indeed, one quotation can be found in the Caius manuscript in that portion that seems to have been borrowed from the London lectures.[50] Since Ceffons gives no precise references, it is difficult to know whether he was referring to the lectures contained in the Caius manuscript or to the earlier London lectures. The latter would appear more likely, a conclusion supported by the fact that from this period on we encounter many references to the *Lectura prima* but few references to the *Lectura Londoniensis.* It should also be noted here that Ceffons' quotations from Wodeham do not appear among earlier citations and thus reflect a fresh reading. It must be added, however, that Ceffons only had access to or was only interested in the prologue to the London lectures, whether he read it in its original form in the London lectures (which seems likely) or in the *Lectura secunda.*

A contemporary of Ceffons who read the *Sentences* at Paris in the same year (1348–49) was HUGOLINO MALABRANCHA OF ORVIETO, a conservative Austin Friar whose devotion to the theology of Augustine was matched only by Bradwardine and Rimini.[51] For Hugolino, Wodeham is an important authority, one whose opinions are to be weighed alongside those of Ockham, Holcot, Rimini, and Vargas. However, he is

---

[49] Ceffons, *Sent.* I, q. 18 (on dist. 2) (Troyes 62, fol. 45ra): "Ad illud arguit sic Adam in *prima lectura.* . . ." Ibid. (Troyes 62, fol. 45vb): "Contra hoc sunt argumenta alterius opinionis quae recitat Adam in *prima lectura.*" Ceffons, *Sent.* I, q. 20 (on dist. 3) (Troyes 62, fol. 47rb): "Primam conclusionem probat Adam, et est argumentum Scoti, L. IV, dist. 45, q. 3, et Ockham. . . ." Ceffons, *Sent.* I, q. 21 (on dist. 3) (Troyes 62, fol. 47va): "Sed tamen videtur mihi cum aliis quod oppositum potest teneri. Unde arguitur, sic[ut] per Adam. . . ." Ibid.: "Ad hoc dicat Adam quod omnis actus incomplexus qui natus est causare evidentiam. . . ." Ibid. (Troyes 62, fol. 48ra): "Ergo ea posuerunt Adam, Chatton, et Gregorius. . . ."

[50] In question 18 (Troyes 62, fol. 45vb) Ceffons cites Wodeham's and Chatton's discussion of Aureol's seven examples of mistakes in vision based on experience. This material is found in Cambridge, Caius 281, fols. 113^r–113^v (prol., q. 3) and in fol. 118^v (prol., q. 4).

[51] On Hugolino's sources see: A. Zumkeller, *Hugolin von Orvieto und seine theologische Erkenntnislehre,* Cassiciacum, ix.2 (Würzburg, 1941), pp. 255–262; D. Trapp, "Augustinian Theology," *Augustiniana,* VI, 222–223.

more critical of Wodeham's thought than was Ceffons. Furthermore, his interests lie with the theology of Wodeham, not his epistemology. Hugolino returns to the one topic in Wodeham touched on by Halifax, Rosetus, Rimini, Vargas, and Mirecourt, namely the fruition and dilectation of God, the psychological nature of that act, and the power of man to create it.[52] Hugolino does not borrow his material on Wodeham from someone else but reflects his own reading of the Oxford lectures, either in the full redaction or in that form in which they appeared in the *Lectura secunda*.

C. Parisian Theology, 1349–1364

Our sources for Parisian theology in the fifteen years between 1349 and 1364 are severely limited. Few works remain from those lecturing and writing in this period. This paucity of documentation should not be attributed solely or even primarily to the Black Death. In contrast to England, where the plague terminated the careers of a large number of distinguished intellectuals, all of those known to us at Paris seem to have survived it, including Autrecourt and Mirecourt. However, by 1350 most of those whose names had dominated the history of the University of Paris in the 1340's had left Paris, and their place was taken by those less well-known to us, whose style of writing differed markedly.

The Franciscan masters, James of Spinello and Astensius, remained at Paris during these years, but their works, of which only fragments survive, were written before 1349.[53] Our best access to their thought still lies in the comments about them by their contemporaries.[54] No doubt because of the importance of its content, the work of Nicholas of Oresme fared better. But what remains are the Aristotelian commentaries and the scientific treatises, not his theology. He failed to leave behind him a *Sentences* commentary, and his short treatise on the *communicatio idiomatum* never cites contemporary sources.

---

[52] Hugolino, *Sent.* I, dist. 1, q. 1, a. 4 (Paris, B. N. lat. 15 840, fols. 23vb and 24va); *Sent.* I, dist. 1, q. 5, a. 4 (Paris, B. N. lat. 15 840, fol. 37va).

[53] The only fragment of Spinello's Commentary discovered to date is found in Madrid, Univ. 58 (118 Z 16), fols. 107^v–122^v. I hope in a future article to describe the content of that work. The *principium* and *collatio* of Astensius of St. Colombe can be found in Graz, Univ. 836, fols. 81^r–90^r.

[54] For example, in Ceffons, who read the *Sentences* in the same year as Astensius and was also familiar with Spinello, or in the anonymous commentary found in Vat. lat. 986, to be discussed below.

More important for our purposes is JOHN OF RIPA, who studied under (and eventually criticized) Astensius. In his *Lectura* and in the *Conclusiones* extracted from it, Ripa makes only veiled references to scholastic authorities after Scotus and Aureol. André Combes had established that Ripa was familiar with the thought of Ockham, Bradwardine, and Rimini.[55] To those sources Janet Coleman has recently added Burley, Francis of Marchia, John Dumbleton, and possibly Roger Swineshead.[56] Of these earlier writers Ripa relies most heavily on the Parisian doctors: Burley, Marchia, and Rimini. However, these figures are seldom cited in the text of Ripa itself.[57] In his magisterial *Determinationes* Ripa was more inclined to name contemporaries (usually by initial) and once mentions Rimini.[58] However, nowhere in his works have I found a citation from Wodeham.

Even more cautious and uncontroversial was the Augustinian, JOHN KLENKOK, lecturing at Oxford in 1354–55.[59] Although I have only glanced at his Commentary on the *Sentences,* it is unlikely that he would have mentioned Wodeham. Klenkok's work is a sober, technical *Expositio litteralis,* a form of presentation which, unlike the more speculative *quaestio* form, provided little or no opportunity for references to contemporary opinion. In any event, Klenkok's work provides no clue to the reputation of Wodeham at Paris in these years.

Another commentary on the *Sentences* available to us is that of the Augustinian FACINUS DE AST (1361–63).[60] It is marked by an absence of citations from contemporary authorities or authors, either in the text or in the margins. Cautiously, Facinus does not appear to cite any scholastic

---

[55] John of Ripa, *Lectura super primum sententiarum. Prologi quaestiones I & II,* ed. A. Combes, Textes philosophiques du moyen âge, VIII (Paris, 1961).

[56] J. Coleman, "Jean de Ripa, O.F.M. and the Oxford Calculators," *MedStud,* XXXVII (1975), 130–189.

[57] In referring to Ripa's numerous citations from Rimini, Coleman (pp. 133, 141) was referring to citations of Rimini's position, not his name. Coleman has, however, found one passage (Paris, B. N. lat. 15 369, fol. 248vb) in which Marchia and Burley are cited by name in the text. The name of Rimini appears once in the *Conclusiones,* but it was introduced by the extractor, not by Ripa.

[58] John of Ripa, *Determinationes,* ed. André Combes, Textes philosophiques du moyen âge, IV (Paris, 1957), p. 228. For references to contemporaries see pp. 160, 308, 310, and 323.

[59] For an excellent discussion of Klenkok's work see D. Trapp, "Augustinian Theology," *Augustiniana,* VI, 223–239.

[60] On Facinus, see Trapp, "Augustinian Theology," *Augustiniana,* VI, 239–242. I have examined Erfurt, CA 2° 115 for fourteenth-century references, but without success.

author later than Scotus, although he was speculative and creative in his own right, as was Ripa (the citations from Facinus in Hiltalingen and Langenstein reflect this). This is possibly a distinguishing feature of commentaries in this period.

Such caution is less evident in the commentary of the Italian Carmelite MICHAEL AIGUANI, who lectured on the *Sentences* at Paris in 1362–63.[61] Among the authors later than Scotus, Michael mentions Mayronnis, Landulph, Monachus (Albus or Niger?), and his fellow Carmelites Paul of Perugia and Osbert Pickingham. Of these only Pickingham is English, and he is no doubt included more for his Order than for his country of origin. Neither Ockham nor Wodeham, nor any of the other English doctors, for that matter, are cited by Michael.

Another author who probably belongs to this period at Paris is the Lotharingian Franciscan, ANDREW OF NEUFCHATEAU.[62] Andrew was familiar with the articles of Paris compiled between 1347 and 1354.[63] He also seems to be the Andrew referred to in a work that can be dated around 1365 or shortly before.[64] Andrew's work, not among the great contributions to the history of medieval thought, is distinguished in part by the total absence of references to authorities later than the twelfth century.

Since so few fourteenth-century authors are mentioned in the works of this period, we cannot assume Wodeham was neglected for any special reason. But there is a more important problem here. What is one to make of this almost total reluctance to mention recent authors? Was it a fear of controversy, a fear of possible condemnation? Or were the commentaries of this period left in their original, bachelor form as read, in which the discussion, particularly the identification, of contemporary opinion was strongly discouraged?

I think we can dismiss the idea that we are dealing with a return to an earlier, more conservative style of commentary as part of a reaction of

---

[61] For the life and writings of Aiguani see B. M. Xiberta, *De scriptoribus*, pp. 324–393.

[62] The first book of the *Sentences* of Andreas of Novo Castro was printed in Paris in 1514. No manuscripts of it have been discovered. Book II would appear to be contained in one manuscript, Colmar 232, at least the work is attributed to Novo Castro on the cover, and the style is almost identical with that found in the printed edition of book I. On Andrew see: H. Elie, *Le complexe significabile* (Paris, 1936), pp. 229–252; A. de Novo Castro, *De conceptione Virginis gloriosae*, ed. T. Szabó, Bibliotheca Franciscana Scholastica Medii Aevi, Vol. XVI (Quaracchi, 1954), 103–232.

[63] Andrew of Neufchâteau, *In primum sententiarum*, dist. 45, q. 6 (Paris, 1514), fol. 216^r.

[64] Vat. lat. 986, fols. 15^r, 94^v, 97^v.

insecurity or repentance occasioned by the trauma of the Black Death.⁶⁵ Neither Hugolino nor Ceffons, both of whom witnessed the event, had any such reaction to it. Nor should we consider this style a product of an atmosphere of caution born out of the condemnation of 1347, although this possibility seems more likely. Those responsible for the condemnation of Mirecourt and the preparation of the new Parisian articles were concerned about statements of the author, not about whom he quoted. Moreover, although Ripa cites little recent opinion, his Commentary was sufficiently creative and controversial to bring about a condemnation of certain of his theses. If we are safe in assuming the surviving commentaries to be typical of those written in this period, we must assume that we are dealing with a practice possibly promoted through a more rigorous application of the university statutes discouraging bachelors from citing (and disagreeing with) living masters. In this case it was interpreted as a prohibition against citing any of the *moderni*, a phrase that originally meant "contemporary" but which was coming to mean any author later than Scotus.

D. The Return of Marginalia, 1365–1400

The period after 1365 witnessed two important changes at the University of Paris. German scholars, who had always been present at Paris but who had not ranked among the leading figures at the university since the days of Albert, dominated the theological faculty until 1380, in quality if not in actual numbers. Further, the practice of structuring *Sentences* commentaries around the various conflicting opinions of previous and contemporary authors, and placing one's own ideas in such a controversial setting, was renewed.

One of the first works to evidence this return to citation is the anonymous *Sentences* Commentary contained in Vat. Lat. 986, probably written some time between 1360 and 1365.⁶⁶ In all, this author cited 38

---

⁶⁵ Millard Meiss argued for a change in mood in the art of Florence and Siena from 1350 to 1375, part of which was a return to a more conservative style. See *Painting in Florence and Siena after the Black Death* (Princeton, 1951). Some scholars, however, have argued that many of the characteristics to which Meiss pointed can be found before 1348 and thus cannot be attributed to a psychological reaction to the Black Death.

⁶⁶ This anonymous commentary could not have been written much before 1360. The author quotes from John of Ripa, who read the *Sentences* at Paris in 1354–55 or 1355–56, and Amandus of Artesio, who was a regent master in theology at Paris during the period 1362–65 and under whom the author of the commentary in Vat. lat. 986 studied and probably was promoted.

writers later than Scotus, many of them English. He was familiar with Burley, Ockham, Chatton, Rodington, Fitzralph, Grafton, Wodeham, Kilvington, Bradwardine, Halifax, Pickingham, and Langeley. He quoted Adam on the ubiquity and immutability of God in a passage that is not cited elsewhere.[67] Thus the author must have had access to the Wodeham texts.

GOTTSCHALK OF NEPOMUK, a Bohemian Cistercian lecturing on the *Sentences* at Paris in 1365–66, cited several English theologians among his fourteenth-century sources, principally Ockham and Halifax.[68] In the portions of Gottschalk I have read, I have come across no direct reference to Wodeham, although he may have been intended among the *alii* who held opinions also maintained by Ockham.

A contemporary of Gottschalk, JOHN HILTALINGEN OF BASEL, was even more candid and conscious of his sources.[69] Reading in the same year,[70] Hiltalingen stocked his pages with abundant references to contemporary scholastic opinion, a habit for which the historian of fourteenth-century thought is extremely grateful. Not since Ceffons had there been such generous citation of English authors. Hiltalingen was familiar with Ockham, Fitzralph, Holcot, Wodeham, Kilvington, Bradwardine, Halifax, Pickingham, Aston, and Brinkel. The proportion of citations within the English group is interesting. Chatton is missing and seems to have dropped from the list of notable English doctors.

---

[67] Vat. lat. 986, fol. 22va.

[68] The only manuscript of Gottschalk is in Krakow, Bibl. Jag. 1499. In particular, see fols. 36ra, 50va, 50vb, and 102vb–103ra.

[69] On the life and writings of Hiltalingen see: D. Trapp, "Hiltalinger's Augustinian Quotations," *Augustiniana*, IV (1954), 412–449; "Augustinian Theology," *Augustiniana*, VI, 242–250.

[70] A. Zumkeller and D. Trapp have made a persuasive case that John of Basel read the *Sentences* at Paris in 1365–66; see: D. Trapp, "Augustinian Theology," *Augustiniana*, VI, 261–262; "Hiltalinger's Augustinian Quotations," *Augustiniana*, IV, 412–413; A. Zumkeller, "Hiltalingen, Johannes," *Neue Deutsche Biographie*, IX, 162. This dating, however, is not without problems. Hiltalingen cites (Clm 26711, fol. 67^r) Conrad of Ebrach ("Magister Conrad in sua lectura ... verum non fuit magister cum posuit"), and K. Lauterer has convincingly dated Conrad's bachelor lectures at Bologna in 1368–69; cf. "Konrad von Ebrach," *Analecta Sacri Ordinis Cisterciensis*, XVII (1961), 189–191. Furthermore, Hiltalingen repeatedly cites John of Braculis, who read at Paris in 1370–71, and even quotes from Braculis' *Quaestiones disputatae*. Finally, the Augustinian Simon of Cremona read at Paris in 1365–66, and it would have been unusual for two Augustinians to be reading in the same year. Consequently, either Hiltalingen read later than has been thought or, more likely, his Commentary was revised and expanded ca. 1375.

By contrast, Fitzralph is given great prominence, second only to Bradwardine. Indeed, one has to go back to Rimini to find another author who considered Fitzralph so important. When we recall the prominent place Fitzralph held in Wodeham's Oxford lectures, and the prominent place Wodeham held for both Rimini and Hiltalingen, one may conclude that some of the interest in Fitzralph was mediated through Wodeham or, at the very least, their names and reputations remained linked. Holcot, who was not mentioned at all in Rimini or Vargas, and who began to appear as an authority in the commentaries of Mirecourt, Hugolino, and Ceffons, came into his own in Hiltalingen's Commentary, where he appeared as an important source. Similarly Kilvington and Bradwardine, mentioned occasionally in earlier commentaries, held prominent places in the commentary of Hiltalingen.

Damasus Trapp, who has painstakingly counted the references in the pages of Hiltalingen, noted 27 references to Wodeham. Moreover, Hiltalingen on occasion cited Wodeham according to the title of a lecture series, such as *Lectura secunda,* and was the first since Rimini to do so. I have been able to trace down most of these references, and because they are so numerous and exact, they give us a clear insight into what lectures and sections of Wodeham were being read in the third quarter of the fourteenth century at Paris.

As we might expect, the first quotation from Adam that occurs in Hiltalingen is on the issue of fruition.[71] The reference is to a passage in the Oxford bachelor lectures criticized by Wodeham's *socii*. It is impossible to tell which redaction of the Oxford lectures Hiltalingen was using, since he summarized Wodeham's position, using much of Wodeham's language, rather than quoting the passage verbatim.

Many of Hiltalingen's citations from Wodeham seem to have been

---

[71] John Hiltalingen, *Lectura,* I, q. 3 (München, Staatsbibl. Clm 26711, fols. 42va–42vb): "... et sic posset secundum eum [Thomas of Strasbourg] consequentia negari, summendo ipsum primo modo dicto in distinctione. Sed Adam, q. 1 prologi vel una [in] dubio: 'probo primo,' dicit, 'quod capacitas animae est finita, quia ipsa non est nisi essentia animae. Secundo, anima repleri potest de forma receptabili in ipsa secundum intentionem, sicut vas corporale secundum extensionem, et hoc loquendo sine miraculo novo. Tertio, dicit, 'quod anima non potest tantum repleri sicut nec vas quin virtute divina et per novum miraculum plus capere posset.' Quarto, ponit quod imaginari potest, sicut in materialibus, quod quamvis repleri possit per qualitatem vel formam aliquam sive praemium vel meritum unius speciei, posset tamen recipere formam aliam speciei superioris, et sic iterum patet quid esset dicendum ad rationem secundum istum modum istius doctoris [Adam] iste modus non placet Roseto." Cf. Clm 26711, fol. 284ra.

taken from later authors. One of his references to Wodeham was taken from the pages of Rosetus.[72] Others may have come through the lost *Sentences* Commentary of Hiltalingen's Augustinian contemporary, Bonsembiante Badoer.[73] Hiltalingen also relied on Gregory of Rimini for some of his references to Wodeham. At one point he refers to a passage in Wodeham that appears in Gregory, and while Hiltalingen's reference is incorrect, Gregory's is exact.[74] Most of Hiltalingen's quotations from Wodeham, however, do not occur elsewhere and thus reflect Hiltalingen's firsthand familiarity with texts.

Trapp called attention to this critical precision of citation in Hiltalingen when he pointed to Hiltalingen's correction of a reference in Wodeham to Aquinas' *Summa theologiae*. The reference in the text Hiltalingen was using was incomplete and inaccurate, and eventually Hiltalingen was able to locate an appropriate place in Thomas' work.[75] However, the better manuscripts of Wodeham did not need correcting on this point. The proper passage in the *Summa theologiae* is I, q. 55, a. 3 (not I, q. 85, a. 4). In the earliest text "a. 3" had an extra mark behind it that was rendered by later scribes as "a. 33," an impossible reference that encouraged some scribes to leave that portion of the reference blank, to be filled in later by the correct number. Moreover, in some manuscripts the first part of the reference, namely "q. 55" was corrupted to "q. 25."[76]

---

[72] München, Staatsbibl., Clm 26711, fols. 42va–42vb.

[73] Ibid., fols. 98ra, 106rb, and 135va. Bonsembiante, or Bonsemblans, is an important figure whose biography demonstrates the ties that existed between scholastic theologians, in this case of Ockhamist inclination, and Italian humanism. He was a close friend of Petrarch and called his attention to the beauty of Arquà in the Euganean hills southwest of Padua, where Petrarch bought property and where he died. Of the scholastic corpus of Bonsemblans, all that remains are the four *principia,* found in two manuscripts (München, Clm 26711, fols. 397–406, and Vat. lat. 981, fols. 91–105), and his *Quaestiones diversae,* which seems to have been his *Vesperiae.* (Vat. lat. 981, fols. 71^v–74^v, 75^r–97^v). On Bonsemblans, see: F. Ehrle, *Der Sentenzenkommentar Peters von Candia* (Münster i. W., 1925), pp. 50–56; R. Arbesmann, *Der Augustiner-Eremitenorden* (Würzburg, 1965), pp. 61–69 (also in *Augustiniana,* XIV (1964), 302–310); and Neal Gilbert, "Ockham, Wyclif, and the 'Via Moderna'," *Antiqui und Moderni,* Miscellanea Mediaevalia, Vol. 9 (Berlin, 1974), pp. 121–122 (of 85–125); and F. Stegmüller, *RepSent,* p. 68, n. 162.

[74] Ibid., fol. 44va. Hiltalingen was not always exact. On fol. 135va he cites Adam, "libro 3, q. 14." Book III had only twelve questions. Hiltalingen probably meant "dist. 14," as he had written on fol. 135ra. Cf. also fol. 98rb.

[75] See Trapp, "Hiltalinger's Augustinian Quotations," p. 432.

[76] The earliest reading occurs in Vat. lat. 955, fol. 15^r (end of Prol., q. 2). There the reading is ". . . per doctorem communem . . . parte prima, q. 55, a. 3^i." The *Ordinatio* version in Paris, Univ. 193, fol. 12rb reads the same, except it has "a. 33". The abbreviation of Wodeham contained in Naples VII C 53, fol. 6va reads: ". . . per Tho., par. 1, q. 25 [or 29?], a.33."

This problem further helps us identify the text of the Oxford lectures used by Hiltalingen.[77] Hiltalingen, in this passage and elsewhere, concentrates on the *dubia* in the prologue of Wodeham rather than the proper structure of the questions. This, in combination with his reading of "q. 25" rather than "q. 55" suggests he may have been using the form of Wodeham's Oxford lectures contained in the Naples manuscript, which is the *Extractio* of Wodeham's work read at Cologne before 1348.[78] Many, perhaps all of Hiltalingen's firsthand references from the Oxford lectures come from this form of Wodeham's work, a text inferior to either the *Ordinatio* or the post-1334 redaction.

Most of Hiltalingen's references to Wodeham show a favorable attitude, though on occasion Hiltalingen rejected Wodeham's views.[79] In both cases, Wodeham was, for Hiltalingen, one of the major doctors among the *moderni*.

In his reference to Wodeham's *Lectura secunda*, Hiltalingen uses that title in a way that would seem to contradict Gregory's usage. Hiltalingen refers to Adam, *Lectura secunda,* book 3, dist. 1, q. 2, a. 2.[80] As it stands, the reference probably contains a scribal error. It cannot be a reference to the Oxford lectures, since the issue under discussion is epistemological and is not found in that work. Although "book III, dist. 1" might appear to be a reference to the London lectures, the issue under discussion is more appropriate to the prologue, not to the first distinction. If, as seems most likely, the Arabic "3" was a scribal error for "1", then the reference does accord with material found in the Caius manuscript, dist. 1, q. 2, a. 2. Inasmuch as this reference is not found in

---

[77] Hiltalingen's familiarity with the Oxford lectures can be seen by looking at Clm 26711, fols. 42va–42vb, 44ra–45ra, 45rb, 46ra–46vb, 59rb, 95rb, 120rb, 131va, 132rb, 135ra, 138rb, 284ra, 284rb, 284vb, 285va, 341rb, 381rb.

[78] Naples VII C 53.

[79] Favorable in tone are: Clm 26711, fols. 42va–42vb, 44va, 45ra (twice), 45rb, 46va–46vb, 59rb, 140rb (where Adam is placed with Gregory). For less favorable citations, see: Clm 26711, fols. 98ra, 131va, 138rb (where Adam is opposed to Gregory), and 381rb.

[80] Clm 26711, fol. 98ra: "Secundum corollarium contra Adam et ipsum [Bonsimilantem] quam impossibile est intellectum terminari secundum cognitionem vel cognitiones diversarum specierum tam impossibile est ipsum terminari perceptione vel perceptionibus solo numero distinctis. Ex quo patet contra primum notabile[m] Bonsimilantis, ubi supra probatur...." Fol. 98rb: "Primum probari ex rationibus Adam, lectura 2^a, libro 3°, distinctione prima, quaestione 2, articulo 2, et rationibus Gregorii, libro primo, distinctione 1, quaestione ultima, articulo tertio, tertia et quarta conclusionibus, et secundum patet, quia...." The question under discussion is (fol. 96va ff.): "Utrum a speciebus quibus visibiliter mittitur spiritus sanctus obiective vitaliter causaliter immutari possit intellectus et sensus."

Rimini, it would appear that Hiltalingen still had direct access to a text that resembled Caius 281. Moreover, this provides independent support that the Caius manuscript contains the work that Parisian theologians knew as Wodeham's *Lectura secunda*.

After Hiltalingen, it would appear that Wodeham was familiar to everyone lecturing in the theological faculty at Paris from whom we have extant works. He is quoted by the Cistercian JAMES OF ELTVILLE, who lectured on the *Sentences* at Paris in 1369–70. Again, Eltville reflects his own reading of Wodeham, since he refers to a passage in the Oxford lectures that is not cited by anyone earlier.[81]

Similarly, the Cistercian bachelor reading in the following year, CONRAD OF EBRACH, was familiar with Wodeham.[82] In his first and fourth books on the *Sentences* Conrad cited Wodeham six times, mostly from the first, third, and fourth books of the Oxford lectures.[83] One exception is the reference: "Vide de hac materia Adam in prima, dist. 7, q. 1 et 2."[84] *Prima* in this statement has to refer to *Lectura prima* and not to the first book of some lecture series. Moreover, the context concerns the divine attributes and the divine essence—material normally included in book I—and the Oxford lectures of Wodeham do not treat the seventh distinction of book I except obliquely in dist. 33, q. 5. The reference in Conrad, however, seems to parallel the Caius manuscript, fols. 190^v–201^v (book I, dist. 7, qq. 1 and 2). If the designation *Lectura prima* refers to the London lectures and is not a post-Rimini reference to the lectures contained in the Caius manuscript (called *Lectura secunda* in Rimini), then we have additional information on the content of the London lectures.

The quotations Conrad took from the Oxford lectures are too brief to establish the redaction used. Nevertheless, the fact that he refers to passages not cited previously suggests that he also had direct access to the texts of Wodeham, both the Oxford lectures and the *Lectura prima*. In the

---

[81] James of Eltville, *Lectura*, IV, q. 1 (Cambrai 570, fol. 213ra). Father Trapp graciously permitted me to consult his microfilm copy of this manuscript.

[82] For a study of the life and writings of Conrad see: K. Lauterer, "Konrad von Ebrach S. O. Cist.," *Analecta Sacri Ordinis Cisterciensis*, XVII (1961), 151–214; XVIII (1962), 60–120; XIX (1963), 3–50.

[83] Conrad of Ebrach, *Sent.* I, dist. 17, q. 3 (Krakow 1279, fol. 42va): "Hoc Adam et Occam." *Sent.* I, dist. 22–26, q. un. (Krakow 1279, fol. 45vb): "Vide de hac materia Adam in prima [lectura], dist. 7, q. 1 et 2 in mediata." *Sent.* I, dist. 40–41, q. 2 (Krakow 1279, fol. 54rb): "Haec est opinio Adae in tertia quaestione." *Sent.* IV, dist. 14–23, q. 3 (Krakow 1279, fol. 178ra), in combination with Halifax.

[84] Krakow 1279, fol. 45vb.

following year DIONYSIUS OF MONTINA, an Augustinian associated closely with the Cistercians (a frequent occurrence in this period), also cited Wodeham.[85]

Lest one get the impression that Wodeham was a special property of the Augustinians and Cistercians in this period, it is well to note that the next three authors to mention Wodeham whose works have survived are secular. PIERRE D'AILLY, one of the most significant theologians of his generation and one of the few Frenchmen of reputation at Paris in the second half of the fourteenth century, referred to Wodeham in the context of seven different questions in books I and IV of his *Sentences* Commentary.[86] His references are all from the Oxford lectures.[87] However, they do not point to a fresh reading of Wodeham. Unlike d'Ailly's citations of Bradwardine, Fitzralph, and Holcot, he seldom indicates a specific place in Wodeham where his reference can be found. Moreover, he only refers to Wodeham on issues for which Wodeham had become a common source. Therefore, although d'Ailly continues to publicize Wodeham as a major authority and may even have read him himself, the evidence suggests that he did not have a firsthand knowledge of this English author.

By contrast, a contemporary of d'Ailly at Paris, HENRY TOTTING OF OYTA, had a knowledge of Wodeham perhaps unmatched since Gregory of Rimini. Moreover, he had a respect for Wodeham unequalled in the fourteenth century. Not only did he refer to both Wodeham's Oxford and London lectures in his writings,[88] but he also edited an *abbreviatio* of the Oxford lectures which was eventually printed in the early sixteenth century.[89] Oyta's abbreviation of Wodeham's Oxford lectures, the subsequent history of which deserves a separate treatment, was probably not done at Prague, as Albert Lang conjectured, but at Paris around

---

[85] A. Zumkeller, *Dionysius de Montina,* Cassiciacum, ix. 2–3 (Würzburg, 1948), p. 39.

[86] For example, see Pierre d'Ailly, *Quaestiones super libros sententiarum cum quibusdam in fine adjunctis* (Strassburg, 1490; Reprint: Frankfurt, 1968), I, q. 2; I, q. 12; I, q. 14; IV, q. 1; IV, q. 2; IV, q. 3; IV, q. 5.

[87] Although d'Ailly rarely designates a particular place in Wodeham, the content of the references points to the Oxford lectures. However, in one place (I, q. 14) d'Ailly does refer specifically to Adam, III, q. 6, which again coincides with the Oxford lectures.

[88] For example, Henry Totting of Oyta, *Lectura Parisiensis* (Clm 8867, fol. 20ra): "Item tertio Adam, Lectura Lundoniensis, quaestione 9 prologi, articulo tertio sic arguit...." This reference does not correspond to the structure of the Caius manuscript, although the passage may be there, possibly having been reused by Wodeham in his *Lectura secunda*.

[89] Cf. Appendix Four.

1375.⁹⁰ Lang had based his conclusion on the passage in the third book of Oyta's abbreviation of the Oxford lectures referring to the king of Bohemia and to Pope Gregory XI.⁹¹ The second reference dated the work to Gregory's pontificate, 1370–1378; the first reference supposedly located the place of writing in Bohemia. As was stated in the first chapter, Wodeham himself had used the example of the king of Bohemia when he was in Oxford, and it appears in all copies of the *Ordinatio* and dates before 1334. Two of the three extant copies of the *Ordinatio* are still in Paris and the third one was probably derived from Paris. The capitulation used by Oyta and the section titles he placed at the bottom of his folios are based directly on the form of the *Ordinatio* and in many places are directly borrowed. Similarly, the redaction that Oyta used, as Michalski recognized, is the *Ordinatio,* although Michalski referred to it as the "middle edition." From this we may conclude that sometime between 1373 (before which Oyta was at Prague and Avignon) and 1378 (the end of Gregory's pontificate) Oyta went to Paris to study and, while there, undertook the task of putting the essence of Wodeham's work into a briefer, more accessible form.

Before turning to the significance of the Parisian origin of Oyta's abbreviation of Wodeham and its subsequent history, we must note the others at Paris in this period who were familiar with Wodeham's work. JOHN OF WASIA, reading *secundum alios* at Paris in 1376, based his Commentary on Alphonsus Vargas (book I) and on John of Mirecourt (books II–IV).⁹² His citations are abundant, but mostly derived through Vargas or Mirecourt. Either directly or through others he was familiar with Ockham, Fitzralph, Chatton, Rodington, Holcot, Wodeham, Kilvington, Buckingham, and Osbert, alongside a large number of Parisian doctors. By contrast, HENRY OF LANGENSTEIN OF HESSE, an important figure both at Paris and Vienna, returned to the practice of quoting almost no fourteenth-century sources in his *Sentences* Commentary.⁹³ However, in keeping with a growing tradition in the late fourteenth century, Henry read *secundum alium* the lectures of a close friend, James of Eltville, to the community of monks at the Cistercian

---

⁹⁰ A. Lang, *Heinrich Totting von Oyta,* BB, xxxiii.4–5 (Münster i.W., 1937), p. 56.

⁹¹ Oyta Abbreviation (Paris, 1512), fol. 121ᵛᵇ. Cf. chapter one, pp. 16–17.

⁹² For a description of the Commentary of Wasia, see D. Trapp, "Augustinian Theology," *Augustiniana,* VI, 214–215. The information on Wasia was taken from that source.

⁹³ See: Alençon 144; N. Steneck, *Science and Creation in the Middle Ages: Henry of Langenstein (d. 1397) on Genesis* (Notre Dame, 1976).

monastery of Eberbach, where James was abbot. That commentary, as we know, included references to the thought of Wodeham. Shortly before that time, PETER OF CANDIA, reading at Paris around 1378, also cited Wodeham.[94]

Indicative of a wider reading is the *Sentences* Commentary of the Carmelite, JOHN BRAMMART, composed in 1380.[95] Brammart was familiar with the Oxford lectures, cites the *Lectura secunda,* and may also have known the London lectures. His frequent quotations of passages from Wodeham not cited elsewhere demonstrate a first-hand knowledge of some of the Wodeham texts.[96] Other references to Wodeham, however, appear to have been taken from the pages of Gregory and Hugolino.

Brammart's reference to Wodeham's *Lectura secunda* (and I have found only one reference so far) poses something of a problem.[97] As it stands, the reference could only fit Wodeham's bachelor lectures at Oxford. Unfortunately, the reference is only to Wodeham's opinion, and there is no quotation from Wodeham that can be checked. The context of the discussion in Brammart, however, does correspond to the section in Wodeham's Oxford lectures supposedly designated, though the use of the title *Lectura secunda* to designate Wodeham's bachelor lectures at Oxford is strange and does not accord with the usage of either Rimini or Hiltalingen.

Another solution is possible. If one reads "quaest. 4" in place of "quaest. 14", then the reference would correspond to the structure of the Caius manuscript and would designate a place where the same material can be found. Indeed, this passage in Wodeham's *Lectura secunda* had already been extensively quoted in the pages of Rimini, through whom Brammart may have become familiar with Wodeham's position on this

---

[94] F. Ehrle, *Der Sentenzenkommentar Peters von Candia,* Franziskanische Studien, ix (Münster i.W., 1925), p. 96 ff.

[95] B. M. Xiberta, *De scriptoribus,* pp. 425–431.

[96] John Brammart, *Lectura*, Florence, Bibl. Naz., II, II, 281, fol. 72^r (Xiberta, 425), where Hugolino is said to follow the opinion of Adam; Wilhering 87, fol. 36va; Wilhering 87, fol. 38rb: "Arguit Ockham, cuius est opinio, dist. 1, q. 6. . . . Multa facit argumenta Adam, quaestione 12 primi . . ."; Wilhering 87, fol. 42rb; Wilhering 87, fol. 44^r (Xiberta, 425); Wilhering 87, fol. 49va: "Concordant Ockham et Adam . . ."; Wilhering 87, fol. 61rb: ". . . Scoti, dist. 2 primi, et recitatur ab Adam, dist. 2 . . ."; Wilhering 87, fol. 62ra: ". . . ponit Adam, secunda distinctione, quaestione prima primi . . ."; Wilhering 87, fol. 126va: "Et latius, si volueris, in Adam et Gregorio videas"; Wilhering 87, fol. 164vb: "Sed Holcot dicit . . . et concordant Adam et Eliphat. . . ."

[97] John Brammart, *Lectura*, Wilhering 87, fol. 34ra: "Et haec est determinatio Ockham, dist. 1, q. 2, et Adae in Lectura secunda circa eandem distinctionem, q. 14."

issue.⁹⁸ This interpretation is supported by another passage in Brammart that shows he knew material from Wodeham's London lectures, either directly or, more likely, by way of the *Lectura secunda* of Wodeham as quoted in the pages of Rimini. In question eight on whether the existence of God is self-evident, Brammart discusses cognition and refers to the fourth question of Adam's prologue.⁹⁹ In content and form this cannot refer to Wodeham's bachelor lectures at Oxford but must either refer to the London lectures or to the work contained in the Caius manuscript. However, the identical quotation from Wodeham occurs in Rimini, where the full reference reads: "Adam in secunda lectura, quaestione 4 prologi."¹⁰⁰ It seems probable, therefore, that both references are to the Caius *Lectura* and that Brammart's understanding of *Lectura secunda* corresponds to Gregory's, i.e., the work contained in the Caius manuscript. Indeed, it may well be that Brammart's sole acquaintance with Wodeham's *Lectura secunda* was through the pages of Gregory.

As presented by Brammart, Wodeham appears in close association with Ockham, Gregory, Hugolino, Holcot, and Halifax. Whatever differences the modern historian might find between the Augustinians, Gregory and Hugolino, and such English doctors as Ockham, Holcot, Wodeham, and Halifax, the Carmelite Brammart was largely unaware of them. For him, these theologians were often in agreement, and he depends heavily on their thought, although he disagrees with them at times.

In contrast to Brammart, who seems to have known Wodeham's works in their unabbreviated form, the ANNOTATOR of the *Lectura* of John of Ripa, writing also around 1380, seems to have known only the abbreviation of Wodeham. At many points he preferred Wodeham's thought to the arguments of Ripa he was glossing.¹⁰¹ PETER PLAOUT, reading at Paris in 1391–93, frequently cited English authors, such as Campsale, Halifax, and Heytisbury. He was also familiar with Wodeham, whom he cited on occasion.¹⁰²

---

⁹⁸ Gregory of Rimini, *Super primum sententiarum* (Venice, 1522), 25 H–L: "Adam in secunda lectura, libro 1, dist. 1, quaest. 3." In the Caius manuscript the third question in distinction 1 is actually designated as question 4.

⁹⁹ John Brammart, *Lectura,* Wilhering 87, fol. 52ᵛᵇ: "Nec valet ratio ipsius Adae, quaestione 4 prologi."

¹⁰⁰ Gregory of Rimini, *Super primum sententiarum,* 36 G–H.

¹⁰¹ John of Ripa, *Lectura super primum sententiarum. Prologi quaestiones I & II*, ed. A. Combes, Textes philosophiques du moyen âge, viii (Paris, 1961), pp. 240, 248, 249, 257, 260, 261, 262, 263, 266, 267, 268, 271. Cf. Appendix three in the same work.

¹⁰² Paris, B. N. lat. 3074, fol. 50ᵛ: "Unde et Adam pulchre tractat istam materiam videat magis aut per se qui voluerit." This reference and the information on Plaout

With the German exodus from Paris in the years after 1380, a fuller knowledge of Wodeham was carried eastward. MARSILIUS OF INGHEN, who had played an important role in the Arts Faculty at Paris and had studied theology there under James of Eltville, made some use of Wodeham in his *Sentences* Commentary delivered at Heidelberg in 1393-95.[103] Surprisingly, he does not quote Wodeham by name in his discussions of fruition, the habit of grace, or quantity in the Eucharist—all places where one would expect to see Wodeham's arguments brought forward. However, since Marsilius seldom refers to opinions of fourteenth-century doctors, his mention of Wodeham is of greater significance. He quotes Wodeham on the issues of God's foreknowledge in relation to future contingents and on sacramental causality.[104] It may well be that Marsilius' familiarity with Wodeham, restricted to the Oxford lectures, was mediated through the Cistercians and was heavily indebted to the Augustinians. At one point Marsilius credits James of Eltville for his knowledge of a particular argument from Wodeham.[105] Moreover, the most frequent fourteenth-century source cited in his commentary is the Augustinian, Thomas of Strasbourg. Marsilius even refers to Gregory of Rimini as *frater magister noster Gregorius,* a phrase one would expect to hear only from an Austin Friar.[106]

The reputation of Wodeham was disseminated elsewhere in German-speaking lands, particularly at Vienna. The Carmelite ARNOLD OF SEHNSEN, who became dean of the theological faculty at Vienna in 1407, read the *Sentences* at Vienna in 1401 or 1404 and quoted from the fourth book of Wodeham's Oxford lectures.[107] Another early fifteenth-century Viennese theologian, PETER REICHER OF PIRCHENWART, who was a disciple of Peter of Pulka, cited Wodeham frequently.[108] Pirchenwart is

---

come from P. Glorieux, "L'année universitaire 1392–1393 à la Sorbonne à travers les notes d'un étudiant," *Revue des sciences religieuses,* XIX (1939), 429–482; the reference to Wodeham appears on p. 438.

[103] On Marsilius see G. Ritter, *Studien zur Spätscholastik,* I: *Marsilius von Inghen und die okkamistische Schule in Deutschland,* Sitzungsberichte der Heidelberger Akademie der Wissenschaften, Philosophisch-historische Klasse, iv (Heidelberg, 1921).

[104] Marsilius of Inghen, *Sent.* I, q. 40 (dist. 38–39), a. 2 (Strassburg, 1501), fol. 167^v refers to Adam, [Oxon.] III, q. 2, dub. 2, concl. 7. Marsilius, *Sent.* IV, q. 1, a. 3 (fol. 475^v) refers to Adam, [Oxon.] IV, q. 2, dub. 1.

[105] Marsilius, *Sent.* IV, q. 1, a. 3 (fol. 475^v): "Dicit magister meus bonae memoriae, magister Jacobus de Erbaco...."

[106] Marsilius, *Sent.* I, Proem., q. 2, a. 3 (fol. 13^r): "frater magister noster Gregorius."

[107] See Xiberta, *De scriptoribus,* pp. 472–476.

[108] München, Staatsbibl. Clm. 3768, pp. 160–161; Vat. lat. 1119, fol. 97^r; Clm 3768, pp. 280–284; Vat. lat. 1119, fols. 174^v–176^v.

especially interesting because, alongside his familiarity with such English theologians as Wodeham, Holcot, and Halifax, he relied heavily on the Cistercians, James of Eltville and Gottschalk of Nepomuk. There is an unexplored line from Gregory of Rimini, through Gottschalk of Nepomuk, to Pirchenwart that may hold some important clues to the development of the *via Gregorii* in the years between Hugolino and Biel.[109] The favorable citation Pirchenwart gives Wodeham in his fourth book on the *Sentences* may go much deeper and in a direction that leads to Biel. An anonymous Vienna commentary, found in Vienna, Bibl. Nat. 4892 and 14212 and ascribed to Peter of Pirchenwart, opens with a question borrowed from Wodeham's Prologue to his Oxford lectures.[110]

Given the universality with which Wodeham was quoted at Paris, one does not need to trace further the individual lines through which Wodeham was transmitted to the German universities. However, one would have to say that Inghen, Langenstein, and most especially Oyta played major roles in that transmission.

One might expect that with the Thomist revival in the fifteenth century a more negative assessment of Adam Wodeham was introduced into scholastic literature. While the full dimensions of this problem have yet to be explored, the evidence for it, at least in the early part of the fifteenth century, appears slight. John Capreolus at Paris, the *princeps Thomistarum*, used Adam as one of his major sources for understanding earlier scholastic theology. Apart from his citations from John of Ripa, Capreolus showed little or no acquaintance with theologians in the

---

[109] According to Trapp, *Augustiniana*, VI (1956), 251–252, Gottschalk read *secundum Gregorium*. Doucet, *Commentaires sur les Sentences. Supplément au Répertoire de M. Frédéric Stegmueller* (Quaracchi, 1954), p. 34, noted the importance of the citations from Gottschalk in Pirchenwart. Others may have thought the connection between Rimini and Pirchenwart was even stronger. One of the München manuscripts of Pirchenwart, Clm 3768, is attributed to a Georgius of Rimini, and another manuscript, St. Paul im Lavanttal, Stiftsbibliothek ms. 28-5-7, is attributed to Gregorius de Arumpno. For Biel's references to Wodeham, see, e.g., *Collectorium circa quattuor libros Sententiarum,* Vol. I, ed. W. Werbeck and U. Hofmann (Tübingen, 1973), pp. 83, 95, 113, 196, 200, 204, 354, 373, 714. On the *via Gregorii* see H. A. Oberman, "Headwaters of the Reformation: *Initia Lutheri—Initia Reformationis*," in *Luther and the Dawn of the Modern Era*, ed. H. A. Oberman (Leiden, 1974), pp. 69–85.

[110] According to Stegmüller, *RepSent.*, p. 514, n. 1384, Vienna, Bibl. Nat. 4892 is ascribed: "Forte est Petri de Pirchenwart." If true, this would add the first three books to what we already possess from Pirchenwart. The opening question in another manuscript of this work, Vienna, Bibl. Nat. 14212, appears to be verbatim the first question of Wodeham's Prologue.

second half of the fourteenth century. His intellectual world was composed primarily of the generation after Thomas, namely those active from Henry of Ghent to Peter Aureol. His principal adversaries were those influenced by Scotus, a group that for him included Durand of St. Pourçain and Aureol. The two figures between Aureol and Ripa upon whom he most depended were Adam Wodeham and Gregory of Rimini.

Capreolus appears to have been familiar only with the *Lectura Oxoniensis,* but his knowledge of it was extensive and exact. He cited long sections from that work and utilized as counterarguments the opinions of theologians with whom he was unfamiliar and whom he borrowed from the pages of Wodeham.[111] In this way Capreolus cited the opinions of Wodeham's Benedictine *socius*[112] as well as the opinion of Fitzralph, whom Capreolus knew only as a "quidam Hibernicus."[113]

Capreolus' judgment of Wodeham was far from negative. He criticized him in the name of Thomas on a variety of issues, particularly on the nature of the will and on quantity. However, he also cited Wodeham favorably and, when responding to positions with which he disagreed, was often satisfied simply to quote Wodeham's response.[114] Again we find that Capreolus, like so many authors in the preceding generation, considered Wodeham to be an important source and a significant authority who could be attacked, but who could also be used to support Thomistic opinions.

E. THE SPANISH CONTRIBUTION

The dissemination of scholastic thought into Spain is an unwritten chapter in the history of medieval (or for that matter European) intel-

---

[111] John Capreolus, *Defensiones theologiae divi Thomae Aquinatis,* vol. I (Turin, 1900), pp. 108–109, 113–115; 199–200, 211–212; 200–201, 215–216; 287–288, 297–299; vol. II (Turin, 1900), pp. 102–103, 118–120; 114–116, 129; 144, 447; vol. III (Turin, 1902), pp. 95–96, 109–117; 260, 289–290; 364–378; 426–429, 434–445; vol. IV (Turin, 1903), pp. 210–211, 226–228; 234–235, 242–245; 412–413, 419–420; vol. V (Turin, 1904), pp. 167–168, 172–173; 179–183, 198–205; 214–215, 225–227; 217–218, 231–233.

[112] Ibid., vol. V (Capreolus, *Sent.* III, dist. 14, q. 1), pp. 179–183, 198–205. Capreolus read Wodeham closely enough to note that the *socius* to whom Wodeham refers in *Lectura Oxon.,* III, q. 1, was the same figure referred to in *Lectura Oxon.,* prol., q. 2.

[113] Ibid., vol. I, pp. 200–201, 215–216; vol. III, pp. 364–378; vol. V, pp. 214–215, 225–227.

[114] E.g., Ibid., vol. III, p. 444: "ut Adam dicit et bene", "bene et sufficienter solvit Adam", "solutio quam ponit Adam bona est et sufficiens." See also vol. IV, pp. 226–228, 242–245.

lectual history. The ecclesiastical archives of Spain, not easily accessible and insufficiently catalogued, are among the last unexplored treasure troves of medieval documents in western Europe. A significant portion of the manuscripts in those archives comprise scholastic philosophy and theology at a time when Spain's universities did not offer a recognized program of theological study. A large number of those scholastic manuscripts are from fourteenth-century theologians among whom the English are well represented. In a period in which very little higher teaching outside the field of law was going on in Spain, and in which many scholastic manuscripts were imported rather than locally produced, convents and cathedrals collected a sizeable number of highly technical works in scholastic theology. Half of the English theologians with extant works between Ockham and Langeley (1318-45) are represented in Spain. What explains this strong interest in scholastic theology, particularly in the English doctors?

Cultural ties between France and the regions of Catalonia and Navarre already existed in the early Middle Ages but grew much stronger in the twelfth and thirteenth centuries. Both Cluny and Citeaux had a network of affiliated monasteries or daughter houses spread throughout northern Spain from Catalonia to Galicia. Similarly, the mendicant orders maintained close ties with Spain. For the Dominicans it was their place of origin, and the Franciscans early established convents throughout the northern part of the country. Young novices, first from the mendicants and later from the Cistercian houses, traveled north to Paris for their university education. By the second quarter of the fourteenth century some, such as Alphonsus Vargas of Toledo, were establishing important reputations at Paris. Even for those whose careers at Paris were less distinguished, there must have been a strong desire to bring home to their convent libraries and teaching programs the best and latest from the Parisian classrooms. Authors of the period 1330-1350 are particularly well represented. Two of the finest manuscripts of Mirecourt are in Spain, one beautifully illuminated.[115] One of the only three surviving copies of Wodeham's complete *Ordinatio* is found today in Spain, and it is the only copy that is extensively illuminated.[116] This copy of Wodeham's *Ordinatio* was imported from Paris by one of the oldest Franciscan convents in Spain, Tarazona. There it remained until the convent was

---

[115] Salamanca 1863 (formerly Madrid, Palacio 568) and Toledo, Cabildo XIII 39.

[116] Tarazona, Cat. 7. The manuscript is written in a mid-fourteenth century Parisian cursive. For a complete description see appendix 1.

closed and its library moved to the cathedral. Although it was one of the best witnesses to the text of Wodeham's first Oxford lectures (in some ways *the* best), it seems to have been unrelated to the development of interest in Wodeham in Spain, which centered around the abbreviation of Oyta and was fostered not by the Franciscans but by the Augustinian Hermits.

If one looks at Catalonia, Navarre, and Languedoc as one cultural region, the Oyta abbreviations found in that area constitute 25 percent of all the extant manuscripts of that work: two at Toulouse, one at Pamplona, and one at Barcelona. Even if one assumes there was less destruction of manuscripts in Spain, there must have been a strong demand for Wodeham's work to explain such a high proportion of manuscripts outside Paris and Germany, where one would expect to find them. A clue is provided by the subject index that appears in some of the manuscripts and was eventually included in the printed edition. It was compiled by the Spanish Augustinian, master Peter Garini, on behalf of his confrere and benefactor, Apparicius of Burgos.[117] In all probability this index was done at Paris, since Garini felt obliged to identify Burgos as "of the Spains," probably to distinguish it from Bourges. This would not have been necessary if he were writing in northern Spain. Both Spanish manuscripts of Oyta's abbreviation contain Garini's index, and it was probably through Spanish Augustinians studying at Paris in the fifteenth century that Wodeham was carried southward into Spain.

At the beginning of the sixteenth century, the publication of Oyta's abbreviation in Paris owed its form to this Spanish interest in Wodeham. When John Major acquired a text of Oyta's abbreviation to publish he did not use a copy from Paris (assuming one was accessible to him) but rather borrowed a copy from Peter Menenes, a student from Portugal.[118]

---

[117] Barcelona, Catedral 38, fol. 183^r: "Tabula super opus Adae composita per rev. magistrum Petrum Garini ordinis Eremitarum Sancti Augustini." Cf. V. Doucet, *Commentaires sur les sentences. Supplément au répertoire de M. Frédéric Stegmueller* (Firenze, 1954) p. 8. In his introduction to his *tabula* Garini gives the circumstances behind its composition. (Pamplona, Catedral 1, fol. 180^r): "Quamquam obligatus rogationibus ... praedilecti in Christo et religione sacra heremitarum sancti Augustini confratris et socii Apparicii de Burgis Hyspaniarum abbreviatum opus Adae super Sententias ... per alphabetum tabulare praesumpsi. ..."

[118] From John Major's introduction to the 1512 edition of Oyta's abbreviation of Wodeham's *Sentences* Commentary: ". . . sed illustris viri et eruditi Petri Menenes Lusitani in theosophia [!] bacchalarii exemplar procuravimus mediocriter castigatum quod imitari pro maiori parte elaboravimus curantes ut tabula alphabetica ad folia et columnas adderetur."

That manuscript, like those in Pamplona and Barcelona, contained the subject index, which Major printed as well, only changing the references from citing questions and articles (as in the manuscripts) to citing folios and columns of the printed text. Thus the printed edition of Oyta's abbreviation was based on the Spanish tradition and followed the form that that work had taken through the labors of those south of the Pyrenees. What Paris had given to Spain it received back by way of the Augustinians and improved with the subject index.[119]

Copies of Wodeham's *Sentences* Commentary, probably in the form of Oyta's abbreviation, must have become plentiful in the fifteenth century. Manuscripts of the abbreviation exist today in parts of Europe where few if any of the original texts of Wodeham are found and where manuscripts of Oyta's works are also lacking. There must, therefore, have been a widespread demand for this work. Although John Major tends to exaggerate at times, he asserts that Wodeham's works could be found in libraries everywhere and in the most polished manuscript productions.[120] When one reflects on the tendency for a printed work to supplant manuscript copies (as happened with the *Sentences* commentaries of Andrew of Neufchâteau, Marsilius of Inghen, and Pierre d'Ailly), the number of extant copies of Oyta's abbreviation bespeaks a large audience in the fifteenth century.

In addition to revealing the origins of the exemplar used in the preparation of the printed edition of Wodeham, Major included in his introduction a number of details about Wodeham's life. Major had access to information about Wodeham not contained in the text he edited, for beyond knowing that Wodeham had spent time at London and Oxford (information he could have derived from Oyta's abbreviation), he also knew that Wodeham had lived at Norwich (not mentioned in Oyta's abbreviation).[121] Major was also aware of the way in which Wodeham's redactions were designated in the fourteenth and fifteenth

---

[119] The Augustinian Hermits took a similar editorial interest in Ockham's other major English disciple, Robert Holcot. The editor of the early printed edition of Holcot was the Augustinian Hermit, Augustinus von Regensburg.

[120] From John Major's introduction to the 1512 edition of Oyta's abbreviation of Wodeham's *Sentences* Commentary: "In omnibus librariis et in caracteribus optimis Adam invenimus. . . ."

[121] Ibid.: ". . . Goddam alias Voddam, professione minoritanus, Oxoniensis achademiae (quae ea in tempestate viros celebres emisit) doctor, Londonis anglorum regia, Oxoniae et Norwici plurimum moratus, quibus in locis duas sententiarum lecturas peregit. . . ." The references to the Norwich lectures that occur in Wodeham, *Sent.* I, d. 33, q. 2 and *Sent.* III, q. 12, are absent in the Oyta abbreviation.

centuries. The phrase "duas sententiarum lecturas peregit" was probably based on the fact that Wodeham was sometimes cited according to the *Lectura prima* and sometimes according to the *Lectura secunda*. It would appear, therefore, that Major's information was derived from traditions about Wodeham and from the form in which Wodeham's redactions were cited in the late fourteenth century. Thus one cannot use Major as a way of separating out the redactions of Wodeham's *Sentences* Commentary as they were written.

It is hard to say whether John Major's strong sympathy for the Ockhamist tradition was nurtured through his reading of Wodeham, or whether his desire to publish Wodeham resulted from an earlier commitment to Ockham's thought. In any event, Major had the highest regard for Wodeham, placing him among the two or three greatest English men of letters, after Bede and Alexander of Hales.[122] Even granting the scholastic bias of Major, it is surprising that Wodeham so impressed Major as to displace such names as Alcuin, John of Salisbury, and John Duns Scotus. For Major, Ockham and Wodeham stood at the summit of learning, and it was through Major and the publication of Wodeham that "nominalism" was best represented at Paris on the eve of the Reformation.

F. Some Conclusions

Subsequent references to Wodeham's works, particularly those of Rimini, have shed some light on our understanding of the redactions of Wodeham's Commentary. Through Rimini we have outside evidence confirming the authenticity of the lectures contained in the Caius manuscript as an integral work of Wodeham, separate from the Norwich, Oxford, and London lectures. Rimini was familiar with the text of the work contained in the Caius manuscript, which he knew under the name *Lectura secunda*.

Rimini also provides us with additional indications, outside the remarks of Wodeham and Oyta, as to the contents of the London lectures. The prologue of that work was devoted almost exclusively to problems of

---

[122] Ibid.: "Etsi pro secundo aut tertio loco inter angliae litteratos certaverit a duobus, sic ei resistitur ut quotum locum inter eos optinuerit a musis nondum accepi. Primam sedem iam diu venerabilis Beda. . . . Etsi sedem secundam septuaginta annis Alexander Halensis iure quaedem optimo vendicaverit ab Okam et Adamo pro eadem dimicatum est, sed ob veterum maiestatem et ut lite pendente nihil innovetur secundo adhuc loco gaudeat Okam ampullosus et diffusus Adam digestus et resolutus."

epistemology. Much of that material has survived in the *Lectura secunda*. This, in turn, tells us that the *Lectura secunda,* or the Caius manuscript, is a combination of material from (a) the London lectures, (b) the post-1334 redaction of the Oxford lectures, and probably (c) new material that was not delivered previously.

It is interesting that the *Lectura secunda* and a short treatise on indivisibles are the only manuscripts of Wodeham that have survived in England.[123] Should that paucity of Wodeham manuscripts be explained through the destruction of manuscripts in England in the early modern era, either through the dissolution of the monasteries or the Puritan revolution? I think not. Twenty to thirty percent of the extant manuscripts of Ockham, Holcot, and Bradwardine exist in England. There is no reason to suppose that the manuscripts of Wodeham or of any of the other English theologians who are poorly represented in England would have had a strikingly higher rate of destruction. The conclusion seems to be that although there certainly must have been at one time a larger number of Wodeham manuscripts in England, Wodeham was proportionately more popular on the Continent (especially in Paris) than in England.

That conclusion is borne out when we look at the references to Wodeham's thought. In England, only Holcot, Halifax and Rosetus cite Wodeham by name, although one senses Wodeham's presence in the pages of Bradwardine and Buckingham. At Paris, on the other hand, Wodeham is cited everywhere. Some of that disparity must be attributed to the decline of Oxford after the Black Death and the unrivaled prominence of Paris in the third quarter of the fourteenth century.

Wodeham was known in Paris by 1342 and possibly a little earlier. Given the close relationship between Paris and Oxford, there were many ways knowledge of Wodeham could have crossed the Channel. Buckingham taught at Paris, and there is a tradition that connects Halifax with Paris.[124] Wodeham himself, who was in Basel in 1339, may have visited Paris on his way east.[125] However the transmission took place, by 1342

---

[123] This treatise can be found in London, British Museum, Harley 3243, fols. 63^{rb}(55rb)–64^{vb}(56vb). This text has been edited by John Murdoch and Edward Synan, "Two Questions on the Continuum: Walter Chatton, O.F.M. and Adam Wodeham, O.F.M.," *FcS*, XXVI (1966), 212–288.

[124] For Buckingham in Paris see the remark of Thomas of Krakow in Paris, B. N. lat. 16 409, fol. 23^v. On the possibility of Halifax in Paris see T. Tanner, *Bibliotheca Britannico-Hibernica, sive de scriptoribus . . . commentarius* (London, 1748), 259; W. J. Courtenay, "Some Notes on Robert of Halifax, O.F.M.," *FcS*, XXXIII (1973), 135–142.

[125] *Analecta Franciscana,* II (1887), 177; III (1897), 630, 631, 637.

there were at least three separate works of Wodeham available in Paris: the Oxford lectures, either in the *ordinatio* version or in the post-1334 redaction; the London lectures; and the *Lectura secunda*. Whether we look at the proportion of extant manuscripts or at the proportion of citations, the Oxford lectures were considered to be the most important. In all probability the Norwich lectures were never read at Paris, and the English manuscript(s) appear to have been lost.

Beginning in the middle of the fourteenth century a shift in terminology took place. A new title was introduced, *Lectura prima,* which appears to be a designation for the London lectures, but which may be another term for the *Lectura secunda*. Until more references to Wodeham are discovered in the period from 1360 to 1380, this problem must remain unsolved.

Considering the number of theologians who could quote Wodeham from firsthand knowledge, there must have been a larger number of manuscripts available in the fourteenth century than have survived. For those at the University of Paris, Wodeham was an exciting mind who ranked near the top of the English doctors. Ockham was the only English *modernus* cited more often than Wodeham by Parisian theologians. Of the eleven fourteenth-century English authors quoted by Rimini, Wodeham is second in importance only to Ockham. In the second half of the fourteenth century he is often quoted more than Ockham. Furthermore, Wodeham's reputation arrived on the Continent earlier than that of Holcot, with whom his name is generally linked. Alongside Ockham, Fitzralph, and Bradwardine he stands as one of the four most cited. When we reflect that the citations of Fitzralph and Bradwardine are almost exclusively concerned with the related problems of divine volition and future contingents, the wide breadth of topics on which Wodeham was considered important stands out all the more.

There is one last area where the citations of Wodeham alter our understanding of the development of fourteenth-century thought, indeed of the entire late Middle Ages. Damasus Trapp was among the first to note the close relationship between the Cistercians and the Austin Friars in the second half of the fourteenth century. That close connection has been further documented in this chapter. What has not yet been pointed out is the positive attitude, the high esteem in which Wodeham was held by Augustinians and Cistercians alike. The objections to Wodeham found in the pages of Halifax, Rosetus, and Rimini gave way to praise in Ceffons, Hiltalingen, Eltville, Ebrach, d'Ailly, Brammart, and Inghen. Even Hugolino, who was critical of Wodeham in the area of soteriology, sided with him on a number of issues. In fact, as Hiltalingen pointed out, Hugolino sometimes preferred Wodeham to Rimini.

It would appear, therefore, that one must be very cautious in posing an Ockhamist (or nominalist) vs. Augustinian polarization in the fourteenth century. Wodeham, the chief disciple of Ockham, was also one of the major authorities for even the most conservative of Augustinians. This is further evidence to suggest that the split between the *via moderna* and the *via antiqua,* and even the supposed split between the Ockhamistic logicians and the historical, conservative, Augustinians, had not yet taken place at the end of the fourteenth century.

If Wodeham was seen as a major spokesman for Ockham, he was also his own man. In the minds of Continental theologians in the fourteenth century Wodeham could be and was separated from Ockham. Wodeham is cited on a number of topics where Ockham is ignored and Parisians were aware that on occasion Wodeham disagreed with Ockham. However, Wodeham and Ockham were often associated in Parisian citations, as they had been associated in life, and much of the thought of Ockham was interpreted through the writings of Wodeham. He remained throughout the fourteenth century the chief spokesman, after the Venerable Inceptor, for the Ockhamist Tradition.

CHAPTER FOUR

WODEHAM'S ACADEMIC CAREER

Having established the order of Wodeham's writings, their approximate dates, and the external evidence that bears upon his chronology, we are now in a position to reconstruct his academic career with some degree of probability. There are two periods in Wodeham's life about which we have information from his writings: (1) his days as a young student, toward the end of his philosophical training and the beginning of his study in theology; and, (2) his reading of the *Sentences* at various places in the last years of his theological study. The chronologies of these two periods fit perfectly, which permits us to surmise a pattern that can be conjecturally traced into those portions of his life for which we have no direct evidence.

A. THE EARLY YEARS

Wodeham was born in the area of Southampton.[1] Assuming his academic career followed the outlines of Franciscan education set forth in chapter two, and working back from the dates of his Oxford lectures and his theological study under Chatton, we can place the date of Wodeham's birth in 1298 or somewhat earlier. We do not know at what age he entered the Franciscan Order. However, in view of his close connection with Ockham and Chatton by 1321, we must assume he had joined the Order several years before. He probably professed at the Franciscan convent at Southampton or at Winchester. Since he apparently began the study of theology under Chatton in 1321, the last four years of his philosophical study can be tentatively placed in the period 1317–1321.

1. *Studies under Ockham and Chatton*

Toward the end of his philosophical training Wodeham came in contact with and probably studied under Ockham.[2] Where this took

---

[1] L. Wadding, *Annales Minorum*, VIII (1932), p. 162: "... frater Adamus Vodehamensis, diocesis Wintoniensis, comitatus Southamptonensis. ..."
[2] See Prologue to William of Ockham's *Summa Logicae* (Vatican, Ottoboni 2071, fol. 1ra): "... sub cuius ferula me fuisse fateor non verecunde in hac scientia et aliis pluribus

place is not certain. Wodeham was aware that Ockham maintained (or perhaps was required to defend) positions at Oxford he later abandoned, but this does not necessarily mean Wodeham studied philosophy at Oxford while Ockham was there.[3] As was argued earlier, it is unlikely that in Wodeham's day Franciscans were studying philosophy at the Oxford convent. Wodeham could have been informed about Ockham's Oxford teaching by Ockham or someone else at a later date. If Wodeham studied philosophy under Ockham, as he claimed to have done, this must have occurred at some place other than Oxford, after Ockham had finished his theological studies. Ockham never lectured on Aristotle at Oxford.

The most likely location for Wodeham's study with Ockham between 1320 and 1324 is London. Although we cannot be certain, it is reasonable to assume that in the second quarter of the fourteenth century the English Provincial Chapter followed the French practice of requiring friars to study philosophy at a custodial school and to begin their theological work before going to a *studium generale* (Paris, Oxford, or Cambridge) to complete the study of theology.[4] Having been born near Southampton, Wodeham, like Ockham, belonged to the diocese of Winchester and the custody of London. The last four years of Wodeham's philosophical study would most likely have been spent in the appropriate custodial

---

professorem eiusdem ordinis praelibati." Because this phrase is found only in this manuscript, Ph. Boehner, S. Brown, and G. Gál have questioned its authenticity and have placed it in the critical apparatus in both the original edition, Franciscan Institute Publications, Text Series, No. 2 (St. Bonaventure, N.Y., 1957), p. 3, and in the new edition (St. Bonaventure, N.Y., 1974), p. 5. Boehner acknowledged, however, the antiquity and general high quality of Ottoboni 2071, and such a personal remark is not out of character in Wodeham. It is possible, therefore, that the phrase might be authentic. The idea found in the earlier literature that Ockham dedicated his *Summa* to Wodeham has been disproven.

[3] In discussing the formal distinction *in divinis*, Wodeham noted that Ockham in his Commentary on the *Sentences* accepted Scotus' argument, "licet aliter tenuerit respondendo in scholis" (Paris, Univ. 193, fol. 121rb). Wodeham does not say he heard that response, nor does *in scholis* necessarily imply Oxford, unless *respondendo* is taken in the technical sense to refer to respondency (the stage immediately before one became *sententiarius*) or disputes before one fulfilled the requirements for inception. The *reportator* of Chatton used the phrase *in scholis* to describe lectures that we know were not given at Oxford (Paris, B. N. lat. 15 887, fol. 37 + 32vb). However, Wodeham probably meant Oxford, for he made a similar remark about Fitzralph in *Lectura Oxon.* III, q. 6 (Paris, Univ. 193, fol. 193ra): "Praeterea sic arguit Fir., licet respondendo in scolis tenuerit illam responsionem. . . ."

[4] See chapter two, notes 11 and 13.

school, the Franciscan convent in London. It was there, in all probability, that Wodeham and Ockham met.

Fr. Gedeon Gál, working largely from other evidence, has also conjectured that Ockham went to the London convent to teach philosophy immediately after completing his theological training at Oxford.[5] These were particularly productive years for Ockham. While in London he commented on the logic of Aristotle, wrote his *Summa Logicae*, revised his commentary on the first book of the *Sentences*, wrote his commentary on Aristotle's *Physics*, and probably held his quodlibetic debates.[6] Ockham's effect on the young Wodeham was immediate and lasting. By 1321 or, at the latest, 1322, Wodeham was an enthusiastic supporter of Ockham's thought and was already siding with Ockham against Chatton. Wodeham may have acted as Ockham's secretary and eventually did act as his editor.

There can be little doubt that Wodeham studied theology with Chatton in 1321–23, probably at London. Wodeham attended and made a *reportatio* copy of lectures on the *Sentences* delivered by Chatton before 1324, since Wodeham showed his copy of Chatton's lectures to Ockham before Ockham left England.[7] Although Wodeham was eventually familiar with at least two commentaries on the *Sentences* by Chatton, works now designated as Chatton's *Reportatio* and his *Lectura*, the quotations Wodeham gave from the lectures he audited and showed to Ockham cannot be found in the *Lectura* but do correspond exactly with the text of the *Reportatio*, a work otherwise known to have been written in 1321–23 at an English convent other than Oxford.[8] Unfortunately

---

[5] William of Ockham, *Summa Logicae*, pp. 47*–56*.

[6] C. K. Brampton, "The Probable Order of Ockham's non-polemical Works," *Traditio*, XIX (1963), 469–483.

[7] Vat. lat. 955, fol. 161ᵛ: "Ad 14 respondet Ockham quod iste male . . . ;" and in the margin, to be inserted after "Ockham", is: "manu sua in margine reportationis meae." A. Pelzer, *Codices Vaticani Latini*, II, 1, p. 402, thought that the reference was to Adam's *reportatio* of Ockham's lectures. The correct interpretation, however, was achieved by Gedeon Gál and Stephen Brown in their introduction to the critical edition of William of Ockham, *Scriptum in librum primum Sententiarum. Ordinatio*, Vol. I (St. Bonaventure, N.Y., 1967), pp. 29*–30*.

[8] Chatton's *Reportatio* was dated by L. Baudry, "Gauthier de Chatton et son commentaire des sentences," *AHDL*, XIV (1943–45), 337–369. The dating is based on the fact that in the third book Chatton cited as recent the papal constitution *Ad conditorem canonum*, which was published on December 8, 1322, but failed to cite the constitution *Cum inter nonnullas* that appeared on November 12, 1323. Working on the assumption that Chatton gave these lectures across a two-year period, Baudry arrived at the biennium 1321–22 (books I & II) and 1322–23 (books III & IV). C. K. Brampton, "Gauthier de Chatton et la provenance des mss. lat. Paris Bibl. Nat. 15886 et 15887," *EF*, XIV

Wodeham's copy is not among the two extant manuscripts of the *Reportatio*. If ever recovered, we would have not only a work in Wodeham's own hand, but it would have in the margin, at least at one place, the autograph comments of Ockham as well.

The theological lectures of Chatton that Wodeham audited between 1321 and 1323 could not have been given at Oxford, and therefore Wodeham must have begun his theological study at another center, most likely the custodial school at London, where he need only have continued beyond his philosophical study. It can also be conjectured that Ockham, Chatton, and Wodeham were resident together in the same Franciscan convent, probably London, throughout most if not all the years between 1321 and 1324.[9] It is true that Wodeham might have travelled to another town to show Chatton's lectures to Ockham, but there is no reason to suppose he did. In fact, the apparent close interrelation between Chatton's *Reportatio* and Ockham's *Quodlibets* suggests that they were composed at the same time and in the same place, where a rapid exchange of argument and counterargument was possible.[10] Although much of this must remain conjecture, it seems certain that Wodeham began the study of theology in 1321. For this training he did not move to the Franciscan convent at Oxford or Cambridge but remained at the custodial school, possibly because of his personal attachment to Ockham, or because of the intellectual excitement generated by the lectures and disputes of

---

(1964), 200–205, and G. Gál in William of Ockham, *Summa Logicae*, p. 55*, have established on the basis of the numerous references to opinions *in villa* that Chatton's *Reportatio* must have been written in England but could not have been delivered before an Oxford audience. The parallel passages that establish the fact that Wodeham showed his copy of Chatton's *Reportatio* to Ockham are Wodeham, *Lectura Oxon.* I, dist. 17, q. 5 (Vat. lat. 955, fols. 160^r–161^r) and Chatton, *Reportatio* I, dist. 17, q. 2 (Paris, B. N. lat. 15 887, fol. 37+48vb). This material is not found in the *Lectura* at the appropriate place, I, dist. 17, qq. 6–7 (Florence, Bibl. Naz., conv. soppr. C V 357, fols. 150^r–152^r). For Wodeham's citation of Chatton's *Lectura* compare Wodeham, *Lectura Oxon.* I, dist. 33, q. 2, a. 2 (Vat. lat. 955, fol. 183^r) with Chatton, *Lectura*, I, dist. 2, q. 6, a. 4 (Florence, Bibl. Naz., conv. soppr. C V 357, fol. 79vb; Paris, B. N. lat. 15 886, fol. 126va). For a discussion of Wodeham's use of Chatton's *Lectura* see Hester G. Gelber, *Logic and the Trinity: A Clash of Values in Scholastic Thought, 1300–1335*, unpublished doctoral dissertation, University of Wisconsin (Madison, 1974), pp. 197–205.

[9] G. Gál was the first to recognize that Chatton, Wodeham, and Ockham had to be in the same place between 1321 and 1323. See his introduction to William of Ockham, *Summa Logicae*, pp. 47*–56*.

[10] Fr. Joseph Wey, who is presently editing Ockham's *Quodlibeta*, has noted several places where Ockham answers criticisms raised in Chatton's *Reportatio*. See also V. P. Zoubov, "Walter Catton, Gerard d'Odon et Nicolas Bonet," *Physis*, I (1959), 261–278; J. E. Murdoch and E. A. Synan, "Two Questions on the Continuum: Walter Chatton (?), O.F.M. and Adam Wodeham, O.F.M.," *FcS*, XXVI (1966), 212–288.

Ockham and Chatton, but most probably because he was required to do so by his superiors.

Wodeham was not a silent student in Chatton's lectures. He apparently raised objections and counterarguments at times and was answered by Chatton either then or on a subsequent day. Wodeham's objections were invariably on points of Aristotelian philosophy, which he may have continued to study with Ockham. The official *reportator* of Chatton's lectures noted Wodeham's objections and Chatton's replies.[11] From this we may conjecture that Wodeham possessed an ability and a self-confidence that exceeded his years or at least exceeded the bounds of quiet respect normally shown by beginning students of theology.

After Ockham's departure for Avignon in 1324 Wodeham continued his study of theology. We know that Wodeham was in residence at Oxford during part of the period 1326–29. His thorough knowledge of the original version of Fitzralph's commentary on the *Sentences* suggests he attended those lectures, probably given in 1326–27.[12] We also know that Wodeham attended a disputation of Fitzralph (no doubt at Oxford) while Fitzralph was a bachelor of theology.[13] Since Fitzralph was in Paris in 1329–30 and incepted shortly after his return to Oxford, this disputation would have had to have taken place between 1326 and 1329, before which Fitzralph was not a bachelor of theology and after which Fitzralph was not at Oxford as a bachelor.

Wodeham no doubt heard other lectures in these years at Oxford. John of Rodington was probably reading the *Sentences* as bachelor in this period. Moreover, Wodeham's time at Oxford overlapped with one or more of the Franciscan lectors who may have fulfilled their regency during this period: Robert Leicester, Walter Foxley, Henry Cruche, and John Ratford.

2. *The Norwich Lectures*

By 1328 Wodeham had completed his seven years of theological study

---

[11] Paris, B. N. lat. 15 887, fol. 37+65ʳᵃ.

[12] Wodeham distinguishes the original version of Fitzralph's *Sentences* Commentary from a corrected version that Fitzralph was working on in 1330–31 while he was *magister regens*. See above, chapter two, pp. 76–78.

[13] Wodeham, in revising his Oxford lectures, altered a reference to Fitzralph in the text that read "unus doctor" to read "nunc doctor, tunc baccalarius," thus revealing a more intimate knowledge of the circumstances of Fitzralph's remark. In the following quotation the marginal and interlinear additions of Wodeham are placed in parentheses. Vat. lat. 955, fols. 41ʳ–41ᵛ: "(Responsio Hyb.) Ad primum respondet et bene in disputatione unus (nunc) doctor (tunc baccalarius) quod quamdam testat. . . ."

and was eligible to read the *Sentences* at a custodial school.¹⁴ This Wodeham did at Norwich, in 1328–29 or 1329–30. He cannot have given those lectures before 1328 because he would not have had sufficient years of theological study, and he could not have given them after 1330, since in 1330–31 he was lecturing at Oxford and referring back to his Norwich lectures.¹⁵ By 1330 Wodeham was also familiar with Chatton's *Lectura*, which was composed between 1323 and 1330.¹⁶

Michalski's conviction that the Norwich lectures postdate the Oxford lectures has no foundation. That idea may have been suggested to him by the order in which John Major placed Wodeham's residences: London, Oxford, and Norwich.¹⁷ Michalski was aware that Wodeham referred to his Norwich lectures at the end of book III of his Oxford lectures, but Michalski insisted on viewing that remark as a later interpolation, despite

---

¹⁴ The practice of reading the *Sentences* at a *studium generale* other than Paris, Oxford, or Cambridge, or at a custodial school (of which there were seven in England) was made mandatory in the legislation for the Franciscans in 1336. This constitution of Benedict XII, however, was probably only making official what had been common practice for several years. Inasmuch as we know Wodeham read at Norwich before reading at Oxford and we know that Norwich was one of the custodial schools, we may infer that this custom was perhaps being observed as early as 1328. Before reading elsewhere, however, it would have been necessary for the candidate to have completed the seven years of theological study required of those who held the M.A. degree and thus to have reached the stage of being opponent and respondent in theological disputations. The practice of reading elsewhere before reading at a major *studium generale* may not have been limited to the Franciscans. We know that Gregory of Rimini taught (and may even have read the *Sentences*) at Bologna, Padua, and Perugia before reading at Paris. *CUP*, II, p. 557 (no. 1097); cf. D. Trapp, "Gregory of Rimini Manuscripts. Editions and Additions," *Augustiniana*, VIII (1958), 425–443.

¹⁵ Wodeham, *Lectura Oxon*. I, dist. 33, q. 2 (Vat. lat. 955, fol. 185ʳ; Paris, Maz. 915, fol. 108ᵛᵃ; Paris, Univ. 193, fol. 124ʳᵃ); *Lectura Oxon*. III, q. 12 (Paris, Maz. 915, fol. 199ʳ; Paris, Univ. 193, fol. 207ᵛᵇ).

¹⁶ Since Chatton cited Ockham's *Summa Logicae* in his *Lectura*, it must have been written after 1323, when Ockham's *Summa* was completed. For the dating of Ockham's *Summa* see the introduction by G. Gál, William of Ockham, *Summa Logicae*, pp. 47*–56*. Moreover, since Wodeham cited Chatton's *Lectura* in book I of his Oxford lectures on the *Sentences*, the former must have been completed before 1330; see above, note 8. As was suggested in chapter two, pp. 70–71, there is a distant possibility that Chatton's *Lectura* is not his bachelor lectures at Oxford but an example of *Quaestiones ordinariae super Sententias*. In this connection one should note Wodeham's statement in his Oxford lectures, IV, q. 5 (Paris, Maz. 915, fol. 216ʳᵃ; Paris, Univ. 193, fol. 220ᵛᵇ): "Nota tamen quod ipse [Chatton] post tempus magisterii sui posuit in Determinatione quam et ego ipse tunc, sicut et priores alias, audivi dum legit Sententias ab eo. . . ." It is not clear whether the "dum legit Sententias" goes with the "tunc" and the "post tempus magisterii" or with the "priores alias".

¹⁷ See *Vita Adae* in the introduction to Oyta's abbreviation of Wodeham's *Sentences* Commentary (Paris, 1512).

its similarity to other cross references in the Oxford lectures that Michalski took to be authentic.[18]

The content of the Norwich lectures cannot be determined exactly. We know that they included (and may have been composed solely of) commentary on the last three distinctions of book III and on much of book IV of the *Sentences*. Through those distinctions he dealt with the Ten Commandments[19] and the logic of the Trinity, which may have evolved naturally out of a discussion of the first commandment.[20] In the fourth book he treated baptism and the other sacraments,[21] and at some point in the Norwich lectures he dealt with the problem of velocity and motion.[22]

During his time at Norwich Wodeham met Ralph Pigaz, who may also have been lecturing at Norwich preparatory to his becoming the lector at the Franciscan convent at Cambridge around 1329. According to Wodeham, Pigaz shared Wodeham's views on the Trinity, which differed sharply from Chatton's.[23] Unfortunately, the lectures of Pigaz and the Norwich lectures of Wodeham are not known to have survived.

3. *The London Lectures*

The London lectures cannot at present be dated precisely. They were given in the period 1328–1332, but their exact chronological relation to the Norwich and Oxford lectures is conjectural. All that we know for certain is that they occurred before Wodeham lectured on book III of the

---

[18] Michalski, "Le problème de la volonté à Oxford et à Paris au XIVe siècle," *Studia Philosophica*, II, 243–244.

[19] *Lectura Oxon.* III, q. 12 (Paris, Maz. 915, fol. 199^r): "Ad argumentum principale satis apte respondet Magister ibidem in littera, et in hoc tempore plus non durante finiuntur conclusiones super tertium nisi quod alibi in lectura Norvicensi super tres ultimas distinctiones prosecutus sum quaestiones de praeceptis decalogi sigillatim."

[20] *Lectura Oxon.* I, dist. 33, q. 2 (Vat. lat. 955, fol. 185^r; Paris, Maz. 915, fol. 108va; Paris, Univ. 193, fol. 124ra).

[21] *Lectura Oxon.* IV, q. 1 (Paris, Univ. 193, fol. 209va); IV, q. 3 (Paris, Univ. 193, fol. 214va): ". . . quae tamen legendo apud Norwicensem prosecutus sum singula per d.[blank space] quarti de baptismo et aliis sacramentis." *Lectura Oxon.* IV, q. 6 (Paris, Univ. 193, fol. 223va): ". . . sicut notavi in quarto lecturarum Norw., eadem dist. [= 14], 1."

[22] *Lectura Oxon.* III, q. 11 (Paris, Univ. 193, fol. 203va).

[23] *Lectura Oxon.* I, dist. 33, q. 2 (Paris, Univ. 193, fol. 124ra; Tar. 7, fol. 89vb; Paris, Maz. 915, fol. 108va; Vat. lat. 955, fol. 185^r): "Aliud dubium: an sufficiat illa distinctio de deitate singulorum et singulis deitatis quam tenet Pigam, et mihi multum placuit, tum quia bene accessit ad veritatem, tum forsitan quia multum concordabat sententiae quam prius tenueram in lectione Norvicensi."

Sentences at Oxford.[24] That leaves three possibilities: that the London lectures preceded the Norwich lectures; that they occurred in between the Norwich and Oxford lectures; or that they occurred in between the second and third books of the Oxford lectures as a result of a year's absence from Oxford. Each of these possibilities needs to be examined closely.

The case for placing the London lectures before the Norwich lectures is weak. In its favor one can only suggest that reading on the first thirteen distinctions of book III might naturally precede reading on the last three distinctions and on book IV. Moreover, if the passage in the *Lectura secunda* that refers to a future treatment of univocity were originally from the London lectures, then that might point ahead to the Norwich lectures.[25] However, we know that Pigaz, who was Cambridge lector around 1329, was at Norwich with Wodeham. That contact probably preceded Pigaz' regency, since after 1330 Wodeham was at Oxford. Moreover, a reference in the third book of Wodeham's Oxford lectures suggests that a *determinatio* of Chatton at Oxford, shortly after Chatton's regency (1329–30), followed closely upon Wodeham's London lectures.[26]

If the London lectures are placed between the Norwich and Oxford lectures, they would have been given in 1329–30 or, at the latest, in 1330–31. There is much to be said for this hypothesis. In the *Lectura Oxoniensis*, book I, dist. 33, q. 5 Wodeham refers to an opinion he held at London.[27] While that reference need not be a reference to the London

---

[24] There are no references "in tertio Londoniense" in books I and II of the Oxford lectures, but they are frequent from the opening of book III until the end of book IV.

[25] *Lectura secunda*, dist. 25, q. 1 (Cambridge, Caius 281, fol. 246va).

[26] Wodeham, *Lectura Oxon.* III, dist. 14, q. 11 (Paris, Maz. 915, fol. 193va; Paris, Univ. 193, fol. 203ra), referring to what he eventually describes as "Chatton in quadam determinatione Oxon. quod continuum non componitur ex partibus divisibilibus," says that ". . . quae audivi postquam illam materiam Londoniae pertractavi." This determination or another like it is referred to elsewhere by Wodeham, *Lectura Oxon.* IV, q. 10 (Vat. lat. 1110, fol. 128^v). Cf. also *Lectura Oxon.* IV, q. 5 (Paris, Maz. 915, fol. 216ra; Paris, Univ. 193, fol. 220vb): "Nota tamen quod ipse post tempus magisterii sui posuit in Determinatione quam et ego ipse tunc, sicut et priores alias, audivi dum legit Sententias ab eo. . . ."

[27] *Lectura Oxon.* I, dist. 33, q. 5 (Paris, Univ. 193, fol. 133ra; Vat. lat. 955, fol. 200^r; Paris, Maz. 915, fol. 118va; Tar. 7, fol. 96va; Erfurt 2° 133, fol. 84va): ". . . nolo hoc ponere nec reputo hoc ponendum, sed volo potius sustinere personam esse aeque simplicem sicut essentiam vel personalem proprietatem. Ideo nolo dicere quod persona includat relationem et essentiam de virtute sermonis loquendo, nec quod constituatur quod resultet ex proprietate et essentia, sed volo dicere quod est essentia et est proprietas. Et hoc idem dico de proprietate quod ipsa est essentia et ipsa est proprietas. Et propterea teneo istam viam quam alias tetigi Londoniae. Ad istam quam hic teneo, scilicet quod

lectures (it could, for instance, refer to an opinion he held and expressed while studying under Chatton), it could be construed as such. Moreover, one finds at the end of book II in Paris, Univ. 193 a statement by Wodeham that he had previously treated many questions that properly belong to book II, such as motion, time, the continuum, and individuation.[28] This might be a reference to the London lectures, which we know treated the continuum, but it might also be a reference to the Norwich lectures, which we know dealt in part with velocity and motion. If we place the London lectures before book I of the Oxford lectures, it would permit us to divide the content of the Oxford lectures more evenly across a biennium, with one year devoted to book I and one year devoted to books II–IV. It would also bring the dating of Wodeham's lectures on books III and IV at Oxford more within the time of Chatton's Oxford residency.

There are other indications, however, that the London lectures were given during a year that interrupted Wodeham's lectures at Oxford. The statement at the opening of book III raises the possibility that Wodeham is beginning at distinction fourteen because he had left off in London at distinction thirteen.[29] More compelling is the fact that there are abundant references to the London lectures in books III and IV of the Oxford lectures, all of which observe the form "in tertio Lond.", and yet there are no references to London in book II, and the sole reference in book I does not use the form "in tertio Lond."[30] When one considers that the

---

nomen proprium primi suppositi in diversis et ita de aliis. . . ." The Vatican and Erfurt manuscripts have "sub disiunctione" in place of "Londoniae".

[28] Paris, Univ. 193, fol. 174[rb]: "Explicit secundus liber, alias enim multas quaestiones secundi de motu, de tempore, de continuo et de individuatione et similibus alias seriosius pertractavi."

[29] Paris, Maz. 915, fol. 167[r]: "Circa istum librum tertium, quia alias Londoniae toto anno pertractavi quaestiones 13 primarum distinctionum, ideo nunc incipio a distinctione 14."

[30] Wodeham, *Lectura Oxon.* III, dist. 14, q. 1 (Paris, Maz. 915, fol. 170[v]): ". . . similiter, d. 4 in tertio Londoniense." Ibid., III, dist. 14, q. 11 (Paris, Univ. 193, fol. 203[ra]; Paris, Maz. 915, fol. 193[va]): ". . . contra hoc positas in tertio Londoniense, dist. 13." Ibid., IV, q. 5 (Paris, Maz. 915, fol. 212[r], and Bruges 172, fol. 12[r]): ". . . sicut probavi in tertio Londoniense." Paris, B. N. lat. 15 892, fol. 153[r] at this point reads: ". . . sicut alibi probavi, scilicet quarto Londoniense," but this is later corrected to "tertio Londoniense." Ibid. (Paris, Maz. 915, fol. 212[r]; Bruges 172, fol. 12[r]; Paris, B. N. lat. 15 892, fol. 153[r]): ". . . sicut prius dictum est, et probatum est diffuse in tertio Londoniense." Ibid. (Paris, Maz. 915, fol. 213[r]; Bruges 172, fol. 13[r]; Paris, B. N. lat. 15 892, fol. 154[r]): ". . . sicut in tertio Londoniense, in prima distinctione, quaestione secunda, respondendo ad obiectionem 14 secundi [Bruges: tertii] articuli." While much of the evidence from the Wodeham manuscripts speaks for itself regardless of the date and place at which

topic of quantity is discussed in book II of the Oxford lectures and was also a major concern of the London lectures, it is strange that Wodeham did not refer back to his treatment at London, if the London lectures actually occurred previously. Indeed, in the post-1334 rewriting of selected questions from book I of the Oxford lectures, Wodeham added references to the London lectures that are absent in the first redaction.[31] When Wodeham explains the need for his renewed discussion of quantity and the continuum in book III of the Oxford lectures, he gives the impression that his most recent and complete treatment of the problem had been in his London lectures, not book II, q. 7 of the Oxford lectures.[32] Placing the London lectures between books II and III of the Oxford lectures would make Wodeham's relationship with Chatton develop progressively from respectful disagreement, to direct criticism, to a heated controversy.

There is one other indication that Wodeham's lectures on books I and II at Oxford might have occurred in one academic year. In books I and II Wodeham discusses at set stages the *principia* of books III and IV, as if other bachelors had reached those points at the appropriate time during the year and Wodeham had not.[33] A glance at the structure of the Oxford lectures and the Caius College manuscript confirms that Wodeham tended to linger on early distinctions and then move ahead by uneven leaps.[34]

---

particular comments were made, the order—and thus the dating—of the London (and Norwich) lectures depend on whether the cross references were original to the Oxford lectures or were added later. I have yet to discover a reference to the London lectures (or to the Norwich lectures) in Vat. lat. 1110. This suggests that the cross references may have been added by Wodeham while preparing the *ordinatio* edition of his Oxford lectures before 1334. However, they explain otherwise unusual omissions in the original text. For example, all manuscripts that contain book III, including Vat. lat. 1110, omit questions on the first thirteen distinctions of book III, an omission, as Wodeham explains, that resulted from his having already lectured on these distinctions at London.

[31] A marginal reference to "3° Lond. d. 13" in Vat. lat. 955, fol. 19^v does not occur at that point in Paris, Maz. 915, fol. 12va, nor Paris, Univ. 193, fol. 15ra. A reference to the London lectures in Cambridge, Caius College 281, fol. 143ra, does not occur at the corresponding section in Vat. lat. 955, fol. 27^v.

[32] Wodeham, *Lectura Oxon.* III, dist. 14, q. 11 (Paris, Maz. 915, fol. 193va), in referring to a recent *determinatio* of Chatton at Oxford, says: "... quae audivi postquam illam materiam Londoniae pertractavi."

[33] *Lectura Oxon.* I, dist. 17, q. 6 (Vat. lat. 955, fol. 163^v; Paris, Maz. 915, fol. 97^v) also applies to the "principium tertii libri." Similarly, II, dist. 1, q. 5 (Vat. lat. 1110, fol. 20^r; Paris, Maz. 915, fol. 145^r), which is devoted to his principial debate with his *socii* over the beatific vision, also applies to the "principium etiam quarti."

[34] In the Oxford lectures, Wodeham devoted fourteen questions to the first distinction of book I, skipped distinctions 4, 5, and 7, jumped from distinction 8 to 17, and then

The abundant references to the London lectures in books III and IV of the Oxford lectures as compared with the total absence of any clear-cut reference in books I and II (which is two-thirds of the Oxford *Lectura*) could be persuasive if it were not for the fact that there are no other known examples of an interruption of a university baccalaureate. That raises one other possibility that needs to be considered. Could Wodeham have lectured on books III and IV before lecturing on books I and II, for at Paris we have several examples of later books being read before book I?[35]

A theory that Wodeham read on books III and IV before he read on I and II only further complicates the problem of the absence of any certain reference to the London lectures in the *Lectura Oxoniensis* I and II. Furthermore, there are abundant cross references, both in Vat. lat. 1110 and in the *Ordinatio*, which indicate that: (1) the Oxford lectures began with a prologue that probably contained only two questions; and, (2) this was followed by books I, II, III, and IV, in that order.[36] Cross references could, of course, have been inserted later, but they are of sufficient number and integrally involved with the structure of individual questions to make this unlikely.

Despite the imprecision on its date, we do know a considerable amount about the London *lectura*. They occupied an entire year and were devoted

---

from 17 to 33. Within the nine questions on distinction 33 he applied some of these to cover, as well, distinctions 4, 5, 7, 11, 12, 27, and 36. This erratic pattern was continued. All the questions of book II were devoted to distinction 1, and many of them refer back to the seventeenth distinction of book I. Wodeham begins book III with distinction 14 because, having covered the first thirteen in the London lectures, he supposedly will cover the remaining ones at Oxford. But all the questions of book III of the Oxford lectures are on distinction 14. The Caius College manuscript appears to be on the first two books of the *Sentences*. Having introduced book II on fol. 173^r, however, Wodeham immediately returns to his unfinished questions and distinctions from book I.

[35] For a discussion of this problem as it concerns the commentaries of Peter Aureol (1316–18), Gregory of Rimini (1342–44), and Facinus de Ast (1361–63), see D. Trapp, "Augustinian Theology," *Augustiniana*, VI (1956), 266–267.

[36] The following cross references are only a small sample of those that occur throughout the Oxford lectures. Prologue, q. 2 (Vat. lat. 955, fol. 10^r; Paris, Maz. 915, fol. 6va) refers to the Prologue, q. 1; I, q. 1 (Paris, Maz. 915, fol. 11va) refers to Prol., q. 2; II, q. 5 (Paris, Maz. 915, fol. 145ra) refers to Wodeham's Principium I = Prima lectio; II, q. 5 (Paris, Maz. 915, fol. 153vb) refers to book I, dist. 1, q. 9; II, q. 5 (Paris, Maz. 915, fol. 147vb) refers to book II, q. 3; II, q. 6 (Paris, Maz. 915, fol. 155ra) refers to book I, q. 1; II, q. 7 (Paris, Maz. 915, fol. 158rb) refers to book I, q. 1; II, q. 7 (Paris, Maz. 915, fol. 158rb) refers to book II, q. 5; II, q. 8 (Vat. lat. 1110, fol. 33^r; Paris, Maz. 915, fol. 159va) refers to Principium I; II, q. 8 (Paris, Maz. 915, fol. 162vb) refers to book II, q. 5; III, q. 1 (Vat. lat. 1110, fol. 44^v; Paris, Maz. 915, fol. 170ra) refers to Prol., q. 2; III, q. 1 (Vat. lat. 1110, fol. 45^v; Paris, Maz. 915, fol. 171ra) refers to book I, q. 1 and book II, q. 5.

to the first thirteen distinctions of book III.[37] They were not, in all probability, a full commentary on the *Sentences*. The prologue was devoted to questions of epistemology and evident knowledge of theological truth. These issues received extensive treatment in questions 2,[38] 7,[39] and 9.[40] We also know that Wodeham exercised a certain degree of freedom in his selection of questions to be drawn from the Lombard text, a freedom present in the Oxford lectures as well. At London he took the occasion of Lombard's discussion of the Incarnation to examine the issues of quantity, indivisibility, and the continuum, defending Ockham's position against the atomists and probably criticizing the position of Walter Chatton.[41] Wodeham seems to have been proud of his London lectures, and they must have brought him a certain degree of fame. They circulated as a separate work throughout the fourteenth century, and Wodeham preferred to direct his readers to his arguments there rather than incorporate them in detail in the second half of his Oxford lectures. As we have seen, Wodeham did use material from the prologue of the London lectures in the construction of his *Lectura secunda*, a work in which he also used material from his bachelor lectures at Oxford. How much of the London lectures appears in the *Lectura secunda* and how much of the material that was borrowed was also revised are impossible to determine at this time.

B. The Oxford Lectures

By the summer of 1330 Wodeham had completed the necessary nine years of theological study required of those who, like the mendicants, did not take the arts degree. He probably began lecturing on the *Sentences* at

---

[37] Wodeham, *Lectura Oxon.* III, dist. 14, q. 1 (Paris, Maz. 915, fol. 169rb; Paris, Univ. 193, fol. 124vb): "Circa istum librum tertium, quia alias Londoniae toto anno pertractavi quaestiones 13 primarum distinctionum, ideo nunc incipio a distinctione 14." Since there were at least nine questions in the prologue of the London lectures and some distinctions were given more than one question, the "13" applies to "distinctionum" rather than "quaestiones."

[38] Discussed by Gregory of Rimini, *Super secundum sententiarum*, dist. 16 & 17, q. 3, a. 1 (Venice, 1522), II, 88 B.

[39] Discussed by Gregory of Rimini, *Super primum sententiarum*, Prol., q. 3, a. 1 (Venice, 1522), I, 13 J–K.

[40] Discussed by Henry Totting of Oyta, *Quaestiones sententiarum* (Paris lectures), q. 1 (Krakow 1362, fol. 20^r; München, Clm 8867, fol. 20^r).

[41] Wodeham, *Lectura Oxon.* III, dist. 14, q. 11 (Paris, Maz. 915, fol. 193^v); Ibid., IV, q. 5 (Paris, Maz. 915, fol. 212^r; Bruges 172, fol. 12^r); Ibid. (Paris, Maz. 915, fol. 213^r; Bruges 172, fol. 13^r).

Oxford in the following year, 1330–31. As was suggested at various points in chapter two, the chronological limits within which the Oxford lectures could have taken place is limited. The reference to John XXII places them before the end of 1334.[42] Moreover, Chatton was still present in Oxford when Wodeham lectured on book III, and we know that Chatton was in Avignon by January, 1333.[43] For the *terminus a quo*, Wodeham's references to Fitzralph make it clear that 1330 is the earliest date at which Wodeham could have begun his Oxford lectures.[44]

Whether London is placed before or in the middle of the Oxford lectures, the latter must have begun in the fall of 1330. If we place the London lectures first and divide the biennium evenly between book I and books II–IV, that biennium could not have been 1331–33, since in the second year Wodeham's lectures on book III would have occurred after Chatton left England. Working on that assumption, our biennium would have to be 1330–32. If we take the other assumption, that the London lectures occurred in between books II and III of the Oxford lectures, then Wodeham's lectures on III and IV could have occurred as late as 1332–33 since Chatton would still have been in England in the fall of 1332 when book III was read. According to this theory we would have: Oxford I and II (1330–31), London III, pt. 1 (1331–32), and Oxford III, pt. 2 and IV (1332–33). Wherever one places the London lectures, Wodeham's lectures on book I fall in the academic year 1330–31. This dating is further confirmed by the close correspondence between the opinions of Wodeham's Dominican *socius* and the opinions of Robert Holcot, who we know was reading in 1330–31.[45]

1. *Collationes, Protestatio, Principia, and Quaestiones*

Having established the year in which Wodeham began his lectures on the *Sentences* at Oxford, we can now turn to the exercises and lectures that filled that year. The steps that began the entire process of reading the *Sentences* as well as the steps initiating the reading of individual books followed a prescribed routine, established by university statute. Some of the results of Wodeham's participation in these prescribed events have survived and should therefore be examined.

---

[42] See above, chapter one, pp. 15–16.
[43] See above, chapter two, pp. 72–73.
[44] See above, chapter two, pp. 76–77.
[45] See above, chapter two, pp. 100–106.

The opening exercise, or *principium*, of the newly-appointed bachelor began with a *collatio*. Although the term itself designates several different types of university exercises, the *collatio* in this context was a sermon delivered by the candidate before the theological masters and fellow bachelors on the eve of his opening lecture on each of the books of the *Sentences*. In these sermons the candidate usually demonstrated his extensive knowledge of the Bible along with his ability to make puns and hide references to himself and others in scriptural texts.[46] All four Oxford *collationes* of Wodeham have survived. Following fourteenth-century practice, Wodeham chose opening texts for his sermons that contained some references to his own name, thus providing a signature or indication of authorship for the work that followed.

Collationes became, in the fourteenth century, an interlace of puns, subtle meanings, and hidden references—things that no doubt delighted the audience that knew the personalities involved. Many of these hidden references, especially the "heraldic" mystifications, as they have been called, are lost on the modern reader who lacks the inside knowledge through which to interpret them. One must be careful, however, not to compensate and read more into the Biblical texts of a *collatio* than was intended. Wodeham provides a good case in point. His opening Scriptural line was "Ista est lex Adam, Domine Deus, 2 Reg. 7," which Damasus Trapp read as "This is the Writ of Adam Lord God[ham], his Second *Lectura*: King's [year] 7 (Edward III: 1327–77) = 1334," and thus inferred that Adam's true name was Godham, that he was probably a nobleman, that this work constituted his second lectures, and that they were written in 1334.[47] But in most manuscripts, including what is probably Wodeham's autograph, his name is spelled "Wodeham". Godham or Goddam is probably a Continental variant or corruption. We also know that the *Ordinatio* is not the *Lectura secunda* and that it was not read in 1334. Nor is there any reason to suppose Wodeham had aristocratic origins. Had Wodeham wished to imply that this was his *Lectura secunda* or *Lectura tertia* of 1330, he could not have found a sentence that included his name in 2 Reg. 3 or 3 Reg. 3.

---

[46] For a discussion of fourteenth-century *collationes* and what has been termed the "heraldic" mystifications or allusions in them, see D. Trapp, "Peter Ceffons of Clairvaux," *RTAM*, XXIV (1957), 105–107, and "Augustinian Theology," *Augustiniana*, VI (1956), 269–272. See also B. Smalley, *English Friars and Antiquity* (Oxford, 1960), p. 135, and André Combes' introduction in Jean de Ripa, *Lectura super primum sententiarum, Prologi quaestiones I & II* (Paris, 1961), p. xxxi.

[47] Trapp, "Augustinian Theology," *Augustiniana*, VI, 271.

Wodeham's *collationes* were included in the *ordinatio* edition, but they are absent in Vat. lat. 1110 and in the post-1334 redaction of the bachelor lectures at Oxford. The *Lectura secunda*, as we shall see, contains *collationes* for books I and II of that work, again using texts that contain the name "Adam."[48] The incipits and explicits for the *collationes* of the Oxford bachelor lectures have been given in appendix one.

In the official academic procedure and occasionally in the manuscript version of a *Sentences* commentary, the first *collatio* was followed by a *protestatio* (profession of faith), a statement made by the candidate assuring the faculty that his subsequent lectures would not contain definitive pronouncements but rather probable arguments, *non assertive*, appropriate for a scholastic exercise.[49] The candidate usually added that if any statements were found not to be in keeping with catholic faith, he would gladly abandon them and subject himself to the correction of the theological faculty.

Very few of these statements have survived, probably because their content followed a standard form and did not reflect the creative ability or the style of the author, or possibly because some bachelors failed to make the *protestatio*. Richard Kilvington, lecturing on the *Sentences* within a few years of Wodeham, is one who failed to make the required *protestatio* and substituted instead an *apologia* after he had lectured to avoid possible charges of presumption or even of heresy.[50]

The *protestatio* of Wodeham has not survived intact, but there may be a fragment of it buried in his introductory comment in the post-1334 redaction of his Oxford lectures.[51] In any event, the statement served the same purpose and is the type of statement that would have been part of the *protestatio*.

Each *collatio* was followed by a principial lecture in which the bachelor engaged his fellow *baccalarii* or *socii* in debate. Like the *collatio*, the

---

[48] Cambridge, Caius 281, fols. 105ra–105va and 173rb–173vb.

[49] For a discussion of the *protestatio* see D. Trapp, "Clm 27034: Unchristened Nominalism and Wycliffite Realism at Prague in 1381," *RTAM*, XXIV (1957), 340, 349.

[50] Richard Kilvington, *Lectura*, at the end of *collatio* I(?) (Erfurt, CA 2° 105, fol. 134rb): "Ego, Richardus de Kilvyngton Eboracensis dyocesis, debita protestatione praemissa nunc pro tunc, revoco in hiis scriptis et correctioni sacrosanctae Romanae ecclesiae et doctorum meorum universitatis Oxoniensis ubi primi mundi universitatibus ceteris viget amplius decor clerici penitus me submitto. . . ."

[51] Vat. lat. 955, fol. 1^v: "In nomine Domini incipit brevis collectio Wodeham super Sententias apud Oxoniam . . . quae si quid contineat repraehensibile contra fidem vel mores, contra eius intentionem est et ex nunc illud abicit et retractat et quorum intererit benevolentiae subicit corrigendum."

principium for each book was given before the theological faculty, although a copy of the lecture could be circulated among the bachelors in advance.[52] At Oxford as well as Paris there were normally only as many bachelors reading in one year as there were regent masters, and no religious order could have more than one regent master with voice and vote in congregation and usually no more than one bachelor reading the *Sentences* in any one year.[53]

This reading of the *Sentences* at Oxford, as was pointed out in chapter two, occupied nine months of the academic year: October to July, during which there were to be four principal debates at designated intervals.[54] The bachelors for the year gave their *principia* in a set sequence.[55] The candidate who began the sequence usually had to wait until the *principium* of book II before responding to the criticisms against his position. The other candidates could begin by attacking the arguments of previous bachelors. In some years the topic of the *principia* seems to have been set, and a clear distinction made between the *principium* of a bachelor and the first question of his subsequent commentary on the *Sentences*.[56] The evidence we have from Wodeham, however, suggests that the procedure in his year or years was somewhat less formal.

If there were principial lectures in 1330–31 separate from the opening lectures on the books of the *Sentences*, then we no longer possess those of Wodeham or, at most, we have only one.[57] The references in Wodeham to the opinions of his fellow *baccalarii* and the completeness of the *ordinatio* edition suggest the strong possibility that there were no principial lectures separate from the first lecture of the Commentary and that the *socii* were engaged at particular points in the course of the Commentary on the

---

[52] See D. Trapp, "Peter Ceffons of Clairvaux," *RTAM*, XXIV (1957), 104–105.

[53] Note the ordering of those appointed to read the *Sentences* at Paris in *CUP*; see also A. G. Little, "The Franciscan School at Oxford," *AFH*, XIX (1926), 822, 826, 831. Only the Dominicans at Paris, who possessed two chairs of theology, could have two bachelors reading in the same year.

[54] Little, *AFH*, XIX, 826; Trapp, *RTAM*, XXIV, 104.

[55] H. Rashdall, *The Universities of Europe in the Middle Ages*, rev. ed. F. M. Powicke and A. B. Emden (Oxford, 1936), I, 477; F. Ehrle, *I più antichi statuti della facoltà teologica dell' Università di Bologna*, Universitatis Bononiensis Monumenta, Vol. I (Bologna, 1931), pp. clxxxvii, 23.

[56] For example, the principial material grouped at the end of Thomas of Strasbourg's Commentary on the *Sentences* (Venice, 1564), II, fols. 210^r–217^v; D. Trapp, *RTAM*, XXIV, 105.

[57] Vat. lat. 869, fols. 215rb–217va.

Sentences.⁵⁸ It would appear that the opening question of the prologue of Wodeham's Commentary on the *Sentences* should be considered his *principium* for the first book. Wodeham, in later questions, refers to it as such.⁵⁹ Moreover, Wodeham's response to his fellow *socii* does not appear in the first question of each book but is spread throughout the Commentary.

The first *quaestio prologi* treats a wide variety of topics, chief among them the capacity of the soul for beatitude. The tone of this opening question is formal, perhaps reflecting the atmosphere of a principial lecture. Throughout the question Wodeham does not refer to any of his *socii*, but he does indirectly refer to Fitzralph.⁶⁰ In the second question of the prologue, which is basically a continuation of the material of question 1, the tone is less formal, more personal, and the opinions of the *socii* begin to appear alongside references to Fitzralph.

For Wodeham, the end of the prologue is not the end of the discussion of this principial topic, namely the capacity of the soul for beatitude. He continues it in book I, dist. 1, q. 1 in which Ockham appears for the first time. After that question Wodeham leaves his opening topic and occupies himself with issues more appropriate to the structure of the first book of the *Sentences*. While a variety of subjects are addressed, the most important ones are the fruition of God, the freedom of the will, the nature of God, the habit of grace, and the Trinity. In the second book, which was begun as early as the spring of 1331 or as late as the fall of 1331, he occupied himself with the issues of grace and merit, although he returned at times to the principial topic of the capacity of the soul. In books three and four, respectively, he addressed the problem of future contingents and sacramental theology.

Wodeham engaged his *socii* at several points in questions that are part of the regular structure of the work. The two major places are in the second question of the prologue and in the fifth question of book two, where one has the impression that Wodeham's colleagues had already begun their commentaries on the fourth book of Lombard's *Sentences*.⁶¹

---

⁵⁸ *Socii* are mentioned in book I, prol., q. 2; I, dist. 17, q. 3; II, q. 3; II, q. 5; II, q. 6; II, q. 7; II, q. 8; III, q. 1; IV, q. 4.

⁵⁹ Cf. I, prol., q. 2; II, q. 5; II, q. 8; and III, q. 1.

⁶⁰ Vat. lat. 955, fol. 4ʳ; Paris, Maz. 915, fol. 3ʳᵃ. The argument is ascribed to a "quidam doctor" in the text, but the doctor is identified in the margin of the Vatican manuscript as "Yber".

⁶¹ Book II, q. 5, which extensively records Wodeham's controversy with the Carmelite, Skelton, and Grafton, begins (Vat. lat. 1110, fol. 20ʳ; Paris, Maz. 915, fol. 145ʳᵃ): "Quinto quaero circa distinctionem primam secundi libri et principium quarti. . . ."

In one respect, the Oxford lectures of Wodeham do not have the appearance of bachelor lectures, although we know they were. As a general rule, bachelors were encouraged to keep controversy to a minimum, engaging their fellow *socii* in debate only in the four *principia* and, even there, referring to them obliquely. In the subsequent edition of the commentary "opponents" might be identified in the margin, opposite the text reference. Fortunately for the history of fourteenth-century thought, this policy was not always followed and may not even have been enforced before the Parisian condemnations of 1347.[62] Many bachelors criticized current opinions that could be identified easily by their audience. Wodeham is a leading example of this freedom. His *socii* are identified in the margin and in the text of the *reportatio* and *ordinatio* of books I and II.[63] More surprisingly, he questioned the conclusions and arguments of his immediate academic superiors, in particular, Walter Chatton, the Franciscan lector at Oxford probably in the previous year and presumably still resident at the Oxford convent, and Richard Fitzralph, a doctor of high reputation and soon-to-be Chancellor of the University.

2. *Wodeham's Style and Structure*

The structure of the individual questions of Wodeham's *Sentences* Commentary corresponds to what has been called the English "essay" style.[64] In fact, Wodeham is one of the principal examples of that style. Moreover, Wodeham lectured on the *Sentences* at a time in which the form of *Sentences* commentaries was undergoing transformation. Wodeham was one of the last English scholastics in the fourteenth century to attempt to relate the questions that interested him to specific distinctions in Lombard's text. Writing at about the same time, Robert Holcot was among the first to abandon Lombard's distinctions and to discuss a limited number of questions under each of the four books.

---

[62] No adequate attempt has been made to date all the pertinent legislation in this matter nor to assess its effect on actual practice. There are a sufficient number of commentaries with references to *socii* throughout the period to indicate that a more combative attitude was tolerated and may even have been encouraged at times. If the condemnation of 1347 was aimed at toning down the scope and aggressiveness of university debate, particularly among the bachelors, it was only temporarily effective. By 1365 references to contemporary opinions again become common.

[63] E.g., Vat. lat. 955, fol. 149^v; Vat. lat. 1110, fols. 16^r, 25^r, 27^r, 27^v; Paris, Maz. 915, fols. 90vb, 145ra.

[64] D. Trapp, "Augustinian Theology," *Augustiniana*, VI, 231.

Little has been written about the changing structure and style of *Sentences* commentaries in the fourteenth century, and although the subject deserves separate study, a few remarks may be appropriate as a background to Wodeham's style.[65] In the second and third decades of the fourteenth century scholastic authors gradually ceased to comment on all distinctions in Lombard's four books of the *Sentences*. In this movement towards a briefer, more flexible structure in which contemporary theological and philosophical interests rather than the outline of Lombard's work would determine the form of commentaries, England took the lead. There are several possible reasons for this development. Oxford may have preceded Paris in reducing the bachelor's reading of the *Sentences* from two years to one academic year (nine months). This shorter lecture period made commenting on most distinctions of Lombard all but impossible. There also seems to have been in the early fourteenth century, particularly at Oxford, an increased speculative activity and a creative interest in a limited number of topics that required fuller treatment at the expense of other sections in Lombard's *Sentences*.

Whatever the causes, a shift in structure took place in English *Sentences* commentaries between 1320 and 1335. Ockham and Chatton were still wedded to the *distinctiones* structure and attempted, at least in the early sections of their commentaries, to devote at least one question to each distinction. By contrast, Richard Fitzralph discarded the distinctions and simply arranged the questions that interested him in an order that corresponded to the four-book structure of Lombard. The Franciscans may have held on longer to the *distinctiones*. One finds them in John of Rodington and Adam Wodeham. But the general tendency was to abandon the *distinctiones* and to lengthen those few, carefully selected questions that caught the imagination of the author and his contemporaries. This latter tendency characterizes the structure of the commentaries of Holcot, Halifax, Kilvington, Buckingham, the Monachus Niger, Langeley, Aston, and Osbert Pickingham. Considering the time at which Wodeham was writing, his structure is surprisingly traditional, indeed close to Ockham's structure. The use of *conclusiones*, so important in

---

[65] See P. Glorieux, "Sentences," *DTC*, XIV (1939), cols. 1860–1884; H. Rashdall, *The Universities of Europe in the Middle Ages*, I, 476–477; P. Glorieux, *Répertoire des maîtres en théologie de Paris au XIIIe siècle* (Paris, 1933), I, 22; E. Ypma, *La Formation des Professeurs chez les ermites de saint-Augustin: 1256–1354* (Paris, 1956), pp. 36, 81–123; G. Leff, *Paris and Oxford Universities in the Thirteenth and Fourteenth Centuries* (New York, 1967), pp. 160–177; A. Combes in Jean de Ripa, *Lectura super primum sententiarum, Prologi quaestiones I & II* (Paris, 1961), pp. xx–xxv; P. Vignaux and A. Combes in Jean de Ripa, *Conclusiones* (Paris, 1957), pp. 7–8, 13–14.

Continental commentaries, is no further developed in Wodeham than in Ockham.⁶⁶

If Wodeham had not yet abandoned the *distinctiones* structure (although he clearly had trouble working within it), he shared with his contemporaries the tendency to lengthen individual questions and to adopt a rambling, highly elaborate structure that permitted multiple digressions and *dubia* and also permitted a more flowing, essay approach to theological questions. Although Holcot had abandoned the *distinctiones* structure, the arrangement of individual questions in Wodeham and Holcot is similar. This newer style is at times difficult for the modern reader to follow, although it does have a logic to it. It owes something to the lengthy questions of Scotus, Aureol, and Ockham, but it is also far more willing to introduce a variety of topics under one question and allow a topic to be developed at length.

C. Baccalarius Biblicus et Formatus

By the spring of 1333 at the latest, Wodeham had completed his Oxford lectures on the *Sentences*. We have almost no knowledge of the fruits of Wodeham's intellectual activity in the years between those lectures and the fulfillment of his regency necessary to make him a master of theology. He must have remained in Oxford for the required two years following the completion of his lectures on the *Sentences*. During the period he probably produced the *ordinatio* edition of his Oxford lectures. Some of that process had probably already taken place while Wodeham was lecturing on the *Sentences*. We know from a comment in book I that Wodeham worked closely with his *scriptor*, at the older Franciscan convent within the walls of Oxford, while Wodeham resided in the newer buildings outside the walls along the Thames.⁶⁷ If Wodeham visited his

---

⁶⁶ On the *conclusiones* structure see: Jean de Ripa, *Conclusiones* (Paris, 1957), pp. 7–8, 13–14; W. J. Courtenay, "John of Mirecourt and Gregory of Rimini on Whether God Can Undo the Past," *RTAM*, XXXIX (1972), 243–245.

⁶⁷ Wodeham, *Lectura Oxon*. I, dist. 2, q. 1, dub. 5 (Vat. lat. 955, fol. 105ʳ): "Verbi gratia, aliquando volo intrare villam [Oxford] tam intersim disputationi quam ut loquar scriptori. Et potest esse quod indigerem ire ad loquendum cum scriptore, dato quod nulla tunc fieret disputatio. Et potest etiam tunc ita esse quod oporteret me tunc intrare villam pro disputatione audienda, dato quod nisi haberem facere cum scriptore." Eccleston's comment that the Franciscans lived some distance from the schools of theology may well reflect the way the Franciscans saw their situation, as Wodeham's remark suggests; cf. *Tractatus Fr. Thomae de Eccleston De adventu Fratrum Minorum in Angliam*, ed. A. G. Little (Paris, 1909), p. 33. Little took a different view of their situation, *AFH*, XIX, 804–805; *The Grey Friars*, pp. 12–28.

scriptor frequently, as he suggests, we can assume that some, perhaps most, of the process of revision and polishing was going on simultaneously with his Oxford lectures.

During the two years of Oxford residence following his lectures on the *Sentences*, Wodeham must have commented on some book of the Scriptures and participated in disputations. Little has listed commentaries on the Song of Solomon and on Ecclesiasticus, but these are no longer extant and may have been products of his year or years as Oxford regent master later in the decade.[68] We know only that Wodeham spent two more years at Oxford before completing his theological studies.

D. THE OXFORD REGENCY

By 1335 Wodeham had completed his theological study at Oxford, and by 1339 he had completed his regency as Franciscan lector. Exactly when this regency took place is difficult to determine. He was already master of theology when he went to Basel in 1339 to consult with James de Porta on some miracles purported to have happened there.[69] If by the second quarter of the fourteenth century a new lector was appointed annually, as would seem to be the case, then one can conjecture from the date of Chatton's regency that Wodeham was *magister actu regens* at Oxford during the academic year 1337–38, or 1338–39.[70]

During his regency Wodeham would have lectured on the Bible, and it is to this period that either his commentary on *Song of Songs* or on *Ecclesiasticus* belongs. If the *Lectura secunda* is an example of *Quaestiones ordinariae*, which seems at present unlikely, then this work would also belong to the period of Wodeham's regency.

E. WODEHAM'S LAST YEARS

We have only two pieces of information on Wodeham after he left Oxford. We know that he visited Basel in the summer of 1339. How long

---

[68] Little, *The Grey Friars*, p. 173.

[69] *Analecta Franciscana*, II, 177; Little, *The Grey Friars*, p. 173.

[70] Little, *AFH*, XIX, 831. The statutes clearly require a two-year regency, but there are too many names in the list of Franciscan lectors at Oxford for each to have waited for his predecessor to finish his term. If one divides the list of 67 names into the century 1248–1348 the average regency would have been a year and a half, but those in the thirteenth century were longer and consequently those in the fourteenth century must have been shorter, at least as far as the vote in congregation was concerned. In the period from 1253 to 1270 the average is nearly three years; from 1270 to 1300 the average is a year and a half; from 1300 to 1348 the average is approximately one year. In the fourteenth century there was either continual overlapping or the period of regency had been reduced to one year.

he lingered in the upper Rhein valley and whether he took that opportunity to visit Ockham in Munich is not known.

Unlike Ockham, Wodeham did return to England, for it was there that he died. The last twenty years of his life are undocumented. He survived the plague in 1348–49, although the date of his death in 1358 coincides with another, albeit less severe, outbreak. At the end of his life he was a resident at the Franciscan convent at Babwell, just outside the walls of Bury St. Edmunds in East Anglia. It was there that his career, both academic and religious, came to a close.

F. Epilogue

The foregoing study can in part be viewed as a work of intellectual cartography. In the relatively unexplored land of the *Sentences* commentaries of Adam Wodeham it has tried, if only in a tentative way, to describe the major features, to discern how these relate to one another, and to give some impression of the number and variety of persons encountered there, many of whom are unfamiliar to historians of medieval thought. As with anyone who maps out unknown territory, the author is only too well aware that he may on occasion have concentrated on the wrong features or may have misperceived the topographical relations. He is also aware that the purpose of all such early attempts is only to function as a point of departure, to be altered and perfected, as the land becomes better known. He is aware too that others, unknown to him, have probably explored the same material at various times and will have noticed other features and may have a different perception of how the whole should look. But if this study makes the Wodeham corpus less unknown, less treacherous in appearance, less complicated, it may encourage other explorers, particularly if, as is hoped, the riches to be gained through the study of Wodeham far outweigh the difficulties encountered in working with the texts. In the future, if the work has served its purpose, this map will no longer suffice and will become only an interesting note in the historiography of the problem.

This study, then, should help bring that time closer. The riches that lie in Wodeham's writings awaiting the scholar of fourteenth-century thought should now be obvious from the earlier chapters. Few writers had Wodeham's reputation in the late Middle Ages; few were as frequently read or as frequently cited; and few had the wealth of citations and references within the text or on the margins of their commentaries as are found in Wodeham. In fact, Wodeham probably cites more fourteenth-century authors than any other scholastic of his century, save John of Basel, who had the advantage of living a full generation later. In Wodeham the historian of late medieval thought cannot only find his way back into the personalities and writings that made Oxford in Wodeham's generation the intellectual center of Europe, but can also come into contact with the theologian who may be both the beginning and central figure within the development of Ockhamism in the late Middle Ages.

APPENDIX 1

REPORTATIO ET ORDINATIO OXONIENSES

A. Reportatio(?) Oxoniensis

1. Description of Manuscript: Vat. lat. 1110

Vatican Library, Cod. Vat. lat. 1110, fols. 1^r–135^v (books II–IV); fols. 136^r–141^r (tabula quaestionum). Paper; 14th century; gothic cursive of Franciscan provenance; one column, varying between 45 and 51 lines. Same hand for text and marginalia. No *collationes*. Text different from and shorter than *Ordinatio*. Appears to be a *reportatio* of Wodeham's Oxford lectures but one copied after Wodeham became *magister regens* and possibly after his death (see last sentence on fol. 141^r). For further description, see *Codices Vaticani Latini*, Vol. II, ed. A. Pelzer (Vatican, 1931), pp. 727–729.

2. Incipits, Explicits, and List of Questions

Incipit II (fol. 1^r): "Circa illud quod dicit Magister, distinctione prima secundi libri, videlicet quod creatura rationalis facta est ad laudandum Deum, cetera, quaero (fols. 1^r–4^r): Utrum creatura rationalis meritorie Deo serviendo proficiat ad augmentum gratiae sine omni novo addito praecedenti. Et probatur primo quod sic, quia secundum Augustinum ad Bonifacium et ponitur libro secundo, dist. 27 [26], 'non gratiam Dei aliquid praecedit meriti humani, sed ipsa meretur augeri, ut aucta mereatur perfici'. Sed si hoc sit verum. . . ."

II, q. 2 (fols. 4^r–10^v): "Secundo quaero: Utrum augmentum gratiae fiat per compositionem gratiae novae cum gratia praecedenti."

II, q. 3 (fols. 10^v–17^r): "Tertio circa istam distinctionem quaero: Utrum creatura rationalis habens gratiam possit mereri suam gratiam augmentari."

II, q. 4 (fols. 17^r–20^r): "Quarto circa distinctionem praedictam quaero: Utrum viator operibus meritoriis insistendo ex hiis Deo carior fiat."

II, q. 5 (fols. 20^r–28^r): "Quinto quaero circa distinctionem primam secundi libri et principium quarti: Utrum praesupposita gratia baptismali viator per merita sua possit pertingere ad maximam gratiam viae sibi possibilem."

II, q. 6 (fols. 28^r–31^r): "Sexto quaero: Utrum viator existens in gratia ultra omnem gratiam habitam vel habendam possit proficere ad maiorem per instantaneas causationes actuum volendi omnia peccata venialia pro futuro vitare."

II, q. 7 (fols. 31^r–33^r): "Septimo quaero: Utrum Deus possit creare aliquam finitam caritatem qua non possit creare maiorem vel aliquam ita magnam secundum extensionem quod non possit maiorem illa producere, et sic de similibus."

II, q. 8 (fols. 33^r–36^r): "Octavo quaero: Utrum secundum proportionem caritatis viae succedat pro praemio proportionaliter magnitudo gloriae."

II, q. 9 (fols. 36^r–40^v): "Nono quaero de deminutione caritatis: Utrum, scilicet propter demerita, minuatur."

II, q. 10 (fols. 40^v–43^v): "Utrum caritas decrescat ad crementum cupiditatis."

Explicit II (fol. 43^v): ". . . credo posse contingere quod sic agendo mereatur, et quod non est transgressor, sed potius executor praecepti in oculis Dei. Ad argumenta principalia huius quaestionis responsum est superius in primo articulo quaestionis. Explicit liber secundus magistri Adae Wodeham."

Incipit III (fol. 43^v): "Circa dist. 14 libri tertii in qua Magister tractat de scientia animae Christi quaero (fols. 43^v–48^r): Utrum anima Christi habeat vel habuerit scientiam aequalem cum Deo. Videtur quod sic, quia anima Christi habet scientiam tantam vel maiorem quantam Deus et non maiorem constat; ergo aequalem."

III, q. 2 (fols. 48^r–52^r): "Secundo circa distinctionem praedictam quaero: Utrum ipsum verbum Dei sit sibi ipsi quamvis non animae sibi unitae scientia futurorum contingentium."

III, q. 3 (fols. 52^r–56^v): "Utrum cum determinata verbi praescientia stet quod futura praescita sint ad utrumlibet contingentia."

III, q. 4 (fols. 56^v–59^r): "Utrum anima Christi vel angelus sciant aliqua futura contingentia per revelationem sibi possibilem fieri ab ipso verbo, vel etiam scire possint."

III, q. 5 (fols. 59^r–62^v): "Quinto circa distinctionem 14 quaero: Utrum alicuius contingentis futuri absoluta revelatio sequens tollat contingentiam."

III, q. 6 (fols. 62^v–66^r): "Sexto quaero: Utrum Deus existenti in gratia possit revelare quod talis sit finaliter damnandus."

III, q. 7 (fols. 66^r–70^r): "Septimo circa hanc distinctionem 14 quaero: Utrum animae Christi vel angelo beato possit in verbo revelari aeternitas suae beatitudinis."

III, q. 8 (fols. 70^r–72^v): "Octavo quaero: Utrum Gabrieli potuit in verbo verbi incarnatio revelari."

III, q. 9 (fols. 72^v–75^r): "Nono circa istam distinctionem 14 quaero: Utrum per revelationes possibiles fieri in verbo posset aliquis sufficienter dirigi in volendis."

III, q. 10 (fols. 75^r–83^v): "Decimo quaero circa hanc distinctionem 14: Utrum anima Christi in verbo Dei cui unitur distincte videre valeat infinita."

III, q. 11 (fols. 84^r–88^r): "Undecimo circa distinctionem 14 quaero: Utrum anima Christi possit in verbo cui unitur distincte cognoscere minimas particulas corporis quod informat."

III, q. 12 (fols. 88^r–92^r): "Duodecimo circa hanc distinctionem quaero: Utrum anima [Christi] per unionem ad verbum sit ipsa omnipotens."

Explicit III (fol. 92^r): "Quod autem additur de foetore latrinae est refugium ad vulgare inconveniens propter defectum boni argumenti. Nam ita horrendum est piis auribus quod optimum donum quod umquam impressit Deus animae Christi vel alicui beato est vilius quam stercus muscae. Et tamen hoc alii habent concedere, quia stercus muscae est vera substantia quae pari ratione dicetur excedere quodlibet accidens in bonitate infinita, sicut ipsi dicunt de excessu infinito cuiuscumque creaturae finitae respectu alicuius creaturae finitae, et pari ratione dicam eis illas incomparabiliter excedere et excedi. Nihil ergo valoris continet argumentum de foetore latrinae. Ad argumentum principale satis aperte respondet Magister, ibidem in littera, et sic terminatur liber iste. Explicit liber tertius fratris Adae Wodeham doctoris in theologia sacra."

Incipit IV (fol. 92^v): "Circa principium quarti libri qui est principaliter de sacramentis et effectibus eorundem, quaero hanc quaestionem (fols. 92^v–98^r): "Utrum aliqua creatura possit creare caracterem vel gratiam vel aliquam creaturam. Quod sic primo per auctoritatem Augustini. . . ."

IV, q. 2 (fols. 98^r–102^v): "Secundo circa idem quaero: Utrum posse creare gratiam vel aliquid aliud repugnet creaturae propter virtutis accidentiae insufficientiam."

IV, q. 3 (fols. 102^v–105^v): "Tertio quaero: Utrum omni rite suscipienti sacramentum baptismi vel confirmationis conferatur gratia salutaris."

IV, q. 4 (fols. 105^v–108^r): "Circa sacramentum eucharistiae quaero: Utrum corpus Christi realiter sub speciebus quae fuerunt accidentia panis et vini contineatur."

IV, q. 5 (fols. 108^r–115^r): "Secundo quaero circa istam materiam: Utrum quantitas terminata panis consecrandi sit alia res extra animam realiter distincta a substantia et qualitate."

IV, q. 6 (fols. 115^r–119^r): "Circa sacramentum poenitentiae quaero primo: Utrum sacramentum poenitentiae sit necessarium ad delendum peccatum mortale post baptismum commissum."

IV, q. 7 (fols. 119^r–120^v): "Utrum actus poenitentiae requisitus ad deletionem peccati mortalis sit meritorius vitae aeternae."

IV, q. 8 (fols. 120^v–125^v): "Utrum quilibet qui commisit peccatum mortale teneatur secundum legem Dei communem de illo conteri."

IV, q. 9 (fols. 125^v–128^v): "Utrum poenitentia sit formaliter vel virtualiter velle cavere peccatum quodlibet in futuro."

IV, q. 10 (fols. 128^v–132^r): "Utrum ille qui peccavit mortaliter in opere exteriori teneatur plus poenitere de opere exteriori et interiori simul quam de interiori solum."

IV, q. 11 (fols. 132^r–134^v): "Utrum aliqua poena infernalis possit esse insensibilis in damnato."

IV, q. 12 (fols. 134^v–135^v): "Utrum sit maxima gloria possibilis in beato."

Explicit IV (fol. 135^v): "Ad tertium dico quod anima nihil agente, sed sola Deo ipsa possit simul cum hoc videre Deum et intelligere, nec auderem contrarium dicere, cum etiam secundum philosophiam 'intelligere' sit pati, non agere, et dato quod 'intelligere' esset agere, adhuc dico quod eo ipso quod res quae nata est esse sibi intellectio vel visio informaret animam, ipsa intelligeret vel videret, et per consequens quod ipsa tunc ageret visionem; et tunc adhuc sequitur idem."

"Et sic finitur quartus liber fratris Adae Wodeham, doctoris in theologia, qui legit Oxoniae anno Domini MCCCXXXII."

Explicit Tabula (fol. 141^r): "Explicit tabula super quartum librum fratris Adae Wodd[am] magistri in theologia de ordine fratrum minorum, et est anglicus natione, vel fuit."

B. Ordinatio Oxoniensis

1. *Description of Manuscripts*

a. Bruges, Bibl. de la Ville, Ms. 172, fols. 1ra–26ra (book IV). Parchment; 14th century; gothic bookhand with cursive elements, similar to hand of Paris, Université 193; provenance: Cistercian monastery of Dunes (near Bruges); two columns of 56–58 lines each. Contains *collatio* IV. Questions lack letter system and corresponding summaries. Manuscript also contains an abbreviated version of Wodeham's second redaction of the Oxford lectures. For further description see: *Catalogue général des Manuscrits des Bibliothèques de Belgique,* Vol. II: *Catalogue des Manuscrits de la Bibliothèque de la Ville de Bruges,* ed. A. de Poorter (Gembloux & Paris, 1934), pp. 222–223.

b. Paris, Bibl. Mazarine, Ms. 915, fols. 1ra–229va (books I–IV). Parchment; 14th century; rounded gothic bookhand similar in character to *Littera Parisiensis,* but probably of German origin; once belonged to the Dominican convent in Paris; two columns of 59–65 lines each. Contains *collationes* I–IV. For further description see: *Catalogue général des Manuscrits des Bibliothèques publiques de France. Paris. Catalogue des Manuscrits de la Bibliothèque Mazarine,* ed. A. Molinier, Vol. I (Paris, 1885), pp. 427–428.

c. Paris, Bibl. de la Université (Sorbonne), Ms. 193, fols. 3ra–233^{ra}(184ra) (books I–IV); fols. 233^{ra}(184ra)–239^{rb}(190rb) (tabula quaestionum). Parchment; 14th century; gothic bookhand with cursive elements; provenance unknown, probably French; two columns of 55–68 lines each. Contains *collationes* I–III. The last section of the manuscript is misnumbered. Folio 156^r is written as 106^r, and thus all remaining folios run fifty behind the proper foliation until fol. 182, where the numbering skips from 131 to 133, making the numbers run forty nine behind the proper foliation. The system of marginal summaries is dropped after IV, q. 5. For further description see: *Catalogue général des Manuscrits des Bibliothèques publiques de France. Université de Paris et Universités des Departments,* ed. C. Beaulieux (Paris, 1918), pp. 57–58.

d. Tarazona, Bibl. de la Catedral, Cod. 7, fols. 1ra–204va (books I–IV). Parchment; 14th century; gothic bookhand, possibly copied at Paris; belonged to Franciscan convent at Tarazona; two columns of 50–53 lines each. Contains *collationes* I–IV.

e. Vatican Library, Cod. Vat. lat. 955, fols. 1^r–208^v (text) (book I); fols. 208^v–217^r (tabula quaestionum). Parchment; second quarter of the 14th century (probably between 1332 and 1340); gothic cursive bookhand of

English Franciscan provenance; one column of 42–56 lines. Contains *collatio* I. Numbered by page and folio. Page numbers given in same hand as marginalia. For further description see: *Codices Vaticani Latini,* Vol. II, ed. A. Pelzer (Vatican, 1931), pp. 400–402.

2. *Incipits, Explicits, and List of Questions*

	Maz. 915	Univ. 193	Tar. 7	Vat. lat. 955
Incipit collatio I: "Ista est enim lex Adam, Domine Deus. II Reg. 7. Mirari solent mundi sapientes et lucris tantum saecularibus et commodis temporalibus inhiantes sacrae Scripturae deditos. . . ."	1ra	3ra	1ra	1^r
Explicit collatio I: ". . . id est Domine Deus, omni creator, terribilis et fortis, iustus et misericors, qui solus es bonus, solus rex, solus praestans, solus iustus et omnipotens et aeternus, qui liberas Israel ab omni malo, custodi partem tuam et sanctifica, scilicet theologos etsi simus peccatores, Domine Deus virtutum, converte nos et ostende faciem tuam et salvi erimus. Psal. 89. Quod nobis praestare dignetur auctor ipse salutis, qui cum Patre et Spiritu Sancto vivit et regnat, Deus per omnia saecula saeculorum. Amen."	1va	3va	1rb	1^v
Incipit prol., q. 1: "Utrum, secundum quod [Maz.: sicut] tactum est in collatione, studium sacrae theologiae [Maz.: scripturae] sit meritorium vitae aeternae. Quod non, quia finis per se et immediatus talis studii non est nisi scire vel credere. Non est autem credere solummodo, quia sine tali studio multi plurimum pollent fide, sicut innuit Augustinus . . . ."	1va	3va	1rb	1^v
Explicit Prol., q. 1: ". . . qui huic scientiae praeponunt nosse seipsos quam scientiam, qui apponit dolorem peregrinationis ex desiderio patriae et conditoris. Hic ibi."	5ra	7rb	4va	7^r
Prol., q. 2: "Secundo pro complemento distinctori materiae [Maz.: difficultatis modo] tactae in dubiis nondum solutis quaero: Utrum studium Sacrae Scripturae impositum alicui in foro poenitentiae pro omissione contraria sit meritorium."	5ra	7rb	4va	7^r

	Maz. 915	Univ. 193	Tar. 7	Vat. lat. 955
Dist. 1, q. 1: "Circa primam distinctionem quaero primo pro distinctori solutione sexti et septimi dubii primae quaestionis: Utrum pro studio sacrae theologiae ex caritate procedente debeatur pro mercede visio Dei et eius fruitio."	10rb	12vb	9ra	16^r
Incipit dist. 1, q. 2: "Utrum fruitio beatifica differat ab ipsa anima. Quod non, quia ubi pauciora, etc. Sed ad hoc quod aliquis fruatur Deo sufficit quod Deus ipse sit praesens ipsi animae. Talis enim praesentia oppositi sufficit ut anima se ipsa diligat. Ad oppositum: fruitio est actus elicitus; igitur non est ipsa anima. In ista quaestione prima conclusio est ista: Quod nec in via nec in patria est anima fruitio Dei, quia fruitio libere causatur ab anima, sed nihil libere causatum in anima est ipsa anima."	13rb	16rb	11va	21^r
Explicit dist. 1, q. 2: "Respondetur quod 'verum' in antecedente non potest supponere nisi personaliter, et non materialiter, quia non est aliquod probatum quod faceret eum stare materialiter, sicut est in ista propositione: 'verum est passio'; in ista propositione solum potest stare materialiter, sed non in ista verum est."	15ra	18ra	12vb	23^v
Dist. 1, q. 3: "Utrum fruitio [Vat.: frui] realiter distinguatur ab omni cognitione."	$15^{ra}-$ 17ra	$18^{ra}-$ 20ra	$12^{vb}-$ 14va	23^v- 26^v
Dist. 1, q. 4: "Utrum fruitio realiter [Maz.: rerum] distinguatur a delectatione."	$17^{ra}-$ 19vb	$20^{ra}-$ 23rb	$14^{va}-$ 16vb	26^v- 31^r
Dist. 1, q. 5: "Viso de delectatione beatifica, utrum sit fruitio, quaerendum est in generali: Utrum generaliter omnis delectatio sit dilectio vel odium, seu volitio aut nolitio."	$19^{vb}-$ 20vb	$23^{rb}-$ 24rb	$16^{vb}-$ 17va	31^r- 32^v
Dist. 1, q. 6: "Utrum voluntas necessario vel libere principiet actus suos."	$20^{vb}-$ 29vb	$24^{rb}-$ 35rb	$17^{va}-$ 25rb	32^v- 47^r
Dist. 1, q. 7: "Iuxta hoc quaero: Utrum voluntas sola sit causa effectiva suae volitionis liberae supposita communi Dei influentia vel concausatione."	$29^{vb}-$ 31vb	$35^{rb}-$ 37vb	$25^{rb}-$ 26vb	47^r- 51^r
Dist. 1, q. 8: "Utrum voluntas possit simul et subito producere actum voluntarium meritorie et libere dilectionis." Vat.: "Utrum voluntas possit subito et simul producere actum meritorie dilectionis."	$31^{vb}-$ 36vb	$37^{vb}-$ 44ra	$26^{vb}-$ 31rb	51^r- 60^r

	Maz. 915	Univ. 193	Tar. 7	Vat. lat. 955
Dist. 1, q. 9: "Utrum voluntas libere possit subito suspendere actum suum sive ab actu habito cessare."	36vb– 40rb	44ra– 48rb	31rb– 34ra	60^r– 65^v
Dist. 1, q. 10: "Decimo quaero circa distinctionem primam in speciali qualiter voluntas se habeat respectu fruitionis [Maz.Tar.: volitionis fruibilis] causandae respectu Dei clare visi, et sic quaestio in forma: Utrum creatura rationalis clare videns Deum necessario diligat ipsum."	40rb– 48va	48rb– 58ra	34ra– 41ra	65^v– 80^v
Dist. 1, q. 11: "Undecimo circa distinctionem primam quaero: Utrum solus Deus sit licite a creatura rationali ultimate fruibilis."	48va– 53rb	58ra– 64ra	41ra– 45rb	80^v– 87^v
Dist. 1, q. 12: "Duodecimo circa primam distinctionem quaero: Utrum haec sit possibilis: creatura rationalis fruitur una persona divina non fruendo alia."	53rb– 58ra	64ra– 69va	45rb– 51va	87^v– 93^v
Dist. 1, q. 13: "Tertiodecimo circa distinctionem primam quaero occasione secundae [Maz. Tar.: tertiae] conclusionis quaestionis 12: Utrum liceat filium Dei plus diligere vel frui eo quam patrem vel spiritum sanctum."	58ra– 60rb	69va– 72va	49rb– 51va	93^v– 98^r
Dist. 1, q. 14: "Quartodecimo principaliter circa distinctionem primam et ultimo quaero cuius potentiae actus sit ipsa fruitio et sit ipsa quaestio in hac forma: Utrum fruitio beatifica sit actus intellectus."	60rb– 62ra	72va– 74va	51va– 53ra	98^r– 100^v
Dist. 2, q. un.: "Circa distinctionem secundam quaero duo. Primum erit de unitate [Maz. Tar.: deitate] essentiali; secundum erit de eius trinitate personali. Prima igitur quaestio sit haec: Utrum in entibus sit tantum unus Deus."	62ra– 66rb	74va– 79rb	53ra– 56va	100^v– 106^v
Dist. 3, q. un.: "Circa distinctionem tertiam quaero: Utrum mens humana sit imago trinitatis increatae sicut in rebus aliis factis propter hominem est vestigium eiusdem trinitatis."	66rb– 71vb	79rb– 85va	56va– 61rb	106^v– 114^v
Dist. 6, q. 1: "Circa distinctionem sextam, ubi inquiritur [Maz.: movetur] an ex hoc quod voluntas Dei est natura sive essentia Dei sequatur quod si verbum Dei natura Dei filius est, quod voluntate Dei filius sit, quaero primo: Utrum a parte rei in divinis sit aliqua non-identitas inter naturam Dei et voluntatem divinam et ita de ceteris perfectionibus quae ponuntur in Deo vel Deus nec moveat quod pluraliter loquar antequam habeatur	71vb– 73vb	85va– 87va	61rb– 62vb	114^v– 117^r

	Maz. 915	Univ. 193	Tar. 7	Vat. lat. 955
quod ibi sit pluralitas, sine enim hac improprietate loquendi non potest homo in hac materia leviter exprimere illud quod vellet." The line ". . . est, quod voluntate Dei filius . . ." was dropped in Vat. and Maz.				
Dist. 6, q. 2: "Secundo circa eandem distinctionem sextam ad maiorem evidentiam eorum quae dicta sunt in praecedenti quaestione quaeritur: Utrum Deus sit realiter et per se primo modo sapiens vel intelligens et sic de similibus." Maz. and Vat.: "Secundo circa eandem distinctionem ad maiorem evidentiam dictorum quaero: Utrum Deus sit essentialiter et per se primo modo sapiens vel intelligens et sic de similibus."	73vb– 76vb	87va– 91ra	62vb– 65ra	117^{r}– 121^{r}
Dist. 8, q. un.: "Circa distinctionem octavam quaero: Utrum solus Deus sit immutabilis."	76vb– 79va	91ra– 94ra	65ra– 67rb	121^{v}– 126^{r}
Dist. 17, q. 1: "Circa distinctionem 17 quaeram de caritate et primo de eius necessitate, secundo principaliter de eius augmentatione et deminutione. De primo quaero primo: Utrum gratia seu caritas sit viatori necessaria ad salutem."	79va– 84ra	94ra– 99ra	67rb– 70vb	126^{r}– 135^{v}
Dist. 17, q. 2: "Secundo iuxta priorem titulem quaero: Utrum caritas seu gratia increata sine alio possit sufficere ad salutem."	84ra– 87va	99ra– 102vb	70vb– 73va	135^{v}– 143^{v}
Dist. 17, q. 3: "Tertio circa distinctionem 17 quaero: Utrum de peccatore possit fieri non peccator et acceptus Deo sine tali habitu sibi infuso per gratiam increatam."	87va– 91rb	102vb– 106va	73va– 76va	143^{v}– 151^{r}
Dist. 17, q. 4: "Secundo principaliter inquiram in hac distinctione 17 de augmento caritatis et aliarum formarum ubi primo quaero: Utrum caritas vel alia forma augmentabilis augmentetur per deminutionem contrarii sui."	91rb– 95rb	106va– 110rb	76va– 79rb	151^{r}– 159^{r}
Dist. 17, q. 5: "Quinto circa distinctionem 17 quaero: Utrum in augmentatione caritatis vel alterius formae gradus omnis praeexistens corrumpatur cum novus gradus inducitur ita videlicet [Maz.: oportet] intelligendo [Maz.: intelligere] quod in omni instanti sit totaliter nova forma."	95rb– 97va	110rb– 112va	79rb– 81ra	159^{r}– 163^{v}
Dist. 17, q. 6: "Sexto circa distinctionem 17 primi libri et principium libri tertii quaero: Utrum omnis bonus motus voluntatis meritorie augmentatius caritatis ad quem homo	97va– 101rb	112va– 116rb	81ra– 84ra	163^{v}– 171^{v}

	Maz. 915	Univ. 193	Tar. 7	Vat. lat. 955
tenetur debeat vel possit ex caritate procedere collata ex merito redemptoris." "... Residuas quaestiones huius materiae de augmentatione formarum quaere in principio secundi statim post collationem in secundum (Vat.: eundem)." This final comment is in the text of Vat. and margin of Univ. It is absent in Maz. and Tar.		116rb		171^v
Dist. 33, q. 1: "Circa distinctionem 33 primi ubi inquiritur utrum proprietates personarum divinarum sint ipsae personae et sint etiam divina essentia, quaero primo pro hac materia et pro secunda distinctione primi et pro multis distinctionibus tertii in quibus agitur de incarnatione personae unius sine alterius incarnatione: Utrum Deus essentialiter unus sit personaliter trinus."	101rb– 106rb	116rb– 122ra	84ra– 88rb	171^v– 181^v
Dist. 33, q. 2: "Secundo quaero pro distinctione quarta primi: Utrum Deus genuerit Deum."	106rb– 109rb	122ra– 124vb	88rb– 90rb	181^v– 186^r
Dist. 33, q. 3: "Tertio circa distinctionem 33 quaero iterum pro quarta distinctione: Utrum aliqua sit certa regula vel ars per quam solvi possint communiter paralogismi facti et talibus similes circa materiam trinitatis."	109rb– 113vb	124vb– 128vb	90rb– 93va	186^r– 192^v
Dist. 33, q. 4: "Quarto circa distinctionem 33 quaero pro distinctione quinta primi libri: Utrum divina essentia generet vel generetur."	113vb– 117va	128vb– 132rb	93va– 96ra	192^v– 198^v
Dist. 33, q. 5: "Quinto quaero circa distinctionem 33 pro distinctione 7 primi: Utrum potentia generandi possit communicari filio in divinis."	117va– 120rb	132rb– 134va	96ra– 97vb	198^v– 202^v
Dist. 33, q. 6: "Sexto circa distinctionem 33 pro distinctione 11 quaero: Utrum spiritus sanctus posset distingui a filio si non procederet ab eo."	120rb– 122rb	134va– 135rb	97vb– 98rb	202^v– 203^v
Dist. 33, q. 7: "Septimo quaero pro distinctione 12 circa istam 33 distinctionem: Utrum pater et filius sint unum principium spirans spiritum sanctum."	122rb– 123vb	135rb– 136vb	98rb– 99rb	203^v– 205^v
Dist. 33, q. 8: "Octavo circa distinctionem 33 quaero pro distinctione 26 et 27: Utrum personae divinae primo et adequate distinguantur ab invicem semetipsis."	123vb– 126ra	136vb– 138vb	99rb– 100va	205^v– 208^r
Dist. 33, q. 9: "Ultimo circa distinctionem 33 quaero pro istamet distinctione: Utrum	126ra– 126rb	138vb– 139ra	100va– 100vb	208^v

	Maz. 915	Univ. 193	Tar. 7	Vat. lat. 955
omne idem patri sit omnibus modis idem patri." Explicit I: ". . . similitudo qua Sortes albus est similis Platoni albo, vel dissimilitudo qua idem Sortes albus est dissimilis Socrati nigro, sint omnino idem; non tamen ideo est Sortes albus illi similis, cui est dissimilis, nec econtra."	126rb	139ra	100vb	208^v

	Maz. 915	Univ. 193	Tar. 7
Incipit collatio II: "Hic est liber generationis Adam. Solent inquiri tituli librorum in principiis lectionum, cui inquisitioni circa secundum librum Sententiarum prae manibus iam habendum imprimis satisfacio quod titulus talis est: Hic est liber generationis Adam. . . ."	126rb	139ra	101ra
Explicit collatio II: ". . . Hic est igitur liber generationis Adam, quia de ipsa et de eius circumstantiis quae ipsam ordinant, deformant vel reformant liber secundus totus protrahitur ut praedixi ad profectum et doctrinam audientis et legentis quatenus in via regulamur per gratiam in futuro pertingamus ad gloriam quam nobis praestare dignetur, etc."	126vb	139rb	101ra
Incipit II, q. 1: "Circa illud quod dicit Magister, prima distinctione secundi libri, cap. 6, quod creatura rationalis facta est ad laudandum Deum, ad serviendum ei, ad fruendum eo, in quibus proficit ipsa, non Deus, Deus enim perfectus et summa bonitate plenus nec augeri nec minui potest, et cap. sequenti dicitur in hoc proficit serviens non iste cui servitur quaero ad perficiendum materiam de augmentatione caritatis inchoatam per alias quaestiones, dist. 17 primi libri: Utrum creatura rationalis meritorie serviendo Deo proficiat ad augmentum gratiae seu caritatis, sine omni novo addito gratiae praecedenti. Nam quod proficiat in augmento gratiae per servitia debita Deo exhibita patet auctoritatibus iam praetactis."	126vb	139rb	101ra
II, q. 2: "Secundo quaero: Utrum profectus vel augmentum gratiae fiat per compositionem gratiae novae cum gratia praecedenti."	131vb– 136rb	142va– 147ra	103rb– 106va

	Maz. 915	Univ. 193	Tar. 7
II, q. 3: "Tertio circa istam distinctionem quoad materiam de augmentatione formarum quaero: Utrum creatura rationalis habens gratiam possit mereri suam gratiam augmentari."	136rb– 142va	147ra– 151vb	106va– 110va
II, q. 4: "Quarto circa distinctionem primam secundi quaero: Utrum viator operibus meritoriis insistendo ex hiis carior Deo fiat."	142va– 145ra	151vb– 153vb	110va– 112rb
II, q. 5: "Quinto quaero circa distinctionem primam secundi et principium quarti: Utrum praesupposita [Univ.: supposita] gratia baptismali viator per merita sua possit pertingere ad gratiam maximam viae sibi possibilem."	145ra– 155ra	153vb– 161va	112rb– 119ra
II, q. 6: "Sexto quaero: Utrum viator existens in gratia ultra omnem gratiam habitam vel habendam possit proficere ad maiorem per instantaneas causationes actuum volendi omnia pro futuro peccata venialia devitare."	155ra– 157va	161va– 164rb	119ra– 121va
II, q. 7: "Septimo quaero circa distinctionem primam secundi: Utrum Deus possit creare [Maz.: causare] finitam [Maz.: fieri] caritatem aliquam qua non possit creare maiorem vel aliquam aliam ita magnam secundum extensionem quod non possit maiorem illa producere, et sic de similibus."	157va– 159va	164rb– 166rb	121va– 123rb
II, q. 8: "Octavo quaero: Utrum secundum proportionem caritatis viae succedat pro praemio proportionaliter magnitudo gloriae."	159va– 163ra	166rb– 169rb	123rb– 126ra
II, q. 9: "Nono quaero de deminutione caritatis: Utrum, scilicet propter demerita, minuatur."	163ra– 166rb	169rb– 172rb	126ra– 129ra
II, q. 10: "Iuxta hoc quaeri potest decimo ad complementum distinctionis materiae praecedentis quaestionis: Utrum caritas decrescat ad decrementum [sic!] cupiditatis."	166rb– 168vb	172rb– 174rb	129ra– 131ra
Explicit II: ". . . aestimo posse contingere quod sic agendo mereatur, et quod non est transgressor sed potius executor praecepti in oculis Dei. Ad argumenta principalia quaestionis huius decimae est responsum in primo articulo [Maz.: principio] quaestionis. Explicit secundus liber." To which Univ. adds: "alias enim multas quaestiones secundi de motu, de tempore, de continuo, et de individuatione et similibus alias seriosius pertractavi."	168vb	174rb	131ra
Incipit collatio III: "In funiculis Adam traham eos. Osee 11. Intellectualis oculi naturale desiderium sed ignorantiae tenebris obumbrati licet impossibile legibus obligati caligantis aciei circumfert obtuitus, et nunc	169ra	174rb	131va

	Maz. 915	Univ. 193	Tar. 7
incomplexa rerum formetur notitia intuendo et abstrahendo. ..."			
Explicit collatio III: "... si direxerit ad eum: cor suum spiritum illius et flatum ad se trahet, Iob 34, in via per gratiam, in patria per gloriam, quod nobis concedat Christus Dei filius cuius ad praesens notitiam quaerimus, qui cum patre et spiritu sancto vivit et regnat. Amen."	169rb	174vb	131vb
Incipit III, q. 1: "Circa istum librum tertium, quia alias Londoniae toto anno pertractavi quaestiones 13 primarum distinctionum, ideo nunc incipio a distinctione 14 in qua Magister tractat de scientia animae Christi et eius potentia et eius scientia. Quaero primo et eadem forma qua quaerit Magister: Utrum anima Christi habuerit et habeat sapientiam aequalem Deo. Videtur quod sic, quia anima Christi habet sapientiam tantam vel maiorem quantam Deus et non maiorem constat; ergo aequalem."	169rb– 173va	174vb– 179ra	131vb– 136rb
III, q. 2: "Secundo circa illud quod dicit Magister principaliter in ista distinctione 14 capitulo penultimo quod anima Christi et angeli in verbo Dei cognoscunt futura et quod anima Christi in verbo cui unita est liquidius et praesentius omni creatura scit omnia quae Deus quaero primo: Utrum ipsum verbum Dei sit sibi ipsi quamvis non animae sibi unitae scientia futurorum contingentium."	173va– 176rb	179ra– 181vb	136rb– 139rb
III, q. 3: "Secundo circa istam materiam quaero: Utrum cum determinata verbi praescientia stet quod futura praescita sint ad utrumlibet contingentia."	176rb– 180ra	181vb– 186ra	139rb– 143rb
III, q. 4: "Viso quomodo verbum Dei cui unita est anima Christi [Maz.: antichristi] est certa et infallibiliter praescientia futurorum restat inquirere: Utrum anima Christi [Maz.: antichristi] vel angeli sciant futura aliqua contingentia per revelationem sibi possibilem fieri ab ipso verbo vel etiam scire possint."	180ra– 181vb	186ra– 187vb	143rb– 145ra
III, q. 5: "Quinto quaero circa istam distinctionem 14: Utrum alicuius [Univ. add. prius] contingentis futuri absoluta revelatio sequens tollat contingentiam [Univ. add. revelati]."	181vb– 183vb	187vb– 188va	145rb– 147vb
III, q. 6: "Sexto quaero circa praesentem distinctionem 14 [Maz.: scilicet]: Utrum Deus vel verbum Dei existenti in gratia possit revelare quod talis finaliter sit damnandus."	183vb– 185ra	188va– 193vb	147vb– 150rb
III, q. 7: "Septimo circa hanc distinctionem 14 quaero: Utrum animae Christi vel angelo beato [Maz.: angeli	185ra– 186vb	193vb– 195rb	150rb– 153va

	Maz. 915	Univ. 193	Tar. 7
beati] possit in verbo revelari aeternitas suae beatitudinis."			
III, q. 8: "Octavo quaero: Utrum Gabrieli [Maz. & Tar.: Gabriel] potuerit in verbo verbi incarnatio revelari."	186vb– 188ra	195rb– 197ra	153va– 155vb
III, q. 9: "Nono quaero circa istam distinctionem 14: Utrum per revelationes possibiles fieri in verbo posset aliquis [Univ.: possit quis] sufficienter dirigi in volendis."	188ra– 189rb	197ra– 198va	155vb– 157vb
III, q. 10: "Decimo quaero circa distinctionem 14: Utrum anima Christi in verbo Dei cui unitur distincte videre valeat infinita."	189rb– 193rb	198va– 203ra	157vb– 163ra
III, q. 11: "Undecimo circa hanc distinctionem quaero [Univ.: quaeritur]: Utrum anima Christi possit in verbo cui unitur distincte cognoscere minimas partium [Univ.: partes accidentium] sibi inhaerentium vel minimas particulas corporis quod informat."	193va– 196rb	203ra– 205va	163ra– 166ra
III, q. 12: "Duodecimo quaero circa hanc distinctionem 14 de potentia animae Christi: Utrum per unionem ad verbum ipsa sit omnipotens."	196rb– 199ra	205va– 207vb	166ra– 169ra
Explicit III: "Quod autem additur de foetore latrinae est refugium ad vulgare, inconveniens propter defectum boni argumenti. Et ita poterit econtro dici argumenti [Tar. *om.* argumenti] quod maximum inconveniens est [Univ. & Tar. *om.* est]. Et ita horrendum piis auribus est dicere quod optimum donum quod umquam impressit Deus animae Christi vel alicui beato [Maz.: alicuius beati; Tar.: alicui] vilius [Maz.: melius] est in infinitum quam stercus unius [Maz. & Tar. *om.* unius] muscae. Et tamen hoc habet arguens ut videtur concedere, quia stercus muscae est vera substantia quae [Univ. *om.* quae] pari ratione dicetur [Maz.: diceretur] tunc [Univ.: et credetur] excedere quodlibet accidens in bonitate [Tar.: beatitudine] infinita [Maz. & Tar.: infinitae], sicut ipse dicit [Univ.: dicis; Tar. *om.*] de excessu infinito cuiuscumque creaturae finitae respectu alicuius creaturae finitae. Et pari ratione dicam sibi illas incomparabiliter excedere et alias [Univ. & Tar. *om.* alias] excedi [Tar.: exceditur]. Nihil ergo valoris continet argumentum sed foetorem abhominationis [Univ.: sed foetoris et abhominationis; Maz.: de foetorum et abhominationibus], sicut si arguatur [Univ.: argueretur; Tar.: Item posset argui] contra articulum fidei de Dei immensitate [Tar.: infinito] sic: si Deus est ubique, igitur est in stercore canis vel in posterioribus eius; consequens horrent aures [Univ.:			

	Maz. 915	Univ. 193	Tar. 7
horret auris; Maz.: horrentur aures]; igitur, etc. Ad argumentum principale satis [Univ. *om.* satis] apte respondet Magister, ibidem in littera, et in hoc tempore plus non dante [Maz.: durante] finiuntur quaestiones [Maz. & Tar.: conclusiones] super tertium, nisi quod alibi in lectura Norvicensi super [Univ.: similiter] tres ultimas [Tar.: tertium ultima] distinctiones [Univ.: quaestiones tertii libri] prosecutus sum quaestiones [Tar.: conclusiones] de praeceptis decalogi sigillatim."			

	Maz. 915	Univ. 193	Tar. 7	Bruges 172
Incipit collatio IV: "In funiculis Adam traham eos. Osee XI. Samaritanus noster ita homini primo pro se et suis omnibus a latronibus [Tar.: a lateribus; Maz.: colateribus] gratuitis spoliato et plagis impositis naturalibus vulnerato miserationis [Brg.: miserans]...."	199ra	—	169va	1ra
Explicit collatio IV: "... usque ad inventionem eius, nam si dixerit [Maz.: duxerit] ad eum cor suum, etc. Iob 34. Trahat, inquam, in via per gratiam, in patria per gloriam, ad quam nos perducat qui sine fine vivit et regnat. Amen."	199rb	—	169vb	1ra
Incipit IV, q. 1: "Iuxta istam lectionem [Brg.: quaestionem] circa principium quarti de sacramentis [Univ.: de substantia sacramenti] quaero, et simul circa distinctionem 6 tertii libri ubi in principio fit mentio [Maz. *om.* fit mentio] de sacramento et re sacramenti: Utrum aliqua creatura possit in effectum sacramenti praecise [Maz. *om.* praecise] productibilem per creationem. Et hoc est expressius quaerere: Utrum aliqua creatura possit creare caritatem [Tar.: caracterem; Maz. & Brg.: creationem] vel gratiam vel aliam creaturam."	200ra– 204rb	207vb– 211va	169vb– 174vb	1rb– 5rb
IV., q. 2: "Secundo circa idem quaero: Utrum posse creare gratiam vel aliquid aliud repugnet propter virtutis activae insufficientiam cuilibet creaturae."	204rb– 207vb	211va– 214va	174vb– 178ra	5rb– 8va

	Maz. 915	Univ. 193	Tar. 7	Bruges 172
IV, q. 3: "Tertio quaero: Utrum omni [Univ. & Brg.: homini] rite suscipienti sacramentum baptismi vel confirmationis conferatur gratia salutaris."	207vb– 210ra	214va– 215vb	178rb– 179vb	8va– 10ra
IV, q. 4: "Circa sacramentum eucharistiae quaero primo: Utrum corpus Christi realiter sub speciebus quae fuerunt panis et vini contineatur."	210ra– 211vb	215vb– 217rb	179vb– 181va	10ra– 11va
IV, q. 5: "Secundo circa istam materiam quia multae difficultates pendent ex identitate vel distinctione quantitatis a substantia et qualitate quaero: Utrum quantitas terminata panis consecrandi sit aliqua vera res extra animam distincta realiter a substantia et qualitate cuius est."	211vb– 217ra	217rb– 221rb	181va– 186vb	11va– 16ra
IV, q. 6: "Circa sacramentum poenitentiae quaero: Utrum sacramentum poenitentiae sit necessarium ad delendum peccatum mortale post baptismum commissum."	217ra– 219va	221rb– 223va	186vb– 190rb	16ra– 18ra
IV, q. 7: "Secundo circa eandem materiam quaero: Utrum actus poenitentiae requisitus ad deletionem culpae [Univ.: peccati] mortalis sit meritorius vitae aeternae."	219va– 220va	223va– 224va	190rb– 191vb	18ra– 18vb
IV, q. 8: "Tertio quaero propter conditionem implicatam praecedenti quod: Utrum quilibet qui commisit peccatum mortale teneatur secundum legem Dei communem de illo conteri."	220va– 223vb	224va– 227va	191vb– 196ra	19ra– 21va
IV, q. 9: "Quarto quaero circa materiam de poenitentia: Utrum vera poenitentia sit formaliter vel virtualiter velle cavere peccatum quodlibet in futuro."	223vb– 225vb	227va– 229rb	196ra– 199ra	21va– 23ra
IV, q. 10: "Quinto quaero circa materiam de poenitentia: Utrum ille qui peccaverit [Univ.: peccat] mortaliter in opere exteriori teneatur plus poenitere de opere exteriori et interiori simul quam de interiori solo."	225vb– 227vb	229rb– 231rb	199ra– 201vb	23ra– 24va
IV, q. 11: "Utrum aliqua poena infernalis possit esse insensibilis in damnato."	227vb– 228vb	231rb– 232rb	201vb– 203va	24va– 25rb
IV, q. 12: "Ultimo autem nunc circa istum quartum quaero: Utrum sit maxima gloria possibilis in beato."	228vb– 229va	232rb– 233ra	203va– 204va	25rb– 26ra
Explicit IV [Maz. & Tar.]: "Ad tertium etiam dicendum: mihi videtur quod anima nihil agente, sed solo Deo ipsa possit simul cum hoc videre Deum et intelligere, nec auderem	229va		204va	

	Maz. 915	Univ. 193	Tar. 7	Bruges 172
contrarium tenere, cum etiam secundum philosophiam 'intelligere' [Tar. *om.* contrarium . . . intelligere] sit pati, non agere; et dato quod 'intelligere' esset agere, adhuc probavi in primo libro quod eo ipso quod res quae nata est esse sibi [Maz.: ibi] intellectio vel visio informaret animam, ipsa intelligeret vel videret; et per consequens quod ipsa tunc ageret visionem. Residuum [Tar.: residuis] quae tangit ille materialiter contra me in suis replicationibus dimitto ultra prosequi, tum quia excusat quod contra mentem suam fuit mihi reputatus, tum quia eorum solutio satis potest colligi ex praescriptis in diversis locis praesentis lecturae, et praecipue [Maz.: praecise] ex secundo, tum tertio quia non restat locus ulterius mutuo contra invicem replicandi. Hic igitur sit finis praesentis opusculi et laborum. Ad laudem omnipotentis domini nostri Iesu Christi, cui sit cum patre et spiritu sancto honor et gloria per omnia saecula saeculorum. Amen. Explicit lectura reverendi et subtilis bachalarii fratris Adae Wodeham ordinis fratrum minorum."				
Explicit IV [Univ. & Bruges]: "Ad tertium etiam dicendum: videtur mihi quod anima nihil agente, sed solo Deo ipsa possit simul cum hoc videre Deum et intelligere, nec auderem contrarium tenere, cum etiam secundum philosophiam 'intelligere' sit quoddam pati; et dato quod anima ageret visionem suam, idem sequitur." Univ.: "Et sic finis. Amen." Bruges: "Explicit scriptura fratris."		233ra		26ra

C. Erfurt-Lüneburg Subredaction

1. *Relation of manuscripts to one another and to Ordinatio I*

The text contained in the Erfurt and Lüneburg manuscripts follows the pre-1334 version of Wodeham's Oxford lectures and appears to be a subredaction of the *Ordinatio* text of book I. In those places where the first and second redactions differ, these manuscripts follow the reading of the earlier text. However, in form and content they are not identical with the manuscripts discussed above. They differ in the arrangement of the questions. Moreover, they possess several readings that are unique to these two manuscripts.

Of the two manuscripts Lüneburg is the earlier, having been copied around 1350. It originally circulated as an unbound series of quires, some of which were lost before binding. Although the order of questions in the Erfurt manuscript differs from that of the Lüneburg manuscript, both the Lüneburg and the Erfurt manuscript (which may have been copied from the Lüneburg manuscript before it was bound) shed some light on the textual groupings within Wodeham's *Primum Sententiarum*. Invariably the prologue and the first distinction circulated as one unit, as did the material on grace contained in distinction 17 and the material on the trinity contained in distinction 33. Distinctions 2, 3, 6, and 8 circulated separately and could be inserted wherever it pleased the scribe or compiler.

The Lüneburg and Erfurt manuscripts, therefore, give us a view into the ways the various sections of the first book circulated before they were frozen into the *ordinatio* format. It is difficult to say which version represents the way in which the questions were read to the Oxford audience. It should be noted, however, that the Erfurt manuscript ends book I on the topic that begins book II, namely the augmentation of grace, and refers the reader ahead. The early date of the Lüneburg manuscript, reflecting a period when the *sexterni* of the *Primum Sententiarum* were still circulating separately, supports the rapid dissemination of Wodeham's thought on the Continent, especially in Germany.

2. *Description of Manuscripts and Order of Questions*

a. Erfurt, Wissenschaftliche Bibliothek der Stadt (Stadtbücherei Erfurt), Cod. Ampl. 2° 133, fols. 1ra–130^r (book I); fols. 130^r–133^v (subject index). Parchment; late 14th century; German gothic bookhand; north German Franciscan provenance, having belonged to Franciscan convents in Faldern and Verden; two columns of 68–69 lines each. Contains *collatio* I. Arrangement of the manuscript by topics rather than distinctions. For further description see W. Schum, *Beschreibendes Verzeichniss der Amplonianischen Handschriften-Sammlung zu Erfurt* (Berlin, 1887), pp. 87–88.

Incipit collatio I (fol. 1ra): "Ista est lex Adam, Domine Deus. II Reg. 7. Mirari solent mundi sapientes et lucris tantum temporalibus et commodis inhiantes sacrae Scripturae deditos...."

Explicit collatio I (fol. 1rb): ". . . Domine Deus, omni creator, terribilis et fortis, iustus et misericors, qui solus es bonus, rex, solus praestans, solus iustus et omnipotens et aeternus, qui liberas Israel ab omni malo, custodi partem tuam et sanctifica, scilicet theologos etsi sumus peccatores, Domine Deus virtutum, converte nos et ostende faciem tuam et salvi erimus. Quod nobis praestare dignetur, qui cum Patre et Spiritu Sancto vivit."

Incipit prol., q. 1 (fol. 1rb): "Utrum studere in theologia sit meritorius. Quod non, quia per se finis studii theologiae nec est scire nec credere, quia credere non est in libera potestate nostra. ..."

Explicit prol., q. 1 (fol. 4rb): "... qui huic scientiae praeponunt nosse seipsos quam substantiam, quae apponit dolorem peregrinationis ex desiderio patriae et conditoris."

Incipit prol., q. 2 (fol. 4rb): "Utrum studium sacrae scripturae impositum alicui in foro poenitentiae per omissionem contrarii sit meritorium. Videtur quod non, quia. ..."

Incipit I, dist. 1, q. 1 (fol. 9rb): "Utrum pro studio sacrae scripturae ex caritate procedente debeatur pro mercede visio Dei et eius fruitio."

Incipit I, q. 2 (fol. 12rb): "Utrum fruitio beatifica differat ab ipsa anima. Quod non, quia ubi pauciora sufficiunt, etc. Sed ad hoc quod aliquis fruatur Deo sufficit quod Deus ipse sit praesens ipsi animae, talis enim praesentia sufficit ut anima se ipsa diligat. Ad oppositum: fruitio est actus elicitus. In ista quaestione prima conclusio est ista: Quod nec in via nec in patria est anima fruitio Dei, quia fruitio libere causatur. ..."

Explicit I, q. 2 (fol. 13vb): "... dicitur quod 'verum' in antecedente non potest supponere nisi personaliter, non materialiter, quia non est aliquod probatum quod faceret eum stare materialiter, sicut est in ista propositione: 'verum est passio', solum potest stare materialiter, licet non in ista verum est."

Explicit I (dist. 17, q. 6) (fol. 130^r): "... nisi vel sic procedat ex gratia vel per gratiam ad beatitudinem sit acceptus. Residuum quaestionis huius de augmentatione formarum quaere in principio secundi. Explicit primus Adae Wodeham." Cf. Vat. lat. 955, fol. 171^v and Paris, Univ. 193, fol. 116rb.

Order of Questions:
Prol., qq. 1–2 (fols. 1rb–9rb)
I, dist. 1, qq. 1–14 (fols. 9rb–61vb)
I, dist. 6, qq. 1–2 (fols. 62ra–67va)
I, dist. 33, qq. 1–9 (fols. 67va–92ra)
I, dist. 2, q. un. (fols. 92ra–97ra)
I, dist. 3, q. un. (fols. 97ra–103vb)
I, dist. 8, q. un. (fols. 103vb–107ra)
I, dist. 17, qq. 1–6 (fols. 107ra–130^r)

b. Lüneburg, Ratsbücherei der Stadt, Hs. theol. 4° 29, fols. 1ra–249vb (book I). Paper; ca. 1350 (watermark similar to Mŏsin–Traljić 5802); cursive bookhand; hand of the marginal scribe similar to text scribe of Vat. lat. 955; manuscript belonged to Franciscan convent at Lüneburg; two columns (with exception of fol. 177) of 36–46 lines per column. Initials rubricated up to fol. 17. Marginal notes in a different hand from text scribe. The manuscript is defective, and some quires were disarranged at time of binding. Absent are *collatio* I; prol., q. 1; dist. 2; and dist. 17, q. 2. The proper arrangement of the faulty quires in dist. 33 is provided in the list of questions. The manuscript was water-damaged at an early date, since some of the marginal notes in a 14th-century hand were written after the water damage. Rich marginalia, similar in some respects to Vat. lat. 955. For further description see forthcoming: I. Fischer, *Handschriften der Ratsbücherei Lüneburg*, Vol. II, pt. 2: *Die theologischen Handschriften: Quartoreihe.*

Incipit prol., q. 2 (fol. 1ra): "Utrum studium Scripturae impositum alicui in foro poenitentiae propter omissionem peccati contrariam[?] sit meritorium. Et videtur quod non. ..."

Incipit I, dist. 1, q. 1 (fol. 10vb): "Utrum pro studio Sacrae Scripturae ex caritate procedente debeatur pro mercede visio Dei et eius fruitio. Quod non. ..."

Incipit I, dist. 1, q. 2 (fol. 17rb): "Utrum fruitio beatifica differat ab ipsa anima. Quod non, quia ubi pauciora sufficiunt, etc. Sed ad fruitionem sufficit praesentia Dei ipsi animae, quia talis praesentia sufficit animae ut anima se ipsa diligat. Ad oppositum: fruitio est actus elicitus. In ista quaestione conclusio prima est ista: Quod non in via nec in patria est anima fruitio Dei, quia fruitio libere causatur ab anima. ..."

Explicit I, dist. 1, q. 2 (fol. 20vb): "Respondetur quod 'verum' in antecedente non potest supponere nec personaliter nec materialiter, quia non est aliquod probatum quod faceret eum stare materialiter, sicut est in ista propositione: 'verum est passio', solum potest stare materialiter, licet non in ista verum est."

Explicit I (dist. 8) (fol. 249vb): "... sicut de natura assumpta, quilibet concedit, quod sit composita. Explicit."

Order of Questions:
 Prol., q. 2 (fols. $1^{ra}-10^{vb}$)
 Dist. 1, qq. 1–14 (fols. $10^{vb}-124^{vb}$)
 Dist. 17, qq. 1, 3–6 (fols. $125^{ra}-164^{vb}$)
 Dist. 6, qq. 1–2 (fols. $165^{ra}-174^{ra}$)
 Dist. 33, q. 1 (fols. $174^{ra}-176^{vb}$, $178^{ra}-180^{vb}$, $189^{ra}-194^{rb}$)
 Dist. 33, q. 2 (fols. $194^{rb}-196^{vb}$, $205^{ra}-207^{vb}$)
 Dist. 33, q. 3 (fols. $207^{vb}-212^{vb}$, $181^{ra}-185^{rb}$)
 Dist. 33, q. 4 (fols. $185^{rb}-188^{vb}$, $197^{ra}-201^{ra}$)
 Dist. 33, q. 5 (fols. $201^{ra}-204^{vb}$, $213^{ra}-214^{vb}$)
 Dist. 33, qq. 6–9 (fols. $214^{vb}-233^{vb}$)
 Dist. 3, q. un. (fols. $233^{vb}-244^{va}$)
 Dist. 8, q. un. (fols. $244^{va}-249^{vb}$)

APPENDIX 2

COLLECTIO BREVIS, OR THE SECOND REDACTION

A. Description of Manuscripts

1. Bruges, Bibl. de la Ville, Ms. 172, fols. 27^r–110^v (books I–IV). Parchment; 14th century; gothic cursive of English provenance (different scribe from fols. 1^r–26^r); belonged to Cistercian monastery of Dunes (near Bruges); two columns of 48 lines each. Contains *collatio* I and the *introductio/protestatio* that belong to this redaction. This portion of the manuscript is an abbreviated version of the second redaction. Certain questions are lacking: I, dist. 6, qq. 1–2; I, dist. 33, qq. 1–9; II, q. 7; IV, qq. 2–12. Text increasingly abbreviated as one moves towards end, and it stops with book IV, q. 1. This manuscript, while it does contain the introductory material at the beginning of book I, does not have the introductory phrasing for each question but instead begins immediately with "utrum". For further description see: *Catalogue général des manuscrits des Bibliothèques de Belgiques*, vol. II: *Catalogue des manuscrits de la Bibliothèque de la Ville de Bruges*, ed. A. Poorter (Gembloux & Paris, 1934), pp. 222–223.
2. Florence, Bibl. Naz., conv. soppr. A III 508, fols. 147va–154vb (*Lectura Oxon.* I, dist. 1, q. 6). Parchment; 14th century; Italian bookhand; belonged to Franciscan convent of Santa Croce in Florence; two columns of 62 lines each. No *collatio*. Manuscript also contains (fols. 135ra–147rb) Wodeham's *Tractatus de indivisibilibus*. These questions of Wodeham occur between the *Sentences* Commentary (*Opus correctum*) of Richard Fitzralph and the questions of Adam Junior. The manuscript also contains the questions of Monachus Niger. On fols. 154vb–161ra one finds another question: "Utrum ab eo in quod magis quam ex quo denominetur mutatio." The question may be by Wodeham and contains a discussion of velocity, quantity, and the continuum, but the structure of the question more closely resembles the style of Robert Holcot rather than that of Wodeham.
3. Florence, Bibl. Naz., conv. soppr. B VII 1249, fols. 1ra–174rb (books I–IV). Parchment and paper; late 14th or early 15th century; Italian cursive bookhand, similar to (or identical with?) the scribe of Florence, Bibl. Naz., conv. soppr. C V 357, which contains the *Sentences* Commentary of Walter Chatton; belonged to the Franciscan convent of Santa Croce in Florence; two columns of 51–57 lines each. Contains *collatio* I. Manuscript also contains (fols. 132ra–143vb) Wodeham's *Tractatus de indivisibilibus*. This manuscript cannot be a copy of Paris, B. N. lat. 15 892. For example, in book I, dist. 17, q. 3, a. 3, the Florence text is longer than the Paris text and parallels the first redaction. Moreover, Florence has distinction 3, which does not occur in the Paris manuscript.

4. Paris, Bibl. Nat., Cod. lat. 15 892, fols. 1ra–174ra (books I–IV). Parchment; 14th century; gothic rounded bookhand: *Littera Parisiensis*; two columns of 59–60 lines each. No *collationes*. Manuscript belonged to the Sorbonne Library. This manuscript cannot be a copy of Florence, Bibl. Naz., conv. soppr. B VII 1249. The Paris manuscript has two questions that are lacking in the Florence manuscript. Moreover, the Paris manuscript has a number of lines that were omitted in the Florence manuscript, *per homoeoteleuton*.
5. Vatican Library, Cod. Vat. lat. 955 (marginalia), fols. 1^r–217^r (book I). Parchment; second quarter of the 14th century (probably between 1334 and 1342); gothic cursive of English Franciscan provenance. For further description see *Codices Vaticani Latini*, Vol. II, ed. A. Pelzer (Vatican, 1931), pp. 400–402.

B. Incipits, Explicits and List of Questions

	Bruges 172	Flor. B VII 1249	Paris B.N. 15 892
Incipit collatio I: "Ista est enim lex Adam, Domine Deus. II Reg. 7. Mirari solent mundi sapientes et lucris tantum temporalibus [F: et commodis saecularibus] inhiantes Sacrae Scripturae deditos...."	27ra	unnumbered	absent
Explicit collatio I: "... Domine Deus, omni creator, terribilis et fortis, iustus et misericors, qui solus es bonus, praestans, solus iustus et misericors, omnipotens et aeternus, qui liberas Israel ab omni malo, custodi partem tuam et sanctifica, scilicet theologos etsi simus peccatores, Domine Deus virtutum converte nos et ostende faciem tuam et salvi erimus. Quod nobis praestare dignetur potest Dei filius. Amen."	27va	unnumbered	absent
Introductio/protestatio: "In nomine Domini incipit brevis collectio Wodham super Sententias apud Oxoniam extracta ex lectionibus suis et ex alibi occurrentibus [Vat.: lectionibus suis alibi et ex occurrentibus aliis postea], dum se disponeret et etiam dum legebat, quae si quid [B. *om.* quid] contineat repraehensibile contra fidem vel mores, contra eius intentionem est [B. *om.* est], ex nunc illud abicit et retractat et quorum intererit benevolentiae subicit corrigendum."	27va	absent	absent
Incipit prol., q. 1: "Utrum, sicut tactum est in collatione, studium Sacrae Scripturae [Flor.: theologiae] sit meritorium vitae aeternae. Quod non quia finis talis studii per se et immediatus non est nisi scire vel credere. Non est autem credere solummodo, quia sine tali studio multi plurimum pollent fide, sicut innuit Augustinus...."	27va	1ra	1ra

APPENDIX 2

	Bruges 172	Flor. B VII 1249	Paris B.N. 15 892
Explicit prol., q. 1: ". . . qui huic scientiae praeponunt nosse seipsos quam scientiam, quae apponit dolorem peregrinationis ex desiderio patriae et conditoris. Hic ibi."	32va	4va	6ra
Prol., q. 2: "Secundo pro complemento distinctori materiae tactae in dubiis nondum solutis prioris quaestionis quaero: Utrum studium Sacrae Scripturae impositum alicui in foro poenitentiae pro satisfactione omissionis culpabilis contrariae sit meritorium vitae aeternae."	32va– 41ra	4va– 10ra	6ra– 12va
Dist. 1, q. 1: "Circa primam distinctionem ubi tractat Magister de frui et uti quaero pro distinctori [P: ulteriori] solutione sexti [B add. et septimi] dubii primae quaestionis prologi: Utrum pro studio sacrae theologiae [P: Scripturae] ex caritate [P: studio] procedente [B om.] debeatur pro mercede Dei visio et eius [P: huius] fruitio."	41ra– 46ra	10ra– 12va	12va– 15va
Incipit dist. 1, q. 2: "Secundo circa distinctionem primam quaero [B om. secundo . . . quaero]: Utrum fruitio beatifica sit qualitas distincta ab anima, cognitione, et delectatione. Quod non, probo plura non sunt ponenda ubi pauciora sufficiunt sed, etc., quia sufficit quod anima sine qualitate superaddita sicut noviter dilectio adhuc quod noviter diligat, sicut albedo de novo est similitudo propter novam ponendi[?] albedinis. Contra: fruitio est actus elicitus a voluntate; anima non sic; ergo, etc."	46ra	12va	15va
Explicit dist. 1, q. 2: ". . . nam de signis nec de figuris nec de numeris nullus homo necessaret[?] de propositionibus."	48va	15ra	18ra
Dist. 1, q. 3: "Tertio circa primam distinctionem quaero: Utrum frui distinguatur realiter ab omni cognitione."	48va– 50ra	15ra– 16vb	18ra– 20ra
Dist. 1, q. 4: "Quarto circa distinctionem primam quaero: Utrum fruitio realiter distinguatur a delectatione."	50ra– 52vb	16vb– 19rb	20ra– 22va
Dist. 1, q. 5: "Viso de delectatione beatifica utrum sit fruitio, quaerendum est consequenter in generali: Utrum omnis delectatio sit dilectio vel odium, seu volitio aut nolitio; et potest argui pro et contra sicut in praecedenti quaestione."	52vb– 53ra	19rb– 21rb	22va– 23rb
Dist. 1, q. 6: "Utrum voluntas necessario vel libere principiet actus suos."	53ra– 58vb	21rb– 30ra	23rb– 32rb
Dist. 1, q. 7: "Iuxta hoc quaero septimo: Utrum voluntas sola sit causa effectiva suae volitionis liberae supposita communi Dei influentia vel concausatione."	58vb– 60ra	30ra– 31vb	32rb– 34va

	Bruges 172	Flor. B VII 1249	Paris B.N. 15 892
Dist. 1, q. 8: "Utrum voluntas possit subito et simul producere actum voluntarium [F *om.* voluntarium] suum meritorie dilectionis." Bruges: "Utrum voluntas possit simul et semel producere meritorium actum."	60ra–63rb	31vb–35ra	34va–38va
Dist. 1, q. 9: "Utrum voluntas libere possit subito suspendere actum suum sive ab actu habito [P *om.* habito] cessare."	63rb–66ra	35ra–38ra	38va–42ra
Dist. 1, q. 10: "Circa primam distinctionem quaero decimo in speciali: Utrum omnis creatura rationalis clare videns Deum necessario diligat ipsum."	66ra–70va	38ra–39va	42ra–43va
Dist. 1, q. 11: "Quaero undecimo circa primam distinctionem: Utrum solus Deus sit licite a creatura rationali ultimate fruibilis."	70va–72va	39va–42va	43va–46va
Dist. 1, q. 12: "Utrum haec sit possibilis: creatura rationalis fruitur [B: fruatur] una persona divina non fruendo alia."	72va–74va	42va–45va	46va–49va
(Dist. 33, q. 1): "Utrum Deus sit essentialiter unus et personaliter trinus."	—	—	49va–52va
Dist. 1, q. 13: "Quaeritur tertiodecimo circa distinctionem primam: Utrum liceat filium Dei plus diligere vel frui eo quam patrem vel spiritum sanctum."	74va–76rb	45va–48ra	52va–55ra
Dist. 1, q. 14: "Quaero quartodecimo circa distinctionem primam et ultimo: Utrum fruitio beatifica sit actus intellectus [B *add.* vel voluntatis]."	76rb–76vb	48ra–49va	55ra–56rb
Dist. 2, q. un.: "Utrum in entibus sit unus Deus."	76vb–78ra	49va–53rb	56rb–60ra
Dist. 3, q. un.: "Circa distinctionem tertiam quaero: Utrum mens humana sit imago trinitatis increatae sicut in rebus aliis factis propter hominem est vestigium eiusdem trinitatis."	78ra–79rb	53rb–56va	60ra–63ra
Dist. 6, q. 2: "Circa distinctionem 6 quaero primo: Utrum a parte rei in divinis sit aliqua non-identitas inter naturam Dei et voluntatum Dei, et ita de ceteris perfectionibus quae ponuntur in Deo. Et istam transeo, quia est de formalibus de quibus sufficit in materia de trinitate. Circa eadem distinctionem quaero secundo: Utrum Deus sit essentialiter ipse primo modo sapiens vel intelligens, et sic de similibus."	—	56va–57vb	63ra–64ra
Dist. 7, q. 1: "Circa distinctionem 7 quaero: Utrum certa regula vel ars per quam solvi possunt paralogismi communiter facti et talibus similes circa materiam trinitatis possit dari."	—	57vb–60vb	64ra–67ra
Dist. 7, q. 2: "Utrum essentia divina generet vel generetur."	—	60vb–62va	67ra–68rb

	Bruges 172	Flor. B VII 1249	Paris B.N. 15 892
Dist. 7, q. 3: "Utrum potentia generandi in Deo patre cadat sub omnipotentia."	—	62va–63vb	68rb–69rb
Dist. 7, q. 4: "Utrum filius possit generare."	—	—	69rb–69va
Dist. 7, q. 5: "Utrum spiritus sanctus posset distingui a filio si non procederet ab eo."	—	63vb–64rb	69va–69vb
Dist. 7, q. 6: "Utrum pater et filius sint unum principium spirans spiritum sanctum."	—	64rb–65vb	69vb–71rb
Dist. 7, q. 7: "Utrum personae divinae primo et adequate distinguantur ad invicem semetipsis."	—	65vb–67rb	71rb–72va
Dist. 8, q. un.: "Circa distinctionem 8 quaero: Utrum solus Deus sit immutabilis."	79rb–80rb	67rb–69rb	72va–74va
Dist. 17, q. 1: "Circa distinctionem 17 quaero de caritate et primo de eius necessitate, secundo de eius augmentatione. Et de primo quaero: Utrum gratia seu caritas sit viatori necessaria ad salutem."	80rb–81ra	69rb–73rb	74va–78va
Dist. 17, q. 2: "Secundo quaero: Utrum caritas sive gratia increata sine alio possit sufficere ad salutem."	81ra–81va	73rb–75vb	78va–81rb
Dist. 17, q. 3: "Tertio quaero circa distinctionem 17: Utrum de peccatore possit fieri non peccator et acceptus Deo sine tali habitu sibi infuso per gratiam increatam."	81va–82ra	75vb–78rb	81rb–83vb
Dist. 17, q. 4: "Quaero secundo principaliter circa istam distinctionem 17 de augmento caritatis et aliarum formarum ubi primo quaero: Utrum caritas vel alia forma augmentabilis augmentetur per deminutionem sui contrarii."	82ra–83rb	78rb–79vb	83vb–85va
Dist. 17, q. 5: "Quaero adhuc circa distinctionem 17: Utrum in augmentatione caritatis vel alterius formae omnis gradus praeexistens corrumpatur cum novus gradus inducitur ita scilicet intelligendo quod in omni instanti sit totaliter nova forma."	83rb–84va	79vb–80va	85va–86rb
Dist. 17, q. 6: "Sexto quaero circa distinctionem 17: Utrum omnis bonus motus voluntatis meritorie caritatis augmentativus ad quem homo tenetur debeat vel possit ex caritate procedere collata ex merito redemptoris."	84va–85vb	80va–82ra	86rb–87vb
Explicit I: ". . . quod talis modus non est meritorius beatitudinis nisi procedat ex gratia vel per gratiam ad beatitudinem acceptus."	85vb	82ra	87vb
Incipit II, q. 1: "Utrum creaturae rationales meritorie serviendo Deo proficiant ad augmentum gratiae sine omni novo addito gratiae praecedenti."	85vb–87ra	82ra–83rb	88ra–89ra
II, q. 2: "Secundo quaero: Utrum profectus vel augmentum gratiae fiat per compositionem novae gratiae cum gratia praecedenti."	87ra–88va	83rb–85va	89ra–91va

	Bruges 172	Flor. B VII 1249	Paris B.N. 15 892
II, q. 3: "Quaero tertio circa istam distinctionem quoad materiam de intensione formarum: Utrum creatura rationalis habens gratiam possit mereri suam gratiam augmentari."	88va–90rb	85va–88va	91va–95ra
II, q. 4: "Quaero quarto circa istam distinctionem: Utrum viator operibus meritoriis insistendo ex hiis carior Deo fiat."	90rb–91va	88va–90va	95ra–97ra
II, q. 5: "Quaero quinto circa distinctionem primam secundi et principium quarti: Utrum praesupposita gratia baptismali viator per merita sua possit pertingere ad maximam gratiam viae."	91va–93rb	90va–91rb	97ra–97vb
II, q. 6: "Quaero sexto: Utrum viator existens in gratia ultra omnem gratiam habitam vel habendam possit proficere ad maiorem per instantaneas causationes actuum volendi omnia pro futuro peccata venialia alia devitare."	93rb–94vb	91rb–92rb	97vb–98vb
II, q. 7: "Quaero septimo: Utrum Deus possit creare finitam caritatem aliam vel aliquam qua non possit maiorem creare vel ita magnam producere secundum extensionem quod non possit maiorem illa producere, et sic de similibus."	—	92rb–93vb	98vb–100ra
II, q. 8: "Quaero octavo: Utrum secundum proportionem caritatis viae succedat pro praemio proportionaliter magnitudo gloriae."	94vb–95va	93vb–95va	100ra–102ra
II, q. 9: "Quaero nono de deminutione caritatis, scilicet: Utrum per demerita minuatur."	95va–96vb	95va–98rb	102ra–104va
II, q. 10: "Quaero ultimo: Utrum caritas decrescat ad crementum cupiditatis."	96vb–98ra	98rb–99vb	104va–106rb
Explicit II: "Ad argumenta principalia responsum est superius in primo articulo istius quaestionis."	98ra	99vb	106rb
Incipit III, q. 1: "Utrum anima Christi habeat sapientiam aequalem Deo."	98ra–99ra	103ra–104vb	106rb–108rb
III, q. 2: "Utrum ipsum verbum Dei sit sibi ipsi quamvis non sit animae sibi ipsi unitae scientia futurorum contingentium."	99ra–99vb	104vb–108ra	108rb–111va
III, q. 3: "Secundo circa istam materiam quaero: Utrum cum determinata verbi praescientia stet quod futura sint ad utrumlibet contingentia."	99vb–101ra	108ra–112ra	111va–115vb
III, q. 4: "Viso quomodo verbum Dei cui unica est anima Christi est certa et infallibiliter praescientia futurorum restat inquirere: Utrum anima Christi vel angeli sciat futura aliqua contingentia per revelationem sibi possibilem fieri ab ipso verbo etiam scire possunt."	101ra–101vb	112ra–114ra	115vb–118rb

	Bruges 172	Flor. B VII 1249	Paris B.N. 15 892
III, q. 5: "Quaero quinto circa istam distinctionem: Utrum alicuius contingentis futuri absoluta revelatio sequens tollat contingentiam."	101vb– 102va	114ra– 116va	118rb– 121rb
III, q. 6: "Sexto quaero circa praesentem distinctionem 14: Utrum Deus vel verbum Dei existenti in gratia possit revelare quod talis finaliter sit damnandus."	102va– 103rb	116va– 118rb	121rb– 123rb
III, q. 7: "Quaero septimo circa distinctionem hanc 14: Utrum animae Christi vel angelo beato possit in verbo revelari aeternitas suae beatitudinis."	103rb– 104rb	118rb– 120vb	123rb– 126ra
III, q. 8: "Quaero octavo: Utrum Gabrieli potuerit in verbo verbi incarnatio revelari."	104rb– 105ra	120vb– 122ra	126ra– 127rb
III, q. 9: "Quaero nono circa istam distinctionem 14: Utrum per revelationes possibiles [P: ponentes] fieri in verbo posset aliquis sufficienter dirigi in volendis."	105ra– 105va	122ra– 123vb	127rb– 129rb
III, q. 10: "Quaero decimo circa hanc distinctionem 14: Utrum anima Christi in verbo Dei cui unitur distincte videre valeat infinita."	105va– 107vb	123vb– 128va	129rb– 134ra
III, q. 11: "Quaero duodecimo [sic] circa istam distinctionem 14: Utrum anima Christi possit in verbo cui unitur distincte cognoscere minimas particulas corporis quod informat."	108ra– 108vb	128va– 130va	134ra– 136rb
III, q. 12: "Quaero adhuc circa distinctionem 14: Utrum per unionem ad verbum ipsa sit omnipotens."	108vb– 109va	130va– 131vb	136rb– 137rb
Explicit III: "Ad secundum respondet per illud quod dictum est ad sextum."	109va	131vb	137rb
Incipit IV, q. 1: "Circa principium quarti de sacramentis quaero: Utrum aliqua creatura possit creare gratiam vel aliam creaturam."	109va– 110ra	144ra– 148vb	137vb– 143vb
IV, q. 2: "Utrum creare gratiam vel aliquid aliud repugnet propter virtutis activae insufficientiam cuilibet creaturae."	110ra– 110va	148vb– 152rb	143vb– 148ra
IV, q. 3: "Utrum homini rite suscipienti sacramentum baptismi vel confirmationis conferatur gratia salutaris."	—	152rb– 154ra	148ra– 150rb
IV, q. 4: "Utrum corpus Christi realiter sub speciebus quae fuerunt panis et vini contineatur."	—	154ra– 155vb	150rb– 152va
IV, q. 5: "Utrum quantitas terminata panis consecrandi sit alia res vera extra animam distincta realiter a substantia et qualitate cuius est."	—	155vb– 160vb	152va– 158rb
IV, q. 6: "Utrum sacramentum poenitentiae sit necessarium ad delendum peccatum mortale, an sufficit contritio."	—	160vb– 163rb	158rb– 161rb
IV, q. 7: "Utrum actus poenitentiae requisitus ad deletionem culpae mortalis sit meritorius vitae aeternae."	—	163rb– 164va	161rb– 162va

	Bruges 172	Flor. B VII 1249	Paris B.N. 15 892
IV, q. 8: "Utrum quilibet qui commisit peccatum mortale teneatur secundum legem Dei communem de illo conteri."	—	164va–168ra	162va–166va
IV, q. 9: "Utrum poenitentia sit formaliter vel virtualiter velle cavere peccatum quodlibet in futurum [sic]."	—	168ra–170rb	166va–169rb
IV, q. 10: "Utrum ille qui peccavit mortaliter in opere exteriori teneatur plus poenitere de opere exteriori et interiori simul quam de interiori solo."	—	170rb–172va	169rb–171vb
IV, q. 11: "Utrum aliqua poena infernalis possit esse insensibilis damnatis."	—	172va–173vb	171vb–173rb
IV, q. 12: "Utrum sit maxima gloria possibilis in beato."	—	173vb–174rb	173rb–174ra
Explicit IV: "Ad secundum, ad tertium etiam dicendum: videtur mihi quod anima nihil agente sed solo Deo ipsa possit simul cum hoc videre Deum et intelligere, nec auderem contrarium tenere, cum etiam secundum philosophiam 'intelligere' sit quod pati, et dato quod anima ageret visionem suam, idem sequitur. Et sic finis. Amen. "Explicit lectura fratris Adae Wodeham."	—	174rb	174ra

APPENDIX 3

LECTURA SECUNDA

A. Description of Manuscript

Cambridge, Gonville and Caius College, Ms. 281 (674), fols. 105ra–250vb (book I). Parchment; 14th century; gothic bookhand of English provenance, and one hand throughout; two columns of 53–59 lines each. *Collationes* I–II (but not the same as in the *Lectura Oxon.*). The work contains some questions from the London and Oxford lectures, and may contain questions from the Norwich lectures as well. The manuscript is defective at various points. Dist. 1, q. 3 is missing; there seems to be a section or a question missing in the opening part of distinction 17; and the text breaks off on fol. 250^v. For further description see: M. R. James, *A Descriptive Catalogue of the Manuscripts in the Library of Gonville and Caius College*, Vol. I (Cambridge, 1907), pp. 330–331.

B. Incipits, Explicits, and List of Questions

Incipit collatio I (fol. 105ra): "Hic est liber generationis Adam. Gen. 5. Intellectualis oculi naturale desiderium, licet ignorantiae tenebris obumbrati, licet impotentiae legibus obligati caligantis. ..."

Explicit collatio I (fol. 105va): "... qui cum patre et spiritu sancto vivit et regnat."

Incipit prol., q. 1 (= ? *Lect. Lond.*, prol., q. 2) (fols. 105va–108vb): "Utrum, actui scientiae in nobis, necessario praesupponatur aliqua simplex apprehensio realiter distincta a omni sensatione."

Prol., q. 2 (fols. 108vb–112vb): "Utrum anima nostra in via naturaliter cognoscere possit actus suos cognitionibus intuitivis realiter distinctis ab abstractivis."

Prol., q. 3 (fols. 113ra–115rb): "Utrum notitia intuitiva sensitiva vel intellectiva possit naturaliter causari vel conservari sine existentia rei visae."

Prol., q. 4 (fols. 115rb–119ra): "Quarto quaero de articulo omisso prioris quaestionis: Utrum per visionem causetur 'esse aliquod apparens' vel 'esse visum' distinctum a visione et visibili."

Prol., q. 5 (fols. 119ra–123rb): "Utrum viator possit, stante statu viae, apprehendere Deum apprehensione aliqua simpliciori et propria."

Prol., q. 6 (fols. 123rb–128rb): "Habito ex quinta quaestione quod Deus potest, sine visione sui, causare abstractivam simplicem sui, nunc sexto quaero et ultimo quoad prologum: Utrum Deus, sine visione sui, possit immediate causare in intellectu omnem evidentiam complexam quam potest causare mediante visione sui."

Dist. 1, q. 1 (= *Lect. Lond.*, prol., q. 7) (fols. 128va–132rb): "Quoniam secundum beatum Augustinum, *De doctrina christiana* . . . , iam quaerendum est de ipso actu sciendi qui est actus iudicativus . . . et primo quaero iuxta auctoritatem allegatam: Utrum actus sciendi habeat pro obiecto immediato res vel signa, id est complexum in mente, vel re[s] significata[s] per complexum."

Dist. 1, q. 2 (fols. 132rb–137va): "Habito ex praecedenti quaestione quod scientia realis causata per apprehensiones tantum rectas habet pro obiecto 'sic esse a partis rei' et non complexum, nec tantum 'sic esse sicut significatur per conclusionem', sed etiam 'sicut significatur per praemissas', dummodo sit scientia evidens evidentia intrinseca, iam restat descendere in speciali ad notitiam theologicam ubi primo quaero: Utrum aliqua scientia theologica sit scibilis scientia proprie dicta."

NB: The second article of this question (fols. 134va–137va beginning at "Secundo principaliter") may have been intended as the third question of dist. 1.

Dist. 1, q. 4 (fols. 137va–145vb): "Quarto et ultimo quaero circa istam distinctionem: Utrum fruitio sit qualitas realiter distincta a cognitione et delectatione."

    Art. 1 (Cf. *Lect. Oxon.* I, dist. 1, q. 2) (fols. 137vb–139vb): "An fruitio distinguatur realiter ab anima."

    Art. 2 (Cf. *Lect. Oxon.* I, dist. 1, q. 3) (fols. 139vb–142va): "De articulo secundo quaero in speciali: Utrum frui realiter distinguatur ab omni cognitione."

    Art. 3 (Cf. *Lect. Oxon.* I, dist. 1, q. 4) (fols. 142va–145vb): "Circa tertium articulum propositum in quarta quaestione quaero in speciali: Utrum fruitio realiter distinguatur a dilectione."

Dist. 2, q. 1 (fols. 145vb–149vb): "Capitulo tertio distinctionis secundae dicit Magister quod ad assertionem fidei qua ibi opponitur unitatem essentialem stare cum trinitate personali utendum est rationibus catholicis adversus garulos ratiocinatores, et non tantum auctoritatibus . . . occasione primo quaero: An ille et alii fidei articuli possint evidenti ratione probari."

Dist. 2, q. 2 (fols. 149vb–153vb): "Iam declaratum est ex primo articulo prioris quaestionis quod beati possunt evidenter demonstrare articulum . . . quod Deus est trinus et unus et ita de aliis veritatibus creditis necessariis. Nunc secundo quaero: An aliquod obiectum contineat virtualiter illam notitiam scientificam."

Dist. 2, q. 3 (fols. 153vb–159ra): "Iuxta praecedentem quaestionem quaero: Utrum deitas vel aliqua alia entitas simpliciter simplex contineat virtualiter plures conceptus simplices et absolutos quorum unus sit conceptus eius quidditativus et alius denominativus, id est dicibilis de ipso tantum secundo modo dicendi per se."

Dist. 2, q. 4 (fols. 159ra–161rb): "De quarto articulo principali quaero in speciali: Utrum deitas contineat virtualiter plures conceptus proprios positivos simplices et mere absolutos quorum unus sit de Deo praedicabilis in quid, et alter in quali, ut quod pluribus conceptibus talibus possit concipi."

Dist. 3, q. 1 (fols. 161rb–165rb): "Circa distinctionem tertiam ut dicit Magister secundum Apostolum quod 'invisibilia Dei a creatura mundi per ea quae facta sunt intellecta conspiciuntur,' quaerendum de qualiter Deus sit cognoscibilis a nobis ex cognitione creaturarum tam complexe quam incomplexe ubi primo quaero: Utrum ex effecti[bu]s possit evidenter probari quod aliquid individuale [Ms.: in divinis] in universo sit simpliciter primum ens."

Dist. 3, q. 2 (fols. 165rb–169rb): "De secundo articulo quaero in speciali: Utrum sit evidenter probabile quod simpliciter incausabile sit tantum unicus numero."

Dist. 3, q. 3 (fols. 169rb–169vb): "Visis de viis quibus probari solet unitas Dei... quaeri posset: Utrum unitas Dei specifica probari possit."

Dist. 3, q. 4 (fols. 169vb–173rb): "Consequenter quaero: Utrum Deum esse innotescat tantum discursive ab effectibus vel sit per se notum."

Collatio II (fols. 173rb–173vb)

Incipit (fol. 173rb): "Lectio in secundum librum sententiarum. Hic est liber generationis Adam. Gen. 5. Ut in principio primi tactum est materia libri sententiarum est quadruplex generatio duplicis Adam, et sicut liber primus est liber generationis novissimi Adam, id est filii Dei . . . sic est hic secundus liber. . . ."

Explicit (fol. 173vb): ". . . quia misericordiam volui et non sacrificium et scientiam Dei non [sic!] plus quam holocausta, quam scientiam nobis tribuat, qui cum patre et spiritu sancto vivit et regnat. Amen."

Dist. 3, q. 5 (Cf. *Lect. Oxon*, I, dist. 3) (fols. 173vb–176vb): "Iuxta lectionem circa principium secundi continuando materiam primi qui est de Deo et sancta trinitate, et specialiter tertiae distinctionis primi . . . quoad conclusiones in qua tractatur de imagine et vestigio trinitatis quaero: Utrum in homine de quo principaliter tractatur in secundo sit imago Dei et trinitatis sicut in ceteris creaturis factis propter hominem, ut habitum est in lectione est vestigium Dei et trinitatis."

Dist. 4 (fols. 176vb–180va): "Circa distinctionem quartam, quae multum dependet ex significatione et suppositione alia et alia concreti et abstracti, quaero: Utrum respectu solius Dei praedicetur vere abstractum de concreto dicendo scilicet 'Deus est deitas' vel 'Deus est trinitas' vel huiusmodi."

Dist. 5 (Cf. *Lect. Oxon*. I, dist. 33, q. 4) (fols. 180va–183rb): "Utrum essentia divina generet vel generetur."

Dist. 6, q. 1 (Cf. *Lect. Oxon*. I, dist. 6, q. 1) (fols. 183rb–188va): "Circa distinctionem sextam ubi inquiritur an ex hoc quod voluntas Dei est natura sive essentia Dei, sequatur quod si verbum Dei, natura Dei, filius Dei quod voluntate Dei filius sit, quaero primus: Utrum a parte rei in divinis sit aliqua non-identitas inter naturam Dei et voluntatem divinam et ita de ceteris perfectionibus quae ponuntur in Deo vel Deus nec moveat quod pluraliter loquor antequam habeatur quod ibi sit pluralitas. Sine enim hac improprietate loquendi non potest homo in hac materia leviter exprimere id quod vellet."

Dist. 6, q. 2 (fols. 188va–190va): "Secundo circa istam distinctionem sextam, supposito quod sapientia quae Deus est et volitio quae Deus est, et sic de aliis, sint omnino idem a parte rei, quaero: Utrum saltem ratione distinguantur inter se et ab essentia."

Dist. 7, q. 1 (Cf. *Lect. Oxon.* I, dist. 33, q. 5) (fols. 190va–198vb): "Circa distinctionem septimam quaero: Utrum potentia generandi possit communicari filio in divinis."

Dist. 7, q. 2 (fols. 198vb–201vb): "Secundo ad maiorem declarationem materiae introductae quaestione praecedenti quaero: Utrum conceptus essentiae quo immediate est Deus significabilis et conceptibilis sit intensio communis informans subiective intellectum nostrum."

Dist. 7, q. 3 (fols. 201vb–205vb): "Tertio quaero: Utrum conceptus communis essentiae quo immediate concipimus Deum sit conceptus deitatis."

Dist. 7, q. 4 (fols. 205vb–206ra): "Supposito ad praesens quod [res] singularis tam sensibilis quam intelligibilis sit cognoscibilis cognitione sibi propria ab intellectu et prius causaliter quam commune, quaero de ordine generationis cognitionum universalium: Utrum communiores praecedant ordine minus communes aut econtro."

Dist. 8 (fols. 206ra–210rb): "Circa distinctionem octavam quaero primo: Utrum Deus sit conceptibilis a nobis conceptu substantiae vel essentiae."

Dist. 9 (fols. 210rb–213ra): "Circa distinctionem nonam, ubi tractatur de coaeternitate patris et filii, quaero: Utrum cum coaeternitate illa stet quod pater praecedat filium origine vel natura."

Dist. 10 (fols. 213ra–215vb): "Circa distinctionem decimam quaero: Utrum stent simul quod spiritus sanctus libere producatur et tamen necessario."

Dist. 11 (Cf. *Lect. Oxon.* I, dist. 33, q. 6) (fols. 215vb–216vb): "Circa distinctionem 11 quaero: Utrum spiritus sanctus possit distingui a filio si non procederet ab eo."

Dist. 12 (Cf. *Lect. Oxon.* I, dist. 33, q. 7) (fols. 216vb–219rb): "Circa distinctionem 12 quaero: Utrum pater et filius sint unum principium spirans spiritum sanctum."

Dist. 13 (fols. 219rb–219va): "Circa distinctionem 13 quaero: Utrum spiratio spiritus sancti sit generatio."

Dist. 14 (fols. 219va–219vb): "Circa distinctionem 14 quaero: Utrum spiritus sanctus detur in propria persona vel tantum in donis creatis."

Dist. 15 (fol. 220ra): "Circa distinctionem 15 quaero: Utrum quaelibet persona divina possit mittere vel mitti."

Dist. 16 (fol. 220ra): "Circa distinctionem 16 quaero: Utrum divina persona visibiliter mittatur."

Dist. 17, q. 1 (fols. 220ra–225vb): "Circa distinctionem 17 circa invisibilem spiritus sancti missionem . . . quaero primo: Utrum praeter[?] spiritum sanctum invisibiliter missum et datum necesse sit ponere aliquam qualitatem, puta caritatem creatam, inhaerentem animae, ad hoc quod anima sit cara et Deo accepta."

NB: Art. 2 = q. 2.

Dist. 17, q. 3 (Cf. Cologne *Extractio*, I, q. 21, dub. 1) (fols. 225vb–226rb): "Tertio circa hanc materiam restat inquirendum: Utrum simul stent quod caritas quae est qualitas quaedam supernaturalis informet animam viatoris et tamen quod Deus non acceptet eum ad vitam aeternam."

Dist. 17, q. 4 (fols. 226va–228rb): "Quarto et ultimo circa hanc materiam restat inquirendum: Utrum sit de facto et de lege communi omni actui meritorio caritas data supponatur."

Dist. 18 (fol. 228rb): "Quaero: Utrum in illo cui datur spiritus sanctus oporteat esse mutationem."

Dist. 19 (fol. 228rb): "Circa distinctionem 19 quaero: Utrum quaelibet persona sit in alia per circumincessionem."

Dist. 20 & 19 (fols. 228rb–229va): "Circa distinctiones 20 et 19 simul quaero: Utrum divinae personae sint inter se propter [Ms.: de inesse per] circumincessionem aequales secundum magnitudinem vel potentiam."

Dist. 21 (fols. 229va–229vb): "Circa distinctionem 21 quaero: Utrum solus pater sit Deus."

Dist. 22 (fols. 229vb–232vb): "Circa distinctionem 22 quaero: Utrum viator possit aliquod nomen imponere ad distincte significandum divinam essentiam."

Dist. 23 (fols. 232vb–235rb): "Circa distinctionem 23 quaero: Utrum hoc nomen 'persona' sit nomen primae intentionis vel secundae."

Dist. 24, q. 1 (fols. 235rb–238rb): "Circa distinctionem 24 ubi tractatur . . . nomina numeralia, puta unus, duo, tres . . . in divinis, quaero primo de unitate: Utrum unitas a qua Deus dicitur unus sit aliquid accidens in Deo vel additum sibi."

Dist. 24, q. 2 (fols. 238rb–246va): "Secundo quaero: Utrum trinitas personarum divinarum sit verus numerus."

Dist. 25 (fol. 246va): "Circa distinctionem 25 esset conquaerendum, sicut communiter hic tractatur: Utrum ab ultimis constitutivis personarum in divinis possit abstrahi aliquis conceptus positivus unus communis in quid talibus ultimis constitutivis."

Dist. 26, q. 1 (fols. 246va–249vb): "Circa distinctionem 26 quaero: Utrum personae divinae per [sic] seipsis primo personaliter distinguantur."

Dist. 26, q. 2 (fols. 249vb–250vb): "Viso quod personae divinae sint personae relative, quaero secundo: Utrum in divinis, hoc non obstante, sit aliqua persona absoluta."

Explicit (fol. 250vb): ". . . sicut propter hoc quod 'homo' significat plures homines, non oportet quod illa nomina, quae praenominantur de hoc nomine 'homo' sine signo universali, praedice[n]tur de se. Et proportionaliter dic de remotione. Et circa hoc quaere C[hatton] in primo, dist. secunda, quaest. quinta, articulo primo. Et improba-."

APPENDIX 4

FRAGMENTA ET ABBREVIATIONES SIVE EXTRACTIONES

A. Vat. Lat. 869

Vatican Library, Cod. Vat. lat. 869, fols. 214vb–217va (*collatio* II and a unique question). Parchment; 14th century; cursive bookhand with English elements; two columns of 47–54 lines each. For further description see *Codices Vaticani Latini*, Vol. II, ed. A. Pelzer (Vatican, 1931), pp. 242–254.

Incipit collatio II (fol. 214vb): "Hic est liber generationis Adam. Gen. 5. Solent inquiri in principiis lectionum tituli librorum. Cui inquisitioni circa secundum librum Sententiarum prae manibus iam habendum imprimis satisfactio quia titulus est talis: hic est liber, etc."

Explicit collatio II (fol. 215ra): "... in futuro per gloriam, quod nobis concedat qui cum patre et spiritu sancto vivit et regnat in saecula saeculorum. Amen."

Incipit quaestio (fol. 215rb): "Iuxta materiam tactam in collatione de productione primi Adam et aliarum rerum in reali subsistentia, primo quaero de principio productivo quantum ad sui scientiam sub hac forma: Utrum verbum Dei fuerit sibi ipsi ab aeterno scientia futurorum contingentium vel rerum ab ipso producibilium. Quod aliter quae[ro]: Utrum Deus ab aeterno novit res producibiles libere."

Explicit quaestio (fol. 217va): "... et talia possunt adhuc non praesciri fore nec numquam fuisse praescitum fore, quod posset probari multis[?]. Sed pro nunc dimitto donec aliud occurrat."

Incipit replicatio (fol. 217va): "Iste sunt replicationes per istum modum quod filius in divinis non producitur de memoria patris elicitive contra hoc arguo tripliciter...."

Explicit [imperfect] replicatio (fol. 217vb): "... praeterea nulli complexo."

B. The Cologne *Extractio*

1. *Description of Text*

This work is an abbreviation of Wodeham's *Lectura Oxoniensis* and belongs to the genre of *Lecturae secundum alium*. It was read between 1334 and 1348, probably at the Franciscan convent in Cologne. The name of the compiler is not known. The author added some of his own comments and questions to Wodeham's text and altered one passage to fit a Cologne audience.

The structure of the work differs from Wodeham's Commentary. While Wodeham's questions often contained *dubia*, the *Extractio* makes the *dubia* a major structural feature of the work through which almost every question is divided into a series of subquestions. Several of the *dubia* do not appear in Wodeham's version. Since many of the *dubia* are not in a question-form, only a selected few have been included in the list of questions.

2. *Description of Manuscripts*

a. Hannover, Stadtbibliothek, Hs. 1, fols. 1ra–47vb, 69va–75ra, 76^v (book I, dist. 17, q. 1—IV). Parchment; 14th century, probably the third quarter. Text copied by two scribes. The first hand (fols. 1ra–34rb) is a rounded, university bookhand, similar to that of Mazarine 915. The second hand (fols. 34rb–47vb, 69va–75ra, 76^v), which for III, qq. 10–12, follows the *ordinatio* text instead of the Cologne *Extractio*, is thinner, more cursive, and less professional. Two columns of 51–53 lines each, except 76^v, which has one column. Probably three quires missing at the beginning of the present manuscript, the first folio of which opens in mid-sentence in the last half of book I, dist. 17, q. 1 and which was numbered in an earlier collection as fol. 37^r. For further description see: C. L. Grotefend, *Verzeichniss der Handschriften und Incunabeln der Stadt-Bibliothek zu Hannover* (Hannover, 1844), p. 1.

Incipit (fol. 1ra): "de potentia Dei ordinata secundum legem nunc concurrentem non potest a voluntate. . . ."
Explicit I (fol. 9vb): ". . . nisi procedat ex gratia vel per gratiam sic acceptus ad beatitudinem. Explicit extractio primi sententiarum Adae de Whodan."
Incipit II (fol. 9vb): "Utrum creaturae rationales, meritorie serviendo Deo, proficiant ad augmentum gratiae sine omni novo addito gratiae praecedenti."
Explicit II (fol. 19ra): ". . . Ad argumenta principalia responsum est superius in prima conclusione primi. Finis secundi libri sententiarum per Adam."
Incipit III (fol. 19ra): "Utrum anima Christi habeat aequalem sapientiam Deo."
Explicit III (fol. 44rb): ". . . ab omnibus proportionibus illis quibus prior et in talis quantitatibus proportionibus est satisfaciendo semper, etc."
Incipit IV (fol. 44rb): "Utrum aliqua creatura possit in effectum sacramenti praecise productibilem per creationem, teneo quod non, quia. . . ."
Explicit IV (fol. 75ra): ". . . de ista difficultate quaerere primo, dist. 17. Et hoc toto isto quarto. Laudetur Deus. Amen. Explicit quartus abbreviatus Adae, et per consequens totus super quattuor libros."

b. Naples, Bibl. Naz., Cod. VII C 53, fols. 1ra–108ra (books I–IV); fols. 108ra–109va (tabula quaestionum). Parchment; one hand of the 14th century: rounded bookhand similar to Littera Neapolitana; Italian Franciscan provenance, once belonging to S. Giovanni a Carbonara di Napoli; two columns of 43 lines each. Folio numbers skip from 87 to 89. For further description see Cesare Cenci, *Manoscritti francescani della Biblioteca Nazionale di Napoli*, Spicilegium Bonaventurianum, VII; Vol. I (Florence, 1971), p. 412.

Incipit I (fol. 1ra): "Utrum studium sacrae theologiae sit meritorium vitae aeternae."
Explicit I (fol. 58vb): ". . . nisi procedat ex gratia vel per gratiam acceptus ad beatitudinem. Explicit scriptum primum sententiarum."
Incipit II (fol. 58vb): "Utrum creaturae rationales, meritorie serviendo Deo, proficiant ad augmentum gratiae sine omni novo addito gratiae praecedenti."
Explicit II (fol. 72vb): "Ad argumenta principalia responsum est superius in prima conclusione primi articuli. Finis secundi."
Incipit III (fol. 72vb): "Utrum anima Christi habeat aequalem sapientiam Deo."
Explicit III (fol. 93vb): "Ad argumentum principale satis aperte patet in littera de qua assumitur, igitur, etc."
Incipit IV (fol. 93vb): "Utrum aliqua creatura possit in effectum sacramenti praecise productibilem per creationem, sive: Utrum aliqua creatura possit creare."
Explicit IV (fol. 108ra): "Et hoc sufficit ad propositum meum, quia nolo quod sit necessarium sed possibile."

3. List of Questions

	Napl.	Hanv.	Approximate parallel in *Lect. Oxon.*
I, q. 1: "Utrum studium sacrae theologiae sit meritorium vitae aeternae."	1ra	—	Prol., q. 1
"Secundus articulus est movere dubia."			
Dub. 1: "Utrum anima possit devenire, ad tantum meritum quod non possit ulterius."	1va	—	
Dub. 2: "Utrum aliquis possit mereri in vita."	2rb	—	
Dub. 4: "Utrum omissio actus boni ad quem quis requiritur sit tantum demeritoria quantum ponemus esset meritoria."	3ra	—	
Dub. 5: "Utrum actus de se meritorius impositus alicui in foro poenitentiae pro satisfactione culpae contrariae sit ei meritorius."	3ra	—	Prol., q. 2
Dub. 6: "Utrum divina visio sit possibilis creaturae."	5ra	—	
Dub. 7: "Utrum actus quo beatus videt verbum differat a verbo vel sit idem quod verbum."	5va	—	
Dub. 8: "Utrum eodem actu beatus viderat verbum et creaturam in verbo."	6rb	—	
Dub. 9: "Utrum viator ex gratia communis viatoribus possibili ex puris naturalibus	6va	—	

	Napl.	Hanv.	Approximate parallel in *Lect. Oxon.*
possit vitare omne peccatum tam morale quam veniale."			
Dub. 10: "Utrum intellectus finitus vel creatus possit videre obiectum infinitum quod est Deus."	7ra	—	
Dub. 11: "Utrum clara visio Dei et beata fruitio inferat gaudium infinitum."	7vb	—	
I, q. 2: "Circa primam distinctionem quaero: Utrum fruitio differat ab anima."	8ra	—	I, dist. 1, q. 2
I, q. 3: "Secundo quaero: Utrum fruitio realiter distinguatur ab omni cognitione."	8vb	—	I, dist. 1, q. 3
I, q. 4: "Utrum fruitio realiter distinguatur a delectatione."	9va	—	I, dist. 1, q. 4
Dub. 1: "Utrum delectatio beatifica sequatur visionem Dei immediate vel mediate aliquo actu voluntatis."	10ra	—	
Dub. 2: "Utrum volitio vel delectatio possit esse praecognitio voliti."	10rb	—	
Dub. 3: "Utrum obiectum sit causa immediata delectationis."	10rb	—	
Dub. 4: "Utrum delectatio beatifica sit actus reflexus habens visionem et delectationem Dei pro obiecto."	10va	—	
Dub. 5: "An omnis beatitudo sit in unico actu quae sit visio Dei et delectatio."	10vb	—	
Dub. 6: "Utrum omnis delectatio vel tristitia sit volitio vel nolitio."	11ra	—	I, dist. 1, q. 5
I, q. 5: "Utrum voluntas necessario vel libere principiat [sic] actus suos."	11ra	—	I, dist. 1, q. 6
I, q. 6: "Utrum sola voluntas sit causa effectiva suae volitionis supposita communi [influentia vel con]causatione Dei."	15vb	—	I, dist. 1, q. 7
I, q. 7: "Utrum voluntas simul et subito possit producere actum voluntarium meritorie et libere dilectionis."	16rb	—	I, dist. 1, q. 8
I, q. 8: "Utrum Deus sit essentialiter unus et personaliter trinus."	17rb	—	I, dist. 33, q. 1
I, q. 9: "Utrum aliqua sit certa regula vel ars per quam solvi possunt [sic] paralogismi quae fiunt circa materiam trinitatis."	20vb	—	I, dist. 33, q. 3
I, q. 10: "Utrum voluntas libere possit subito suspendere actum suum vel cessare ab actu."	24ra	—	I, dist. 1, q. 9
I, q. 11: "Utrum creatura rationalis clare videns Deum necessario diligat eum."	26ra	—	I, dist. 1, q. 10
I, q. 12: "Utrum solus Deus sit licite a creatura rationali ultimate fruibilis."	32ra	—	I, dist. 1, q. 11

	Napl.	Hanv.	Approximate parallel in *Lect. Oxon.*
Art. 3: "Utrum aliquod aliud a Deo sit licite fruibile fruitione beatifica ultimata."	34ra	—	
I, q. 13: "Utrum haec sit possibilis: creatura rationalis fruitur una persona divina non fruendo alia."	34va	—	I, dist. 1, q. 12
I, q. 14: "Utrum fruitio beatifica sit actus intellectus."	36rb	—	I, dist. 1, q. 14
I, q. 15: "Circa distinctionem secundam quaero: Utrum in entibus sit tantum unus Deus."	37ra	—	I, dist. 2
Dub. 1: "Utrum unitas Dei possit demonstrari."	37rb	—	
Dub. 2: "Utrum eiusdem effectus possint esse plures causae rationales aequales eiusdem ordinis."	37rb	—	
Dub. 3: "Utrum unitas ... probari possit per hoc quod effectus eiusdem non possunt esse plures causae totales."	37vb	—	
Dub. 5: "An possint esse plures causae finales totales respectu eiusdem effectus."	38rb	—	
I, q. 16: "Circa distinctionem tertiam quaero: Utrum in mente humana sit imago trinitatis increatae sicut in rebus aliis factis propter hominem est vestigium eiusdem trinitatis."	38vb	—	I, dist. 3
Dub. 2: "Utrum secunda pars imaginis, scilicet actualis intellectio, gignatur a prima, scilicet a memoria."	39rb	—	
Dub. 3: "Utrum actualis cognitio seu intellectio manens in mente subiective possit cessare esse intellectio."	40ra	—	
Dub. 4: "Utrum amor procedat a notitia."	40vb	—	
Dub. 5: "Utrum voluntas possit diligere incognitum."	41rb	—	
Dub. 6: "Utrum partes imaginis creatae sint aequales."	42ra	—	
I, q. 17: "Circa distinctionem sextam quaero: Utrum in divinis sit aliqua non-identitas inter naturam divinam et voluntatem divinam et ita de aliis perfectionibus quae ponuntur in Deo vel quae sunt in divinis."	42va	—	I, dist. 6, q. 1
I, q. 18: "Utrum Deus sit per se primo sapiens."	43rb	—	I, dist. 6, q. 2
I, q. 19: "Utrum solus Deus sit immutabilis."	44vb	—	I, dist. 8
I, q. 20: "Utrum caritas vel gratia sit viatori necessaria ad salutem."	45vb	1ra	I, dist. 17, q. 1
I, q. 21: "Utrum gratia increata sive caritas sine alio possit sufficere ad salutem."	48va	2va	I, dist. 17, q. 2

	Napl.	Hanv.	Approximate parallel in *Lect. Oxon.*
Dub. 1: "Utrum simul stent quod caritas est quaedam qualitas supernaturalis informans animam viatoris et tamen quod Deus non acceptet eam ad vitam aeternam."	49rb	—	Cf. *Lect. Sec.*, dist. 17, q. 3
Dub. 2: "An praeter caritatem increatam sit ponenda aliqua caritas informans creata."	49va	—	
Dub. 3: "Utrum omnis actus meritorius diligendi Deum propter se et proximum propter Deum principiet partialis a caritate infusa."	50va	—	
Dub. 4: "Utrum omnes actus eiusdem speciei cum actu meritorio sint meritorii de facto."	50vb	—	
Dub. 5: "Utrum, supposito quod omnis actus quem caritas principiat sit alterius speciei ab isto quem sola voluntas principiat, vel si non omnis saltem aliquis, utrum omnis actus eiusdem speciei cum isto actu sit meritorius secundum leges Dei ordinatas."	50vb	—	
I, q. 22: "Tertio quaero circa distinctionem 17: Utrum de peccatore fieri possit non peccator et acceptus Deo sine tali habitu sibi infuso per gratiam increatam."	51va	4vb	I, dist. 17, q. 3
I, q. 23: "Utrum caritas quae est forma augmentabilis vel quaecumque alia forma augmentetur per deminutionem sui contrarii."	54vb	6vb	I, dist. 17, q. 4
I, q. 24: "Utrum in augmento caritatis vel alterius formae gradus omnis praeexistens corrumpatur cum novus introducitur ita videlicet intelligendo quod in omni instanti sit totaliter nova forma."	56rb	8ra	I, dist. 17, q. 5
I, q. 25: "Utrum omnis bonus motus voluntatis meritorie augmentatius caritatis ad quem homo tenetur, debeat, vel possit ex caritate procedere, collata ex merito redemptoris."	57rb	8va	I, dist. 17, q. 6
II, q. 1: "Utrum creaturae rationales, meritorie serviendo Deo, proficiant ad augmentum gratiae sine omni novo addito gratiae praecedenti."	58vb	9vb	II, q. 1
II, q. 2: "Utrum augmentum gratiae fiat per compositionem [Hanv.: additionem] novae gratiae cum praecedenti gratia."	59vb	10rb	II, q. 2
II, q. 3: "Utrum creatura rationalis possit mereri gratiam suam augeri."	61rb	11va	II, q. 3

	Napl.	Hanv.	Approximate parallel in *Lect. Oxon.*
II, q. 4: "Utrum viator operibus meritoriis insistendo fiat ex hiis Deo carior."	62vb	12rb	II, q. 4
II, q. 5: "Utrum praesupposita gratia baptismali viator possit per merita sua pervenire ad maximam gratiam viae sibi possibilem."	63ra	12va	II, q. 5
II, q. 6: "Utrum viator existens in gratia ultra omnem gratiam habitam vel habendam possit proficere ad maiorem per instantaneas causationes actuum volendi omnia peccata venialia pro futuro devitare."	63va	12vb	II, q. 6
II, q. 7: "Utrum Deus possit creare aliquam caritatem qua non possit maiorem causare, et sic de aliis formis."	64va	13va	II, q. 7
II, q. 8: "Utrum secundum proportionem caritatis viae succedat pro praemio proportionaliter magnitudo gloriae."	65vb	14va	II, q. 8
II, q. 9: "Utrum caritas deminuatur per demerita."	67vb	15vb	II, q. 9
II, q. 10: "Utrum caritas decrescat ad crementum cupiditatis."	71ra	17vb	II, q. 10
III, q. 1: "Utrum anima Christi habeat aequalem sapientiam Deo."	72vb	19ra	III, q. 1
III, q. 2: "Utrum divinum verbum sit sibi ipsi, quamvis non animae sibi unitae, scientia futurorum contingentium."	74ra	19vb	III, q. 2
III, q. 3: "Utrum cum determinata verbi praescientia stet quod futura sint ad utrumlibet contingentia."	77va	22rb	III, q. 3
III, q. 4: "Utrum anima Christi vel angeli scire possint futura contingentia aliqua creatura per revelationem possibilem sibi fieri a verbo."	82va	26ra	III, q. 4
III, q. 5: "Utrum alicuius futuri contingentis absoluta revelatio tollat contingentiam."	83rb	28ra	III, q. 5
III, q. 6: "Utrum verbum divinum existenti in gratia possit revelare quod talis finaliter sit dampnandus."	86ra	—	III, q. 6
III, q. 7: "Utrum animae Christi vel angelo beato possit in verbo revelari aeternitas suae beatitudinis."	88ra	—	III, q. 7
III, q. 8: "Utrum Gabrieli in verbo potuerit incarnatio verbi revelari."	89rb	30va	III, q. 8
III, q. 9: "Utrum per revelationes possibiles fieri in verbo posset aliquis sufficienter dirigi in agendis."	90ra	31va	III, q. 9
III, q. 10: "Utrum anima Christi in verbo cui unitur valeat distincte videre infinita."	91ra	33rb	III, q. 10

	Napl.	Hanv.	Approximate parallel in *Lect. Oxon.*
III, q. 11: "Utrum anima Christi possit in verbo cui unitur distincte cognoscere minimas particulas corporis quod informat."	93rb	39va	III, q. 11
III, q. 12: "Utrum anima Christi per unionem ad verbum sit omnipotens."	93va	43va	III, q. 12
IV, q. 1: "Utrum aliqua creatura possit in effectum sacramenti praecise productibilem per creationem; sive: Utrum aliqua creatura possit creare."	93vb	44rb	IV, q. 1
IV, q. 2: "Utrum posse creare gratiam vel aliquid repugnet cuilibet creaturae propter insufficientiam virtutis activae."	96rb	45ra	IV, q. 2
IV, q. 3: "Tertio quaero: Utrum omni rite suscipienti sacramentum baptismi vel confirmationis conferatur gratia salutaris."	98ra	—	IV, q. 3
IV, q. 4: "Utrum corpus Christi realiter contineatur sub speciebus quae fuerunt panis et vini."	99ra	45vb	IV, q. 4
IV, q. 5: "Utrum quantitas panis consecrandi sit aliqua res distincta vera extra animam realiter a substantia et qualitate distincta."	99vb	46rb	IV, q. 5
IV, q. 6: "Utrum sacramentum poenitentiae sit necessarium ad delendum peccatum mortale commissum post baptismum."	101ra	47va	IV, q. 6
IV, q. 7: "Utrum actus poenitentiae requisitus ad deletionem culpae mortalis sit meritorius vitae aeternae."	103ra	69vb	IV, q. 7
IV, q. 8: "Utrum quilibet qui commisit peccatum mortale teneatur secundum legem communem de illo conteri."	103vb	70va	IV, q. 8
IV, q. 9: "Utrum vera poenitentia sit formaliter vel virtualiter velle cavere omne peccatum in futuro."	105rb	71va	IV, q. 9
IV, q. 10: "Utrum quis teneatur plus poenitere de opere interiori et exteriori simul quam de interiori solo."	106vb	72va	IV, q. 10
IV, q. 11: "Utrum aliqua poena infernalis possit esse insensibilis damnato."	107rb	74ra	IV, q. 11
IV, q. 12: "Utrum sit maxima gloria possibilis in beato."	107vb	74vb	IV, q. 12

C. The Oyta *Abbreviatio*

1. *List of Edition and Manuscripts*

A. Printed Edition: Paris, 1512

B. Manuscripts:

Barcelona, Bibl. Cat., Ms. 38, fols. 1^r–156^v (books I–IV); fols. 167^r–183^r (index).
Berlin, Staatsbibl., Hs. theol. lat. 2° 534, fols. 1^r–217^r (books I–IV); fols. 217^r–229^v (index).
Klosterneuburg, Stiftsbibl., Hs. 296, fols. 1^r–268^v (books I–IV); fols. 268^v–280^v (index).
Krakow, Bibl. Jagiellonska, Ms. 1176, fols. 1^r–267^v (books I–IV).
Krakow, Bibl. Jagiellonska, Ms. 1195, fols. 1^r–285^v (books I–IV).
Krakow, Bibl. Jagiellonska, Ms. 1197, fols. 341^r–351^v (index).
Mainz, Stadtbibl., Hs. I 53 A, fols. 71^r–103^r (book IV).
Pamplona, Bibl. Cat., Ms. 1, fols. 1^r–178^r (books I–IV); fols. 181^r–202^v (index).
Paris, Bibl. Nat., Ms. lat. 15 893, fols. 1^r–198^v (books I–IV).
Paris, Bibl. Nat., Ms. lat. 15 894, fols. 1^r–160^v (books I–IV).
Paris, Bibl. Mazarine, Ms. 916, fols. 1^r–128^v (books I–IV).
Paris, Bibl. Mazarine, Ms. 917, fols. 1^r–194^v (books I–IV).
Reims, Bibl. de la Ville, Ms. 504, fols. 1^r–182^v (books I–IV).
Rouen, Bibl. de la Ville, Ms. 581 (A 285), fols. 1^r–249^r (books I–IV); fols. 249^r–260^v (index).
Toulouse, Bibl. de la Univ., Ms. 246, fols. 1^r–210^r (books I–IV); fols. 210^r–219^v (index).
Toulouse, Bibl. de la Univ., Ms. 247, fols. 1^r–242^v (books I–IV).
Vienna, Bibl. Nat., Hs. 4371, fols. 18^r–54^v (book I).

2. *Incipits, Explicits, and List of Questions* (foliation according to the 1512 edition):

Incipit collatio I (fol. 1ra): "Ista est enim lex Adam, Domine Deus. Secundo regum septimo. Mirari solent mundi sapientes et lucris tantum saecularibus et commodis temporalibus inhiantes sacrae Scripturae deditos. . . ."
Explicit collatio I (fol. 1va): ". . . Domine Deus, omnium creator, terribilis, fortis, iustus et misericors, qui solus es bonus, solus rex, solus praestans, solus iustus, omnipotens, et aeternus, qui."
Incipit prol., q. 1 (fols. 1va–4va): "Iesus Christus totius Scripturae sacrae principium atque finis esse dinoscitur ipsius, igitur gratia directrice humiliter postulata, quaero circa principium libri sententiarum: Utrum studium sacrae Scripturae sit meritorium vitae aeternae."
Prol., q. 2 (fols. 4va–8va): "Utrum studium sacrae Scripturae impositum alicui in foro poenitentiae sit meritorium."
I, dist. 1, q. 1 (fols. 8vb–10rb): "Utrum pro studio sacrae theologiae ex caritate procedente debeatur pro mercede visio Dei et eius fruitio."

I, dist. 1, q. 2 (fols. 10rb–11va): "Utrum fruitio beatifica sit qualitas distincta ab ipsa anima."

I, dist. 1, q. 3 (fols. 11va–13ra): "Utrum fruitio realiter distinguitur ab omni cognitione."

I, dist. 1, q. 4 (fols. 13ra–15va): "Utrum fruitio realiter distinguatur a delectatione."

I, dist. 1, q. 5 (fols. 15va–16va): "Utrum sit fruitio quaeritur in generali: Utrum omnis delectatio vel tristitia sit dilectio vel odium seu volitio aut nolitio."

I, dist. 1, q. 6 (fols. 16va–23va): "Utrum voluntas necessario vel libere principiet suos actus."

I, dist. 1, q. 7 (fols. 23va–24vb): "Utrum sola voluntas cum Dei influentia seu concausatione communi sit causa effectiva suae liberae volitionis."

I, dist. 1, q. 8 (fols. 24vb–28ra): "Utrum voluntas possit simul et subito producere actum voluntarium meritorie et libere dilectionis."

I, dist. 1, q. 9 (fols. 28ra–30ra): "Utrum voluntas libere possit subito suspendere actum suum sive ab actu habito cessare."

I, dist. 1, q. 10 (fols. 30ra–37ra): "Utrum creatura clare videns Deum necessario diligat ipsum."

I, dist. 1, q. 11 (fols. 37ra–40va): "Utrum solus Deus licite a creatura rationali ultimate sit fruibilis."

I, dist. 1, q. 12 (fols. 40va–45ra): "Utrum haec sit possibilis: creatura rationalis truitur una persona divina non fruendo alia."

I, dist. 1, q. 13 (fols. 45ra–46rb): "Utrum liceat filium Dei plus diligere quam patrem vel spiritum sanctum seu eo plus frui."

I, dist. 1, q. 14 (fols. 46rb–47vb): "Utrum fruitio beatifica sit actus intellectivus."

I, dist. 2, q. un. (fols. 47vb–51ra): "Utrum in entibus sit tantum unus Deus."

I, dist. 3, q. un. (fols. 51ra–55va): "Utrum mens humana sit imago trinitatis increatae sicut in rebus aliis factis propter hominem et vestigium eiusdem trinitatis."

I, dist. 6, q. 1 (fols. 55va–57va): "Utrum a parte rei in divinis sit aliqua nonidemptitas inter naturam Dei et voluntatem divinam, et ita de ceteris perfectionibus quae ponuntur in Deo vel Deus, nec moveat quod pluraliter loquor antequam habeatur quod ibi sit pluralitas, sive enim hac improprietate loquendi non potest homo in hac materia leviter exprimere illud quod vellet."

I, dist. 6, q. 2 (fols. 57va–58rb): "Utrum Deus sit realiter et per se primo modo sapiens et intelligens, et sic de similibus."

I, dist. 8, q. un. (fols. 58rb–60ra): "Utrum solus Deus sit immutabilis."

I, dist. 17, q. 1 (fols. 60ra–63rb): "Utrum caritas seu gratia sit viatori necessaria ad salutem."

I, dist. 17, q. 2 (fols. 63rb–65vb): "Utrum caritas seu gratia increata sine alio sufficere possit ad salutem."

I, dist. 17, q. 3 (fols. 65vb–67vb): "Utrum de peccatore possit fieri non peccator et acceptus Deo sine habituali gratia infusa."

I, dist. 17, q. 4 (fols. 67vb–69rb): "Utrum gratia vel alia forma augmentabilis augmentetur per deminutionem sui contrarii."

I, dist. 17, q. 5 (fols. 69rb–70vb): "Utrum caritatis vel alterius formae omnis gradus praeexistens corrumpatur cum gradus novus introducitur ita videlicet intelligendo quod in omni instanti fiat nova forma."

I, dist. 17, q. 6 (fols. 70vb–73rb): "Utrum omnis motus bonus voluntatis meritorie augmentativus caritatis ad quem homo tenetur debeat vel possit ex caritate procedere collata ex merito redemptoris." Fol. 73rb: "Residuas quaestiones huius materiae de augmentatione formarum quaere in principio secundi."

I, dist. 33, q. 1 (fols. 73rb–78vb): "Utrum Deus essentialiter unus sit personaliter trinus."

I, dist. 33, q. 2 (fols. 78vb–81ra): "Utrum Deus genuerit Deum."

I, dist. 33, q. 3 (fols. 81ra–82vb): "Utrum sit aliqua regula vel ars per quam consequenter solvi possint paralogismi facti circa materiam trinitatis et talibus similes."

I, dist. 33, q. 4 (fols. 82vb–85ra): "Utrum essentia divina generet vel generetur."

I, dist. 33, q. 5 (fols. 85ra–86vb): "Utrum potentia generandi possit communicari filio in divinis."

I, dist. 33, q. 6 (fols. 87ra–87vb): "Utrum spiritus sanctus possit distingui a filio si non procederet ab eo."

I, dist. 33, q. 7 (fols. 87vb–89ra): "Utrum pater et filius sint unum principium spirans spiritum sanctum."

I, dist. 33, q. 8 (fols. 89ra–90vb): "Utrum personae divinae primo et adequate distinguantur ab invicem seipsis."

I, dist. 33, q. 9 (fol. 91ra): "Utrum omne idem patri sit omnibus modis idem patri."

Explicit I (fol. 91ra): ". . . sicut licet similitudo qua Sortes albus est similis Platoni albo, et dissimilitudo qua Sortes est dissimilis Socrati nigro, sint omnino idem; non tamen ideo est Sortes albus illi similis cui est dissimilis, nec econverso, etc."

Incipit collatio II (fol. 91rb): "Hic est liber generationis Adam. Solent inquiri tituli librorum in principiis lectionum, cui inquisitioni circa secundum librum sententiarum prae manibus iam habendum imprimis satisfactio quod titulus talis est: Hic est liber generationis Adam. . . ."

Explicit collatio II (fol. 91va): ". . . Hic est igitur liber generationis Adam, quia de ipsa et de eius circumstantiis quae ipsam ordinant, deformant vel reformant, liber secundus totus pertrahitur ut praedixi ad profectum et doctrinam audientis et legentis, quatenus in via regulamur per gratiam, in futuro pertingamus ad gloriam, quam nobis praestare, etc."

Incipit II, q. 1 (fols. 91va–93vb): "Circa illud quod dicit Magister, prima distinctione secundi libri, cap. 6, quod creatura rationalis facta est ad laudandum Deum, ad serviendum ei, ad fruendum eo, in quibus proficit ipsa, non Deus, quacro ad perficiendum materiam de augmentatione caritatis inchoatam dist. 17 primi libri: Utrum creatura rationalis, meritorie serviendo Deo, proficiat ad augmentum gratiae seu caritatis sine omni novo addito gratiae praecedenti."

II, q. 2 (fols. 93vb–95ra): "Utrum profectus vel augmentum gratiae fiat per compositionem novae gratiae cum gratia praecedenti."

II, q. 3 (fols. 95ra–99ra): "Utrum creatura rationalis habens gratiam possit mereri suam gratiam augmentari."

II, q. 4 (fols. 99ra–99vb): "Utrum viator operibus meritoriis insistendo ex hiis carior Deo fiat."

II, q. 5 (fols. 99vb–104vb): "Utrum supposita gratia baptismali viator per merita sua possit pertingere ad maximam gratiam viae sibi possibilem."

II, q. 6 (fols. 104vb–106vb): "Utrum viator existens in gratia ultra omnem gratiam habitam vel habendam possit proficere ad maiorem per instantaneas lectiones actuum volendi omnia pro futuro peccata venialia devitare."

II, q. 7 (fols. 106vb–107rb): "Utrum Deus possit creare finitam qualitatem qua non possit creare maiorem intensive vel aliquam magnitudinem qua non possit maiorem producere extensive."

II, q. 8 (fols. 107rb–109va): "Utrum secundum proportionem caritatis viae succedat pro praemio proportionabiliter magnitudo gloriae."

II, q. 9 (fols. 109va–113ra): "Utrum caritas propter demerita minuatur."

II, q. 10 (fols. 113ra–115ra): "Utrum caritas decrescat ad crementum cupiditatis."

Explicit II (fol. 115ra): "Unde aestimo esse posse contingere quod aliquis sic augendo mereatur, et quod non est transgressor sed potius executor praecepti in oculis Dei. Ad argumenta principalia responsum est in primo articulo."

Incipit collatio III (fol. 115ra): "In funiculis Adam traham eos. Osee 11. Intellectualis oculi naturale desiderium, licet ignorantiae tenebris obumbrati, licet impositio legibus obligati caligantis aciei circumfert obtuitus, et nunc incomplexa rerum formatur notitia intuendo et abstrahendo...."

Explicit collatio III (fol. 115rb): "... si dixerit ad eos: cor suum spiritum illius et flatum ad se trahet, Iob 34, in via per gratiam, in patria per gloriam, quam nobis concedat Dei filius, cuius ad praesens notitiam quaerimus, qui cum patre, etc."

Incipit III, q. 1 (fols. 115va–118ra): "Circa tertium librum, quia alias Londoniae toto anno pertractavi quaestiones 13 primarum distinctionum, nunc incipio a distinctione 14 in qua Magister pertractat de scientia animae Christi et eius potentia, et de eius scientia. Quaero primo sicut quaerit Magister: Utrum anima Christi habeat et habuerit sapientiam aequalem Deo."

III, q. 2 (fols. 118ra–119rb): "Utrum verbum Dei sit sibi ipsi quamvis non animae unitae sibi scientia futurorum sibi contingentium."

III, q. 3 (fols. 119rb–122va): "Utrum cum determinata praescientia verbi stet quod futura praescita sunt ad utrumlibet contingentia."

III, q. 4 (fols. 122va–123vb): "Utrum anima Christi vel angeli sciant vel scire possint aliqua futura contingentia per revelationem sibi possibilem fieri ab ipso verbo."

III, q. 5 (fols. 123vb–125rb): "Utrum alicuius prius contingentis futuri absoluta revelatio sequens tollat contingentiam revelati."

III, q. 6 (fols. 125rb–127ra): "Utrum Deus, existenti in gratia, possit revelare quod ipse finaliter sit damnandus."

III, q. 7 (fols. 127ra–128vb): "Utrum beato possit revelari in verbo aeternitas suae beatitudinis."

III, q. 8 (fols. 128vb–130rb): "Utrum Gabrieli incarnatio verbi potuerit in verbo revelari."

III, q. 9 (fols. 130rb–132rb): "Utrum per revelationes possibiles fieri in verbo possit quis sufficienter dirigi in volendis."

III, q. 10 (fols. 132rb–135rb): "Utrum anima Christi cui unitur distincte valeat videre infinita."

III, q. 11 (fols. 135rb–136ra): "Utrum anima Christi [possit] cui in verbo unitur distincte cognoscere minimas partes accidentium sibi inhaerentium vel minimas partes corporis quod informat."

III, q. 12 (fols. 136ra–136rb): "Utrum per unionem ad verbum ipsa sit omnipotens."

Explicit III (fol. 136rb): "Sed sicut hic non valet ex eo quod istae lineae non sic uniuntur secundum logum quod ex eis fiat longius, sic etiam nec valet ibi ex eo quod illi gradus non uniuntur sic quod ex eis in eadem parte subiecti fiat intensius. Ad primum principale satis respondet Adam in littera. Et sic est finis tertii."

Incipit IV, q. 1 (fols. 136va–138vb): "Circa principium quarti quaeritur: Utrum aliqua possit in effectum sacramenti praecise productibilem per creationem. Et hoc est expressius quaere: Utrum aliqua creatura possit creare gratiam vel aliam creaturam."

IV, q. 2 (fols. 138vb–140ra): "Utrum posse creare gratiam vel aliquid aliud repugnet creaturae propter virtutis insufficientiam."

IV, q. 3 (fols. 140ra–141vb): "Utrum homini rite suscipienti sacramentum baptismi vel confirmationis conferatur gratia salutaris."

IV, q. 4 (fols. 141vb–142vb): "Utrum corpus Christi realiter sub speciebus quae fuerunt panis et vini contineatur."

IV, q. 5 (fols. 142vb–143vb): "Utrum quantitas terminata panis consecrandi sit aliqua res una extra animam distincta realiter a substantia et qualitate cuius est."

IV, q. 6 (fols. 143vb–145vb): "Utrum sacramentum poenitentiae sit necessarium ad delendum peccatum mortale post baptismum."

IV, q. 7 (fols. 145vb–146rb): "Utrum actus poenitentiae requisitus ad deletionem peccati mortalis sit meritorius vitae aeternae."

IV, q. 8 (fols. 146va–147rb): "Utrum quilibet qui commisit peccatum mortale teneatur secundum legem Dei communem de illo conteri."

IV, q. 9 (fols. 147rb–148vb): "Utrum poenitentia sit formaliter vel virtualiter velle cavere quodlibet peccatum in futurum [sic]."

IV, q. 10 (fols. 149ra–150va): "Utrum ille qui peccat mortaliter in opere exteriori teneatur plus poenitere de opere interiori et exteriori simul quam de interiori tantum."

IV, q. 11 (fols. 150va–151vb): "Utrum aliqua poena infernalis potest esse insensibilis damnato."

IV, q. 12 (fols. 151vb–152rb): "Utrum sit maxima gloria possibilis beato."
Explicit IV (fol. 152rb): "Ad tertium etiam mihi videtur dicendum quod anima nihil agente, sed solo Deo ipsa possit simul cum hoc videre et intelligere, nec auderem contrarium tenere, cum etiam secundum philosophiam 'intelligere' sit quoddam pati. Et dato quod anima ageret visionem suam, idem sequitur. Et sic finis. Gratias igitur ago tibi, Domine Iesu Christe, qui dixisti per os sancti Iohannis pueri tui . . . . Quoniam tua gratia praeveniente et cooperante ad hoc opusculi de lectura sententiarum Adae conscripti a principio usque ad finem me perducere dignatus es, et quia scribendo et studendo de merito viatoris. . . . Per te, Iesu Christe, salvator et gubernator noster, qui cum patre et spiritu sancto vivis et regnas Deus per omnia saecula saeculorum. Amen."

D. Vat. Lat. 946

Vatican Library, Cod. lat. 946, fols. 22ra–22vb (Prol., q. 1, and I, dist. 2, q. 1). Paper; written between 1338 and 1355; gothic cursive bookhand; two columns of 50–53 lines each. The text is an abbreviation of the opening part of Wodeham's *Lectura Oxoniensis,* highly reduced. For further description see *Codices Vaticani Latini,* Vol. II, ed. A. Pelzer (Vatican, 1931), p. 386.

Incipit (fol. 22ra): "Circa primum librum sententiarum quaeruntur quaestiones. Prima quaestio est: Utrum studium sacrae theologiae sit meritorium vitae aeternae."
Explicit (fol. 22va): "Ad argumentum principale dico quod Apostolus loquitur de idolis et de diis noncupative. Unde subdit nobis autem unus Deus est, quia omnes dii gentium sunt demonia."

APPENDIX 5

TABLE OF QUESTIONS

Since among the various redactions of Wodeham's *Sentences* Commentary the same question can appear under more than one distinction and several different problems can be treated within one question, the following list is arranged alphabetically rather than topically or according to the structure of Lombard's *Sentences*. The appendix reference is given in parentheses.

An aliquod obiectum contineat virtualiter illam notitiam scientificam. I, dist. 2, q. 2 (Ap. III).
An ille et alii fidei articuli possint evidenti ratione probari. I, dist. 2, q. 1 (Ap. III).
Utrum ab ultimis constitutivis personarum in divinis possit abstrahi aliquis conceptus positivus unus communis in quid talibus ultimis constitutivis. I, dist. 25 (Ap. III).
Utrum, actui scientiae in nobis, necessario praesupponatur aliqua simplex apprehensio realiter distincta a omni sensatione. Prol., q. 1 (Ap. III).
Utrum actus poenitentiae requisitus ad deletionem peccati mortalis sit meritorius vitae aeternae. IV, q. 7 (App. IA, IB, II, IVB, IVC).
Utrum actus sciendi habeat pro obiecto immediato res vel signa, id est complexum in mente, vel res significatas per complexum. I, dist. 1, q. 1 (Ap. III).
Utrum alicuius contingentis futuri absoluta revelatio sequens tollat contingentiam. III, dist. 14, q. 5 (App. IA, IB, II, IVB, IVC).
Utrum aliqua creatura possit creare caracterem vel gratiam vel aliam creaturam. IV, q. 1 (App. IA, IB, II, IVB, IVC).
Utrum aliqua poena infernalis possit esse insensibilis in damnato. IV, q. 11 (App. IA, IB, II, IVB, IVC).
Utrum aliqua scientia theologica sit scibilis scientia proprie dicta. I, dist. 1, q. 2 (Ap. III).
Utrum aliqua sit certa regula vel ars per quam solvi possint communiter paralogismi facti et talibus similes circa materiam trinitatis. I, dist. 7, q. 1 (Ap. II); I, dist. 33, q. 3 (App. IB, IC, IVB, IVC).
Utrum anima Christi habuerit et habeat sapientiam [or: scientiam] aequalem Deo. III, dist. 14, q. 1 (App. IA, IB, II, IVB, IVC).
Utrum anima Christi in verbo Dei cui unitur distincte videre valeat infinita. III, dist. 14, q. 10 (App. IA, IB, II, IVB, IVC).
Utrum anima Christi possit in verbo cui unitur distincte cognoscere minimas partium sibi inhaerentium vel minimas particulas corporis quod informat. III, dist. 14, q. 11 (App. IA, IB, II, IVB, IVC).

Utrum anima Christi vel angeli sciant futura aliqua contingentia per revelationem sibi possibilem fieri ab ipso verbo vel etiam scire possint. III, dist. 14, q. 4 (App. IA, IB, II, IVB, IVC).

Utrum animae Christi vel angelo beato possit in verbo revelari aeternitas suae beatitudinis. III, dist. 14, q. 7 (App. IA, IB, II, IVB, IVC).

Utrum anima nostra in via naturaliter cognoscere possit actus suos cognitionibus intuitivis realiter distinctis ab abstractivis. Prol., q. 2 (Ap. III).

Utrum a parte rei in divinis sit aliqua non-idemptitas inter naturam Dei et voluntatem divinam, et ita de ceteris perfectionibus quae ponuntur in Deo. I, dist. 6, q. 1 (App. IB, IC, III, IVB, IVC).

Utrum caritas decrescat ad crementum cupiditatis. II, dist. 1, q. 10 (App. IA, IB, II, IVB, IVC).

Utrum caritas seu gratia increata sine alio possit sufficere ad salutem. I, dist. 17, q. 2 (App. IB, IC–Erf, II, IVB, IVC).

Utrum caritas vel alia forma augmentabilis augmentetur per deminutionem contrarii sui. I, dist. 17, q. 4 (App. IB, IC, II, IVB, IVC).

Utrum communiores praecedant ordine minus communes aut econtro. I, dist. 7, q. 4 (Ap. III).

Utrum conceptus communis essentiae quo immediate concipimus Deum sit conceptus deitatis. I, dist. 7, q. 3 (Ap. III).

Utrum conceptus essentiae quo immediate est Deus significabilis et conceptibilis sit intensio communis informans subiective intellectum nostrum. I, dist. 7, q. 2 (Ap. III).

Utrum corpus Christi realiter sub speciebus quae fuerunt panis et vini contineatur. IV, q. 4 (App. IA, IB, II, IVB, IVC).

Utrum creatura rationalis clare videns Deum necessario diligat ipsum. I, dist. 1, q. 10 (App. IB, IC, II, IVB, IVC).

Utrum creatura rationalis habens gratiam possit mereri suam gratiam augmentari. II, dist. 1, q. 3 (App. IA, IB, II, IVB, IVC).

Utrum creatura rationalis meritorie serviendo Deo proficiat ad augmentum gratiae seu caritatis, sine omni novo addito gratiae praecedenti. II, dist. 1, q. 1 (App. IA, IB, II, IVB, IVC).

Utrum cum coaeternitate illa stet quod pater praecedat filium origine vel natura. I, dist. 9 (Ap. III).

Utrum cum determinata verbi praescientia stet quod futura praescita sint ad utrumlibet contingentia. III, dist. 14, q. 3 (App. IA, IB, II, IVB, IVC).

Utrum deitas contineat virtualiter plures conceptus proprios positivos simplices et mere absolutos quorum unus sit de Deo praedicabilis in quid, et alter in quali, ut quod pluribus conceptibus talibus possit concipi. I, dist. 2, q. 4 (Ap. III).

Utrum deitas vel aliqua alia entitas simpliciter simplex contineat virtualiter plures conceptus simplices et absolutos quorum unus sit conceptus eius quidditativus et alius denominativus, id est dicibilis de ipso tantum secundo modo dicendi per se. I, dist. 2, q. 3 (Ap. III).

Utrum de peccatore possit fieri non peccator et acceptus Deo sine tali habitu sibi infuso per gratiam increatam. I, dist. 17, q. 3 (App. IB, IC, II, IVB, IVC).

Utrum Deum esse innotescat tantum discursive ab effectibus vel sit per se notum. I, dist. 3, q. 4 (Ap. III).
Utrum Deus ab aeterno novit res producibiles libere. (Ap. IVA).
Utrum Deus essentialiter unus sit personaliter trinus. I, dist. 33, q. 1 (App. IB, IC, II, IVB, IVC).
Utrum Deus genuerit Deum. I, dist. 33, q. 2 (App. IB, IC, IVC).
Utrum Deus possit creare finitam caritatem aliquam qua non possit creare maiorem vel aliquam aliam ita magnam secundum extensionem quod non possit maiorem illa producere, et sic de similibus. II, dist. 1, q. 7 (App. IA, IB, II, IVB, IVC).
Utrum Deus, sine visione sui, possit immediate causare in intellectu omnem evidentiam complexam quam potest causare mediante visione sui. Prol., q. 6 (Ap. III).
Utrum Deus sit conceptibilis a nobis conceptu substantiae vel essentiae. I, dist. 8 (Ap. III).
Utrum Deus sit realiter [or: essentialiter] et per se primo modo sapiens vel intelligens, et sic de similibus. I, dist. 6, q. 2 (App. IB, IC, II, IVB, IVC).
Utrum Deus vel verbum Dei existenti in gratia possit revelare quod talis finaliter sit damnandus. III, dist. 14, q. 6 (App. IA, IB, II, IVB, IVC).
Utrum divina essentia generet vel generetur. I, dist. 5 (Ap. III); I, dist. 7, q. 2 (Ap. II); I, dist. 33, q. 4 (App. IB, IC, IVC).
Utrum divinae personae sint inter se propter [Ms.: de inesse per] circumincessionem aequales secundum magnitudinem vel potentiam. I, dist. 19 & 20 (Ap. III).
Utrum divina persona visibiliter mittatur. I, dist. 16 (Ap. III).
Utrum ex effecti[bu]s possit evidenter probari quod aliquid individuale [Ms.: in divinis] in universo sit simpliciter primum ens. I, dist. 3, q. 1 (Ap. III).
Utrum filius possit generare. I, dist. 7, q. 4 (Ap. II); cf. I, dist. 33, q. 5 (Ap. IB).
Utrum fruitio beatifica differat ab ipsa anima. I, dist. 1, q. 2 (App. IB, IC, IVB, IVC).
Utrum fruitio beatifica sit actus intellectus. I, dist. 1, q. 14 (App. IB, IC, II, IVB, IVC).
Utrum fruitio beatifica sit qualitas distincta ab anima, cognitione, et delectatione. I, dist. 1, q. 2 (Ap. II); cf. I, dist. 1, q. 4 (Ap. III).
Utrum fruitio realiter distinguatur ab omni cognitione. I, dist. 1, q. 3 (App. IB, IC, II, IVB, IVC).
Utrum fruitio realiter distinguatur a delectatione. I, dist. 1, q. 4 (App. IB, IC, II, IVB, IVC).
Utrum fruitio sit qualitas realiter distincta a cognitione et delectatione. I, dist. 1, q. 4 (Ap. III); cf. I, dist. 1, q. 2 (Ap. II).
Utrum Gabrieli potuerit in verbo verbi incarnatio revelari. III, dist. 14, q. 8 (App. IA, IB, II, IVB, IVC).
Utrum generaliter omnis delectatio sit dilectio vel odium, seu volitio aut nolitio. I, dist. 1, q. 5 (App. IB, IC, II, IVB, IVC).
Utrum gratia seu caritas sit viatori necessaria ad salutem. I, dist. 17, q. 1 (App. IB, IC, II, IVB, IVC).

Utrum haec sit possibilis: creatura rationalis fruitur una persona divina non fruendo alia. I, dist. 1, q. 12 (App. IB, IC, II, IVB, IVC).
Utrum hoc nomen "persona" sit nomen primae intentionis vel secundae. I, dist. 23 (Ap. III).
Utrum ille qui peccavit mortaliter in opere exteriori teneatur plus poenitere de opere exteriori et interiori simul quam de interiori solo. IV, q. 10 (App. IA, IB, II, IVB, IVC).
Utrum in augmentatione caritatis vel alterius formae gradus omnis prae-existens corrumpatur cum novus gradus inducitur ita videlicet intelligendo quod in omni instanti sit totaliter nova forma. I, dist. 17, q. 5 (App. IB, IC, II, IVB, IVC).
Utrum in divinis, hoc non obstante, sit aliqua persona absoluta. I, dist. 26, q. 2 (Ap. III).
Utrum in entibus sit tantum unus Deus. I, dist. 2, q. un. (App. IB, IC–Erf, II, IVB, IVC).
Utrum in homine sit imago Dei et trinitatis sicut in ceteris creaturis factis propter hominem, ut habitum est in lectione est vestigium Dei et trinitatis. I, dist. 3, q. 5 (Ap. III).
Utrum in illo cui datur spiritus sanctus oporteat esse mutationem. I, dist. 18 (Ap. III).
Utrum ipsum verbum Dei sit sibi ipsi quamvis non animae sibi unitae scientia futurorum contingentium. III, dist. 14, q. 2 (App. IA, IB, II, IVB, IVC).
Utrum liceat filium Dei plus diligere vel frui eo quam patrem vel spiritum sanctum. I, dist. 1, q. 13 (App. IB, IC, II, IVC).
Utrum mens humana sit imago trinitatis increatae sicut in rebus aliis factis propter hominem est vestigium eiusdem trinitatis. I, dist. 3, q. un. (App. IB, IC, II, IVB, IVC).
Utrum notitia intuitiva sensitiva vel intellectiva possit naturaliter causari vel conservari sine existentia rei visae. Prol., q. 3 (Ap. III).
Utrum omne idem patri sit omnibus modis idem patri. I, dist. 33, q. 9 (App. IB, IC, IVC).
Utrum omni [or: homini] rite suscipienti sacramentum baptismi vel confirmationis conferatur gratia salutaris. IV, q. 3 (App. IA, IB, II, IVB, IVC).
Utrum omnis bonus motus voluntatis meritorie augmentativus caritatis ad quem homo tenetur debeat vel possit ex caritate procedere collata ex merito redemptoris. I, dist. 17, q. 6 (App. IB, IC, II, IVB, IVC).
Utrum pater et filius sint unum principium spirans spiritum sanctum. I, dist. 7, q. 6 (Ap. II); I, dist. 12 (Ap. III); I, dist. 33, q. 7 (App. IB, IC, IVC).
Utrum per revelationes possibiles fieri in verbo posset aliquis sufficienter dirigi in volendis. III, dist. 14, q. 9 (App. IA, IB, II, IVB, IVC).
Utrum personae divinae seipsis primo personaliter distinguantur. I, dist. 26, q. 1 (Ap. III).
Utrum personae divinae primo et adequate distinguantur ab invicem semetipsis. I, dist. 7, q. 7 (Ap. II); I, dist. 33, q. 8 (App. IB, IC, IVC).
Utrum [anima Christi] per unionem ad verbum ipsa sit omnipotens. III, dist. 14, q. 12 (App. IA, IB, II, IVB, IVC).

Utrum per visionem causetur "esse aliquod apparens" vel "esse visum" distinctum a visione et visibili. Prol., q. 4 (Ap. III).

Utrum posse creare gratiam vel aliquid aliud repugnet propter virtutis activae insufficientiam cuilibet creaturae. IV, q. 2 (App. IA, IB, II, IVB, IVC).

Utrum potentia generandi in Deo patre cadat sub omnipotentia. I, dist. 7, q. 3 (Ap. II).

Utrum potentia generandi possit communicari filio in divinis. I, dist. 7, q. 1 (Ap. III); I, dist. 33, q. 5 (App. IB, IC, IVC).

Utrum praesupposita gratia baptismali viator per merita sua possit pertingere ad gratiam maximam viae sibi possibilem. II, dist. 1, q. 5 (App. IA, IB, II, IVB, IVC).

Utrum praeter spiritum sanctum invisibiliter missum et datum necesse sit ponere aliquam qualitatem, puta caritatem creatam, inhaerentem animae, ad hoc quod anima sit cara et Deo accepta. I, dist. 17, q. 1 (Ap. III).

Utrum profectus vel augmentum gratiae fiat per compositionem gratiae novae cum gratia praecedenti. II, dist. 1, q. 2 (App. IA, IB, II, IVB, IVC).

Utrum pro studio sacrae theologiae ex caritate procedente debeatur pro mercede visio Dei et eius fruitio. I, dist. 1, q. 1 (App. IB, IC, II, IVC).

Utrum quaelibet persona divina possit mittere vel mitti. I, dist. 15 (Ap. III).

Utrum quaelibet persona sit in alia per circumincessionem. I, dist. 19 (Ap. III).

Utrum quantitas terminata panis consecrandi sit aliqua vera res extra animam distincta realiter a substantia et qualitate cuius est. IV, q. 5 (App. IA, IB, II, IVB, IVC).

Utrum quilibet qui commisit peccatum mortale teneatur secundum legem Dei communem de illo conteri. IV, q. 8 (App. IA, IB, II, IVB, IVC).

Utrum respectu solius Dei praedicetur vere abstractum de concreto dicendo scilicet "Deus est deitas" vel "Deus est trinitas" vel huiusmodi. I, dist. 4 (Ap. III).

Utrum sacramentum poenitentiae sit necessarium ad delendum peccatum mortale, an sufficit contritio. IV, q. 6 (Ap. II); cf. IV, q. 6 (Ap. IB).

Utrum sacramentum poenitentiae sit necessarium ad delendum peccatum mortale post baptismum commissum. IV, q. 6 (App. IA, IB, IVB, IVC); cf. IV, q. 6 (Ap. II).

Utrum saltem ratione distinguantur inter se ab essentia. I, dist. 6, q. 2 (Ap. III).

Utrum, scilicet propter demerita, [caritas] minuatur. II, dist. 1, q. 9 (App. IA, IB, II, IVB, IVC).

Utrum secundum proportionem caritatis viae succedat pro praemio proportionaliter magnitudo gloriae. II, dist. 1, q. 8 (App. IA, IB, II, IVB, IVC).

Utrum simul stent quod caritas quae est qualitas quaedam supernaturalis informet animam viatoris et tamen quod Deus non acceptet eum ad vitam aeternam. I, dist. 17, q. 3 (Ap. III); cf. Cologne *Extractio*, I, q. 21, dub. 1 (Ap. IVB).

Utrum sit de facto et de lege communi omni actui meritorio caritas data supponatur. I, dist. 17, q. 4 (Ap. III).

Utrum sit evidenter probabile quod simpliciter incausabile sit tantum unicus numero. I, dist. 3, q. 2 (Ap. III).

Utrum sit maxima gloria possibilis in beato. IV, q. 12 (App. IA, IB, II, IVB, IVC).
Utrum solus Deus sit immutabilis. I, dist. 8, q. un. (App. IB, IC, II, IVB, IVC).
Utrum solus Deus sit licite a creatura rationali ultimate fruibilis. I, dist. 1, q. 11 (App. IB, IC, II, IVB, IVC).
Utrum solus pater sit Deus. I, dist. 21 (Ap. III).
Utrum spiratio spiritus sancti sit generatio. I, dist. 13 (Ap. III).
Utrum spiritus sanctus detur in propria persona vel tantum in donis creatis. I, dist. 14 (Ap. III).
Utrum spiritus sanctus possit distingui a filio si non procederet ab eo. I, dist. 7, q. 5 (Ap. II); I, dist. 11 (Ap. III); I, dist. 33, q. 6 (App. IB, IC, IVC).
Utrum stent simul quod spiritus sanctus libere producatur et tamen necessario. I, dist. 10 (Ap. III).
Utrum studium Sacrae Scripturae impositum alicui in foro poenitentiae pro omissione contraria [or: pro satisfactione omissionis culpabilis contrariae] sit meritorium. Prol., q. 2 (App. IB, IC, II, IVC); cf. I, q. 1 (Ap. IVB).
Utrum studium sacrae theologiae [or: Scripturae] sit meritorium vitae aeternae. Prol., q. 1 (App. IB, IC–Erf, II, IVB, IVC); cf. I, q. 1 (Ap. IVD).
Utrum trinitas personarum divinarum sit verus numerus. I, dist. 24, q. 2 (Ap. III).
Utrum unitas a qua Deus dicitur unus sit aliquid accidens in Deo vel additum sibi. I, dist. 24, q. 1 (Ap. III).
Utrum unitas Dei specifica probari possit. I, dist. 3, q. 3 (Ap. III).
Utrum vera poenitentia sit formaliter vel virtualiter velle cavere peccatum quodlibet in futuro. IV, q. 9 (App. IA, IB, II, IVB, IVC).
Utrum viator existens in gratia ultra omnem gratiam habitam vel habendam possit proficere ad maiorem per instantaneas causationes actuum volendi omnia pro futuro peccata venialia devitare. II, dist. 1, q. 6 (App. IA, IB, II, IVB, IVC).
Utrum viator operibus meritoriis insistendo ex hiis carior Deo fiat. II, dist. 1, q. 4 (App. IA, IB, II, IVB, IVC).
Utrum viator possit aliquod nomen imponere ad distincte significandum divinam essentiam. I, dist. 22 (Ap. III).
Utrum viator possit, stante statu viae, apprehendere Deum apprehensione aliqua simpliciori et propria. Prol., q. 5 (Ap. III).
Utrum voluntas libere possit subito suspendere actum suum sive ab actu habito cessare. I, dist. 1, q. 9 (App. IB, IC, II, IVB, IVC).
Utrum voluntas necessario vel libere principiet actus suos. I, dist. 1, q. 6 (App. IB, IC, II, IVB, IVC).
Utrum voluntas possit simul et subito producere actum voluntarium meritorie et libere dilectionis. I, dist. 1, q. 8 (App. IB, IC, II, IVB, IVC).
Utrum voluntas sola sit causa effectiva suae volitionis liberae supposita communi Dei influentia vel concausatione. I, dist. 1, q. 7 (App. IB, IC, II, IVB, IVC).

INDEX OF MANUSCRIPTS

Alençon, Bibl. municipale, Ms. 144: 147
Assisi, Bibl. Comunale, Ms. 137: 44
Barcelona, Archivo de la Catedral, Ms. 38: 9, 154–155, 223–228
Basel, Universitätsbibl., Ms. B V 30: 76
Berlin, Staatsbibl., Ms. Theol. lat. 2° 534: 223–228
Bologna, Bibl. Comunale dell' Archiginnasio, Ms. A 921: 132
Bruges, Bibl. publ. de la ville,
  Ms. 172: 12–15, 87, 130, 168, 171, 186, 196–198, 202–209
  Ms. 188: 94
  Ms. 497: 54
  Ms. 503: 91
Cambrai, Bibl. de la ville, Ms. 570: 145
Cambridge, Gonville & Caius College, Ms. 281(674): 9–10, 21, 25–26, 30, 32, 37, 41, 44, 52, 54, 56–57, 59, 61–65, 67, 74, 81, 83, 110, 119, 125–131, 136, 144–146, 148–149, 156–157, 167, 169–170, 174, 210–214
Cambridge, Pembroke College, Ms. 236: 98, 102, 104, 106, 108, 119
Colmar, Bibl. de la ville, Ms. 232: 139
Erfurt, Wissenschaftliche Bibl. der Stadt,
  CA 2° 105: 174
  CA 2° 115: 138
  CA 2° 132: 91–92, 94
  CA 2° 133: 12–13, 167, 198–200
  CA 4° 395: 97
Florence, Bibl. Nazionale,
  Fondo principale, Ms. II II 281: 148
  Fondo dei conventi soppressi, Ms. A III 508: 14, 34–36, 64, 67, 77, 79, 91, 106, 202
  Conv. soppr. B VII 1249: 13, 16, 18–19, 34–35, 37, 77, 87, 109, 202–209
  Conv. soppr. C V 357: 36, 69–71, 163, 202
  Conv. soppr. J VI 20: 108
Fribourg (Switz.), Couvent des Cordeliers, Ms. 26: 91–93
Graz, Universitätsbibl., Ms. 836: 137
Hannover, Stadtbibl., Ms. 1: 14, 30, 133–134, 213, 215–222, 233
Klosterneuburg, Stiftsbibl., Ms. 296: 223–228
Kraków, Bibl. Jagiellońska,
  Ms. 1176: 223–228
  Ms. 1184: 132
  Ms. 1195: 223–228
  Ms. 1197: 223–228
  Ms. 1279: 145
  Ms. 1362: 9, 171
  Ms. 1499: 141
Lilienfeld, Stiftsbibl., Ms. 148: 132
London, British Museum,
  Harley 3243: 62, 157
  Royal 10 C VI: 99–100, 120
Lüneburg, Ratsbücherei, Ms. Theol. 4° 29: 12–13, 59, 83, 133, 198–201
Madrid, Bibl. Nacional, Ms. lat. 65: 74
Madrid, Bibl. de la Univ., Ms. 58 (118 Z 16): 137
Mainz, Stadtbibl., Ms. 1 53 A: 223–228
Milan, Bibl. Ambrosiana,
  Ms. C 281 inf.: 34
  Ms. E 55 inf.: 118
Munich, Bayr. Staatsbibl.,
  Clm 3768: 150–151
  Clm 8867: 9, 146, 171
  Clm 26 711: 92–93, 141–144
Naples, Bibl. Nazionale, Ms. VII C 53: 14, 30, 61, 133–134, 143–144, 213, 215–222, 233
Oxford, Balliol College, Ms. 246: 102, 104, 106, 119
Oxford, Bodleian Library,
  Canon. Misc. 177: 120
  Digby 2: 54
  Digby 24: 54
  Digby 216: 110–111
Oxford, Oriel College, Ms. 15: 77, 106, 108, 120–122
Padua, Bibl. Univ., Ms. 927: 61
Pamplona, Bibl. de la Catedral, Ms. 1: 9, 154–155, 223–228
Paris, Bibl. Mazarine,
  Ms. 915: 8, 10–12, 14, 16–24, 26–31, 33, 37, 44, 58–59, 61–62, 64–66, 70–73, 75, 77, 79–80, 83–84, 87–88, 90–91, 95, 101–103, 105–109, 119, 124–125, 165–171, 176–177, 186–198
  Ms. 916: 223–228
  Ms. 917: 223–228
Paris, Bibl. Nationale,
  Ms. lat. 3074: 149
  Ms. lat. 14 069: 54
  Ms. lat. 14 514: 118–119
  Ms. lat. 14 576: 94
  Ms. lat. 15 369: 138

Paris, Bibl. Nationale—*contd.*
  Ms. lat. 15 561: 91, 94
  Ms. lat. 15 840: 137
  Ms. lat. 15 853: 77, 106
  Ms. lat. 15 880: 33, 118–119
  Ms. lat. 15 883: 132
  Ms. lat. 15 886: 70, 163
  Ms. lat. 15 887: 36, 66, 69, 71, 161, 163–164
  Ms. lat. 15 892: 8, 10–11, 13, 16, 18–21, 23, 25–26, 29–30, 37, 70, 168, 202–209
  Ms. lat. 15 893: 223–228
  Ms. lat. 15 894: 223–228
  Ms. lat. 16 409: 157
Paris, Bibl. de l'Université (Sorbonne), Ms. 193: 9, 12–16, 18–20, 23–31, 36–37, 44, 55–56, 58–66, 71–73, 75, 77, 79–84, 88, 90, 95, 102–103, 106–111, 119, 124–126, 129, 143, 161, 165–169, 171, 186–198, 200
Prague, Universitní knihovna (Universitätsbibl.), Ms. III B 10: 108
Reims, Bibl. de la ville, Ms. 504: 223–228
Rouen, Bibl. municipale, Ms. 581 (A 285): 223–228
Salamanca, Bibl. Univ., Ms. 1863: 153
Sankt Paul im Lavanttal, Stiftsbibl., Ms. 28 V 7: 151
Tarazona, Bibl. de la Catedral, Ms. 7: 9, 12, 15–17, 20, 23–31, 37, 61–62, 77, 81, 83–84, 88, 91, 107–108, 153, 167, 186–198
Toledo, Bibl. del Cabildo, Ms. XIII 39: 153
Toulouse, Bibl. de la Univ.,
  Ms. 246: 154, 223–228
  Ms. 247: 154, 223–228
Troyes, Bibl. municipale, Ms. 62: 136
Vatican Library,
  Vat. lat. 869: 32, 175, 215
  Vat. lat. 943: 33–34
  Vat. lat. 946: 228
  Vat. lat. 955: 8, 10–15, 17, 20–23, 25–26, 30, 33, 37, 52, 55, 58–64, 66–67, 70–72, 76–77, 79–80, 83, 87, 90, 95, 102, 106, 109, 119, 124–125, 128–129, 131, 143, 162–167, 169–170, 174, 176–177, 179, 186–192, 200–202
  Vat. lat. 981: 143
  Vat. lat. 986: 120, 122, 137, 139–141
  Vat. lat. 1110: 8, 10, 13–15, 19–20, 23–26, 29, 37, 59, 64–65, 70, 72–75, 77, 80–81, 84, 86, 89–91, 106–107, 109–111, 125, 167, 169–170, 174, 176–177, 183–186
  Vat. lat. 1111: 33, 118–119
  Vat. lat. 1119: 150
  Vat. lat. 4353: 88, 121
  Vat. lat. 13002: 9, 32
  Vat. lat. 13687: 44
  Borgh. 346: 44
  Chigi (Chis.) B V 66: 120–121
  Ottob. lat. 591: 108
  Ottob. lat. 2071: 160–161
Vienna, Öster. Nationalbibl.,
  Ms. 4371: 223–228
  Ms. 4892: 151
  Ms. 14212: 151
Wilhering, Stiftsbibl., Ms. 87: 148–149

INDEX OF NAMES

The following index is divided into two parts. The first list includes the names of persons up through the sixteenth century. They are listed under their cognomens or places of origin, except for those few who would naturally be sought under their first names. The principal discussion of a person is denoted by *italic* numerals. Page references have not been given when a name appears only in the title of a book or article cited in the notes. Since the entire book is concerned with Adam Wodeham, his name has not been included in this index. The second list consists of modern authors cited from the secondary literature. In both lists, names appearing in the text and notes on the same page have been indicated by page references alone. The running page number form (e.g., 106–109) does not necessarily imply continuous discussion. Because there are few subjects discussed that are not so designated in the table of contents, no separate subject index has been included. Similarly, no bibliography has been provided, since the secondary literature on Wodeham is treated on pp. 7–12, and the index of modern authors will lead the reader to the full bibliographical reference for the secondary literature that has been used.

A. Ancient and Medieval Authors

Abbeville, Gerard of, 51n, 52
Adam of Ely (= Adam Junior?), 32, 35, 120n, 202
Adolph IX, Count of Berg, 134
Aiguani, Michael, 139
Ailly, Pierre d', 43n, *146*, 155, 158
Albert the Great (Albertus Magnus), 43n, 140
Alcuin, 156
Alexander of Hales, 42, 52, 156
Alnwick, William of, 57–58
Ambrose, 41
Anselm of Bec, 41–43, 69, 101n
Aquinas, see Thomas Aquinas
Aristotle, 55, 67n, 161–162
Artesio, Amandus of, 140n
Arumpno, see Gregory of Rimini
Ascoli, James of, 56
Ast, Facinus of, *138–139*, 170
Astensius of St. Colombe, 137–138
Aston, Nicholas, 115, 118n, 120n, *122–123*, 135, 141, 178
Augustine, 41–42, 79, 102n, 103n, 183, 185, 187, 203, 211
Aureol, Peter, *56–59*, 71, 127, 131, 136n, 138, 152, 170n, 179
Autrecourt, Nicholas of, 94–95, 137
Auxerre, William of, 42, 80n

Baconthorp, John, 52
Badoer, Bonsemblans (Bonsembiante), 143–144
Baldeswell, Peter of, 53, *56*
Baldiswell, Roger, 56

Beaufon, Walter, 53, *61–62*, 85
Bede, 1, 156
Benedict XII, 16–17, 29, 83n, 165n
Benedictine *socius*, 19n, 20n, 24–25, *90–95*, 96, 152; see also Monachus Niger
Benson, see Beaufon
Bernard of Clairvaux, 41
Bertrand de la Tour, 75
Biel, Gabriel, 52, 134, *151*
Boethius, 41, 79
Boldon, Uthred of, 93, 94n, 95
Bonaventure, 42–43
Bonettus, Nicolas, 34
Bonsemblans, see Badoer
Braculis, John of, 141n
Bradwardine, Thomas, 1–2, 34, 113n, *117–123*, 132, 135–136, 138, 141–142, 146, 157–158
Brammart, John, *148–149*, 158
Brinkel, Richard, 141
Briton, Lawrence, 83
Brixen, Friedrich von, 133n
Buckingham, Thomas, 1, 115n, 118n, *121–123*, 132, 135, 147, 157, 178
Burgos, Apparicius of, 154
Burley, Walter, 13, *59–60*, 66, 131, 138, 141
Bury, Richard of, 60

Campsale, Pseudo-, 55
Campsale, Richard, 43–44, *60–61*, 68–69, 71, 133, 149
Candia, Peter of, 148
Capreolus, John, 91, *151–152*

INDEX OF NAMES

Caracciolo, Landulph, 131, 135, 139
Carmelite *socius*, 33, 90, 106, 108n, *111*, 176n
Ceffons, Peter, 122n, *135–137*, 140, 141n, 142, 158
Cesena, Michael of, 75
Chatton, Walter, 1, 5, 19n, 22, 34–36, 39, 46, 56–58, 60, 64n, *66–77*, 82–83, 88–89, 101, 104, 112, 121n, 124n, 135, 136n, 141, 147, 160, 161n, 162–169, 171–172, 177–178, 180, 202, 214
Chaucer, 116
Chiterne, William, 106–107
Climiton, see Kilvington
Conington, Richard of, 55
Cornwall, Richard Rufus of, 55
Costesey, Henry of, 65, 85
Cowton, Robert, 46
Crathorn, William, 1, 50n, 76, *95–101*, 105, 107–109, 135
Cremona, Roland of, 52
Cremona, Simon of, 141n
Cruche, Henry, 164

D'Ailly, see Ailly
Dinkelsbühl, Nicholas of, 52
Dominican *socius*, 90, *95–106*, 172
Drayton, Richard, 63
Dumbleton, John, 138
Duns Scotus, see Scotus
Durand of St. Pourçain, 59, 152

Ebrach, Conrad of, 141n, *145*, 158
Eccleston, Thomas, 50n, 66n, 84, 179n
Edward III, 173
Eltville, James of, *145*, 147–148, 150–151, 158
Ely, Adam of, see Adam
Erbaco, James of, see Eltville

Felthorp, Thomas, 85–86
Fishacre, Richard, 52, 54–55
Fitzralph, Richard, 1–2, 5, 15, 20n, 24–25, 33, 34n, 35, 39, 52, 58, 66, 71, *75–82*, 84n, 85, 87, 88n, 89–90, 96, 101, 106, 109, 112, 117, 119n, 120n, 121, 126, 129, 132, 135, 141–142, 146–147, 152, 158, 161n, 164, 172, 176–178, 202
Foxley, Walter, 164

Garini, Peter, 154
Gedeonis, John, 34
Ghent, see Henry of Ghent
Giles of Rome, 70n
Gosford, Roger, 95–96, 100
Grafton, 19n, 90, *106–109*, 141, 176n; see also: Grafton, Edmund and Hugh
Grafton, Edmund, 107–108; see also Grafton and Hugh Grafton

Grafton, Hugh, 53, 106, 108; see also Grafton and Edmund Grafton
Grandisson, John, Bishop of Exeter, 75n
Granton, see Crathorn and Grafton
Grascon, see Grafton
Gratian, 103n
Gregory I, The Great, 41
Gregory IX, 45n
Gregory XI, 16–17, 147

Hales, see Alexander of Hales
Halifax, Robert of, 1, 33, 82n, 117n, *118–120*, 123, 125, 132, 135, 137, 141, 145n, 148n, 149, 151, 157–158, 178
Halton, John, Bishop of Carlisle, 67
Harclay, Henry, 34n, *56–57*
Henry of Ghent, 42, 54–55, 152
Heytisbury, William, 149
Hiltalingen, John, of Basel, 43n, 82n, 92–93, 120n, 122n, 134, 139, *141–145*, 148, 158–159, 182
Holcot, Robert, 1–2, 5, 50n, 89, *95–109*, 112, 118, 119n, 120n, 121n, 132, 135–136, 142, 146–147, 149, 151, 155n, 157–158, 172, 177–179, 202
Hoyo, Nicholas, 25n, 53, 83

Inghen, Marsilius of, *150–151*, 155, 158
Isidore of Seville, 41

Jerome, 41
John XXI, 16, 28–29
John XXII, 15–16, 28–29, 62, 70n, 74, 172
John the Canon, 34

Kilvington, Richard, 1, 47n, *85–89*, 94–95, 110, 113n, 135, 141–142, 147, 174, 178
Klenkok, John, 93, 122n, *138*
Krakow, Thomas of, 118n, 157n

Landulph, see Caracciolo
Langeley, Alexander, 118n, *122*, 135, 141, 153, 178
Langenstein, Henry of, 133, 139, *147–148*, 151
Leicester, Robert, 164
Lombard, Peter, 41–43, 103n, 171, 176–178, 229

Magister Abstractionum, *54–56*, 65
Major, John, 1n, 4, 7, 17, 31, 92, 116, *154–156*, 165
Marchia, Francis of, 131, 138
Marchia, John of, see Ripa
Massa, Michael of, 34n
Mayronnes, Francis, 54, *65*, 79n, 131, 139
Menenes, Peter, 154
Middleton, Richard, 42
Mirecourt, John of, 82n, 93, 118n, 122n, *131–132*, 135, 137, 140, 142, 147, 153

INDEX OF NAMES

Monachus Niger, 35, 54n, *90–95*, 120–121, 139, 178, 202; see also Benedictine *socius* and Roger Swineshead
Montina, Dionysius of, 146

Nepomuk, Gottschalk of, *141*, 151
Neufchateau, Andrew of, *139*, 155
Normannus, John, 93
Northwode, John of, 75n

Ockham, William of, 1–2, 5, 23, 26–27, 34–35, 37, 43–44, 46, 52n, 53, *55–65*, 67n, 68–75, 83, 85, 99n, 100–101, 106, 113–114, 117–118, 123, 131, 133–136, 138–139, 141, 145n, 147, 148n, 149, 153, 155n, 156–164, 165n, 171, 176, 178–179, 181
Odonis, Gerard, 34n, *74–75*
Olivi, Peter John, 46, 52, 131
Orvieto, Hugolino of, 122n, *136–137*, 140, 142, 148–149, 151, 158–159
Oresme, Nicole, 120n, 137
Osbert, see Pickingham
Oyta, Henry Totting of, 1n, 2, 8–9, 11, 14, 16–18, 19n, 28, 30, 72n, 116, 125–127, 134, *146–147*, 151, 154–156, 165n, 171n

Padua, Marsilius of, 119n
Pelagius, 119n, 124n, 125n
Perugia, Paul of, 131, 139
Petrarch, 143n
Pickingham, Osbert, 118n, *122–123*, 135, 139, 141, 147, 178
Pigaz, Ralph, 31n, 61, *65–66*, 85, 166–167
Pirchenwart, see Reicher
Plaout, Peter, 149, 150n
Porta, James of, 180
Pulka, Peter of, 150

Radford, 109n, 110–111
Radford, John, 110–111, 164
Radford, Richard, 47n, 85, 90, 109n, *110–111*
Radford, Thomas, 110–111
Reading, John of, 52, 55, 60, *62–63*
Regensburg, Augustinus of, 155n
Reicher, Peter, of Pirchenwart, 150–151
Reppes, 47n, 53, *83–85*, 90
Reppes, Bartholomew of, 84–85
Reppes, John, 84
Reppes, Richard of, 47n, 53, 84–85
Reppis and Repps, see Reppes

Rimini, Gregory of, 2, 15n, 42, 43n, 91–94, 106, 112, 117n, 118n, 122n, *123–133*, 135–138, 142–146, 148–152, 156, 158–159, 165n, 170n, 171n
Ripa, John of, 11n, 18n, 19n, *138–140*, 149, 151–152, 173n, 179n
Ripa, Annotator of, 149
Rippes, see Reppes
Rideval, John of, 79n, 83
Rodington, John of, 13, *82–83*, 132, 135, 141, 147, 164, 178
Rosetus, Roger, *120–121*, 137, 142n, 143, 157–158
Rufus, Richard, see Cornwall
Ruprecht III, Count of Pfalz, 133n

St. Cher, Hugh of, 52
St. Pourçain, see Durand
St. Victor, Hugh of, 41, 43
St. Victor, Richard of, 79
Salisbury, John of, 156
Scotus, John Duns, 42–44, 56–58, 62–63, 65, 69, 74, 111, 116, 121–122, 134, 136n, 138–141, 152, 156, 161n, 179
Sehnsen, Arnold of, 150
Skelton, William, 1, 24, 47n, 85, 87–88, 90, 96, 106, 108n, 109–110, 127, 176n
Sophista, Richard, 54
Spinello, James of, 137
Strasbourg, Thomas of, 142n, 150, 175n
Swineshead, Richard, *94*n, 120n
Swineshead, Roger, *94–95*, 120n, 121n, 138

Thomas Aquinas, 42–43, 51n, 143, 152
Thornton, Nigel of, 81
Totting, see Oyta
Trevytlam, Richard, 121n
Tricon, see Chatton

Ulcredus and Uthred, see Boldon

Vargas, Alphonsus, of Toledo, 53n, 82n, *131–132*, 135–137, 142, 147, 153

Waleys, Thomas, 79n
Ware, William of, 46
Wasia, John of, 147
Wavere, Nigel of, 47n, 53, *81–82*, 85
Wicierus, 94, 95
Woodford, William, 46, 67n
Wyclif, John, 43n

B. Modern Authors

Alessandri, L., 33n
Arbesmann, R., 143n

Balić, C., 44n, 57n

Baudry, L., 66n, 67n, 70n, 162n
Beaulieux, C., 186
Bihl, M., 45n, 47n, 83n
Birkenmajer, A., 132n

INDEX OF NAMES

Boehner, Ph., 27n, 54n, 113, 161n
Brampton, C. K., 35n, 66n, 67–68, 70n, 71, 113, 162n
Brlek, M., 45n
Brown, S., 23n, 27n, 54n, 62n, 113, 161n, 162n
Buck, A., 43n
Buytaert, E. M., 58n

Callaey, P. F., 46n
Cenci, C., 216
Coleman, J., 94n, 138
Combes, A., 11, 18n, 19, 72n, 138, 149n, 173n, 178n
Courtenay, W. J., 3n, 33n, 44n, 122n, 132n, 157n, 178n

De Rijk, C. M., 54, 55n, 56n, 65
Dettloff, W., 12n
De Vooght, P., 11n
Doucet, V., 9, 32, 84n, 120n, 121n, 154n

Eckermann, W., 53n
Ehrle, F., 9, 11, 143n, 148n, 175n
Elie, H., 139n
Emden, A. B., 24n, 56n, 57n, 61n, 62n, 63n, 65n, 66n, 67n, 68n, 70n, 75n, 81n, 82n, 84n, 85n, 86, 93n, 96n, 99n, 107n, 108n, 109n, 110n, 111, 175n

Fischer, I., 201
Fitzpatrick, N. A., 46n, 66n, 67
Franz, G., 134n

Gál, G., 23n, 27n, 34n, 35n, 54, 55, 57n, 58n, 62n, 63n, 65, 66n, 67n, 68, 70n, 71, 83n, 113, 128n, 161n, 162, 163n, 165n
Gelber, H., 59n, 60n, 69n, 71n, 163n
Gibson, S., 47n, 50n, 98n
Gilbert, N., 143n
Gilson, E., 1
Glorieux, P., 49n, 51–52, 56n, 108n, 150n, 178n
Gössmann, E., 43n
Grotefend, C. L., 216
Guimaraes, Ag. de, 50n
Gwynn, A., 75n

Heynck, V., 63n
Hinnebusch, W. A., 46n, 50n, 52n
Hoffmann, F., 96n, 151n
Hofmann, U., 52n

Isenburg, Wilhelm Karl Prinz von, 134n

James, M. R., 210
Junghans, H., 63n

Knowles, D., 93n

Kraus, J., 56n, 96n
Kürzinger, J., 131n

Lang, A., 11, 15, 17–18, 146–147
Langlois, Ch.-V., 65n
Lappe, J., 94n
Lauterer, K., 141n, 145n
Lechner, J., 82n
Leff, Gordon, 12n, 33n, 63n, 75n, 79n, 178n
Little, A. G., 7n, 35n, 46n, 48, 49n, 50n, 51n, 62n, 67n, 76n, 79n, 82n, 175n, 179n, 180
Lohr, C. H., 60n
Longpré, F., 62n, 63n

Madre, A., 52n
Maier, A., 11, 33, 86, 87, 121n
Maurer, A., 56n, 57n
Mayer, C. P., 53n
Meiss, M., 140n
Michalski, C., 1n, 2, 7–15, 18n, 20–21, 26, 30, 37, 82n, 99n, 119n, 128, 147, 165–166
Molinier, A., 186
Moorman, J. R. H., 84
Murdoch, J. E., 2n, 11, 34, 36, 57n, 62n, 74n, 86n, 157n, 163n

Oberman, H. A., 11n, 52n, 96n, 151n

Pelster, F., 56n
Pelzer, A., 21n, 162n, 183, 187, 203, 215, 228
Pinborg, J., 54
Poorter, A. de, 186, 202
Powicke, F. M., 175n

Rashdall, H., 175n, 178n
Reilly, J. P., 63n
Ritter, G., 150n
Robson, J. A., 11n, 121n, 122n
Rössler, H., 134n
Roth, B., 65n

Salter, H. E., 49n, 99n
Schepers, H., 96n, 97, 99n, 100n, 101n, 107
Schum, W., 199
Smalley, B., 51n, 79n, 96n, 173n
Sommerfeldt, G., 133n
Stegmüller, F., 143n, 151n
Steneck, N., 147n
Synan, E. A., 2n, 11n, 34, 36, 57n, 60n, 62n, 74n, 86n, 157n, 163n
Szabó, T., 139n

Tanner, T., 157n
Tachau-Auerbach, K. H., 77n
Tessier, G., 132n
Trapp, D., 2n, 15n, 25n, 91–92, 94n, 115, 117n, 121n, 122n, 131n, 132, 136n, 138n, 141n, 142n, 143, 145n, 147n, 151n, 158, 165n, 170n, 173, 174n, 175n, 177n

Tweedale, M. M., 82n

Vignaux, P., 178n

Wadding, L., 160n
Weisheipl, J. A., 52, 59n, 60n, 94n, 117n, 121n
Werbeck, W., 52n, 151n
Wey, J. C., 97n, 163n
Wilson, C., 87n

Xiberta, B. M., 115, 123n, 131n, 139n, 148n, 150n

Ypma, E., 53n, 178n

Zimmermann, A., 43n
Zoubov, V. P., 163n
Zumkeller, A., 115, 136n, 141n, 146n

LIBRARY OF DAVIDSON COLLEGE

Books on